Dignity, Character, and Self-Respect

Dignity,

Character,

and

Self-Respect

Edited and with an Introduction by Robin S. Dillon

ROUTLEDGE New York London

Published in 1995 by
Routledge
29 West 35 Street
New York, NY 10001

Published in Great Britain in 1995 by
Routledge
11 New Fetter Lane
London EC4P 4EE

Library of Congress Cataloging-in-Publication Data

Dignity, character, and self-respect / edited by Robin S. Dillon
        p.   cm.
    Includes bibliographical references and index.
    ISBN 0-415-90708-X (cloth)   —   ISBN 0-415-90709-8 (paper).
    1. Self-esteem.   I. Dillon, Robin S.
BJ1533.S3D54   1994   94-20565
179'.9—dc20   CIP

To Jim and Heather

Contents

✢

Acknowledgments   *ix*

1. Introduction   *1*
   Robin S. Dillon

PART I. DIGNITY, PERSONHOOD, AND RIGHTS

2. Dignity   *53*
   Aurel Kolnai

3. Servility and Self-Respect   *76*
   Thomas E. Hill, Jr.

4. Self-Respect and Protest   *93*
   Bernard R. Boxill

PART II. CHARACTER, AGENCY, AND SHAME

5. Self-Respect   *107*
   Elizabeth Telfer

6. Self-Respect Reconsidered   *117*
   Thomas E. Hill, Jr.

7. Self-Respect, Excellences, and Shame   *125*
   John Rawls

8. Shame and Self-Esteem: A Critique   *133*
   John Deigh

9. Shame, Integrity, and Self-Respect   *157*
   Gabriele Taylor

PART III. ARE THERE DIFFERENT KINDS OF SELF-RESPECT?

10. Two Kinds of Respect   *181*
    Stephen L. Darwall

11. Is Self-Respect a Moral or a Psychological Concept?   *198*
    Stephen J. Massey

12. Self-Respect and Autonomy   *218*
    Diana T. Meyers

PART IV. POLITICS

13. Self-Respect: Theory and Practice   *251*
    Laurence Thomas

14. Race, Class, and the Social Construction of Self-Respect   *271*
    Michele M. Moody-Adams

15. Toward a Feminist Conception of Self-Respect   *290*
    Robin S. Dillon

Bibliography   *311*

Index   *320*

✛

Acknowledgments

✛

Since its conception on a Mississippi Riverboat in 1990, many people have contributed to bringing this project to fruition. I am especially grateful to Geoffrey Sayre-McCord for convincing me on that hot New Orleans day to undertake this project and for his help and support during the initial stages of its development. I also wish to thank Cynthia Stark, Diana Meyers, and Hannah Stewart-Gambino for their generous comments on the Introduction; Claudia Card, Mike Martin, Amélie Rorty, Laurence Thomas, Terence Moore, and several anonymous referees for valuable advice on both the organization of the volume and the substance of the Introduction; and the students in my "Politics of Self-Respect" seminar at Lehigh University. The philosophy department of Lehigh University has been very supportive and generous; in particular,

Marianne Napravnik, Marcy Trusko, Ian Peterson, and John Carleton Mitchell worked beyond the call of duty in typing the manuscript.

The essays contained in this collection have all appeared in print before. Their sources are noted at the beginning of each chapter. I would like to express my gratitude to the various presses, journals, and authors who kindly granted permission to reprint, and to Diana Meyers for undertaking the revision of chapter 12.

My editors at Routledge, Maureen MacGrogan, Alison Shonkwiler, and Stewart Cauley, have been wonderfully enthusiastic, helpful, patient, and very forgiving, for which I am most grateful. Special thanks go to Hannah Stewart-Gambino and Myra Rosenhaus for their unflagging support throughout this project. Finally, I want to express my deep appreciation to Jim Dillon and Heather Dillon, for their unfaltering encouragement, interest, and endurance.

1

✢

Introduction

✢

Robin S. Dillon

I

Self-respect is undeniably something of great value. Perhaps those who
lack it know this best: to lose respect for oneself and then struggle to
regain it, to be robbed of one's dignity and to try to live without it, to
have to fight to maintain a sense of one's worth in a world that denies it,
to find that one's self-respect is so fragile that even the most ordinary
events threaten to topple it—to live like this is to be painfully aware that a
strong and confident self-respect is vital to the ability to live a satisfying,
meaningful, flourishing life. How very much it matters that we respect
ourselves, and what happens when we cannot, is also a common theme
in literature. In the great tragedies and epic poems, for example, the
hero who dishonors himself in his own eyes suffers a fate worse than
death with the loss of his self-respect. In contemporary dramas, such as

O'Neill's *The Ice Man Cometh* and Miller's *Death of a Salesman*, characters who have lost all respect for themselves and all possibility of regaining it drive inexorably toward social, spiritual, and physical suicide. The journey in the opposite direction, from degradation and abject despair to a robust sense of worth, is described in *The Autobiography of Malcolm X* and Alice Walker's *The Color Purple*, where the development of self-respect marks, for Malcolm and Celie, the passage from merely surviving to richly living and brings with it love and respect for others. And as Primo Levi's *Survival at Auschwitz* makes clear, where survival itself is at stake, as it was for prisoners in the Nazi death camps, the struggle to maintain self-respect under conditions designed to obliterate human dignity is essential to surviving in any meaningful sense.

One thing made obvious by these works is that the significance of self-respect is not chiefly a matter of an individual's psychological health; it is something of profound moral importance, as philosophers have long recognized. Aristotle, Aurelius, Augustine, Aquinas, Montaigne, Descartes, Pascal, Spinoza, Hobbes, Rousseau, Hume, Hegel, Mill, Nietzsche: all have had something to say about what is variously called "magnanimity," "proper pride," "self-esteem," "a sense of dignity."[1] It was Kant, however, who first made the concept of self-respect a central topic in moral philosophy, and it continues to play an important role in contemporary ethical theory, to a great extent because of the attention given the concept in John Rawls's *A Theory of Justice*.[2] In contemporary moral philosophy the concept turns up in a variety of contexts: in theories of rights and justice, in accounts of virtue and character, in discussions of agency and autonomy, in explanations of moral reasoning, moral motivation, and moral development, in explorations in moral psychology, in applied ethics contexts. In addition, concerns raised by people outside the academy about self-respect in connection with current political movements are reflected within philosophy in feminist theory, gay and lesbian theory, and discussions of racism.

Despite its prominence in moral philosophy, however, there is a difficulty: although philosophers and nonphilosophers alike would agree that respecting oneself is important, it is simply not clear what self-respect *is*, let alone why it matters. Indeed, there is more controversy than consensus about its nature and value, no general agreement concerning necessary and sufficient conditions for self-respect or its relation to other goods or concepts. And there is good reason for the absence of settled opinion about something so widely regarded as morally quite important. For what makes self-respect a theoretically useful concept is also what makes it hard to pin down: it is embedded in a nexus of such profound and profoundly problematic concepts as personhood, rights, equality, justice, agency, autonomy, character, integrity, identity, and the good life. Explaining self-respect thus raises many of the central issues in moral philosophy. And insofar as whether one respects oneself or not has everything to do with both how one lives with others and how one lives with oneself, thinking about self-respect takes us not only to the core of moral theory but also to the heart of moral life. The nature and importance of self-respect thus calls for sustained and focused treatment. Hence this volume, which brings together for the first time a number of the most significant and influential contemporary essays on self-respect. Together these essays show this to be a topic of formidable philosophical concern worthy of further exploration, and they provide an invaluable foundation for that venture. The purpose of this introductory chapter is to set the context for these essays: to locate the contemporary discussions of self-respect within the domain of moral philosophy, identify the issues and questions with which they have been concerned, survey some of the historical background of contemporary analyses, and attend systematically to some of the main themes.

II

Contemporary philosophers have approached self-respect with a variety of interests. Some have been chiefly concerned to better understand its nature and importance.[3] Others have taken up the concept in the course of exploring subjects such as moral standards;[4] intersubjective value;[5] moral relativity;[6] rights;[7] equality;[8] moral motivation and moral reasoning;[9] egoism;[10] personal morality;[11] virtue;[12] integrity;[13] autonomy;[14] self-deception;[15] self-trust;[16] self-sacrifice;[17] forgiveness;[18] emotions in general;[19] particular emotions such as shame, embarrassment, pride, resentment, and indignation;[20] and the nature of a flourishing human life.[21] Numerous discussions of self-respect have been generated by Rawls's invocation of the concept in *A Theory of Justice*, explicating, criticizing, or developing his account.[22] Rawls had utilized the concept in assessing the justice of social institutions; since then, there have been many explorations of the effects of injustice and inequality on self-respect,[23] and discussions of it in the context of oppression and liberation with regard to race, sex, class, and sexual orientation.[24] Philosophers have also found it worthwhile to examine self-respect in the course of dealing with a variety of other issues in applied ethics, such as health care,[25] educational policy,[26] business ethics,[27] workplace ethics,[28] and what Mike Martin calls "everyday morality."[29]

The questions raised by these wide-ranging discussions are, as one might expect, many and varied, and some of the most significant ones have yet to be systematically addressed. A survey of the questions, which tend to fall into five broad areas of concern, gives a sense of the richness of the concept and the investigations of it.[30]

The Analysis of Self-Respect

What kind of a thing *is* self-respect?

Is self-respect a grounded phenomenon? If so, what are its grounds?

Is self-respect an objective or subjective concept? That is, are there objective conditions—for example, moral standards or correct judgment—that a person must meet in order correctly to be said to have self-respect, or is self-respect a psychological phenomenon that gains support from any sort of self-valuing, without regard to correctness or moral acceptability?

Is the concept a substantive or a formal one? That is, is there fairly specific content to the concept of self-respect, as there is to the concept of generosity, or is it less determinate, like the concept of integrity?

Does respecting oneself conceptually require or entail the respect of others?

Is the concept of self-respect invariant across different cultural and historical contexts?

Is self-respect a unified phenomenon, or are there different kinds of it? If the latter, is there a core notion of self-respect?

The Phenomenology of Self-Respect

What is it like to respect oneself or to live in a self-respecting fashion? What is it like to lack or lose self-respect or suffer blows to it, or to have diminished or insecure self-respect? Could self-respecting individuals be unconcerned about whether they respect themselves?

What features of an individual's psychology and experience engender and support self-respect? What features undermine or destroy it?

How is self-respect like and unlike respect for others?

Is self-respect important to anyone who has it? Is it of greater value to certain sorts of individuals or in certain contexts?

How does self-respect involve and affect a person's identity (who and what she is), her self-identity (who and what she takes herself to be), and her "self-ideal" (who and what she thinks she ought to be)? How does it affect who and what she becomes?

Moral Dimensions of Self-Respect

Why and how does self-respect matter morally?

How does it connect with one's values, aims, commitments, and projects, including the moral ones?

Is self-respect something that everyone is morally justified in having, or is it something that only morally good people deserve? Do we have a moral duty to respect ourselves?

What is the relation between self-respect and moral rights?

How is self-respect related to moral virtue(s)?

What is the connection between self-respect and autonomy? Between self-respect and integrity?

What is its role in moral deliberation and motivation? How is it implicated in moral development?

Social Dimensions of Self-Respect

What are the interpersonal dimensions of self-respect? What modes of interaction with others support or undermine it? Is respect for oneself reflection of the respect (or something else) of others, or could it be wholly independent of, even opposed to, others' reactions? Must one believe the grounds of one's self-respect to be something that others value?

How are dimensions of public life, such as rights, the distribution of social goods, and membership or participation in social groups and activities relevant to self-respect? How do social norms, practices, policies, and the structure and functioning of social institutions affect it? Is the justice of such things to be assessed (at least in part) by how they affect self-respect? What does justice require in this regard?

Politics and Self-Respect

How does oppression of various kinds, including institutionalized racism, classism, sexism, and heterosexism, affect the ability of members of oppressed groups to develop and maintain self-respect? Do considerations of self-respect help to clarify what is morally wrong with oppression?

How can we understand self-respect in contexts of oppression so as not to regard as unproblematic the self-valuing of individuals whose understanding of and attitudes toward themselves, their circumstances, and their relations to others may be distorted by oppression?

What factors engender and sustain unproblematic self-respect in contexts of oppression? What responses to oppression or injustice are self-respecting?

How is self-respect relevant to liberation from oppression?

What is politically required to ensure widespread unproblematic self-respect?

III

In her essay included in this volume, Elizabeth Telfer notes that the first question that must be addressed concerning self-respect is: What is it? One surprising aspect of the contemporary discussions is how many different starting-from-scratch analyses there are; another is the significant overlap between accounts of self-respect, on the one hand, and accounts of ostensibly different concepts, such as pride, dignity, and honor, on the other. Reading these accounts, one may have the sense that the same phenomenon is being called by different names and different phenomena by the same name. One way to start making sense of all this is to identify the conceptual family to which self-respect belongs. This approach is especially helpful in identifying discussions in which self-respect makes its appearance incognito, as well as discussions of related concepts that may shed light on self-respect.

To begin the genealogy, self-respect is clearly the conceptual offspring of respect; indeed, "self-respect" is often defined simply as "due respect for oneself." Thus, one strategy for understanding self-respect is explicitly to derive an account of it from a wider analysis of respect. Although most accounts do not employ this strategy, most do test conclusions about self-respect against what it would make sense to say about respect, maintaining, for example, that it is reasonable to respect oneself for x because it would be reasonable to respect someone else for x.[31]

The link to respect identifies further conceptual kin: honor, esteem, and regard, for these are regarded as synonymous with respect. So it is common to identify self-respect with self-esteem, self-regard, and (perhaps less common in contemporary America) with a sense of honor. Antonymous concepts include those in the neighborhood of dishonor, contempt, disregard, and devaluation.

What connects respect, honor, esteem, and regard is their common concern with worth. Regard is the recognition of the worth of an object, esteem the appraisal of the worth, honor the reward for great worth. And the notion of a sense of worth is a common element in contemporary discussions of self-respect; indeed, it is generally regarded as the core of self-respect, if not the whole of it. The Latin for "worth" gives us another conceptual relative: dignity, and thereby a sense of dignity. Conceptual contraries include worthlessness and a sense of worthlessness, ignominy, indignity, humiliation.

Another important member of this family is pride. This is a particularly useful concept, inasmuch as it provides some clues for distinguishing self-respect and self-esteem. Self-respect is treated as synonymous with pride insofar as they both concern "a sense of one's own proper dignity" or "a proper sense of personal dignity and worth," whereas self-esteem (a favorable opinion of oneself) tends to be identified with pride when it is "overweening" or "inordinate."[32] Contraries here include shame, humility, and self-effacement, as well as arrogance, vanity, and self-conceit.

Respect, esteem, regard, honor; dignity, worth; self-esteem, pride—locating self-respect within this family of concepts is, of course, only a first step toward understanding it, for their meanings are often no more transparent than its is. Spelling out those meanings and their implications is part of what generates different analyses of self-respect. One benefit of identifying its close conceptual kin is that discussions of things that seem to have nothing to do with self-respect can now be identified as, in fact, dealing directly or indirectly with it. This is particularly useful when we turn to historical accounts, for although phenomena that we might call "self-respect" have been discussed by philosophers at least since Aristotle, the term itself did not enter the philosophical vocabulary until fairly late.[33]

IV

The contemporary Anglo-American philosophical discussions of self-respect take place within a particular philosophical tradition, and to a large extent they reflect historical accounts of the concepts related to self-respect. In those accounts we can see the significance that forms of self-regard have been taken to have and the diversity of views about their nature and grounds. Four of the accounts—those of Aristotle, Hobbes, Hume and Kant—are particularly worth taking a look at.

Aristotle

For Aristotle, the proper appreciation of one's worth is an essential dimension of the fully virtuous person. In the *Nichomachean Ethics* he explores the nature and value of this appreciation, its grounds, its effect on the individual, and its connection with the opinions of others. The central concept in this account is honor. Aristotle regards a rightful concern with honor both as a virtue in its own right and as the "crown of the virtues" (NE, 1124al).[34] This virtue, *megalopsuchia*,[35] is possessed by the individual who believes, and believes correctly, that he is worthy of great things, especially of "the greatest of external goods," (NE, 1123b20) namely, honor (the esteem and admiration of others) and honors (awards given in recognition of an individual's admirable qualities).[36] The *megalopsuchos* is contrasted with the vain man, who believes he is more worthy than he is, and with the unduly humble man, who thinks he is less worthy than he really is.

The *megalopsuchos* is worthy of honor because he manifests "greatness in every virtue"—those excellences of character and intellect that make for a flourishing life (NE, 1123b30). So *megalopsuchia* is a higher-order virtue; and what makes it a virtue seems to be two things. First, as the *megalopsuchos* has true beliefs about what is deserving of honor and about himself, he manifests admirable correctness of thought and judgment. He also has admirably correct values, for honor is, Aristotle insists, genuinely worthy of pursuit, and virtue is objectively good and demands to be acknowledged as such. The *megalopsuchos* knows the true value of honor and of being worthy of honor, and cares about these as he ought. He also cares about staying and knowing that he stays in the right relation with them. Thus, *megalopsuchia* is not merely a matter of having a good opinion of oneself; it is a self-consciousness of virtue that involves self-knowledge, accurate judgment, correct values, and an appropriate concern for these things.

But *megalopsuchia* involves more than intellectual appreciation of one's virtues; concern for his worthiness reverberates throughout the individual, shaping his values, attitudes, motives, and conduct. And here, too, the virtuousness of *megalopsuchia* is clear. For the *megalopsuchos* is a different sort of person than one who does not recognize or care about his own worthiness. In particular, he is more stably virtuous, inasmuch as *megalopsuchia* involves effective and proper motivation to virtuous conduct. Because the *megalopsuchos* values being worthy of honor and strives to live so as to continue to be worthy, he has an extra layer of motivation with regard to, say, temperate actions: he is moved not only by the proper desire for pleasure, but also by the desire not to dishonor himself by acting self-indulgently. *Megalopsuchia* thus preserves and strengthens the other virtues. By giving him a self-conscious stake in the quality of his character and the conduct of his life, then, *megalopsuchia* effectively ties the individual into the project of living virtuously.

Since honor is a social good, *megalopsuchia* is a social phenomenon, but its relation to the opinions of others is interesting. For Aristotle, what the community regards as honorable is just what it regards as virtuous; but it is not uncommon for public honor to be bestowed on what is not really worthy and withheld from what is. So the *megalopsuchos* has a cautious relationship to public esteem. He does not depend on the opinions of others for his sense of his worth, nor does he seek to be praised. Rather, he knows his own worth and is concerned that others recognized it as well. But not all others; for he values only the esteem of those who are qualified to judge him, namely, those who are similarly virtuous and wise. Of course, there can be no difference between his judgments and theirs, for the standards that determine his worthiness, in his own eyes and in theirs, are wholly social. Still, he is concerned not just with how he appears in his own eyes, but how he appears in theirs. He thus takes the position that, in virtue of his virtues, he is the sort of person whom others who are worthy of honor rightly regard as also worthy of honor, and that it is important to remain and to present the unmistakable appearance of being that sort of person.

Hobbes

Hobbes gives a strikingly different account of self-worth and our regard for it. In *Leviathan* he writes, "The manifestation of the value we set on one another is that which is commonly called honoring and dishonoring. To value a man at a high rate is to *honor* him, at a low rate is to *dishonor* him. But high and low, in this case, is to be understood by comparison to the rate that each man sets on himself" (L, 79).[37] Now it might seem that the value an individual places on himself is the true measure of his worth but in fact, "let a man, as most men do, rate themselves at the highest value they can, yet their true value is no more than it is esteemed by others" (L, 79). What is the basis of that esteem? "The *value* or WORTH of a man is, as of all other things, his price—that is to say, so much as would be given for the use of his power—and therefore is not absolute but a thing dependent on the need and judgment of another" (L, 79).

So there is nothing objective about a man's worth, nor is it intrinsic to him; it is subjective, relative, and variable, set chiefly by factors beyond his control. And virtue has no privileged status here: it is a source of worth only if others value it in a man. Thus no sense can be made on Hobbes's account of the Aristotelian notion of an individual's being *worthy* of honor. Nor need there be any correlation between how someone is valued by others and how he values himself. Although Hobbes does not discuss the basis of self-esteem, we can surmise that, if it has a ground at all, it is the usefulness to an individual of his own powers or the price he wants to be paid for their use, both of which depend on his own variable needs and desires. So although it might make sense to say that an individual does not value himself correctly (e.g., he hasn't the powers he thinks he has), there is no Hobbesian sense to the Aristotelian notion of an individual's valuing himself appropriately or having appropriate regard for his worth. There are only conflicting opinions about value, and the opinions of others are the ones that count.

Not surprisingly, self-esteem and regard for honor are not virtues on Hobbes's account. Indeed, in the state of nature they are quite dangerous. For since all worth is bestowed, and since, although men are naturally inclined to value themselves highly, their self-evaluation is meaningless, men desire to be honored by others and desire it so much that they are willing to use any means, even violence, to get it (L, 106). So "men are continually in competition for honor" (L, 141); self-esteem and desire for the esteem of others are thus among the sources of "quarrel" and eventually war (L, 106). Little wonder that the Laws of Nature—the "convenient articles of peace" suggested by reason (L, 109)—include a ban on pride, which is the desire to be the winner in the competition for honor (L, 127).

In the commonwealth, by contrast with the state of nature, this competition ceases. For to prevent quarrels and war, all private valuation is officially eliminated, a "public rate of worth" is established, and to the sovereign is annexed the power to enforce this valuation scheme and "to give titles of honor, and to appoint what order of place and dignity each man shall hold, and what signs of respect...they shall give one another" (L, 149-150). Dignity, "the public worth of a man...set on him by the commonwealth" (L, 79-80), is the only legitimate worth. In these circumstances, there is non-Aristotelian sense to be made of an individual's valuing himself appropriately or having an appropriate concern for his worth and honor. But appropriate self-valuing is a wholly public good, insofar as it helps to maintain the peace. Whether it has any personal significance or moral value is irrelevant.

Hume

Hobbes and Aristotle represent divergent streams of thought regarding worth, self-valuation, and the valuations of others. Hobbes regards an individual's worth as wholly dependent on the valuations of others and self-valuation as dangerous. An appropriate sense of one's worth is conceptually impossible outside the commonwealth and morally unimportant within it. Aristotle regards worth as objectively grounded; thus, one has either a proper or an improper sense of one's worth, and it is very important, personally and morally, to have a proper sense. Social standards define worthiness, but the opinions of particular others are neither conceptually nor causally necessary for having an appropriate sense of worth. Hume takes an interesting middle way between these two views: worth is both subjective and objective, the perspective and opinions of others are both conceptually and causally necessary for a proper sense of worth, and a proper sense of worth is a morally powerful phenomenon. The focus of Hume's account is the passion Hobbes regarded as dangerous, namely, pride.

"The term, pride," writes Hume in the Second *Enquiry*, "is commonly taken in a bad sense; but this sentiment seems indifferent, and may be either good or bad, according as it is well or ill founded, and according to the other circumstances that accompany it" (E, 314).[38] In the *Treatise* he identifies well-founded pride as the virtuous consciousness of our virtues, which is "essential to the character of honor" (T, 596)[39]—an obvious descendent of Aristotle's *megalopsuchia*. The discussion of virtuous pride is embedded in a subtle and intricate account that traces the transformation of 'natural' pride into 'moralized' pride, a passion whose psychological machinery ensures that concern for "inward satisfaction" becomes a motivation to be moral.

In the *Treatise* Hume describes the passion of pride as an agreeable sensation of satisfaction with oneself that arises from a pleasure produced by something related to the self (T, 278). As a passion generated through the operation of natural causal mechanisms, 'natural' pride is "indifferent"—neither good nor bad, but just what happens to us—and "any thing that gives a pleasant sensation and is related to the self, excites the passion of pride" (T, 288). It thus makes no sense to speak of an episode of this passion as either properly or improperly grounded, nor is there any possibility of distinguishing among 'natural' pride, vanity, conceit, self-applause, self-satisfaction, and self-esteem.[40]

Although we might wish to experience this pleasurable passion continuously, 'natural' pride does not last, nor are we capable of sustaining it on our own. However, there is a secondary source of pride, namely, the opinions of others; and through the natural and inevitable operation of sympathy, they significantly influence our own ideas and passions and dramatically increase the staying power of pride. But they do so with strings attached, strings that transform 'natural' pride into what we might call 'social' pride. "Our reputation, our character, our name are considerations of vast weight and importance; and even the other causes of pride...have little influence, when not seconded by the opinions and sentiments of others" (T, 316). In particular, the esteem of others for us and what is ours is a potent source of and reinforcement for pride; and "nothing is more natural than for us to embrace the opinions of others" in this regard (T, 320). Thus it is that the opinions of others have the power to declare some pride appropriate and some inappropriate: one can be acceptably proud not of what merely pleases oneself alone, but only of what pleases others as well. Thus, subjectivity no longer suffices; sustainable pride involves intersubjective conditions of validity. This pride is social not only because it is generated and sustained in a social context, but also because, in experiencing it, one does not regard oneself from an exclusively private perspective. As social beings, we sustain our pride only if we look at ourselves through others' eyes as well as our own, and how we appear in their eyes matters as much if not more to us than how we appear in our own. This facility in shifting perspectives also underlies the inevitable metamorphosis of 'social' pride into a moral passion.

'Social' pride, like 'natural' pride, would seem to be morally indifferent: if what pleases us is murder and mayhem, then an individual can be properly proud of his skills in these activities. However, Hume maintains that human sociality is naturally and inevitably the domain of the moral, and this affects pride. The disagreements we encounter among the sentiments and judgments of different people in different situations would make communication and stable judgments about important matters impossible "were we to remain constantly in that situation and point of view, which is peculiar to us" (T, 603). The solution is to correct our sentiments and judgments to bring them in line with everyone else's, which requires shifting from our peculiar personal perspectives to take up "steady and general points of view" (T, 581) or "the point of view of humanity" (E, 272), in which the interests of all humans are represented impartially. Here, the moral sentiment judges conduct and character not merely as pleasant or unpleasant, but as virtuous or vicious according to whether or not they tend toward "the good of mankind" (T, 578). Pride, too, is corrected; for moral beings, the only pride worth having is that arising from pleasures that are vetted by the moral sentiment when we survey what is ours from the general point of view. From the moral perspective, then, we can distinguish ill-grounded from well-grounded pride, labeling as vice vanity, overweening conceit, and excessive pride, and calling a due degree of pride or self-esteem virtuous.[41]

For 'natural' pride, the subjectivity of feeling was sufficient; for 'moral' pride, objective validity is essential. Of course, it is still sentiment that judges virtue and vice; that is, worth is still a subjective matter. But our sense of worth is not wholly subjective; based in an objective perspective, it is proper regard for our genuine moral worth.

From the moral perspective, the proper basis for pride is one's character and the conduct manifesting it. What is more, instead of being passive recipients of externally caused pleasure, we become active constructors of pride through self-survey. We continually review our conduct and character, persistently engage in self-examination, systematically reflect on the life we are living. And the survey is evaluative: we step back from ourselves to appraise our actions, judge our character, and assess the shape and direction of our life. We secure our objective self-approbation when we have merit, i.e., when we are virtuous. Since we care about being able to survey ourselves with well-grounded satisfaction, the propensity for self-reflection and self-assessment systematically affects our conduct and character: we try to be people who merit a due degree of pride, i.e., virtuous people. Furthermore, since "no one can well distinguish *in himself* betwixt the vice and virtue, or be certain, that his esteem of his own merit is well-founded" (T, 598), we need the (corrected) opinions of others even more than before, to insure that the lamentable tendency to overvalue ourselves (T, 597) does not distort our characters. But others esteem us only when we do our share for "the good of mankind."

The upshot is that something we naturally seek and value greatly—satisfaction with ourselves—becomes a powerful moral force.

> By a continual and earnest pursuit of a character, a name, a reputation in the world, we bring our own deportment and conduct frequently under review, and consider how they appear in the eyes of those who approach and regard us. This constant habit of surveying ourselves, as it were, in reflection, keeps alive all the sentiments of right and wrong, and begets, in noble natures, a certain reverence for themselves as well as others; which is the surest guardian of every virtue (E, 276).

When a person considers "not only his character with regard to others, but also that his peace and inward satisfaction entirely depend on his strict observation" of the social virtues, and that "a mind will never be able to bear its own survey, that has been wanting in its part to mankind and society" (T, 620), he has, if he's not a foolish knave bent on short-term gain at the cost of long-term happiness (E, 283-4), sufficient motivation to be moral.

Kant

For Aristotle and Hume, the worth of persons is grounded in the quality of their characters, and only the virtuous deserve the appropriately favorable view of themselves that is *megalopsuchia* or proper pride. By contrast, Kant maintains that self-respect is something that all persons, regardless of character, deserve and ought to maintain. Of all the historical accounts, Kant's is the most influential, and with good reason: the concept of respect is one of the cornerstones of his most influential ethics. One of his formulations of the supreme principle of morality— "Act in such a way that you always treat humanity, whether in your own person or in the person of any other, never simply as a means, but always at the same time as an end"[42]—is widely regarded as the preeminent statement of the principle of respect for persons, the simple but powerful idea that all persons as such must be respected.[43] It is also regarded as Kant's major contribution to our understanding of self-respect. This principle declares that we have not only a moral duty to respect others, but also a moral duty to respect ourselves, which requires us to act in certain ways and forbids us from acting in other ways.

However, while the duty of self-respect is a central feature of Kant's ethics, we find throughout his works elements of a richer account.[44] Four distinct forms of self-regard are identifiable, each of which is morally important. Kant's overall account combines elements familiar from Aristotle, Hobbes, and Hume, while making the powerful new concept of respect for one's dignity as a person "the foundation stone" (L, 121) of morality.

Dignity (*Wërde*) is the name Kant gives to a kind of intrinsic worth, which is worth that something has insofar as it has value not *for* someone or some purpose, but in and of itself. Dignity is absolute, incomparable, unconditional worth—the supreme moral value. It contrasts with price, which is relative or conditional worth. Looked at in one way, familiar from Hobbes, human beings have a nonmoral price conditional on our usefulness; but looked at in another way, as beings possessed of morally practical reason, humans have dignity. For as rational beings we are ends in ourselves: our very nature has value in itself. This sets us apart from everything else and gives us a special status, which is marked by calling us *persons* (G, 428; M, 433-4).

Morally practical reason is what Kant calls "humanity in one's person" and what he identifies as autonomy: the power to legislate moral laws for oneself and to act in accord with them, independently of inclination. Because autonomy is the very source of morality, this power of reason and the beings possessed of it have the highest moral value. So autonomy is "the ground of the dignity of human nature and of every rational nature" (G, 436). And respect (*Achtung*) is the appropriate response to dignity (G, 428, 436).

However, Kant identifies several ways in which we are said to be autonomous and so have dignity, and he calls diverse modes of response to dignity "respect." Consider, first, autonomy. This power may or may not be exercised by a being who possesses it; we act morally when we exercise it. And we are said to be autonomous both in virtue of having the capacity to act morally and in virtue of realizing this capacity in morally good action. Thus we have dignity and are worthy of respect both insofar as we possess the capacity for moral goodness and insofar as our actions are morally good.[45] However, different forms of respect are involved in the two cases.

Consider, then, autonomy as a capacity. Insofar as rationality is our very essence as human beings, the rational capacity of autonomy is present in every person, however irrational a particular individual might be. Its presence in us is what gives persons dignity. What is more, all persons have equal dignity—and so are worthy of equal respect—regardless of social status, natural characteristics, or personal merit; in particular, morally bad individuals have the same dignity as the most virtuous. So in virtue of our common rational nature each person has dignity "by which he exacts *respect* from all other rational beings in the world" and "can value himself on a footing of equality" with every other person (M, 434).

Two different forms of respect respond to the dignity grounded in the capacity for autonomy. The more familiar form is that expressed in the Categorical Imperative's command to "treat humanity, whether in our own person or in the person of any other, never simply as a means, but always at the same time as an end." This means that we are obliged to respect all person: to value properly and acknowledge in a practical way the dignity of humanity in every person, ourselves included. The duty of self-respect requires us to act only in ways that are consistent with our status as moral beings and to refrain from acting in ways that abase, degrade, defile, or disavow our dignity. To call this a duty to *respect* ourselves is to say that what is required are not only certain actions and forbearances but also a certain reason for acting. One must act from "an awareness of the sublimity of [one's] moral nature" (E, 435), in order to honor and protect it. The general duty to respect humanity in our own person generates a number of specific duties to treat ourselves as ends. We have duties not to commit suicide or misuse our sexual powers and to abstain from drunkenness, gluttony, and drug abuse, for such actions impair or destroy our humanity or make us appear to be mere animals—beings without dignity. Our highest duties to ourselves involve eschewing lying, self-deception, avarice, and servility, for these vices imply a false valuation of ourselves insofar as they involve subordinating our rational will to our desires. Kant talks about self-respect explicitly only in connection with servility, for this is the open disavowal of our equal dignity as persons, but the principle underlying all of these duties is the same, and fulfilling each of them is a way of respecting our humanity.

Fulfilling the duty of self-respect is morally important as the acknowledgment of the supreme moral value we have as persons; as such it has the same moral significance as our duty to respect other persons. But respecting oneself is also morally important because it is a necessary condition of respecting others. Kant maintains that the duty of self-respect is the most important moral duty, for it constitutes "the supreme condition and the principle of all morality" (L, 121): unless there were duties of respect to oneself, there could be no moral duties at all (M, 416). The explanation for this claim brings into play the second form of self-respect that is grounded in one's capacity for autonomy—reverence for oneself.

The duty of self-respect involves acting in certain ways for certain reasons. But respect is also a feeling. Kant often signals this use of the term by adding *reverentia* after *Achtung;* for example, "Respect [*Achtung*] (*reverentia*) is likewise something merely subjective; it is a feeling of a special kind and not a judgment about an object which it would be a duty to bring about or promote" (E, 401). Reverence for oneself is one of the natural capacities of feeling that "lie at the basis of morality," enabling us to be motivated by the thought of duty. This consciousness of our dignity as persons is "irresistibly forced" from us, and only by feeling reverence for ourselves as the subjects of the moral law can we respond to the claims of morality (M, 398, 402-3). So reverence is the subjective source of morality and the motivational ground of the duty of self respect. And it is clearly insofar as we have the capacity for autonomy that we feel reverence for ourselves (M, 435). Indeed, the capacity can be realized only if we feel reverence.

Now, our dignity as persons cannot be diminished or destroyed unless the capacity for autonomy itself is diminished or destroyed, but it can be debased or defiled by immorality or irresponsibility. In such cases, although our dignity is preserved, our awareness of our dignity may be damaged; it may be difficult to see ourselves as beings with dignity and to feel reverence for ourselves. This is especially true when we violate duties of self-respect (M, 425, 428). To the extent that it is hard to feel reverence for ourselves, it is hard to be moral, since reverence is the source from which the ability to be moral springs. Thus, fulfilling the duty of self-respect is essential for preserving reverence for ourselves; in this way it is a necessary condition for fulfilling our other duties, including the duty to respect others.

All persons have dignity, and so warrant reverence for ourselves and have duties of self-respect, because of our capacity for morally autonomous action. But Kant also maintains that we have dignity and deserve respect insofar as we exercise our autonomy in morally worth actions.[46] This is the third form of self-respect we find in Kant. It is, unlike the other two, an evaluative form, and it has two components: "Humility, on the one hand, and true, noble pride (*Stolz*) on the other are elements of proper self-respect" (L, 126). When a person who has acted morally well judges himself by the standards set by the moral law, recognition that he nevertheless falls short engenders humility, which is "the limitation of the high opinion we have of our moral worth" (L, 127). At the same time, consciousness that he has "honored and preserved humanity in his own person and in its dignity" (C, 88) produces a positive self-assessment, manifest as noble pride. As beings with moral duties that we discharge more or less adequately, we deserve as much self-respect as our performances merit; and proper self-respect—an honest assessment of our true moral worth—enables us to continue striving to be morally good.

Kant uses the term "noble pride" (*Stolz*) also in connection with a fourth form of self-regard, the love of honor, which is the virtue opposed to the vices of self-degradation that violate the duty of self-respect.[47] Love of honor has two aspects. The first involves the desire not to be treated as inferior (E, 465). The second is a desire to be worthy of the admiring respect of others: not only to be good but to appear good as well (E, 464; L, 190). This motivates us to act in ways that make it obvious that we are beings who highly value our duty, thereby honoring the dignity of humanity in us. Insofar as we make manifest our autonomy through "ordinary good conduct" (L, 189), the second aspect of love of honor supports the first, for others who know us as good persons a fortiori know us to be persons to whom they owe equal respect.

The connections among the four forms of self-respect make clear their moral importance. The love of honor is the disposition that motivates us to fulfill our duty of self-respect, which arises from and preserves reverence for ourselves, which in turn helps to make morality possible. When we strive to be morally worthy out of reverence and love of honor—when we aim to honor the dignity in our own person—we feel proper self-respect, which lets us know where we stand morally and keeps us headed in the right direction.

V

The contemporary discussions of self-respect are marked by many of the same concerns as the historical accounts. The diversity in the historical accounts presses the conceptual question: What *is* self-respect? And this continues to be a prominent issue. As an approach to the contemporary accounts, we can address this question by taking a cue from Kant and asking what significance lies in calling it *respect* for oneself.

As its etymology suggests, respect is a mode of apprehending something. Respect is always a *seeing*, a presumed disclosure; what is disclosed is the worth or worthiness of the object. And we appreciate its worth: respect is also a mode of *valuing*. Esteem, too, is a valuing mode, but its etymology implies the bestowal of value on the object by the estimator, while respect implies a response elicited by value already present in the object, a response that is called for, deserved, owed, or due, something the object commands or demands. This gives respect an objective logic: to respect something is to regard it as also worthy of the respect of others. Self-respect, then, involves perceiving and valuing oneself as a being of genuine worth, someone whom others would have reason to respect.

There are ambiguities here, however, for the valuing response that is respect is characterized along two divergent lines running also through "regard" and "appreciation." One line has the mode of response taking the form: "this is *important*; it calls for due consideration in thinking and acting." On the other line, the mode of response takes the form: "This is *good*, of notable quality; it deserves our approbation." So, on the one line, respect, regard, and appreciation involve recognizing the importance of something; on the other, they involve evaluating the quality of something. These two lines are represented historically—most obviously in the contrast between Aristotle's and Hume's accounts on the one hand and the more familiar aspects of Kant's account on the other, but also within the Kantian account—in the identification of two distinct grounds for self-regard: the important fact that one is a person and the quality of one's character and conduct.

With regard to this divergence, contemporary accounts divide into five groups. The first group, represented in this volume by the essays by Thomas E. Hill, Jr., and Bernard R. Boxill, includes those accounts that take the first line, treating self-respect as the proper appreciation of the importance of being a person. On these accounts all persons are entitled to respect themselves. The second group, which includes the essays by Elizabeth Telfer and John Rawls, takes the second line, treating self-respect as grounded in character and conduct. According to these accounts, only those individuals whose character and conduct have merit deserve to respect themselves. A third group of accounts attends to the distinction itself in some way; it includes (a) those that argue, as Stephen L. Darwall does, that these are different kinds of self-respect, (b) those that identify self-respect as regard for the importance of being a person and identify self-esteem as regard for one's quality (the essay by Laurence Thomas is illustrative), and (c) attempts such as Diana T. Meyers's to weave the differences into a unified whole. In the fourth group are revisionary accounts, such as my own, which retain certain elements of accounts in the first group while transforming others. The fifth group includes accounts, such as those by Stephen J. Massey and Michele M. Moody-Adams, which carve up the conceptual territory in ways that do not correspond to the distinction between importance and quality.

The historical accounts differ also about how to categorize the various forms of self-regard. In Kant alone, we find self-respect classified as a duty, a feeling, an assessment of merit, and a motivation; Aristotle's *megalopsuchia* is a complex character trait, Hume's pride a narrower sentiment. Contemporary philosophers, too, disagree about what sort of thing self-respect is. Some identify it as a feeling; others (e.g., Rawls, Thomas, and Moody-Adams) say it is or includes a certain opinion, belief, or conviction; still others (e.g., Boxill, Telfer, Darwall, and Meyers) view it as an attitude, often as one involving particular beliefs, emotions, and dispositions, which must (says Hill) or need not (says Massey) have appropriate grounding. It is regarded as being or including a cognitive disposition (Darwall), an emotional disposition (Telfer), and a disposition to action (Moody-Adams). It is identified as a particular mode of living (Hill), and as comprising a set of distinctive responses to and of expectations about one's own actions and the actions of others (Gabriele Taylor). Nearly all accounts agree, however, that the heart of self-respect is the sense of one's worth.

Since each of these accounts seems limited and yet contains much that rings true, we might do well to characterize self-respect, at least preliminarily, in a fairly broad way, as involving a number of elements related in a variety of ways, leaving open the question of which elements are constitutive of self-respect and which are conditions for or manifestations of it.

One thing strongly suggested by descriptions of individuals who respect themselves and those who don't is that self-respect is not something one has only now and again; it has rather to do with the structure and attunement of an individual's life. It reverberates throughout one's person, affecting the configuration and constitution of one's thoughts, desires, values, emotions, attitudes, dispositions, and actions. We can capture this dimension if we understand self-respect to be a complex and multifaceted phenomenon involving all those aspects of cognition, valuation, orientation, affect, expectation, motivation, action, and reaction that bear on one's worth as a person—that is, on one's dignity as a person as such, the value and significance of one's life, the quality of one's character and manner of living, one's specialness as the particular person one is, and so on.

At the core of this complex, orienting the various elements within it, is one's sense of one's own worth. Like a sense of humor, a sense of worth is a perceptual capacity, that is, a capacity to recognize and understand one's worth (and a lot more besides), and a sensitivity to whatever threatens one's worth and to what might enhance, protect, and sustain it. A sense of worth is also a valuing stance. To have a sense of worth is not simply to recognize that one has worth, but to regard that fact as mattering a great deal. This makes one's sense of worth motivational: it disposes one to protect one's worth when it is threatened, to confirm it when necessary, to enhance it where possible, and to on. A person's sense of worth is thus an engaged, concernful appreciation of her worth, a lived affirmation of it. It is at the same time not so much self-conscious and affectively present as it is a matter of assumption, construal, perspective, and disposition suffusing one's thinking, feeling, and living. Although in some contexts—as when one's rights are challenged, degradation threatens, or circumstances call for taking stock of oneself—one's worth and sense of worth (or lack thereof) may be at the center of one's thoughts and feelings, in calmer contexts the sense of worth may operate as unconsciously as one's sense of the solidness of the ground: completely taken for granted yet informing every move.

Contemporary accounts differ in their characterizations of the beliefs, attitudes, behaviors, and so on, that are central to self-respect, chiefly because of deeper differences concerning (a) the aspect or conception of the self that is the object of respect, and (b) the nature and grounds of the worth of the self or aspect of self. The object of self-respect is variously characterized as a person (that is, as a being with full moral status and a standing in the moral community as an equal among equals), an autonomous agent, a moral agent, an agent living out a particular plan of life, an individual with a certain character and history of conduct, and the particular person one is. But however the self as object is conceived, respect for oneself is generally regarded as the appreciation of one or the other of two kinds of worth: a kind of worth that is unearned, invariable, and inalienable, often called "dignity," and a kind of worth that individuals earn more or less of and that is subject to diminishment and loss as well as enhancement, which may be called "merit."[48] This distinction regarding worth corresponds to the divergent characterizations of respect: respect is viewed both as the response to (the importance of) dignity and as the response to (the quality that is) merit. The grounds for dignity are variously said to include a person's intrinsic nature (as a person, an autonomous agent, a moral agent), or such things as one's status in a rigid social hierarchy, cultural heritage, or identity-conferring membership in a particular class or group. The grounds for merit include an individual's character and conduct insofar as it reveals character, as well as those traits, qualities, abilities, and accomplishments that are important from a moral point of view or from the point of view of the individual's living out her plan of life. The essays in Parts I and II of this volume are grouped in order to highlight some of these differences concerning the object and grounds of self-respect.

VI

The essays in Part I, "Dignity, Personhood, and Rights" develop familiar Kantian themes about dignity and self-respect. As we have seen, for Kant "dignity" is a technical term referring to the unique worth possessed by an end-in-itself. But "dignity" is commonly used in a number of ways. We describe things other than human beings—a magnificent work of art, an ancient and majestic tree, honest labor—as having dignity. Dignity is also the honor that is associated with high rank in an established social hierarchy or is invested in positions or offices of importance. The term is sometimes used synonymously with "respect" and "self-respect," as in "treat people with dignity." In his essay, "Dignity" (chapter 2), Aurel Kolnai explores two sorts of dignity that are typically and uniquely attributed to humans. There is, first, the human dignity that all persons are said to have independently of social status and which is the characteristic moral feature of persons as such. Second, there is the quality of dignity—of being dignified, or expressing dignity—which is characteristic of some individuals but not of others and which is a matter of how one comports oneself.

Kolnai's chief concern is with dignity in the second sense. Individuals possess this quality and are deserving of admiring, even reverential, respect, insofar as their comportment manifests such characteristics as composure, calm self-control, serenity, and quiet invulnerability. All persons are not equal here, for individuals manage this to different degrees, and some not at all; but whether and how they do has much to do with how they regard their human dignity. Human dignity is, of course, the familiar Kantian notion, involving the ideas of the inherent and inalienable value of being a person, the fundamental equality of persons, the respect owed to each and demanded from all, and the moral community in which each person has full moral status. Kolnai's account brings to our attention a new emphasis to be found in contemporary treatments of dignity: the connection between human dignity and basic human rights. As various declarations of human rights affirm, the equality of human dignity is taken to be the basis of the equal moral rights that all persons have as persons, independently of social law, custom, convention, and agreement.[49]

The sheer fact of personhood and its inherent human dignity is the ground of one kind of self-respect, to which every person is entitled. Self-respect in this sense involves the perception and appreciation of oneself as a person—a being with human dignity and human rights—and of one's place as an intrinsically valuable being among intrinsically valuable beings. But what precisely does that involve? Thomas E. Hill, Jr.'s "Servility and Self-Respect" (chapter 3) is the contemporary locus classicus for discussion of the connection between personhood and self-respect. Developing Kant's claim that servility manifests a lack of self-respect, Hill identifies servility as the failure to understand and acknowledge or to value properly the equal basic rights one has just as a person. Self-respect requires respect for one's rights, which in turn requires having certain beliefs about and attitudes toward oneself as a person, one's relation to morality, and one's place in the moral community. (For a similar view, see Thomas, chapter 13). Hill argues that inasmuch as there is a duty to respect the moral law which accords us our rights, all persons have a duty to respect themselves by affirming their moral rights in thought and deed.

As other philosophers have noted, self-respecting individuals have, in addition to dispositions to act, certain emotional dispositions, such as the disposition to feel indignation when their dignity is assaulted through the violations of their rights, or resentment when they are treated by others as inferior—dispositions to react to threats to their dignity and status as persons.[50] In "Self-Respect and Protest" (chapter 4), Bernard R. Boxill also explores the response of a self-respecting person to the threats posed by persistent injustice. In such circumstances, Boxill maintains, protesting violations of one's rights is what self-respect demands, even when such protest is unlikely to ameliorate one's situation. Not only does protest affirm one's rights and personhood in the face of their denial, but it also may be all that enables a self-respecting person to know that he does respect himself, which is knowledge a self-respecting person cannot do without.

Boxill concurs with Hill in regarding our equal basic rights, and thus the worth inherent in being a person, as providing a basis for self-respect. His account is especially notable for emphasizing that it is not enough for self-respect that one believe oneself to have worth and rights as a person; one must have the *confident conviction* that this is so. What protest does is to make manifest to oneself the fact that one does respect oneself and on good grounds, which underwrites and strengthens the requisite confidence.

That human dignity is a ground of self-respect is obvious, but Boxill's emphasis on confidence about one's worth suggests that there is also a connection between self-respect and Kolnai's quality of dignity. Boxill elsewhere describes the person with (the quality of) dignity as one who "radiates so serene a sense that his rights are manifest as to tacitly, but unmistakably and eloquently, call shame on all who refuse to acknowledge them."[51] Such a person would respond to unjust treatment in calmly controlled ways that reveal the inherent invulnerability of his status as a person and his belief in that status. Dignity here is "the sense that one's manifest humanity makes one manifestly worthy of one's human rights."[52] But that is just what respect for oneself as a person involves. That is, while human dignity is the grounds for self-respect, at least part of the quality of dignity is evident and imperturbable confidence in the obviousness of one's worth as a person, i.e., manifest and strong self-respect.

This analysis calls attention to an important aspect of dignity, which Michael Meyer calls its "public availability."[53] To talk of human dignity rather than human worth is to talk about what is perceivable, about the way in which one is *visibly* human and worthy of respect. Similarly, to talk of dignity as a quality is to emphasize not the psychological dimensions of a person's sense of worth but its outward manifestation in how she presents herself to others. Thus, although all human persons have intrinsic worth, it is possible for some humans to be unable, perhaps because of obdurate prejudice, to perceive other humans as beings with dignity equal to their own. The struggle of oppressed people for dignity can be the struggle to be seen as what they are: persons equal to their oppressors. And the quality of dignity—responding to injustice in ways that make clear that *we* know we are persons, even if you refuse to acknowledge this—can be a tool in that struggle.

How important it is that one's dignity be manifest to *oneself* is made clear in recountings of the experiences of prisoners in Nazi death camps. Although dignity as manifest value is something that can be destroyed without destroying the individual's intrinsic worth, personhood, or right to respect, its destruction can in fact destroy the individual. As Primo Levi's memoir of his ordeal in Auschwitz reveals, the definitive aspect of the camps was not death per se, but the annihilation of dignity.[54] One especially brutalizing way in which this was carried out was through what Terrence Des Pres calls "excremental assault," the systematic subjection to filth: being forced to live, work, and sleep in excrement, to remain caked with it, even to eat and drink it. The unmistakable aim here, and the very common effect, was to "destroy our human dignity, to efface every vestige of humanity, to fill us with horror and contempt toward ourselves and our fellows,"[55] and so to obliterate the prisoners' sense of themselves as human beings—as beings with any kind of worth—to reduce them in their own minds to something beneath even brutes, and thus utterly destroy them by maiming and crushing their souls before their bodies died. To survive in the face of such profound humiliation required "holding on to dignity," and that depended "on the daily, never finished battle to remain *visibly* human."[56] Keeping dignity manifest through such monumentally difficult tasks as trying to stay clean preserved self-respect and so preserved life.

One lesson from Boxill and the death camps is that self-respect can be undermined or crushed by the attitudes and treatment of others, and that part of what makes such things wrong is their effect on self-respect. But self-respect can also be nourished by others' attitudes and treatment, and these are good in large part because of this effect. James Wallace has argued, for example, that benevolence, kindness, generosity, and compassion are virtues—traits that "foster good human life in extensive and fundamental ways"—in large part because the expression of them supports the self-respect of their recipients by affirming their intrinsic worth and importance as persons.[57] It also seems clear that significant effects flow in the opposite direction as well. On Hill's analysis, since a person who respects herself understands and properly values her moral status and rights as a person, consistency requires her to respect others on the same grounds as she respects herself. Other things equal, respecting oneself would make it more likely that one would also respect others, although self-deception, moral blindness, or having a distorted view of the moral community and one's place in it—conditions that keep one from seeing or acknowledging that others are like one in the relevant respects—can block the extension of respect to others.

The analyses of self-respect as grounded in personhood, dignity, and basic moral rights raise several questions. First, is there a necessary conceptual connection between rights and self-respect? To suppose there is is to suppose that in a society with no conception of human rights, there could be no self-respect. Joel Feinberg has argued for such a connection;[58] Massey (chapter 11) points out some problems in trying to make this argument. Second, if asserting one's rights in protest of injustice is what self-respect demands, are there ways of doing so that are nevertheless not self-respecting? Meyer and Michael Pritchard have explored this question, identifying dignified and non-dignified ways of manifesting one's sense of dignity.[59] Third, does self-respect necessarily involve a sense of one's equal worth with all persons? To suppose that it does is to suppose that in a rigidly hierarchical society, there could be no self-respect. John Deigh (chapter 8) suggests otherwise. Fourth, if being a person is what gives one dignity and makes one worthy of respect, what is it that makes one a person? Kant's answer, of course, is rational autonomy. The concepts of *human* dignity and *human* rights, however, suggest that the class of respect-worthy beings is in some ways broader and in some ways narrower than the class of rationally autonomous beings. Koyeli Ghosh-Dastidar, noting some differences between Western and Indian ways of conceptualizing personhood, has argued that as the conception of the person varies cross-culturally, so do conceptions of respect and self-respect.[60] I have explored (chapter 15) the ramifications for the concept of self-respect of trans-theoretic variations in the conception of a person. Questions about the ultimate grounds of respect for oneself as a person, of course, inherit the problems connected with one of the deepest and most enduring concerns in moral philosophy: trying to understand what it is to be a person and what it is about persons that makes us matter morally.

VII

Respect for one's dignity as a person is a morally powerful concept; yet it is not the view of self-respect that is prevalent outside of philosophical discussions. To many people, self-respect is something that one earns by aspiring to morally worthy standards of behavior, that takes considerable time and effort to develop, that involves self-restraint and taking responsibility for oneself—something, in short, that is a matter of character rather than personhood. And for Aristotle and Hume, what is of importance for self-regard is not the fact that one is a person, but the kind of person one is. For them, appropriate self-regard is what motivates the individual to become and remain one kind of person rather than another, and it is the satisfaction one deserves to feel for being that kind of person. This view of self-respect is developed in the essays in Part II, "Character, Agency, and Shame."

In "Self-Respect" (chapter 5) Elizabeth Telfer distinguishes two distinct but connected aspects of self-respect—one whose account is more Aristotelian, which she calls "conative self-respect," and the more Humean "estimative self-respect"—both of which are different from respect for oneself as an equal person. Conative self-respect is a motivational character trait constituted by a concern for the dignity of one's character that restrains one from acting in ways that are unworthy of oneself, where unworthiness is defined by certain standards for conduct and character. The standards include both objective ones, some of which are dictated by the moral significance of autonomous agency, and subjective ones, which one sets for oneself or are provided by one's goals, projects, and roles. In Kantian fashion Telfer stresses the importance of the objective standards connected with autonomy and argues that conative self-respect requires due respect for the dignity of autonomous agency. It is unworthy of an autonomous agent to act in ways that disregard autonomy; conative self-respect thus demands autonomous conduct, which in turn requires the virtues of independence, self-control, and tenacity. A person who lacks these qualities cannot have conative self-respect; a person with conative self-respect will regard conduct manifesting dependence or a lack of self-control to be beneath her and contemptible and so will be motivated to refrain from such conduct. In this way she protects and preserves her character and autonomy.

That certain virtues are required if one is to respect oneself is a common claim in recent discussions. For example, Meyers (chapter 12), Jean Hampton, and I concur with Telfer's claim that virtues of autonomy are essential to self-respect.[61] Others have identified self-trust, integrity, courage, self-understanding, and honesty with oneself to be virtues needed for self-respect.[62] Aristotle and Hume view proper self-regard as itself a virtue, but Telfer maintains that while conative self-respect can be a powerful motivation for virtuous conduct and the development of virtuous character, it may be too egoistic to be a virtue itself. Taylor (chapter 9) takes issue with this claim.

Telfer's view that self-respect involves the exercise of autonomy by acting in accord with certain standards is developed along somewhat different lines by Thomas E. Hill, Jr., in "Self-Respect Reconsidered" (chapter 6). In his earlier essay Hill had emphasized our moral responsibility to respect our rights as person. In this essay Hill stresses our responsibility to respect ourselves as autonomous agents. Hill argues that self-respect requires that we exercise our autonomy by developing and committing ourselves to live and judge ourselves by a set of standards for conduct and character. These standards are personal, both in the sense that they need not be moral or be regarded as applying to other people and in the sense that they are normatively self-defining: the values they express are central to one's self-conception, and one stakes one's worth in one's own eyes on living by them. To the extent that it is morally important for persons to live autonomously and to define and appraise themselves as particular individuals—to have and to live by their own values—it is morally objectionable to lack self-respect.

For Telfer and Hill, self-respect is grounded in and responsive to the dignity a person has as an autonomous agent. The second aspect of self-respect that Telfer identifies, estimative self-respect, is merit-based self-respect: a favorable opinion of oneself, grounded in conduct and qualities of character and arising from the belief that one meets those standards that one believes one ought to meet. As with Hume's pride, whether this is a good attitude or not depends on whether the evaluative judgment is correct and the standards appropriate. Someone can have more or less estimative self-respect than she merits, even by her own standards; where she overestimates her merit, she deserves to lose some self-respect. Applying this to Hill's account, an individual would merit estimative self-respect to the extent that she lives in accord with her own standards. Were she to judge herself a failure in this regard, self-contempt or self-disgust would be the result.

Something like estimative self-respect—the personal evaluation of personal worthiness relative to personal standards—is a significant aspect of the account of self-respect that John Rawls develops in *A Theory of Justice*, one chapter of which, "Self-Respect, Excellence, and Shame," appears as chapter 7 of this volume. For Rawls self-respect (or "self-esteem," as he also call it) is the favorable opinion of oneself comprising (a) confidence in the worth of one's "plan of life"—the aims and ideals one seeks to attain and around which one's life is structured—and (b) the assessment of one's character and abilities as well suited to successfully living that life. The judgment that one's activities have merit is one main source of self-respect. Another very important source is the respect of others: "unless we feel that our endeavors are honored by them, it is difficult if not impossible for us to maintain the conviction that our ends are worth advancing."[63] Self-respect is important, Rawls claims, because without it one cannot adequately pursue one's ends or achieve one's goals.

Among other things, a individual's plan of life sets certain standards for character and conduct. Rawls characterizes shame as the emotion people feel when they realize they lack those excellences, moral and otherwise, that their plans of life require. In "Shame and Self-Esteem: A Critique" (chapter 8), John Deigh takes issue with this characterization of shame; in doing so, he brings back into focus questions concerning the nature and sources of worth. Rawlsian "self-esteem" (as Deigh calls it) rests on an agentic conception of worth according to which one earns and loses worth depending on one's actions, and in general on how one conducts one's life. One's sense of worth rises, as self-esteem, and falls, as shame, depending on whether one judges oneself to be more or less a success or failure in the pursuit of one's life plan. But its inability to account for a variety of commonplace cases of shame, Deigh argues, shows that this is not the sense of worth that is connected with shame. Deigh proposes an alternative theory of worth according to which one's sense of worth is predicated not on what one does but on what on *is*, arguing that one's identity is not fully determined by how one conducts one's life but derives, also or in large part, from such things as one's status in a social hierarchy, membership in a particular class, group, or culture, or essential nature as a person. Shame is felt when one betrays what one is, as when one acts as a lesser sort of person. But worth is not lost here, only tarnished; so whereas on the Rawlsian conception shame involves a damaged sense of worth, on Deigh's characterization it involves an undamaged sense of worth, the sense that one *has* worth but that one's behavior gives one the appearance of lesser worth. One of the functions of a sense of worth, on Deigh's characterization, is to preserve congruence between one's real worth and the public appearance of worth.

In "Shame, Integrity, and Self-Respect" (chapter 9), Gabriele Taylor returns to something like conative self-respect to explain how self-respect and shame preserve integrity and identity. Taylor explicitly distinguishes self-respect from self-esteem: the latter she views as a favorable opinion of oneself, the former as involving the motivation to do what protects the self from injury arising from being the object of treatment or the subject of behavior that one views as intolerable. To have self-respect, Taylor maintains, is, in part, to have certain expectations about or standards for one's behavior that themselves are grounded in what one regards as having great value to the life one wants to lead, and especially in those value commitments from which one's normative identity derives. If one violates one's standards and expectations, one experiences shame—the warning recognition that one's values and identity are threatened by what one has done or contemplates doing, or what one is or is in danger of becoming, or what one might give the appearance of being. Shame thus involves the expression of our value commitments. One respects oneself by living in accord with one's standards and expectations, that is, with one's values; and to live by one's values is to have integrity. Respect for oneself thus preserves one's integrity; and to the extent that one's values are self-defining, self-respect preserves one's identity.

These analyses of self-respect raise a number of questions. For instance, Rawls follows Hume in regarding the opinions of others as having a powerful influence on an individual's ability to respect herself; but we might ask, as Robert Yanal does, whether such a dependence manifests rather a lack of self-respect.[64] On the other hand, while Hill and Taylor stress the personal nature of the standards and values involved in self-respect, we might ask whether it is likely or even conceptually possible for a person to believe the grounds of her self-respect to be something that others in no way value. Darwall argues that self-respect that is grounded in character requires intersubjective valuation.[65] A related question is whether there are specific standards that persons must meet in order to be said rightly to respect themselves. In particular, must a person's character and conduct be morally good if they are to merit self-respect? Or could a concern for self-respect put one at odds with morality? The essays by Darwall, Massey, and Meyers in Part III provide very different answers here. What is clear from the analyses of self-respect in relation to character and agency is that, like those concerned with dignity and personhood, questions concerning the grounds of self-respect inherit the problems connected with another of the deep and enduring concerns of moral philosophy: trying to determine what kinds of lives are appropriate for persons to live and what kinds of persons it is good to be.

VIII

The differences between the personhood and character accounts of self-respect, as well as Telfer's distinction between estimative and conative self-respect, naturally prompt the question with which the essays in Part III are concerned: Are there different kinds of self-respect? Likewise, Rawls's synonymous use of the terms "self-respect" and "self-esteem" and Taylor's argument for distinguishing them raise a second question: Are self-respect and self-esteem the same or different? The two questions may not be unrelated; perhaps a difference between self-respect and self-esteem underlies the divergence between the personhood and character accounts. It is thus best to address the second question first.

One difference between self-respect and self-esteem is that moral philosophers tend to talk about the former while psychologists talk almost exclusively about the latter. The significance of this emerges more clearly when we look at how psychologists characterize self-esteem. It should be noted that there is as much disagreement among psychologists about self-esteem as there is among philosophers about self-respect.[66] Nevertheless, many of the psychological accounts agree on several features as characteristic of self-esteem,[67] two of which are significant for our purposes. First, self-esteem has an evaluative dimension, which is identified as a favorable self-appraisal, as an attitude of self-approval, or as involving the belief that one is significant, worthy, capable, or successful. Self-esteem is often treated as if it were not so much grounded or justified as caused (by one's relationships with others, for example); but when grounds for the self-evaluation are identified, they tend to be very wide-ranging—nearly everything that one can call "mine." A number of accounts follow William James's characterization of self-esteem—one of the earliest and considered by many to be definitive—which stresses the role of personal values, standards, and aspirations in self-evaluation. According to James, the individual not only judges his actual performances, capacities, and attributes according to his personal standards, assessing the degree to which what he is and does matches what he aspires to be and do to arrive at a personal estimate of his own worthiness, but he also weighs different aspects of himself differently according to how central those aspects are to his conception of himself.[68] In contrast to James, the followers of G. H. Mead emphasize the importance of communal standards and values to individual self-appraisal, and the degree to which our self-evaluations are reflections of the evaluations others make of us. Here, the limits of social appreciation and approval set constraints on self-esteem.[69]

A second feature of self-esteem is affectivity: it is or it influences how we feel about ourselves. The person who has self-esteem is said to feel good about herself, to like herself, to have feelings of personal worth.

Those who treat self-esteem as involving self-evaluation identify these feelings as the individual's emotional response to her evaluation; others view the feeling as psychologically primitive. The affective dimension of self-esteem is widely regarded as what makes it valuable to individuals and motivationally primary.

A number of philosophers distinguish self-respect from self-esteem in ways that show their debt to psychological theorizing. Thomas (chapter 13), for example, defines self-respect in Kantian terms and characterizes self-esteem along Jamesian lines as the evaluation of one's abilities and behavior as either enabling or not enabling the successful pursuit of one's ends.[70] And as Thomas argues elsewhere, the implications for moral theory of the psychological view of self-esteem are clear: since self-esteem is compatible even with egregious immorality—the evil may esteem themselves as highly as the good, if they value their evil or perceive themselves as good—it has no special moral significance, whereas self-respect has great moral significance.[71]

There are, however, reasons to resist ceding the whole of self-evaluation to psychology. In particular, there are reasons to distinguish a specifically moral kind of self-evaluation whose identification as a form of self-respect marks it as belonging unequivocally in our moral discourse. For we do evaluate ourselves from the moral point of view as well as from other points of view; we assess ourselves in moral terms and appraise the kind of persons we are, morally speaking. This is a distinctive and morally significant kind of self-evaluation. The grounds for such an evaluation are narrower than those for self-esteem, for they are limited to what is relevant to the assessment of the kind of person one is and the kind of life one is leading, morally speaking. And while self-esteem has much to do with achievement and success, the concern in evaluative self-respect is not to pat oneself on the back morally but to assure oneself that one comes up to scratch (Telfer), has not lowered oneself in one's eyes (Hill), has not acted beneath one's dignity (Taylor). What is important is not that we score highly but rather, as Hume puts it, that we be able to "bear our own survey." Nor is it feeling good about ourselves that is definitive of evaluative self-respect, but rather knowing where we stand morally, and knowing this is clearly of great importance in living the moral life.

This view accords with the account Stephen L. Darwall develops in "Two Kinds of Respect" (chapter 10). Darwall's identification of two kinds of self-respect parallels the "this is important"/"this is good" divergence discussed in section V above. The first kind, recognition self-respect, is the regard that all persons are entitled to have for themselves.

Recognition self-respect motivates us to engage in worthy conduct or to eschew unworthy conduct, and to expect respect from others and to be unwilling to tolerate disrespect from them. Respect for oneself as an equal person and respect for oneself as an agent with certain responsibilities are both forms of recognition self-respect. Thus, what is described by the familiar Kantian account and by Boxill's and Hill's accounts is recognition self-respect, as is Telfer's conative self-respect. And Darwall's analysis can be generalized to apply to the sense of worth that Deigh poses in contrast to the Rawlsian conception.

The second kind of self-respect, appraisal self-respect, is the evaluative form of self-respect. It is a positive appraisal of oneself as a person that is merited on the basis of the excellence of one's character. Clearly not all persons merit appraisal self-respect equally, some may fail to merit it altogether, and individuals might sometimes deserve to lose (some of) it. As grounded in our virtues as persons, the idea of appraisal self-respect captures much of Aristotle's *megalopsuchia* and Hume's proper pride, and it is similar to Telfer's estimative self-respect. Rawls's definition of self-respect comes close to appraisal self-respect, but much of his analysis involves a conflation of it with self-esteem. Darwall distinguishes the two by their grounds: those for self-esteem are much wider, encompassing any attributes that one would be pleased to have or regret not having.

Stephen J. Massey argues for a decidedly different way of carving up the conceptual landscape in "Is Self-Respect a Moral or a Psychological Concept?" (chapter 11). Massey argues that there are two concepts of self-respect, a moral or objective concept and a psychological or subjective concept. Subjectively, it is necessary and sufficient for self-respect that one have certain favorable self-regarding evaluative beliefs, attitudes, and feelings. It does not matter for subjective self-respect whether the beliefs are true, nor are there any constraints, moral or otherwise, on what counts as worthy conduct. This is, of course, the psychologists' conception of self-esteem. In contrast, the objective concept requires that one's beliefs, attitudes, and conduct meet objective criteria. Objectively, a person has self-respect only if her favorable self-attitude is grounded in morally appropriate ways, for example, only if she correctly recognizes and values her moral status as a person with equal basic rights, or only if her character, which she regards as good, is truly good.

Massey's analysis raises an important issue concerning the evaluative form of self-respect. The substantive disagreement among individuals, cultures, and moral theories about whether and why persons matter morally, how persons ought to live, and what forms of character and conduct are worthy entails parallel disagreement about what constitutes appropriate grounds for respecting oneself. So what may appear from one perspective to be valuing appropriately what is really of worth about oneself might be seen from another perspective as a failure of self-respect, and it is not obvious that one view is right and the other wrong. This does not mean that self-respect is fundamentally subjective in Massey's sense but it does mean that any account of the evaluative form of self-respect unavoidably rests on, and perhaps owes a defense of, inevitably contestable answers to substantive moral questions about persons and the nature of the moral life.

In her essay on "Self-Respect and Autonomy" (chapter 12), Diana T. Meyers takes issue with the cleavage of self-respect into an objective kind and a subjective kind and proposes a unified account of self-respect. Meyers maintains that respect is a triadic relation holding among attitude, behavior, and object. The term "respect" applies unequivocally when the relation is unqualified or uncompromised, that is, when a respectful attitude is expressed in respectful conduct toward a respect-worthy object. But when any of these elements is inappropriate—for example, when a respectful attitude is directed toward an unworthy object—then respect is compromised. Compromised self-respect can be indecent or pernicious—as when a person respects himself for what he knows is immoral conduct—or innocent—as would be the case if someone understood that all persons have dignity and deserve respect but believed, as the result of social conditioning, that she was something less than a person. But only uncompromised self-respect has the intrinsic goodness we tend to regard as belonging to self-respect.

What is needed if individuals are to avoid compromised self-respect, Meyers argues, is the exercise on their part of personal and moral autonomy. Individuals are more likely to realize the intrinsically valuable correspondence between their self-attitudes and a fully worthy self, and their uncompromised self-respect is likely to be more stable and to have greater instrumental value, when they strive to measure up to standards or to fulfill life plans that they autonomously embrace. In connection with this, Meyers explores the relation between autonomy and self-respect of women in contemporary America who are faced with changing social expectations about women's roles. Given that intrinsically good and personally valuable uncompromised self-respect requires autonomy, it seems clear that to socialize individuals in ways that undermine their ability to be morally and personally autonomous is to inflict serious injury on them and that a society that countenances or encourages such socialization is thereby condemnable.

IX

It is not uncommon for philosophers to argue, as Meyers does, that the moral goodness or justice of a society depends in part on whether it supports or undermines the respect of its members. But the power of this argument depends, of course, on self-respect's being something of great moral importance. It is worth pausing to collect together some of the views about the moral significance and value of self-respect.

We can note first that a confident sense of worth is of great value psychologically; Rawls locates its value, for example, in the zest with which it enables us to pursue our life plans. Not only is its presence life-enhancing, but its absence can be profoundly debilitating and destructive. When the abiding flavor of our lives is shame, self-contempt, or self-hatred, or anxiety, despair, or apathy about our worth; when we experience a profound and pervasive sense of ourselves as inconsequential, inadequate, worthless, not good enough, not as valuable as others, or not as worthy as they of the good things in life; when our lives seem meaningless, our activities of little value, our capabilities minimal, our characters base; when we view ourselves as having continually failed to live in accord with even minimal standards or as having irreparably degraded ourselves—when living is like this, living well is impossible. And to the extent that living well is morally significant, then having a secure sense of worth is morally significant.

However, if Massey is right about subjective and objective self-respect, then not all self-respect will be intrinsically morally desirable: a positive sense of worth that is ill-grounded or morally execrable can be subjectively as uplifting and empowering as objectively valid self-respect. But if we accept Meyers's analysis, then uncompromised self-respect, in addition to having the intrinsic moral value that compromised self-respect lacks, is also more likely to deliver these benefits and so better enables one's life plan to unfold successfully.

The moral value of uncompromised self-respect goes still deeper. As Kant and Hill maintain, recognition respect for oneself as an equal person and bearer of equal rights is the valuing of things that have great moral significance: our profound dignity as persons, our standing in the moral community, the moral law itself as the source of our rights. Recognition respect for ourselves as autonomous agents is likewise the valuing of something of great moral value: the capacity for agency that makes us moral beings in the first place, and our capacity to be self-defining, self-appraising, and self-directing. Similarly, Aristotle, Hume, Rawls, and Darwall remind us in different ways that the objects of uncompromised evaluative self-respect are morally important: our good moral characters, our morally worthy conduct, and our fulfillment of worthy plans of life. And the appropriate appreciation of morally worthy things is intrinsically good. Those whose capacity for recognition self-respect is deformed do not understand things of great consequence for human life; those whose evaluative self-respect is compromised show that they are ignorant of or less concerned than they ought to be about the real worth of things. To engage in and care about respecting oneself—to care about one's human worth—is to respond to the values of human living in such a way that one's life is guided and shaped by value; and maintaining an explicit congruence between self and value is appropriate and good for beings such as ourselves.

Self-respect is also morally valuable insofar as it contributes to the continuation of morality. By situating the individual explicitly in the moral community as a person of profound moral worth among persons of equal dignity, recognition respect for oneself as a person affects how we live with one another; indeed, it would seem to be a condition of living together morally well. Recognition respect for oneself as an agent can be a powerful motivation for morally worthy conduct and the development of a morally worthy character. To the extent that what one values is being a person worthy of respect living a respect-worthy life, rather than merely feeling good about oneself, then recognition self-respect works with uncompromised evaluative self-respect to give individuals a self-conscious stake in the quality of their characters and conduct, which in turn ties them personally into the project of living a morally appropriate life.

Uncompromised evaluative self-respect, as a form of internalized monitoring of one's conduct and character, serves an important function socially but it also serves a profoundly moral function personally. For we are beings for whom the questions, 'What kind of person ought I to be?' and, 'What kind of life is worth living?' inevitably arise. Few things matter more than answering these questions well, and uncompromised evaluative self-respect enables us to know whether we are, in living out our answers, answering well. Moreover, as Hume points out, the concern to deserve and maintain self-respect, to "bear our own survey," is a powerful shaper of our characters, values, attitudes, motives, and conduct, of who and what we become. In providing us with the motivation and means for self-review, self-direction, and self-development, uncompromised evaluative self-respect enables us to be self-critically self-regulating, as persons ought to be. And, inasmuch as recognition self-respect requires staking one's worth on certain self-defining value and uncompromised evaluative self-respect requires not betraying one's value-commitments, they preserve one's integrity and identity.

From the perspective of individual flourishing, then, the various forms of self-respect are profoundly important. Just as significant, if not as obvious, the essays in the final section suggest, is the importance of self-respect to the moral flourishing of society.

X

Issues of self-respect have increasingly become important in public discussions in America about a variety of contemporary social problems. For example, it is impossible to adequately address the crises concerning the African American community, especially in America's inner cities—increasing racial discord and violence; the high rate of Black-on-Black crime and the tragically high death rate of young Black men; the failure of educational systems to meet even minimal needs of African American children; chronic unemployment and welfare dependency; the wasted lives, thwarted talents, and hopeless rage that characterize the Black underclass—without some attention to the self-hatred and crippled self-worth that fuels and is fueled by these conditions.[72] Concerns about self-worth also mark current discussions about a variety of educational issues, such as whether students are harmed or benefited in educational contexts that are segregated or integrated by gender or race, and the related debates over multicultural curricula. Recent discussions about such topics as sexual harassment, affirmative action, and social policies regarding gays and lesbians have all raised self-respect issues. These public discussions about how to deal with the continuing legacies of discrimination, exploitation, injustice, and oppression highlight the political dimensions of self-respect.

Self-respect is often regarded as primarily a personal phenomenon, a matter of the beliefs, attitudes, and conduct of the individual, and whether an individual respects herself or not is often regarded as something for which the individual bears the chief responsibility. However, many of the contemporary discussions recognize that there are substantial social and political dimensions to self-respect. For example, whether individuals respect themselves or not is very much a function of their social relationships and of the structure and functioning of the social institutions among which they live; when those relationships and institutions are unjust, discriminatory, or oppressive, self-respect can be diminished, distorted, or destroyed. Not surprisingly, resistance to injustice and struggles for liberation from oppression also implicate self-respect in a variety of ways. More deeply, the very nature and meaning of self-respect and how it is constituted and secured are subject to social construction, and the evaluation of such constructions involves issues of social justice. The essays in Part IV, "Politics," explore some of the connections among self-respect, justice, oppression, and liberation.

The interest among contemporary philosophers in the social and political dimensions of self-respect owes much to Rawls's attention to them in *A Theory of Justice*. For Rawls, issues of self-respect are at the core of a theory of social justice. Individuals' access to self-respect is, according to Rawls, to a large degree a function of how the basic institutional structure of society defines and distributes the social bases of self-respect, which include the messages conveyed in the structure and functioning of institutions concerning the relative moral worth of citizens, the distribution of fundamental political rights and civil liberties, access to the resources individuals need to pursue their plans of life, the availability of diverse associations and communities within which individuals can seek affirmation of their worth from others, and the norms governing public interaction among citizens. Since self-respect is vital to individuals' ability to pursue and fulfill their life plans and since its bases are social, just institutions and policies must be designed to support rather than undermine self-respect.

In "Self-Respect: Theory and Practice" (chapter 13), Laurence Thomas critically develops some Rawlsian themes in connection with issues of racism and the experience of Blacks in the United States. Thomas maintains that self-respect (i.e., recognition respect for oneself as an equal person) involves not only beliefs about one's moral status but also beliefs about one's social and political status. In particular, it involves the conviction that as a person one is deserving both of just treatment in social and political contexts and of whatever civil and institutional rights, privileges, opportunities, and protections are accorded other citizens in virtue of their being persons. Thus an African American who believes, as Booker T. Washington has been alleged to believe, that Blacks are in virtue of their race alone less deserving of full-fledged citizenship than whites did not have self-respect.

Thomas makes two further points of interest. First, in discussing the civil rights movement he explains how a political movement against social injustice can have the effect of enhancing the self-respect of

members of a group that has been subject to injustice; equally important, he identifies as *the* goal of the civil rights movement the securing
of the self-respect of Blacks (as well as the respect of whites for Blacks).
This suggests that the liberation of a group of people from the oppression of institutionalized injustice involves not only winning freedom and
equality but also liberating self-respect. Second, Thomas holds with
Rawls that since social institutions have a profound effect on how people view themselves, the justice of social institutions must be judged
according to their impact on self-respect. The social institutions of a
given society are fairly arranged if and only if they are conducive to
every member of society having self-respect. A racist society is execrably
unjust precisely because it targets people on the basis of their race in
ways that subvert self-respect.

Many writers have been concerned to identify the effects of injustice
and oppression on self-respect in order to better understand what must
be done to make society just. One thing made clear in these accounts is
the way in which the diminishment of self-respect helps to perpetuate
oppression. In his "Letter from Birmingham Jail," Martin Luther King
poignantly describes the effects of socially sanctioned segregation on the
self-respect of blacks. Most chilling is the "degenerating sense of nobod-
iness" that engenders a hopeless adjustment to segregation and an
inability to see the intolerable as intolerable.[73] Focusing on the "psychological oppression" of women in a patriarchal society, Sandra Bartky calls
attention to the "intimations of inferiority" rampant in a sexist society
that women internalize to become unwitting participants in their own
oppression by coming "to exercise harsh dominion over their *own* self-
esteem."[74] Richard Mohr argues that the continued denial of civil rights
to gays in America, in particular the denial of protection against discrimination in employment and housing, and the de facto demand that
gays stay "closeted"—forcing them to trade dignity and integrity for security—undermines the sense of dignity of gays, often to the point of rendering them unable to see their situation as unjust.[75] But the recognition
of what is degrading, intolerable, and unjust is, of course, a necessary
condition for resisting it.

In "Race, Class, and the Social Construction of Self-Respect" (chapter
14), Michele M. Moody-Adams discusses the influence on self-respect of
socially entrenched discrimination against and devaluation of groups of
people in virtue of their class or race. To better understand this influence, Moody-Adams proposes an account of self-respect that is strikingly
different from other contemporary accounts. The first part of the

account identifies two components of due respect for one's worth: (a) the conviction, and the readiness to act on it, "that one best affirms one's own value by using one's talents and abilities to contribute to one's survival," and (b) an inclination to develop those talents and abilities as far as one is able. This view of self-respect is striking in its attention to the everyday ways in which individuals live self-affirming lives. The second part of her account argues that self-respect is socially constructed. Every society develops intricate patterns of normative views and expectations about selves, self-worth, and appropriate forms of life, and about the social, political, and economic institutions and practices within which individuals may seek to affirm self-respect. These patterns of expectations shape our self-conceptions and our lives and provide the framework within which we recognize, evaluate, and seek to secure and enhance our worth and sense of worth. In a society with a history of race or class discrimination, the socially developed expectations that construct self-respect reflect the devaluation of persons of certain races or classes, with the effect that the capacity of individuals in disfavored groups to have self-respect can be undermined in a variety of ways. Moody-Adams's concluding discussion of aspects of the experience of many Black Americans that have enabled them to preserve self-respect despite such threats points in the direction of social reforms that may be necessary to ensure widespread access to self-respect.

How to preserve or restore self-respect in the face of injustice or oppression has been of concern to many writers. Recall, for example, Boxill's discussion of the significance of protest to that task. Patricia Hill Collins identifies numerous means that Black women have employed in community with one another to create self-definitions that foster self-respect and resistance to oppression.[76] In their inspiring autobiographies, three freedom-fighters—Frederick Douglass, Malcolm X, and Rigoberta Menchu—reflect on the development of their own self-respect as vital to their ability as individuals to participate in monumental struggles against oppression, and prescribe projects and methods to engender liberatory self-respect in their people.[77] In his examination of gay politics, Mohr argues that inasmuch as the heart of the coming-out experience—the "fundament of gays' experience as political creatures"—is the public affirmation of the individual's human dignity, the strategies employed by the gay movement in its struggles for justice must have as their chief goal the assertion of the dignity of gays as gay persons.[78] Mohr also argues that because life in the closet is morally debased and debasing, self-respect requires coming-out, and the maintenance of self-respect by an openly gay individual requires "outing" others (publicly exposing the gay orientation of others without their consent).[79] One conclusion that emerges from these discussions is that the restoration and preservation of self-respect, which is essential to survival under oppression and to liberation from it, is not something an individual does alone but something that must be done in community with others and that requires some form of political activism.

However, even where individuals under oppression develop and maintain self-respect, there may still be problems. For one of the effects of oppression is the inability of individuals to recognize distortions in their sense of worth. It can be the case that the self-conceptions of oppressed people and their understanding of what constitutes appropriate conduct and treatment are thoroughly compromised, or that oppression has diminished not only their self-respect but also their very selves and the abilities they would need to call on in order to have self-respect, so that although they presently respect themselves as far as is possible for them, they do so in ways that reinforce their oppression. Meyers (chapter 12) points out that in some circumstances what self-respect is typically understood to involve may not be what would be effective for liberation. This suggests a need for reconceptualizing self-respect so as not to regard as unproblematic the self-valuings of individuals in contexts of oppression, and to enable self-respect to promote liberation rather than perpetuate oppression.

In the final selection, "Toward a Feminist Conception of Self-Respect" (chapter 15), I undertake such a reconceptualization. Feminists have seen self-respect as essential to the empowerment of women to challenge and change subordinating institutions and practices of patriarchal society. But I argue that insofar as conceptions of self-respect are not informed by an awareness of its political dimensions, they are less than conducive to liberation. Emancipatory theory and practice call for a feminist conception of self-respect; I propose a reconceptualization of recognition self-respect to meet that need. This reconceptualization involves regarding the object of self-respect in a more particularist and communitarian and less generic and individualist way than contemporary accounts have been wont to do; it encourages us to respect ourselves not simply as persons or as certain kinds of persons, but as the particular individual that each of us is, embedded in a network of relationships with other particular individuals whose ability to respect themselves and others profoundly affects our own. The feminist conception also involves a more emotionally engaged mode of valuing oneself and stresses the importance of self-understanding. In proposing this reconceptualizaiton, I call attention to the essential contestability of the central concepts on which contemporary accounts of self-respect rest and the consequent ideological malleability of the concept of self-respect itself, and open the door to further rethinking of self-respect.

XI

In many ways philosophical interest in self-respect is set to enter a new phase, the groundwork for which has been laid by the essays in this volume. There is still much work left to be done in the area of conceptual analysis, but such projects must now proceed from an explicit acknowledgment of the extent to which the concept is complex, contested, profoundly moral, deeply political, and connected to a plethora of philosophically rich topics. There was a time not so long ago when many philosophers, forgetful of what Aristotle, Hume, and Kant had insisted on, regarded work on self-respect as peripheral; but in the past quarter-century the essays in this volume have made it clear that thinking about self-respect is as central to moral philosophy as it has always been to moral life.

Notes

1. Aristotle, *Nichomachean Ethics*, bk. II, ch. 7; bk. IV, ch. 3. Aurelius, *Meditations*, bk. IV, sec. 16. Augustine, *Confessions*, bk. X; *City of God*, bk. XIV, ch. 13. Aquinas, *Summa Theologica*, pt. I-II, Q. 60, Q. 66. Montaigne, *Essays*. Descartes, *The Passions of the Soul*, pt. II, arts. 54, 59, 62, 66; pt. III, arts. 149-164, 190-191, 203-207. Pascal, *Pensees* 100, 147-159. Spinoza, *The Ethics*, pt. III. Hobbes, *Leviathan*, pt. I, ch. 10, ch. 15; pt. II, ch. 18. Rousseau, *Discourse on Inequality*, pt. II; *Emile*. Hume, *A Treatise of Human Nature*, bk. II, pt. I, II; bk III, pt. III, sec. vi; *Enquiry Concerning the Principles of Morals*, sec. IX. Hegel, *Philosophy of History*, pt. II. Mill, *Utilitarianism*, ch. 2. Nietzsche, *Beyond Good and Evil*. For further references, see the essay on "Honor" (especially the section on "Honor as due self-esteem: magnanimity or proper pride,") in Mortimer J. Adler, ed., *Great Ideas: A Syntopicon of Great Books of the Western World* (Chicago: Encyclopedia Britannica, Inc., 1952).

2. John Rawls, *A Theory of Justice* (Cambridge, Mass.: Harvard University Press, 1971). Section 67 appears as chapter 7 of this volume.

3. In this volume see Dillon (chapter 15), Hill (chapters 3 and 6), Darwall (chapter 10), Massey (chapter 11), Moody-Adams (chapter 14), Telfer (chap-

ter 5), and Thomas (chapter 13). See also Robin S. Dillon, "How To Lose Your Self-Respect," *American Philosophical Quarterly* 29 (1992): 125–139; Koyeli Ghosh-Dastidar, "Respect for Persons and Self-Respect: Western and Indian," *Journal of Indian Council of Philosophical Research* 5 (1987): 83–93; Thomas E. Hill, Jr., "Self-Respect," in *Encyclopedia of Ethics*, ed. Lawrence C. Becker and Charlotte B. Becker (New York: Garland Publishing, Inc., 1992); Stephen J. Massey, "Kant on Self-Respect," *Journal of the History of Philosophy* 21 (1983): 57–73; David Sachs, "How To Distinguish Self-Respect from Self-Esteem," *Philosophy and Public Affairs* 10 (1981): 346–360, and "Self-Respect and Respect for Others: Are They Independent?" in *Respect for Persons, Tulane Studies in Philosophy*, vol. 31, ed. O. H. Green (New Orleans: Tulane University Press, 1982), pp. 109–128; Laurence Thomas, "Morality and Our Self-Concept," *Journal of Value Inquiry* 12 (1978): 258–268, and "Rawlsian Self-Respect and the Black Consciousness Movement," *The Philosophical Forum* 9 (1977–1978): 303–314; and Robert J. Yanal, "Self-Esteem," *Noûs* 21 (1987): 363–379. (I include works that purport to deal with self-esteem, since whether this is the same as or differs from self-respect is subject to debate; see section VII below.)

4. H. J. N. Horsburgh, "The Plurality of Moral Standards," *Philosophy* 24 (1954): 332–346.

5. Stephen L. Darwall, *Impartial Reason* (Ithaca: Cornell University Press, 1983).

6. David B. Wong, *Moral Relativity* (Berkeley: University of California Press, 1984).

7. See Hill (chapter 3 of this volume); Joel Feinberg, "The Nature and Value of Rights," *Journal of Value Inquiry* 4 (1970): 243–257; Alan Gewirth, *Reason and Morality* (Chicago: University of Chicago Press, 1978); Virginia Held, "Reasonable Progress and Self-Respect," *The Monist* 57 (1973): 12–27; Loren Lomasky, *Persons, Rights, and the Moral Community* (Oxford: Oxford University Press, 1987); A. I. Melden, *Rights and Persons* (Berkeley: University of California Press, 1977); Diana T. Meyers, "The Politics of Self-Respect," *Hypatia* 1 (1986): 83–100; and Richard D. Mohr, *Gays/Justice: A Study of Ethics, Society, and Law* (New York: Columbia University Press, 1988).

8. See Lynne Balaief, "Self-Esteem and Human Equality," *Philosophy and Phenomenological Research* 36 (1975): 25–43, and Amy Gutman, *Liberal Equality* (Cambridge: Cambridge University Press, 1980).

9. See W. D. Falk, "Morality, Form, and Content," in *Ought, Reasons, and Morality: The Collected Papers of W. D. Falk* (Ithaca: Cornell University Press, 1986), pp. 232–247, and Thomas E. Hill, Jr., "Pains and Projects: Justifying to Oneself," in Hill, *Autonomy and Self-Respect* (Cambridge: Cambridge University Press, 1991).

10. Richmond T. Campbell, *Self-Love and Self-Respect: A Philosophical Study of Egoism*

(Ottawa: Canadian Library of Philosophy, 1979).

11. Michael S. Pritchard, *On Becoming Responsible* (Lawrence, Kans.: University Press of Kansas, 1991), and "Self-Regard and the Supererogatory," in Green, ed., *Respect for Persons*, pp. 139–151.

12. See Stephen D. Hudson, *Human Character and Morality: Reflections from the History of Ideas* (Boston: Routledge & Kegan Paul, 1986), and James D. Wallace, *Virtues and Vices* (Ithaca: Cornell University Press, 1978).

13. See Taylor (chapter 9 of this volume) and Pritchard, *On Becoming Responsible*.

14. Meyers (chapter 12 of this volume).

15. Mike W. Martin, ed., *Self-Deception and Self-Understanding* (Lawrence, Kans.: University Press of Kansas, 1985), and *Self-Deception and Morality* (Lawrence, Kans.: University Press of Kansas, 1986).

16. Trudy Govier, "Self-Trust, Autonomy, and Self-Esteem," *Hypatia* 8 (1993): 99–120.

17. Jean Hampton, "Selflessness and the Loss of Self," *Social Philosophy and Policy* 10 (1993): 135–165.

18. See Jeffrie Murphy and Jean Hampton, *Forgiveness and Mercy* (Cambridge: Cambridge University Press, 1988); Joram Graf Haber, *Forgiveness* (Savage, Md.: Rowman and Littlefield, 1991); and Margaret Holmgren, "Forgiveness and the Intrinsic Value of Persons," *American Philosophical Quarterly* 30 (1993): 341–352.

19. Robert Solomon, *The Passions* (New York: Basic Books, 1977).

20. See Deigh (chapter 8 of this volume), Rawls (chapter 7), Taylor (chapter 9); John Kekes, "Shame and Moral Progress," in *Ethical Theory: Character and Virtue, Midwest Studies in Philosophy* vol. 13, ed. Peter A. French, Theodore E. Uehling, and Howard K. Wettstein (Notre Dame: University of Notre Dame Press, 1988), pp. 282–296; Pritchard, *On Becoming Responsible*; Bela Szabados, "Embarrassment and Self-Esteem," *Journal of Philosophical Research* 15 (1989–1990): 341–349; and Laurence Thomas, *Living Morally: A Psychology of Moral Character* (Philadelphia: Temple University Press, 1989), and "Morality, the Self, and Our Natural Sentiments," in *Emotion: Philosophical Studies*, ed. K. D. Irani and G. E. Meyers (New York: Haven Publishing Corp., 1983), pp. 144–163.

21. See Jon Elster, "Self-Realization in Work and Politics: The Marxist Conception of the Good Life," *Social Philosophy and Policy* 3 (1985–1986): 97–126; Owen Flanagan, *Varieties of Moral Personality: Ethics and Psychological Realism* (Cambridge, Mass.: Harvard University Press, 1991); and Thomas, *Living Morally*.

22. See Deigh (chapter 8 of this volume); Carl Cranor, "Justice, Respect, and Self-Respect," *Philosophy Research Archives* 2 (1976); Norman Daniels, "Equal

Liberty and Unequal Worth of Liberty," in *Reading Rawls: Critical Studies of "A Theory of Justice,"* ed. Norman Daniels (New York: Basic Books, 1975), pp. 253–281; Gerald Doppelt, "Rawls's System of Justice: A Critique from the Left," *Noûs* 15 (1981): 259–307; Robert E. Lane, "Government and Self-Esteem," *Political Theory* 10 (1982): 5–31; Frank Michelman, "Constitutional Welfare Rights and *A Theory of Justice,*" in *Reading Rawls*, pp. 319–347; B. C. Postow, "Economic Dependence and Self-Respect," *The Philosophical Forum* (1978–1979): 181–205; Wayne Proudfoot, "Rawls on Self-Respect and Social Union," *Journal of Chinese Philosophy* 5 (1978): 255–269; Geoffrey Scarre, "Utilitarianism and Self-Respect," *Utilitas* 4 (1992): 27–42; Henry Shue, "Liberty and Self-Respect," *Ethics* 85 (1975): 195–203; Kenneth Strike, "Education, Justice, and Self-Respect: A School for Rodney Dangerfield," *Philosophy of Education* 35 (1980): 41–49; Thomas, "Rawlsian Self-Respect and the Black Consciousness Movement"; and Yanal, "Self-Esteem."

23. See Balaief, "Self-Esteem and Human Equality"; Doppelt, "Rawls's System of Justice"; Victor J. Seidler, *Kant, Respect, and Injustice: The Limits of Liberal Moral Theory* (London: Routledge & Kegan Paul, 1986), and *The Moral Limits of Modernity: Love, Inequality, and Oppression* (New York: St. Martins Press, 1991); and Simone Weil, *The Need for Roots* (London: Routledge & Kegan Paul, 1972) and *Seventy Letters* (Oxford: Oxford University Press, 1965).

24. See Boxill (chapter 4 of this volume), Dillon (chapter 15), Meyers (chapter 12), Moody-Adams (chapter 14); Susan Babbitt, "Feminism and Objective Interests: The Role of Transformation Experiences in Rational Deliberation," in *Feminist Epistemologies*, ed. Linda Alcoff and Elizabeth Potter (New York: Routledge, 1993), pp. 254–264; Sandra Lee Bartky, *Femininity and Domination: Studies in the Phenomenology of Oppression* (New York: Routledge, 1990); Bernard R. Boxill, *Blacks and Social Justice* (Lanham, Md.: Rowman & Littlefield, 1992); Patricia Hill Collins, *Black Feminist Thought: Knowledge, Consciousness, and the Politics of Empowerment* (New York: Routledge, 1990); Gertrude Ezorsky, *Racism and Justice: The Case for Affirmative Action* (Ithaca: Cornell University Press, 1991); Ann Ferguson, "A Feminist Aspect Theory of the Self," in *Science, Morality, and Feminist Theory*, ed. Marsha Hanen and Kai Nielsen (Calgary: University of Calgary Press, 1987), pp. 339–356; Howard McGary, "Reparations, Self-Respect, and Public Policy," in *Ethical Theory and Society*, ed. David Goldberg (N.Y.: Holt, Rinehart, & Winston, 1988); Meyers, "The Politics of Self-Respect"; Mohr, *Gays/Justice* and *Gay Ideas: Outings and Other Controversies* (Boston: Beacon Press, 1992); Postow, "Economic Dependence and Self-Respect"; and Cornell West, *Race Matters* (New York: Vintage Books, 1993).

25. David DeGrazia, "Grounding a Right to Health Care in Self-Respect and Self-

Esteem," *Public Affairs Quarterly* 5 (1991): 301–318.

26. Strike, "Education, Justice, and Self-Respect."

27. David Braybrooke, *Ethics in the World of Business* (Totowa, N.J.: Rowman & Allenheld, 1983).

28. See Diana T. Meyers, "Work and Self-Respect," in *Moral Rights in the Workplace*, ed. Gertrude Ezorsky (Albany: State University of New York Press, 1987), pp. 18–27, and Jerry Cederblom and Charles J. Dougherty, *Ethics at Work* (Belmont, Calif.: Wadsworth, 1990).

29. Mike W. Martin, *Everyday Morality: An Introduction to Applied Ethics* (Belmont, Calif.: Wadsworth, 1989).

30. For a shorter list of questions, most of which are incorporated here, see Hill, "Self-Respect," in *Encyclopedia of Ethics.*

31. There is reason, however, to exercise caution in relying on the concept of respect to make sense of self-respect. For not only does a person's respect or lack of respect for herself reverberate throughout her self and her life in ways and to an extent that another person's respect or lack of it for her does not, but also, not all of the dimensions of respect, even of respect for other persons, translate into modes of self-respect. Consider, for example, respect as discrimination, deference, or politeness.

32. The *Oxford English Dictionary* (Oxford: Oxford University Press, 1971), compact edition, and *The American Heritage Dictionary* (Boston: American Heritage and Houghton Mifflin, 1970), among others, define "pride" in terms of self-respect and self-esteem in just these ways. Cf. Lawrence C. Becker, "Pride," in *Encyclopedia of Ethics.*

33. The O.E.D. reports that "self-respect," understood as "due regard for the dignity of one's person," entered the English language at the end of the eighteenth century, while "self-esteem," defined as "a favorable opinion of oneself," entered in the mid-seventeenth century. Whether anything of significance hangs on the transition to "self-respect" from earlier terms is something that philosophers have not yet addressed. More work needs to be done in identifying the intellectual and political contexts in which concern about self-respect so-called comes to the fore, and in determining whether such concern characterizes particular moments in the Western philosophical tradition.

34. Aristotle, *Nichomachean Ethics*, trans. W. D. Ross, in *The Basic Works of Aristotle*, ed. Richard McKeon (New York: Random House, 1941).

35. Literally, "having a great soul," traditionally translated by the Latin "magnanimity," but also rendered as "proper pride" and as a "high-mindedness" that involves "pride and confident self-respect." For "magnanimity," see *Nichomachean Ethics*, trans. Terence Irwin (Indianapolis: Hackett, 1985) and

Ethics, trans. J. A. K. Thomson (London: Penguin Classics, 1976). Thomson's glossary provides "dignity" and "proper pride" as synonyms. For "proper pride," see the Ross translation. For "high-mindedness," see *Nichomachean Ethics*, trans. Martin Ostwald (Indianapolis: Bobbs-Merrill, 1962). Ostwald's glossary defends this translation as "better suited to rendering the pride and confident self-respect inherent in this concept" (p. 311).

36. *Nichomachean Ethics*, Irwin trans., pp. 408–409.

37. Thomas Hobbes, *Leviathan* (Indianapolis: Bobbs-Merrill, Library of Liberal Arts, 1958).

38. David Hume, *Enquiries Concerning the Human Understanding and Concerning the Principles of Morals*, ed. L. A. Selby-Bigge, 2nd ed. (Oxford: Clarendon Press, 1972).

39. David Hume, *A Treatise of Human Nature*, ed. L. A. Selby-Bigge, 2nd ed. (Oxford: Clarendon Press, 1978).

40. Thus, Hume uses these terms interchangeably throughout Book II of the *Treatise*.

41. Thus in Book III of the *Treatise*, where he discusses the moral point of view, Hume uses these terms discriminately, which he was unable to do in Book II.

42. *Grunlegung zur Metaphysik der Sitten*, in *Kants gesammelte Schriften*, ed. Königliche Preussischen Akademie, 23 vols. (Berlin: Georg Reimer, 1907), vol. 4, p. 429 (hereafter KgS); translated as *Groundwork of the Metaphysic of Morals*, trans. H. J. Paton (New York: Harper Torchbooks, 1964) (hereafter G; Akademie pagination given).

43. Among those who treat this formulation of the Categorical Imperative as a respect-for-persons principle are John E. Atwell, "Kant's Notion of Respect for Persons," in Green, ed., *Respect for Persons*, pp. 17–30; Alan Donagan, *The Theory of Morality* (Chicago: University of Chicago Press, 1977); R. S. Downie and Elizabeth Telfer, *Respect for Persons* (London: George Allen and Unwin, 1969); and Stephen D. Hudson, "The Nature of Respect," *Social Theory and Practice* 6 (1980): 69–90. This view is also a staple of introductory ethics textbooks. But see Carl Cranor, "Kant's Respect-for-Persons Principle," *International Studies in Philosophy* 12 (1980): 19–40, for an argument against this interpretation of the Categorical Imperative.

44. *Die Metaphysik der Sitten*, KgS vol. 6; part II translated as *The Doctrine of Virtue: Part II of the Metaphysic of Morals*, trans. Mary Gregor (Philadelphia: University of Pennsylvania Press, 1964) (cited as M; Akademie pagination); also translated as *Metaphysical Principles of Virtue* in *Ethical Philosophy*, trans. James Ellington (Indianapolis: Hackett Publishing Company, 1983) (cited as E; Akademie pagination). *Kritik der praktischen Vernunft*, KgS vol. 5; translated as *Critique of Practical Reason*, trans. Lewis White Beck (Indianapolis: Bobbs-

Merrill, Library of Liberal Arts, 1956) (cited as C; Akademie pagination). *Eine Vorselung Kant's uber Ethik im Auftrage der Kantgesellschaft*, ed. Paul Menzer; translated as *Lectures on Ethics*, trans. Louis Infield (Indianapolis: Hackett Publishing Company, 1963) (cited as L). For a recognition of some complexity in Kant's account, see Stephen J. Massey, "Kant on Self-Respect."

45. On dignity as grounded in the capacity for autonomy, see G, 435, 439, 440; C, 90. On dignity grounded in the realization of this capacity, see G, 401n, 434, 435, 440; C, 81.

46. See, e.g., G, 401, 434–36, 440; C, 77–79; L, 185–191.

47. See M, 420, 464, 465; L, 185–191.

48. For a useful and influential analyses of these two kinds of worth, see Gregory Vlastos, "Justice and Equality," in *Social Justice*, ed. Richard Brandt (Englewood Cliffs, N.J.: Prentice Hall, 1962), pp. 31–72.

49. On the connection between dignity and human rights, see Michael J. Meyer and William A. Parent, eds., *The Constitution of Rights* (Ithaca: Cornell University Press, 1992).

50. See, e.g., Sachs, "How To Distinguish Self-Respect from Self-Esteem," Thomas, *Living Morally*, and Pritchard, *On Becoming Responsible*.

51. Boxill, *Blacks and Social Justice*, p. 195.

52. Ibid, p. 197.

53. Michael J. Meyer, "Dignity, Rights, and Self-Control," *Ethics* 99 (April 1989): 520–534.

54. Primo Levi, *Survival at Auschwitz: The Nazi Assault on Humanity* (New York: MacMillan, 1958).

55. Terrence Des Pres, *The Survivor: An Anatomy of Life in the Death Camps* (New York: Oxford University Press, 1976), pp. 62–3.

56. Ibid, p. 64.

57. Wallace, *Virtues and Vices*, pp. 152–158.

58. Feinberg, "The Nature and Value of Rights."

59. See Meyer, "Dignity, Rights, and Self-Control," and Pritchard, *On Becoming Responsible*.

60. Ghosh-Dastidar, "Respect for Persons and Self-Respect."

61. See Hampton, "Selflessness and the Loss of Self," and Dillon, "How To Lose Your Self-Respect."

62. See Martin, *Everyday Morality*, and Govier, "Self-Trust, Autonomy, and Self-Esteem."

63. Rawls, *A Theory of Justice*, p. 178.

64. Yanal, "Self-Esteem."

65. Darwall, *Impartial Reason*. But see Hill's response in "Darwall on Practical Reason," *Ethics* 96 (1986): 604–619.

66. Two extensive surveys of the relevant psychological literature concluded that not only is there no universally accepted definition of self-esteem, but there is a great deal of confusion and disagreement among theorists both as to the nature of self-esteem and as to why people need and want it. See L. Edward Wells and Gerald Marwell, *Self-Esteem: Its Conceptualization and Measurement* (Beverly Hills: Sage Publications, 1976), and T. Scheff, *Crisis in the Academic System: Is the Emperor Wearing Clothes?* (unpublished manuscript, University of California, Santa Barbara, 1990), cited in Sheldon Solomon, Jeff Greenberg, and Tom Psyzscznski, "A Terror Management Theory of Social Behavior: The Psychological Functions of Self-Esteem and Cultural Worldviews," *Advances in Experimental Social Psychology* 24 (1991): 93–159.

67. I have drawn here on *The Encyclopedia Dictionary of Psychology*, ed. Rom Harre and Roger Lamb (Cambridge: The MIT Press, 1983); Frank J. Bruno, *The Dictionary of Key Words in Psychology* (London: Routledge & Kegan Paul, 1986); *The Encyclopedia of Psychology*, ed. Raymond J. Corsini (New York: John Willey & Sons, 1984); Stanley Coopersmith, *The Antecedents of Self-Esteem* (Palo Alto: Consulting Psychologists Press, 1981); Morris Rosenberg, *Conceiving the Self* (New York: Basic Books, 1979); and Wells and Marwell, *Self-Esteem.* It should be noted that it is not uncommon to identify self-esteem as an attitude that may be either positive or negative, but I follow common usage in treating self-esteem as an attitude with positive content.

68. William James, "The Consciousness of Self," in *The Principles of Psychology*, vol. 1 (New York: Dover Publications, Inc., 1950 [1890]).

69. George Herbert Mead, *Mind, Self, and Society* (Chicago: University of Chicago Press, 1934).

70. Among those who concur with this way of carving up the territory of self-worth are Govier, "Self-Trust, Autonomy, and Self-Esteem"; Martin, *Everyday Morality*; Sachs, "How To Distinguish Self-Respect from Self-Esteem"; and Axel Honneth, "Integrity and Disrespect: Principles of a Conception of Morality Based on the Theory of Recognition," *Political Theory* 20 (1992): 187–201.

71. Thomas, *Living Morally.*

72. For an eloquent discussion of these issues, see West, *Race Matters*, especially chapter 1, "Nihilism in Black America."

73. Martin Luther King, "Letter from Birmingham Jail," in *Why We Can't Wait* (New York: Penguin Books, 1964), p. 86.

74. Bartky, "On Psychological Oppression," in *Femininity and Domination*, p. 22.

75. Mohr, *Gays/Justice.*

76. Collins, *Black Feminist Thought*, pp. 91–114.

77. Frederick Douglass, *My Bondage and My Freedom* (New York: Dover

Publications, 1969); Malcom X, *The Autobiography of Malcom X*, as told to Alex Haley (New York: Ballantine Books, 1964); *I, Rigoberta Menchu: An Indian Woman in Guatemala* (New York: Verso, 1983).

78. Mohr, *Gays/Justice*, p. 327.
79. Mohr, *Gay Ideas*.

✛

Dignity,
Personhood,
and Rights

✛

2

+

Dignity

+

Aurel Kolnai

Why, however, should it be necessarily wrong to discuss the
nebulous in a businesslike manner?
—Findlay, *Meinong's Theory of Objects and Values*

I. General Approach (Priming, *Grundierung*)

1. The Conceptual Area of Dignity

The English word "Dignity" is a noun directly borrowed from the
Romance (Latin, French); like "Beauty," it is an abstract noun not deriv-
able from a primary English adjective. Just as there is no direct analogue
in English of "beau," "bello," "schön," etc., there is none for "dignus,"
"digne," "digno" or even for "würdig," though the German adjective is
itself derived from the noun "Würde" (dignity). These foreign adjectives
are all capable of a determining genitival or phrasal construction: thus,
"digne d'attention," "digne d'être honoré," "liebenswürdig," "würdig,
gewählt zu werden," etc. For the idea of desert, aptitude, equivalence or
suitability as here expressed, we must use in English some word not connected with "dignity" e.g. the verb "deserve" itself or, especially, the adjec-

This essay was originally published in *Philosophy* 5 (1976). Copyright © 1976 by the Royal
Institute of Philosophy. Reprinted with the permission of Cambridge University Press.

tive "worthy" or sometimes "worth" (an adjective for predicative use): "worthy of being admired," "worth doing," etc., as indeed in German "wert" (small "w") may stand for "würdig" ("liebenswürdig" is closer to "amiable," "liebenswert" to "lovable"). On the other hand, "Dignity" does exactly correspond with "dignitas," "dignité" and "Würde." For the quality of *having dignity*, possessed by that which is "digne," "würdig," etc., "absolutely," without a specifying genitive or clause, we use the term "dignified" (for which German also has "würdevoll"): a word synthetic and somewhat clumsy exactly like "beautiful." From "worthy" or "worth" to "dignified" there seems to be a pretty far cry. But an essential link clearly subsists. Dignity means Worth or Worthiness in some "absolute," autonomized and objectivized, as it were "featural" sense; and it is towards an elucidation of that sense—Dignity as the quality of that which is "dignified"—that I am concerned to make an attempt here.

If Dignity means Worthiness or Value of some kind—perhaps something not far remote from "Worth"—it plainly does not mean Worthiness, Value or the quality of being "good" either in the sense open to any further determination as expressed by "worthy of…" or in the sense of Value or Goodness as a blanket *pro*-concept regardless of any more specific determination. It has a *descriptive content*. Significant kinds of value, goodness, appreciability or desirability may have nothing in particular to do with Dignity. It is, in this respect, on a par with any of the basic moral virtues such as justice, truthfulness, benevolence, chastity, courage, etc., including even integrity or conscientiousness, none of which is synonymous with Moral Goodness or Virtue as such, and each of which, notwithstanding its possible built-in reference to Morality (and moral evaluation) as such, is susceptible of contentual description.

I propose now to examine (i) what appears to be the proper and characteristic *response* we yield to dignity when we sense its presence in an object, (ii) the set of more particular and concrete *features* which may be empirically ascertained to cluster round the phenomenon of Dignity: its conceptual aura or halo as it were.

(i) What is "good" in any sense will evoke a *pro* attitude as such, an attitude appreciative, supporting, bearing a sign of attraction, etc.; what is "pleasant" will evoke liking, desire, delight; what is "instrumentally good" is naturally rewarded by something like appreciative recognition, a response of approbation, and a tendency to choose it; the "beautiful" elicits a response that might be described as delight with a tinge of devotion; and the morally right conduct or good character (moral virtue) compels "approval," i.e., a sort of devoted appreciation with an aspect of volitive approbation to it—a gesture of sanction as it were. Obviously there is a very high degree of overlapping between these modalities of appreciative response; as indeed, on the object side, the pleasant and the beautiful, the morally good and the beautiful, the morally good and the useful, etc., display an intrinsic overlap which only prigs and pedants, slaves of didactic classifications, and fanatics of hierarchy, would deny. Still, the distinctions are natural, ineliminable, and well grounded in our experience of reality. Can we attempt at all to assign, to adumbrate at least, a distinctive response to Dignity (or "the dignified")? Whatever such a response may be, it must bear a close resemblance to our devoted and admiring appreciation for beauty (its "high" forms at any rate) on the one hand, to our reverent approval of moral goodness (and admiration, say, for heroic virtue) on the other. Dignity commands emphatic respect, a reverential mode of response, an "upward-looking" type of the *pro* attitude: a "bowing" gesture if I may so call it. There is less emphasis in the paradigm response to Dignity on delight and satisfyingness than in aesthetic appreciation, and at the same time less on the deontic or mandatory or even on the hortatory aspect of moral approval; and no intentional reference at all to the useful and functionally efficient. In contrast with moral approval as such, it has little, if anything, to do with practical approbation and "action-guiding" rule-obedience in any direct sense. Our experience of Dignity is centrally an experience of "Height": a concept, alas, obscure and insufficiently analyzed, yet widely and intimately familiar to men—except perhaps to consistent and inveterate positivists. But if cautious sobriety and careful fidelity to facts are seen to be the criteria of a positivistic approach, I am all for positivism. I do not imagine that by pointing to the splendid notion of Height I have said anything definitive about our response to Dignity. For one thing, I cannot now embark, in passing, on an elucidation of "Higher" and "Lower." In the second place, our experience of the quality of Dignity, though it presupposes our sense of the distinction between Superior and Inferior (e.g., the Spiritual and the Material, or the Rational and the Instinctual), is by no means identical with it. What is dignified is not necessarily sublime, and Dignity is not just a lesser degree of Sublimity. Our response to the sublime has something awe-struck about it, as if the presence of the sublime edified us but at the same time shocked or crushed us. Whereas, when faced with the quality of Dignity as such we certainly also feel edified but not so much "crushed," overwhelmed or even deeply excited as, rather, tranquillized and perhaps impressed with a sense of *our own* dignity rather than with a sense of our own smallness and triviality. In other

Aurel Kolnai   55

words, the dignified connotes the idea of *verticality* in a more discreet fashion than does the sublime, and connotes, at the same time, a certain idea of *reciprocity*. So far as we recognize Godhead or anything "Divine," we eminently attribute sublimity to it, rather than dignity; on the contrary, even "humanists" in any sense of the word would seldom speak of "human sublimity," whereas the strange concept of "human dignity"—discussed in part II—is one of the notions we seem to be most familiar with in whichever linguistic medium we may live and think.

It looks as if our response to Dignity is the purest "value response" (*Wertantwort*) as such: in particular, less stirring and less impregnated with delight than our aesthetic, less organically connected with approval and with any practical or deontic accent than our moral responses. If Dignity means "being worthy of ...," the completion that most aptly suggests itself would seem to be "worthy of being appreciatively acknowledged *as* worthy to be thus acknowledged and appreciated, *sans plus*."

(ii) What are some of the "more particular and concrete features" that strike us as eminently dignified? No two of us might answer this question in exactly the same way, but I trust that the following attempt at a random enumeration would hardly shock or surprise anybody: at least, not in virtue of anything I include, though very likely as regards my inevitable sins of omission. Here, then, are the features typifying Dignity that most vividly occur to me. First—the qualities of composure, calmness, restraint, reserve, and emotions or passions subdued and securely controlled without being negated or dissolved (*verhaltene Leidenschaft* in German). Secondly—the qualities of distinctness, delimitation, and distance; of something that conveys the idea of being intangible, invulnerable, inaccessible to destructive or corruptive or subversive interference. Dignity is thus comparable, metaphorically, to something like "tempered steel." Thirdly, in consonance therewith, Dignity also tends to connote the features of self-contained serenity, of a certain inward and toned-down but yet translucent and perceptible power of self-assertion: the dignified type of character is chary of emphatic activity rather than sullenly passive, perhaps impassive rather than impassible, patient rather than anxiously defensive, and devoid but not incapable of aggressiveness. So far, the predicates we have listed are largely but by no means exclusively of the moral order: they appear partly to imply wisdom and percipience; and they are chiefly applicable to so-called "human beings," i.e., persons, but again not exclusively so: much dignity in this sense seems to me proper to the Cat, and not a little, with however different connotations, to the Bull or the Elephant. What about the monumentality of some trees and the silent life that animates plants in general? Is not the austere mountainous plateau of Old Castile a dignified landscape, even if we set aside the dignity of the wiry stoic race it has bred and the majestic sonority of the language it has brought alive? And, though man-made, cannot works of art (especially of the "classic," though not exactly "classicistic," type) have a dignity of their own? What we credit with "dignity" here is, above all, the kind of "simplicity" that is not the simplicity of linear monotony or notional perspicuity but, on the contrary, a great complexity of aspects and fullness of significance condensed into a bold stroke, whether suggestive of sweet harmony or of bitter asperity, by an extreme and perhaps undecipherable economy of means. (The Spanish adjectives *escueto*—"spare"—and *adusto*—"dry," "parched"—express it most evocatively.)

In conclusion, I must point to one more, and fairly central, aspect of Dignity, though I have hinted at it already when mentioning "inward power" and the quality of the "monumental." The aspect I have in mind is *weight*; the weight of strong bones rather than of exuberant flesh; the "weight" that impresses itself upon us in some portraits by Rembrandt rather than that which oppresses us in Rubensian opulence. I have also anticipated my reference to it in emphasizing the quality of the self-contained (in German: *das In-sich-Ruhende*). With its firm stance and solid immovability, the dignified quietly defies the world—even though, like everything else, it would have no significance whatever outside the context of the world.

2. Dignity and Value Categories

Dignity obviously should not be identified with Morality. To a large extent, it enters into the category of the aesthetical. An indefinite variety of objects plainly insusceptible of moral appraisal can none the less exhibit dignity. Nor is it possible, conversely, to interpret morality as a sub-class of dignity. Moral virtues as important as benevolence and diligence, or again some forms of self-improvement, are not paradigmatically relevant to dignity. It implies no contradiction to say that X is a morally better but a less dignified person than Y or that Y is a more sinful person than X and yet less prone than X to certain frivolous attitudes which are distinctively opposed to dignity. Again dignity is not a purely aesthetical concept—unless we water down the category of the aesthetic to the point of wanting to say that everything that is intrinsically valuable is *ipso facto* "beautiful"—and that, on the other hand, such basic aesthetical dimensions as grace, shapeliness, intensity and poignancy have little or nothing to do with dignity (cf. the characteristic contrast established by Schiller between *Anmut und Würde*). Does this mean that Dignity must be accorded a primordial categorial status of its own, bordering on the ethical and the aesthetical alike, or intercalated between the two even though merging into both? That question is merely terminological. The phenomenon of Dignity remains the same, whether we choose to call it a participant in both the ethical and the aesthetical realm of values or to erect it into a third realm of value overlapping with both. Two remarks, however, need to made at this point.

(i) When I associate Dignity with "Weight"—I might also speak of solidity, firmness, density or "compactness"—does this not sound as if I had in mind something like an "*ontological*" value, as distinct both from the ethical and the aesthetic? But the phrase "ontological value" has an unsavoury naturalistic tang about it: reminiscent of the Eleatics, Plato, Aristotle and his scholastic copyists and bowdlerizers, of "static" rationalists and "dynamic" vitalists, of historicist and millennarian Utopians. It is not Value that constitutes Being, and not a "more real" Being or a "perfection" of any kind of "nature" *qua* a nature of its kind that we emotively apprehend as value or a "greater" or "higher" value. It is not Power in any sense that we mean by Good or Right, nor does superior Power testify to "truer" Goodness or a more valid Right. I am second to none, be it Reid or Price or Kant, Moore or Prichard or Ross, in my moral hatred of such naturalistic misconceptions. Nevertheless, I do not feel sure at all that the notion of an "ontological value" is nonsensical itself; I believe that we may legitimately inquire into it provided only that we scrupulously abstain from identifying it with the concept of either Reality or Value in general, and strenuously resist any temptation to define either morality or beauty, or indeed dignity itself, in its terms. When we contrast the genuine with the counterfeit, apparent "thisness" or power or value with a mere appearance of it, transparent with merely pretended worth, etc., we are thinking in both ontological and axiological terms with an eye on the peculiar connection—*toto coelo* different from any reductionist confusion or conflation or mutual "collapse" of the two orders of concepts. Thus, when we say in praise of Jones that he "is *a man*," in contrast with being a mere "ghost of a man," a mere puppet, a shadow, a clown, a paper tiger, a mere automaton or flunkey, a hollow dandy or demagogue or mystagogue, we assert the presence in Jones of a "*virtue*" in the full and strong sense of the word, though what we mean is not that Jones is an eminently "virtuous" or righteous or conscientious man, not that he is naturally handsome and captivating without the use of elaborate cosmetics (or an athlete in perfect health). "Ontological value" is not, then, a mere fancy of speculative metaphysics to be lightly dismissed as a "misuse of language"; I certainly would not propose it as a definiens of Dignity—I am myself enamoured of tentative and groping analytical description, and wary of premature definitions, i.e., of all definitions in philosophy—but I *would* risk the surmise that Dignity is not perhaps simply a twilight zone between the region of the ethical and that of the aesthetic but also connotes a specific trait of "ontological value." Far from reductionism—"*Entia* sunt *multiplicanda secundum necessitatem.*"

(ii) Again, I want to draw attention to that sense of Dignity in which it is inherent, not in the character of persons nor in the quality of any extra-human objects but in hierarchical positions or relations such as rank, status, place, function, office and the like: that is to say, the dignity pertaining to "dignitaries." (Cf. "being *in* authority" as distinct from "being *an* authority *on* something" and further, from "having authority.") This is neither dignity as a distinctive personal quality nor dignity in the sense of "human dignity" as ascribed to persons as such, but an aspect of verticality proper to institutionalized and even, to a lesser extent, to informal social coexistence, cooperation and division of labour. I cannot expatiate here on the problems involved by the relations between dignity of office and qualitative dignity.

3. Dignity and Related Qualities

I have spoken above of the kinship and the differentiation between the dignified and the sublime. We might likewise discuss the relation between the dignified and the rational as well as the dignified and the spiritual (i.e., the deep and predominant attachment of some persons to intellectual, moral, religious and artistic themes); and again the close relations, which however do not attain to identity, between the dignified and the noble, the distinguished, or the exquisite. Obviously rational self-control is an integral aspect of dignity; but calculating rationality on the one hand, hard-headed or sweet reasonableness on the other hand, are less so. A spiritual centre of gravity eminently tends to make a person dignified; but dignity does not necessarily involve any marked and specified spiritual interests. We often use the words "dignity" and "nobility" synonymously, but not always: deep contemplation or sustained earnestness is dignified rather than noble, while the lineaments of a living body or even certain modes of gracious and graceful behaviour may more naturally be called noble than dignified. Distinction appears to imply originality and some outstanding achievement more than does dignity; but a measure of easy-going irresponsibility is more compatible with distinction than with dignity (Max Scheler was not only an exceptionally sharp, clever and cultured thinker but a highly distinguished philosopher and perhaps a generous man, but he certainly was not dignified). A dignified bearing may fully strike us as something exquisite; but emphasis on fine quality as such, in whatever respect, pertains to the sphere of the exquisite rather than to that of the dignified.

II. The Quality of Dignity and "Human Dignity"

1. The So-called "Rights of Man"

It is generally held that some fundamental linkage obtains between Dignity and what we somewhat clumsily and misleadingly call "the Rights of Man." A dignified attitude involves respect for such "rights" in others and a claim to one's own "rights" being likewise respected by others—though, according to circumstances, that claim may manifest itself in the form of active assertion, of disdainful silence, or even of charitable admonition or a sympathetic attempt to make the offender understand it. Dignity and the belief in "human rights" converge in the ethical model of human relationships based on mutual respect and indeed tinged with a reverent acknowledgement of the alterity of others and the differentness of individuals. (Of course, what is meant here by "rights" is not "positive" but "natural" rights—a most ambiguous and infelicitous figure of speech—i.e., rights invested with intrinsic evidence and not enacted by legal or other specific stipulations; the ethical validity of legal or conventional rights presupposes such intrinsic principles as *pacta sunt servanda*, or that any wanton or arbitrary interference with another's sphere of autonomy is morally wrong.) Yet the logical status of Dignity and that of the "Rights of Man" sharply contrast with each other.

Dignity is a quality; the concept of dignity is descriptive, though it also bears an essential and inseparable evaluative note. Rights are *not* qualities; their concept is not descriptive but prescriptive—ascriptive if you like, but their ascriptive is parasitic on their prescriptive sense. That rights ought to be respected is a tautology exactly like "Duties ought to be complied with": they just consist *in* that they ought to be respected. Dignity does *not* "consist" in that it ought to be prized, praised, admired or revered. Disrespect of a right constitutes an *offense*; indifference to dignity is only a *defect*, as is any lack of adequate response to a value. (Or, indeed, any impercipiency towards a significant fact.) My mental qualities are just as real as my physical properties, though perhaps they can only be perceived by others through the medium of some kind of behavioural or otherwise physical observation (yet not, of course, "discovered" by a scientist dissecting my brain); my rights are not in any comparable sense "real" and cannot be ascertained by any method of psychological observation. Through the action of environmental or other factors, my dignity (like my knowledge or my courage, or my predilection for or bias against this or that thing) may increase or diminish in the course of time. Whereas, my being accorded some new positive right or my being deprived of one I have possessed does not directly alter my character; and my "human rights," within the meaning of the term, while they can be punctiliously respected or brutally disregarded and trampled upon, cannot at all be conferred upon me or amplified or annulled or lessened: your accomplishment of your duty is not what makes it your duty, and your failure to comply with it does not invalidate that duty. Thus, we feel both that Dignity is somehow consonant with the "Rights of Man" and that the two are situated on entirely different levels. This fact may not pose any noteworthy practical difficulty in our moral striving or even in the work of moral education, but it is likely to give rise to some philosophical puzzlement.

2. The Hybrid Concept of "Human Dignity"

It may be from some such sense of puzzlement that the oddly ambiguous concept of "Human Dignity" has sprung. For "Human Dignity"—the term "Dignity of the Person" would be more correct, and "Dignity inherent in being a Person" more accurate still—seems to share some characteristics of the "Rights of Man" (or "Rights of the Person") and some of Dignity proper (Dignity as a Quality) alike. The concept of "Human Dignity" is properly and principally *ascriptive* rather than *either* descriptive *or* prescriptive. To respect "Human Dignity" is a strict moral obligation on the same footing, if not wholly identical, with the respect due to the "Rights of Man"—quite unlike the reverent response it is right and proper to give to "Dignity as a Quality." Yet "Human Dignity" is not, like the "Rights of Man," reduced to complete vacuity if we remove it from the context of that rigorously owed respect. It has something about it of a faceless and inchoate *quasi*-quality we "ascribe" to persons as such, independently of their distinctive virtues, modes of bearing, and mental levels and attitudes. It demands respect, but its meaning does not consist just in that demand. "Human Dignity" is not, like "Dignity as a Quality," a matter of more or less, not a matter of virtue, accomplishment or refinement; rather, it seems to be something "inalienable" much like "Rights of Man," and yet not quite in the same manner. Whereas the "Rights of Man" can only be disregarded, negated, insulted, violated or "suppressed," "Human Dignity" can actually be impaired and destroyed, temporarily or irreversibly, like any real "quality." If tomorrow I fall into the hands of Communist torturers, they cannot "eliminate" my human rights but only prevent me from exercising them; whereas they can easily make short work of my "Human Dignity," *more so* even than of such inner "Dignity as a Quality" as I may possess, by maltreatment, the administration of certain drugs, and putting me in one of their slave-camps. In a less dismal way even, my "Human Dignity" may well suffer by drunkenness or more sinister drug habits, as well as by grave accidents independent of anybody's guilt. If I am a congenital moron or have my brain permanently crippled by meningitis or am today perhaps the victim of incipient senile dementia, do I really "possess" the same "Human Dignity" as that "possessed" by any other—normal, average, or even slightly sub-standard—"human being"? Thus, there still seems after all to be some rudiment of a "more or less" about "Human Dignity," in a fashion closely similar to the possible "degrees" of free-will and responsibility (i.e., imputability)—greatly contrasting, of course, with the vast scale of gradation proper to the spiritual quality of "inner freedom" or any other mental or physical qualities. Again, if you just gratuitously insult my "Human Dignity" without any action apt to cripple my faculties of self-possession, what happens is much like a mere infraction of my rights: my "Human Dignity" has not really been diminished, but you have yourself, by your lapse into iniquitous or uncivilized conduct, revealed and aggravated your own lack—not of "Human Dignity," to be sure, but of Dignity as a Quality.

Although the "Rights of Man," whatever they are, are not positive (legal, institutional, conventional) rights, we can only conceive of them in a somehow codifiable form: we invariably speak of them in the plural, not in the sense of an indefinitely great number but as if there were four or five or sixteen of them, despite the fact that we cannot without some arbitrary stipulation enumerate them as we can count our fingers and toes, or the departments of France. On the contrary, we never speak of "Human Dignity" except in the singular, similarly as we talk of civic rights but only of citizenship, or of moral virtues but only of (moral) sense, and of conscience. It looks as if we conceived of "Human Rights" as postulates, i.e., specified rules for other people's conduct towards a person, grounded in "Human Dignity," which in its turn were neither a "claim" nor a "quality" but a kind of half-way house between a set of prescriptive claims and the basic quality of being-a-person: a semi-fictitious, semi-real *status* "ascribed" to the person as such.

3. "Human Dignity" and "Dignity as a Quality"

We might feel tempted to interpret "Human Dignity" as a *minimum* of actual dignity (Dignity as a Quality) quasi-automatically, quasi-tautologously "possessed" by everyone in virtue of simply being a person; or again, as the *virtual* presence in everyone of Dignity as Quality, a "perfection" that everyone is "called" to achieve actually, though only some of us do so and in very different degrees, while some of us are conspicuous by their display, again in very different degrees, of features specifically opposed to "Dignity as a Quality," such un-dignity equally presupposing the unquestioned status of "Human Dignity." This would pretty closely correspond to Aranguren's distinction between *moralidad como estructura* (the fact that man is a "moral being," subject to moral categories, exercising moral judgment and an object thereof) and *moralidad como contenido* (the actual morality, the moral value-and-disvalue or goodness and badness of men). Neither of these schemes seems to be altogether satisfactory. "Human Dignity" is not, I think, important *only* in view of its representing a minimum level of actual "Dignity as a Quality"; and I do not feel sure about whether qualitative un-dignity also implies a loss or impairment of "Human Dignity" or, on the contrary, would be impossible in a person who was no longer in possession of his "Human Dignity" or, say, no longer in a state or condition of "Human Dignity." An attempt to elucidate these complex relationships would overreach my present scope. But it seems certain that our "Human Dignity" is threatened mainly by the impact on us of powers alien to our own will, whereas our lack of "Dignity as a Quality" or indeed our un-dignity is mainly our own work: it cannot express itself or come to be except through our own agency. Deficient, alas, in heroic virtue and not of the stuff martyrs are made of, I would most likely ingloriously collapse under torture and fail to stand up to pain, fright and benumbing poisons: I would then be ready to behave, perhaps without even feeling that it matters much, in a fashion incompatible with "Human Dignity." But I venture to believe I would still retain a higher degree of "Dignity as a Quality" than the people of substantially liberal convictions who tend to welcome the ascendancy of a totalitarian tyranny as the fulfillment of Progress or of the "meaning of History," or again as the surge of superior vitality or the Wave of the Future. Let us vary the example. Suppose you could do with my co-operation in a shady but profitable business deal, and offer me as a bribe a packet of twenty fairly good Dutch cigars. I feel tempted for a moment; but such traffic would be beneath my dignity. Realizing, however, that the success of your scheme to a large extent depends on my support, you raise your stingy offer to a promise of 500 Upmans or Partagas. Ah, that's a different matter. "A woman is only a woman, but a good cigar is a smoke," as the young Kipling sang; and I sing, "Honour is only honour, but Havana is heaven." I accept. Perhaps I have come to discern that there are loftier things on earth than the ordinary pedestrian standards of Right and Wrong; or to find out that in the long view your ostensibly crooked scheme is calculated to maximize pleasure in the world, very properly beginning with *my* pleasure. I cynically put up with my loss of dignity or, worse, slur it over in my mind and idealistically explain it away. No doubt, you have been my corrupters. But I am not just corrupted; I am corrupt! My lack or loss of dignity ("Dignity as a Quality"), my un-dignity, my indignity is authentically mine. The question may now be asked: Have I thus also lost my "Human Dignity"? To raise the question is not to answer it. In a way, being now assailed by remorse, I may feel that I "no longer exist morally"; but the position is not quite that. Rather, it is that I do exist morally, and precisely am an immoral wretch. Admittedly, though, you the hatchers of the dishonest enterprise who have invited me to "lend you my aid in this raid" (Kipling again) are at least as immoral as I am, but one would be less disposed to call you moral *wretches*. The distinction between the indignity opposed to "Dignity as a Quality" and the vanishing of "Human Dignity" stands out in bolder relief in your case than in mine.

Of course, to confess to one's own confusion is a cheap and scarcely dignified method of blunting the edge of the confounding objections one may anticipate.

III. The Undignified

1. Bernard Shaw's Short-winded Sense of Dignity

There is a rightly famous, incisive witticism by the late [George] Bernard Shaw, which I am quoting from memory, but I hope with essential accuracy: "See to it that you get what you like, or else you will like what you get." Surely this conveys a plea for Dignity and a warning against the lack of it. Whatever the intrinsic quality of our likes and dislikes themselves, and notwithstanding the prudential as well as the moral necessity of our controlling, repressing, tempering and modulating many of them, there is an elementary, not to say an elemental, feature of dignity about clarifying, developing, pursuing and making valid our personal tastes and choices. Again, albeit I hold that many of the most precious and delightful things (goods, experiences, values, satisfactions, etc.) we "get" in life are such as are meted out to us gratuitously by Chance or

Incident or Providence rather than obtained or attained or achieved by our own pre-existent desire and effective striving, it is true that pliability, unresisting adaptability and unreserved self-adjustment are prototypal opposites of Dignity. (When once as a small boy I had to write in a school essay that "Spring is the pleasantest season"—a cliché I was acquainted with, finding however myself at that time that summer was more pleasant, though I have since come to appreciate a mellow early October day the most—everything in me revolted at the idea that a *taste*, as distinct from a rule of conduct, should be forced upon me.) Thus Shaw seems to be eminently concerned with the dignity of the person: he exhorts the individual to shape his life according to his own vision rather than to allow his inmost preferences to be shaped by circumstantial facts and to fall into slavish dependence on his environment. But the predictive form in which he clothes his admonition—"or else you *will* like what you get," a sanction appended to his counsel rather than an expansion of it—shows his pitiable failure to understand what is most important about Dignity: not to "get what one likes" but to be able to endure what one "gets" without necessarily assenting to it and growing to "like" it. (The Stoic sage put it admirably when he admonished a youth complaining of his father's lack of parental virtues, "Did Nature owe you a good father? No, only a father." He wrote *neither*, "You are wrong; the goodness of fathers is often inscrutable; you are too immature to discern it; you *have* got a good father," *nor* "Make haste to depose your father and fashion unto yourself another that comes up to your standards.") What Shaw does is to erect into an inexorable decree the very dependence on externals of the person he is inciting us to rebel against. Like any Naturalist, he confuses Dignity with Power, Wealth and Success. But, while naturalists of the conservative hierarchical temper taught us to participate in Dignity by admiring the Power, etc., of "our betters," while those of a liberal capitalistic temper improved upon this by announcing that Power, etc., are "anybody's" and thus virtually everybody's, those of the Socialist and fake-realist brand, like Shaw, completed the turn from embellishing Illusion to Utopian Delusion by asserting that Power, etc., can be organized revolution and subversive "conquest" be made actually everybody's. Perhaps people of this cast of mind believe that by the ensuring through a collective agency of everybody's "Human Dignity" (including a sense of individual self-assertion and self-fulfillment) everyone will also acquire Dignity as a Quality or, what comes to the same thing, the concept of "Dignity as a Quality" will lose its point—a view prefigured by the first great apostle of Progress, Condorcet, who confidently foresaw a rationally and scientifically redrawn world in which there would be no opportunity for the exercise of heroic virtue nor any sense in revering it.

The core of Un-Dignity, as I would try to put it succinctly, is constituted by an attitude of refusal to recognize, experience, and bear with, the tension between Value and Reality; between what things ought to be, should be, had better be or are desired to be and what things are, can be and are allowed to be. That refusal, which may take an immense variety of forms, includes of course the now fashionable anathema on our (most happily) incurable "splitness," "alienation" and yearning for (religious and extra-religious, reverentially stated or more specifically pursued) "self-transcendence." It does *not*, of course, include either submission to the existing order of things and the virtue of patience, or a sustained endeavour for reform, improvement and assuagement. Heraclitus may well have had this in mind when he wrote the magnificent words, "Better (or stronger?) is invisible than visible harmony":

ἁρμονίη ἀφανὴς φανεῆς κρείττων

2. The Feature World of The Undignified

I must content myself with a fleetingly sketched and hopelessly incomplete grouping of the relevant dimensions. Questions like how far—how exactly or how roughly—these correspond to the contrary dimensions of Dignity, or how far we might distinguish between mere lack of dignity (in an object in which its presence would be expected) and positive undignity, or the criteria of distinguishing between an awareness and pursuit of dignity which is itself a component of dignity and a pretence of or pretension to dignity which is peculiarly destructive of dignity—these and other fascinating problems about our subject must be entirely forgone here.

Undignified is everything that is antithetic to distance, discretion, boundaries, articulation, individuation and autonomy: the features, then, of confusion, chaos, disorder, unruliness, indiscriminate community or consorting or intimacy, promiscuity, domineeringness and servility, and others down to conspicuous loquacity or (I will not go into this distinction) garrulity. (It need not be emphasized that clarity-seeking simplification has nothing dignified, the rejection of *fausse clarté* and the experience of tints fading into one another, etc., nothing undignified about it.) Another heading under which undignified features may be grouped: brutish and noisy, or even naively unreserved and of-a-piece self-assertion, self-assurance and self-complacency; self-pity, emotionalism, exhibitionism, demonstrativeness, etc. Further, untruthfulness and ungenuineness; hypocrisy, false pretence and the whole empire of the showy, flashy and gaudy, the *Kitsch*, the *cursi*, the *endimanché*, the ornate trash or *camelote*, the *poshlost'* (ponderous platitude). Finally, as opposed to "Weight" or Gravity, all that is levity, frivolity, irrelevance, shallowness, needless triviality. Some clarifications and qualifications would obviously be necessary. Stage-acting and dancing are not as such undignified: a good deal of dignity can in fact enter into them; but whatever is stagey outside the stage connotes un-dignity. Opinions may differ about jazz, "entertainment" in the closer sense of the word, many other frontier zones of art. Wit and brilliance as such are not undignified; humour, far from being undignified, supposes a keen sense of weights; but all forced humour and programme gaiety is undignified. Satire is a problem. (Austin: To pretend to be vulgar often, alas, is to *be* vulgar; but when? Karl Kraus the Viennese satirist, probably the finest writer of standard German prose in this century, in a sort of obsessive hallucination would pour forth pages interlarded with the most hideous Viennese semi-Yiddish and Aryan Viennese "cockney" slang as well as with Prussian barbarisms more reminiscent of New-Yorkese, sometimes in visible but often in more effective invisible quotation marks, without for a moment becoming vulgar. When I use locutions such as "...or I'm a Dutchman" or "You betcher sweet life" or "She is forty if she's a day" or "exquisitely girlish" I fear I am *being* vulgar.) What professions outside the properly criminal ones are undignified as such? One answer is E. Friedell's: that of a *Professor* (university don), because it involves a slow metabolism, a sluggish bowel, a penchant for gradualist doctrines, and pedantry. I wonder.

Two particular aspects, however, seem to me to require express mention.

3. Uncontrolled Passion

No forms of the Undignified that are mainly constituted by loss of self-restraint, enslavement by or half-hearted yielding to a passion, or even a shameless display of it, can, I submit, reach the apex of un-dignity. With the possible exception of Vanity—in which levity and inward dependence on pleasing others rather than passion proper occupy the central point—this applies to all standard passion, however objectionable and beastly, however morbid and devious: to Lust, Avarice, Ambition, craving for Power, Revenge, Anger (and even Cruelty if suffused with anger), rebellious or jingoistic Mob Violence. Shylock's insistence on his pound of flesh has *something* dignified about it. So has Sappho's drastic description of her state of sexual excitement at the sight of some pretty lass (though it cannot even be candid animal amorality, for in another poem she repels the amorous advances of a man in primly graceful terms of chaste indignation). Carlyle, much rather a proto-Fascist than a believer in Democracy, depicts the *terreur* and the excesses of the revolutionary mob with a sense of sublimity rather than with unmixed loathing; and I was myself enough of an aesthete when Englishing and commenting on the texts of some of the crazy visionaries of the Third Reich to betray a certain degree of horrorful fascination. How can we account for this relative privilege of Passion? Not only does a note of dignity attach to the elemental forces of Nature; it is even represented, however dimly and however swamped by un-dignity, in man's implicit avowal of weakness when seized, and swept off his feet, by forces of that order, in his submission to what ought not to be but imperiously *tends* to be above his strength and beyond his control. I have omitted, presumably from a personal sense of shame, the intensest and at any rate most universal of passions, Fear. Cowardice is paradigmatically undignified. Yet a person crying out in pain, trembling with fear, quivering and writhing in anguish, imploring to be spared, etc., is not an incarnation of Un-Dignity. A tragic and thereby a remotely dignified note enters into his picture. His failure to achieve, and even to have striven for, stoic endurance has placed him in its perspective. In his flight from the inexorable Split he dare not face, his awareness of it is set aflame. The "Human Dignity" he has been bereft of—though, as we here presume, not without his own complicity—bears witness to the Qualitative Dignity he has fallen short of and perhaps has come near to achieving. If not the outright coward, the victim of fear is a caricature of the hero and his disfigured countenance may be lit up with an ironic reflexion of martyrdom.

4. The Meretricious

It might be argued that the feature sometimes described as the "meretricious" embodies the culmination of Un-Dignity. There is, within my knowledge, no wholly exact foreign equivalent for the term, seeing that none of the more easily translatable words with their habitat in its neighbourhood—such as "venal," "bribable," "whore-like," "mercenary," or the nouns "toady" or "flatterer," or again "pander" or "pimp"—offer a perfect rendering of the quality in question. The professional harlot (*meretrix*, she who "earns" by selling her carnal intimacy) including her more "classy" variants, or again the pander or procuress, are too narrowly specialized examples; the sales-agent need not have anything meretricious about him; the so-called "good mixer" may or may not have a touch of it; the etymological lineage of "courtesan" (French *courtisan* and Italian *cortigiano*, in English "courtier") may be usefully remembered in the context of "toady" or "flatterer"; perhaps advertisement-writers, "hidden persuaders" and propaganda agents need a fair amount of meretriciousness to excel in their profession, but of course I mean "meretricious" in a less technically restricted context. Anyhow, though commercial advertisements are morally harmless and relatively honest in as much as they overtly offer for sale some commodity which some people may have an interest in acquiring and which the vendor has an obvious and undisguised interest in selling, their study (along with that of *Woman's Own* and similar or more sophisticated magazines) supplies an excellent method for getting acquainted with the objective feature of "the meretricious." "The nylons worthy of *your* legs" or "If your face doesn't really feel clean with cream, yet soap and water is too drying, then Estee Lauder's *New Fresh Water Treatments* were just created for you" may serve as random examples. But the titles of certain (perhaps instructive) popular books may sound even more exciting to the logician: I mean such as *Slimming for You, Your Arthritis* and *Your Sinus Trouble.* The point is not so much the predominance of the appeal to base instincts, even though these are of course most directly liable to crude stimulation by seductive imagery, as the indiscriminate fake-personal mode of address: whereas in injunctions like "Thou shalt not kill" or "Know thyself" the incisive personal form of address patently refers to a universality (of which the concrete singular case is merely the point of application). When my glance first fell on *Your Sinus Trouble* I caught myself imagining for a moment that the author really meant *my* sinus trouble and was anxious to help *me* rather than just anybody suffering from that complaint.

What characterizes the meretricious attitude is the intimate unity of abstract self-seeking and qualitative self-effacement. The meretricious type of person is, ideally speaking, at once boundlessly devoted to the thriving of his life and indifferent to its contents. He wallows in his dependence on his environment—in sharp contrast to the dignity of a man's setting bounds to the impact of its forces and undergoing their influence in a distant and filtered fashion—and places himself at the disposal of alien wants and interests without organically (which implies, selectively) espousing any of them. The tout (including such variants as the slave of fashion, the echolalic loud-speaker, the genius for opportunism, etc.) embodies a parasitical, coreless, not to say ghost-like mode of life; he escapes the tensions of alienation by precipitate fusion and headlong surrender, and evades self-transcendence by the flitting mobility of a weightless self. His peculiar un-dignity resides in his jubilant renunciation of dignity: his spectacular success, that is, in creating around himself a world for his own use from which all reference to dignity *and the missing of it* has been crowded out; in which dignity no longer appears to be crushed but, rather, its very concept appears extinguished.

IV. Some Ethical Problems Concerning Dignity

1. The "Paradoxes" of Self-Assertion and Self-Renunciation

The paradoxes or *aporiae* in question constitute a familiar subject in Ethics or rather the study of Virtues; they originate from Plato's conception of a "hierarchial equilibrium" and Aristotle's medico-moral idea of the "right mean," important new dimensions having been added by the Christian prizing of Humility and the modern shifts of emphasis to Objectivity and the "Critical Tradition" on the one hand, to Individuality on the other. Awareness of this set of problems invades, of course, the areas of Epistemology and especially of Linguistic Logic. Most of the terms implied, such as "Pride" and "Humility," are ambiguous even within their purely descriptive concepts; and according to our own evaluative attitudes and our views about the relation between the descriptive and the evaluative we tend to speak of "true humility," "pride as rightly understood" (cf. the distinctions between "Stolz" and "Hochmut," "fierté" and "orgueil," and the English adjectives "proud" and "prideful"), or "the golden mean between pride and humility," or again the "right kind of pride" and the "right kind of humility" (without necessarily implying that these two should coincide, as if it were desirable that all men should have the same sort of *temperament*).

A few hints must suffice here.

(i) *Personality* and *Impersonality* are equally integral to Dignity in the sense of "personality" interpreted as an intangible and imperturbable inward core, depth and weight, and "impersonality" in the sense of self-detachment, self-transcendence and objectivity. The theme of "personal response to impersonal standards of value," not confined of course within the context of Dignity, may provide the key formula here.

(ii) *Modesty* (in its general sense, not in that of sexual reserve) and its apparent opposite *Exactingness* (i.e., the display of high value claims, making high demands on the quality of objects, being "hard to please" or being "particular," in German "anspruchsvoll") again are both essentially and positively related to Dignity. The "paradoxy" is at least partly resolved by pointing to the distinction between "possession" and "enjoyment" as material and exclusive control of "goods" on the one hand, and as experience, intentional reference and percipience of values on the other. The ideal of Poverty and even of smallness has been praised not by Christians alone (the finely worded formula *Paix et peu* is, I think, of Chinese origin); "scarcity" and "spareness," and a certain disproportion between "being" and "seeming" as a constituent of Dignity we have emphasized earlier. Conspicuous display and ostentation, pomp and circumstance are likely to be undignified unless they have some specific justification in terms of publicly relevant status and "dignitary's" dignity. Yet no one in his five wits, or perhaps even out of them, would praise a man for his "modesty" who would visit only third-rate provincial museums or at the Louvre or the Prado or the National Gallery confine his attention to minor painters and at the Rijksmuseum to the Department of Eighteenth-century Decadence, because these are good enough for him, while everywhere shyly averting his glance from the el Grecos, Rembrandts or Cézannes lest he should enjoy a sight he does not deserve. Another relevant distinction concerns the simplicity of certain kinds of goods as contrasted with poor quality within one given genus. It is more dignified to content oneself with even very plain fare of acceptable standard than to prefer a more elaborate cuisine of fancy dishes ill cooked and made of inferior ingredients. This thesis involves further and fascinating category problems, which however cannot be discussed here any more than the wider problems of thrift and waste, or asceticism and the generous sharing of pleasure, etc.

(iii) *Pride and Humility*, a theme partly merging into but distinguishable from that of Claim to Value or Possession and Modesty, again can no more than be touched upon here. If pride in the sense of "being proud" strikes much the same note of distance, self-contained reserve and inexpugnable integrity that is characteristic of the dignified attitude, pride in the sense of "being prideful" tends to be at variance with dignity in two respects: first, in view of its obvious links with coarse self-assertion and a puffed-up insistence on a privileged status of self as against others; secondly, in view of its likely desiccating and isolating effect on the agent himself which is antithetic to the sense of values, an inseparable aspect of dignity. Again, "being proud *of*" one's own virtues and accomplishments is apt to endanger dignity inasmuch as it tends to transfer emphasis from response to value to the cult of the self as such; and being proud, jealous and centrally (rather than merely peripherally) conscious of one's own dignity borders on self-contradiction and conjures up the danger of a kind of obtrusive un-dignity, seeing that dignity eminently belongs to the type of moral and personal values, which, unlike, e.g., justice, veracity or intellectual probity, are second-order qualities and are acquired—apart from the express removal of certain definite impediments—wholly or mainly indirectly, through the pursuit of values other than themselves and through the agent's response to the same values *present in others*. The relation between Dignity and Humility seems to me to be even more ambiguous—and to show a greater amplitude between the positive and the negative extremes. Humility slanted towards servility and self-annulment (on the mundane plane, conflatable with "the meretricious"), not excluding "hero-worship" and devotional servility—the attitudes of slavish self-abasement and systematic self-negation before the Divine—utterly flies in the face of Dignity. Such devotional postures and all too placid and complacent "I am naught" modes of penitence and prostration are an insult to the dignity of God (conceiving of Him as a sort of Asiatic despot and capricious "Omnipotence," an object of idolatrous adulation); again they proclaim the denial and hopelessness of moral discernment and effort. As Samuel Johnson has splendidly put it, "To find a substitution for violated morality is the leading feature in all perversions of religion." Devout humility of this kind means, indeed, Pharisaism raised to the second power: the self-confessed "sinner" and so-called "publican" priding himself on not being like that Pharisee who is satisfied with his degree of sanctity. In contradistinction, however, to that short-circuited humility, that gesture of craven self-devaluation and as it were nihilistic yearning for ontological absorption, Humility *qua* self-transcendent surrender and submission to "What is higher than ourself" is the very idiom or at any rate the crowning act of Dignity, in that it casts our being into the mould of "due response" to what is "*worthy of...*" (being thus recognized and served). It is not, I think, "perversion" or idolatry and lack of dignity but one of the highest expressions of Dignity I know of that speaks from Péguy's famous prophetic vision—"Heureux ceux qui sont morts pour des cités charnelles..."—of the coming Armageddon (and his own glorious death in action at its decisive turning point):

> ...Heureux ceux qui sont morts dans ce couronnement
> Et cette obéissance et cette humilité.

The great German essayist E. Jünger has aptly if somewhat bizarrely written: "Piety (*Frömmigkeit*) is only possible as a relation between miraculous beings." The inequality it entails may be immense—as it is between God and the Believer, in the religious framework—but it is not the straight inequality between a higher and a lower object which functionally complement each other. In at least every interpersonal context, Dignity connotes reciprocity no less, but rather more strictly, than it does inequality. The Greek idea that the height of our thinking is necessarily proportionate to the height of the object it refers to has caused great confusions in both Philosophy and Religion (e.g., that the objects of geometry are the noblest and most divine, and again that the devotional attitude as opposed to critical and scientific thought confers the greatest and most essential dignity upon us); but neither is the reverse as true as N. Hartmann seems to have thought it to be. We rightly smile when we come across the phrase—a decayed and probably commercialized remnant of religious piety and technically so-called "spirituality"—that "thinking of beautiful things tends to make us beautiful"; but under a ghastly debris it buries a grain of truth. Moreover, the dignity of our thought as "masters" of creation, our thought about lowly and mechanical objects itself, indeed all thought as such, implies a dimension of humility: in all intentional reference to objects, all awareness of facts, howsoever destined to enhance our "possession" of truth and our purposive control of nature and its processes, we cannot but exercise a basic act of humility: that of surrendering to "compulsive evidence" and submitting to the "Sovereignty of the Object." Percipience in its ultimate root is recipience. "Natura non nisi obtemperando vincitur," wrote Francis Bacon truthfully enough but without understanding that our greater honour resides in the obedience rather than in the successes in mastery which it may instrumentally subserve. His earlier namesake, Bacon the Franciscan, had been the worthier founder of science.

2. Moral Dignity and Rule-Morality

So far as Dignity is a moral virtue, or perhaps rather a condensed manifestation of "being a virtuous person," it is a relatively "object-free," "stance-like" (*Haltung*) quality, only secondarily and quasi-occasionally *pursued* by the agent and not directly expressible in terms of rule-obedience. Nevertheless, rules or maxims of conduct may be dignity-inspired and presuppose an awareness of the concept of dignity. "I will behave in a dignified fashion," thus put, sounds comical and unreal; indeed, specifically undignified. (At the other extreme, that of purely directional virtues, "I will be just" is a perfectly normal utterance, since it means nothing but the decision to conform to the purely object-referred duty of justice.) Yet there is nothing comical or morally dubious about a practical reflection like, "No, I will not do this after all: it would be definitely undignified"; or again, "I will rather do as X did in that very similar situation: that was a truly dignified way of insisting on his rightful claim but, the principle being secured, quietly renouncing the personal advantage it might have afforded him."

A paramount concern about one's own dignity impresses us as self-centered, self-important, perhaps self-complacent to the point of hypocrisy, and again as gauche, quirky, beside the point, humourless, priggish, aesthetically as well as morally self-defeating. A person's maintaining or protecting his own "Human Dignity" or indeed the dignity of the office he happens to represent—which is an objective responsibility, and probably a strict obligation—is a quite different matter. But it may well be one of the techniques of civilized coexistence to hint at times that one's own dignity is something slightly funny and to some extent expendable. For this, precisely, is implied in its being secure and invulnerable: such a style of behaviour expresses rather than negates one's dignity itself, as a possession stable and self-evident—organically rooted—enough to allow for a certain latitude of carelessness. The same principle of "tempering and thereby perfecting imperfections" is not in the same sense applicable to the particular moral virtues, especially not to the strictly directional virtues. A man obsessed with exact justice might by occasionally mellowing his strictness and according himself a margin of casual lapses from justice in small matters become a more lovable but not a *juster* man; occasional display by a philanthropist of selfish indifference might make him less of a bore but not a *more benevolent* person.

Nothing, however, could amount to a more fatal misunderstanding of "Dignity as a Quality" than placing it in an antithesis or setting it up as an alternative to plain deontic morality. Suppose X is an eminently and typically dignified person. What characterizes his actions, words and deportment is a *penumbra* of awareness of his own worth, his fidelity to duty and his respect for others' rights and response to others' virtues and to alien values—awareness of this compound of traits as a "self-evident," by no means hidden or denied but conspicuous and yet *under-emphasized* constituent of his being. X *commands trust* not only in the sense that he can be trusted not to lie or to cheat, to honour commitments and claims, but even in the sense that any moral *lapse* he may be guilty or suspected of is *powerless against the basic trust he inspires.* That is not so, as irrationalist and anti-bourgeois romantics would have it, because he (X) is invested with a mystical and unanalysable quality of absoluteness, quasi-divinity, special intimacy with superior Powers, a privilege of experiential depth or anything independent of "ordinary," publicly accessible and applicable criteria and standards of Right and Wrong; but on the contrary, because he is felt to be *penetrated*—rather than merely commanded, controlled, governed or interested—by Morality to the point of being *personally inseparable* from it. Some crazy fanatic or monomaniac "idealist" may in some sense be appreciated or admired, an "amiable rogue" like Gogol's Chichikov who trades in "dead souls" (registered as live serfs) may excite affection, but neither of these is an instance of our dignified X. A man accredited with dignity may commit some deception and yet continue to be respected or trusted, *not* because his admirers place him above the moral law and feel that so fine and daemonic or inwardly powerful and existential a personage cannot be judged by ordinary codes but in the following way. *Either* his "wise and prudent" friends (spectators, valuers) feel that his blameworthy action has had some exceptional justification and is not really blameworthy at all by ordinary standards: i.e., that in its wrongful character under some obvious categorial description it does not express X's character as such and perhaps *does* express it, in X's favour, under a finer though perhaps less patently available categorial description. Or else they feel that he has committed this actually blameworthy action in some particular, morally disabling, circumstances and that the action, though certainly his action and thus imputable and reprehensible, is *uncharacteristic* in the stricter sense of the term. His past and enduring conduct are surer guides to his appraisal, and he continues to deserve trust as if nothing to the contrary had happened. Yet the "intangibility" or "invulnerability" inherent in Dignity as a Quality is a peculiar *quality* rightly and reasonably apprehended as such by the valuer who recognizes its guarantee of future behaviour and accords it "credit" and "implicit trust"; it is not a *fact* vouched for by some immutable "law" of nature or supernature. Dignity as a Quality can go to seed and be lost (whatever the Stoics may have said to the contrary about Virtue) though not, I suppose, to the point of leaving behind no vestige of it at all.

3

+

Servility and Self-Respect

+

Thomas E. Hill, Jr.

Several motives underlie this paper. In the first place, I am curious to see if there is a legitimate source for the increasingly common feeling that servility can be as much a vice as arrogance. There seems to be something morally defective about the Uncle Tom and the submissive housewife; and yet, on the other hand, if the only interests they sacrifice are their own, it seems that we should have no right to complain. Secondly, I have some sympathy for the now unfashionable view that each person has duties to himself as well as to others. It does seem absurd to say that a person could literally violate his own rights or owe himself a debt of gratitude, but I suspect that the classic defenders of duties to oneself had something different in mind. If there are duties to oneself, it is natural to expect that a duty to avoid being servile would have a prominent place among them. Thirdly, I am interested in making sense of Kant's puzzling,

This essay was originally published in *The Monist* 57 (1973). Copyright © 1973 by *The Monist*, La Salle, Illinois 61301. Reprinted by permission.

but suggestive, remarks about respect for persons and respect for moral law. On the usual reading, these remarks seem unduly moralistic; but, viewed in another way, they suggest an argument for a kind of self-respect which is incompatible with a servile attitude.

My procedure will not be to explicate Kant directly. Instead I shall try to isolate the defect of servility and sketch an argument to show why it is objectionable, noting only in passing how this relates to Kant and the controversy about duties to oneself. What I say about self-respect is far from the whole story. In particular, it is not concerned with esteem for one's special abilities and achievements or with the self-confidence which characterizes the especially autonomous person. Nor is my concern with the psychological antecedents and effects of self-respect. Nevertheless, my conclusions, if correct, should be of interest; for they imply that, given a common view of morality, there are nonutilitarian moral reasons for each person, regardless of his merits, to respect himself. To avoid servility to the extent that one can is not simply a right but a duty, not simply a duty to others but a duty to oneself.

I

Three examples may give a preliminary idea of what I mean by *servility*. Consider, first, an extremely deferential black, whom I shall call the *Uncle Tom*. He always steps aside for white men; he does not complain when less qualified whites take over his job; he gratefully accepts whatever benefits his all-white government and employers allot him, and he would not think of protesting its insufficiency. He displays the symbols of deference to whites, and of contempt towards blacks: he faces the former with bowed stance and a ready "Sir" and "Ma'am"; he reserves his strongest obscenities for the latter. Imagine, too, that he is not playing a game. He is not the shrewdly prudent calculator, who knows how to make the best of a bad lot and mocks his masters behind their backs. He accepts without question the idea that, as a black, he is owed less than whites. He may believe that blacks are mentally inferior and of less social utility, but that is not the crucial point. The attitude which he displays is that what he values, aspires for, and can demand is of less importance than what whites value, aspire for, and can demand. He is far from the picture book's carefree, happy servant, but he does not feel that he has a right to expect anything better.

Another pattern of servility is illustrated by a person I shall call the *Self-Deprecator*. Like the Uncle Tom, he is reluctant to make demands. He says nothing when others take unfair advantage of him. When asked for his preferences or opinions, he tends to shrink away as if what he said should make no difference. His problem, however, is not a sense of racial inferiority but rather an acute awareness of his own inadequacies and failures as an individual. These defects are not imaginary: he has in fact done poorly by his own standards and others'. But, unlike many of us in the same situation, he acts as if his failings warrant quite unrelated maltreatment even by strangers. His sense of shame and self-contempt make him content to be the instrument of others. He feels that nothing is owed him until he has earned it and that he has earned very little. He is not simply playing a masochist's game of winning sympathy by disparaging himself. On the contrary, he assesses his individual merits with painful accuracy.

A rather different case is that of the *Deferential Wife*. This is a woman who is utterly devoted to serving her husband. She buys clothes *he* prefers, invites the guests *he* wants to entertain, and makes love whenever *he* is in the mood. She willingly moves to a new city in order for him to have a more attractive job, counting her own friendships and geographical preferences insignificant by comparison. She loves her husband, but her conduct is not simply an expression of love. She is happy, but she does not subordinate herself as a means to happiness. She does not simply defer to her husband in certain spheres as a trade-off for his deference in other spheres. On the contrary, she tends not to form her own interests, values, and ideals; and, when she does, she counts them as less important than her husband's. She readily responds to appeals from Women's Liberation that she agrees that women are mentally and physically equal, if not superior, to men. She just believes that the proper role for a woman is to serve her family. As a matter of fact, much of her happiness derives from her belief that she fulfills this role very well. No one is trampling on her rights, she says; for she is quite glad, and proud, to serve her husband as she does.

Each one of these cases reflects the attitude which I call servility.[1] It betrays the absence of a certain kind of self-respect. What I take this attitude to be, more specifically, will become clearer later on. It is important at the outset, however, not to confuse the three cases sketched above with other, superficially similar cases. In particular, the cases I have sketched are not simply cases in which someone refuses to press his rights, speaks disparagingly of himself, or devotes himself to another. A black, for example, is not necessarily servile because he does not demand a just wage; for seeing that such a demand would result in being fired, he might forbear for the sake of his children. A self-critical person is not necessarily servile by virtue of bemoaning his faults in public; for his behavior may be merely a complex way of satisfying his own inner needs quite independent of a willingness to accept abuse from others. A woman need not be servile whenever she works to make her husband happy and prosperous; for she might freely and knowingly choose to do so from love or from a desire to share the rewards of his success. If the effort did not require her to submit to humiliation or maltreatment, her choice would not mark her as servile. There may, of course, be grounds for objecting to the attitudes in these cases; but the defect is not servility of the sort I want to consider. It should also be noted that my cases of servility are not simply instances of deference to superior knowledge or judgment. To defer to an expert's judgment on matters of fact is not to be servile; to defer to his every wish and whim is. Similarly, the belief that one's talents and achievements are comparatively low does not, by itself, make one servile. It is no vice to acknowledge the truth, and one may in fact have achieved less, and have less ability, than others. To be servile is not simply to hold certain empirical beliefs but to have a certain attitude concerning one's rightful place in a moral community.

II

Are there grounds for regarding the attitudes of the Uncle Tom, the Self-Deprecator, and the Deferential Wife as morally objectionable? Are there moral arguments we could give them to show that they ought to have more self-respect? None of the more obvious replies is entirely satisfactory.

One might, in the first place, adduce utilitarian considerations. Typically the servile person will be less happy than he might be. Moreover, he may be less prone to make the best of his own socially useful abilities. He may become a nuisance to others by being overly dependent. He will, in any case, lose the special contentment that comes from standing up for one's rights. A submissive attitude encourages exploitation, and exploitation spreads misery in a variety of ways. These considerations provide a prima facie case against the attitudes of the Uncle Tom, the Deferential Wife, and the Self-Deprecator, but they are hardly conclusive. Other utilities tend to counterbalance the ones just mentioned. When people refuse to press their rights, there are usually others who profit. There are undeniable pleasures in associating with those who are devoted, understanding, and grateful for whatever we see fit to give them—as our fondness for dogs attests. Even the servile person may find his attitude a source of happiness, as the case of the Deferential Wife illustrates. There may be comfort and security in thinking that the hard choices must be made by others, that what I would say has little to do with what ought to be done. Self-condemnation may bring relief from the pangs of guilt even if it is not deliberately used for that purpose. On balance, then, utilitarian considerations may turn out to favor servility as much as they oppose it.

For those who share my moral intuitions, there is another sort of reason for not trying to rest a case against servility on utilitarian considerations. Certain utilities seem irrelevant to the issue. The utilitarian must weigh them along with others, but to do so seems morally inappropriate. Suppose, for example, that the submissive attitudes of the Uncle Tom and the Deferential Wife result in positive utilities for those who dominate and exploit them. Do we need to tabulate *these* utilities before conceding that servility is objectionable? The Uncle Tom, it seems, is making an error, a moral error, quite apart from consideration of how much others in fact profit from his attitude. The Deferential Wife may be quite happy; but if her happiness turns out to be contingent on her distorted view of her own rights and worth as a person, then it carries little moral weight against the contention that she ought to change that view. Suppose I could cause a woman to find her happiness in denying all her rights and serving my every wish. No doubt I could do so only by nonrational manipulative techniques, which I ought not to use. But is this the only objection? My efforts would be wrong, it seems, not only because of the techniques they require but also because the resultant attitude is itself objectionable. When a person's happiness stems from a morally objectionable attitude, it ought to be discounted. That a sadist gets pleasure from seeing others suffer should not count even as a partial justification for his attitude. That a servile person derives pleasure from denying her moral status, for similar reasons, cannot make her attitude acceptable. These brief intuitive remarks are not intended as a refutation of utilitarianism, with all its many varieties; but they do suggest that it is well to look elsewhere for adequate grounds for rejecting the attitudes of the Uncle Tom, the Self-Deprecator, and the Deferential Wife.

One might try to appeal to meritarian considerations. That is, one might argue that the servile person *deserves* more than he allows himself. This line of argument, however, is no more adequate than the utilitarian one. It may be wrong to deny others what they deserve, but it is not so obviously wrong to demand less for oneself than one deserves. In any case, the Self-Deprecator's problem is not that he underestimates his merits. By hypothesis, he assesses his merits quite accurately. We cannot reasonably tell him to have more respect for himself because he *deserves* more respect; he knows that he has not *earned* better treatment. His problem, in fact, is that he thinks of his moral status with regard to others as entirely dependent upon his merits. His interests and choices are important, he feels, only if he has earned the right to make demands; or if he had rights by birth, they were forfeited by his subsequent failures and misdeeds. My Self-Deprecator is no doubt an atypical person, but nevertheless he illustrates an important point. Normally when we find a self-contemptuous person, we can plausibly argue that he is not so bad as he thinks, that his self-contempt is an overreaction prompted more by inner needs than by objective assessment of his merits. Because this argument cannot work with the Self-Deprecator, his case draws attention to a distinction, applicable in other cases as well, between saying that someone deserves respect for his merits and saying that he is owed respect as a person. On meritarian grounds we can only say "You deserve better than this," but the defect of the servile person is not merely failure to recognize his merits.

Other common arguments against the Uncle Tom, et al., may have some force but seem not to strike to the heart of the problem. For example, philosophers sometimes appeal to the value of human potentialities. As a human being, it is said, one at least has a capacity for rationality, morality, excellence, or autonomy, and this capacity is worthy of respect. Although such arguments have the merit of making respect independent of a person's actual deserts, they seem quite misplaced in some cases. There comes a time when we have sufficient evidence that a person is not ever going to *be* rational, moral, excellent, or autonomous even if he still has a capacity, in some sense, for being so. As a person approaches death with an atrocious record so far, the chances of his realizing his diminishing capacities become increasingly slim. To make these capacities the basis of his self-respect is to rest it on a shifting and unstable ground. We do, of course, respect persons for capacities which they are not exercising at the moment; for example, I might respect a person as a good philosopher even though he is just now blundering into gross confusion. In these cases, however, we respect the person for an active capacity, a ready disposition, which he has displayed on many occasions. On this analogy, a person should have respect for himself only when his capacities are developed and ready, needing only to be triggered by an appropriate occasion or the removal of some temporary obstacle. The Uncle Tom and the Deferential Wife, however, may in fact have quite limited capacities of this sort, and, since the Self-Deprecator is already overly concerned with his own inadequacies, drawing attention to his capacities seems a poor way to increase his self-respect. In any case, setting aside the Kantian nonempirical capacity for autonomy, the capacities of different persons vary widely; but what the servile person seems to overlook is something by virtue of which he is equal with every other person.

III

Why, then, is servility a moral defect? There is, I think, another sort of answer which is worth exploring. The first part of this answer must be an attempt to isolate the objectionable features of the servile person; later we can ask why these features are objectionable. As a step in this direction, let us examine again our three paradigm cases. The moral defect in each case, I suggest, is a failure to understand and acknowledge one's own moral rights. I assume, without argument here, that each person has moral rights.[2] Some of these rights may be basic human rights; that is, rights for which a person needs only to be human to qualify. Other rights will be derivative and contingent upon his special commitments, institutional affiliations, etc. Most rights will be prima facie ones; some may be absolute. Most can be waived under appropriate conditions; perhaps some cannot. Many rights can be forfeited; but some, presumably, cannot. The servile person does not, strictly speaking, violate his own rights. At least in our paradigm cases he fails to acknowledge fully his own moral status because he does not fully understand what his rights are, how they can be waived, and when they can be forfeited.

The defect of the Uncle Tom, for example, is that he displays an attitude that denies his moral equality with whites. He does not realize, or apprehend in an effective way, that he has as much right to a decent wage and a share of political power as any comparable white. His gratitude is misplaced; he accepts benefits which are his by right as if they were gifts. The Self-Deprecator is servile in a more complex way. He acts as if he has forfeited many important rights which in fact he has not. He does not understand, or fully realize in his own case, that certain rights to fair and decent treatment do not have to be earned. He sees his merits clearly enough, but he fails to see that what he can expect from others is not merely a function of his merits. The Deferential Wife *says* that she understands her rights vis-à-vis her husband, but what she fails to appreciate is that her consent to serve him is a valid waiver of her rights only under certain conditions. If her consent is coerced, say, by the lack of viable options for women in her society, then her consent is worth little. If socially fostered ignorance of her own talents and alternatives is responsible for her consent, then her consent should not count as a fully legitimate waiver of her right to equal consideration within the marriage. All the more, her consent to defer constantly to her husband is not a legitimate setting aside of her rights if it results from her mistaken belief that she has a moral duty to do so. (Recall: "The *proper* role for a woman is to serve her family.") If she believes that she has a *duty* to defer to her husband, then, whatever she may say, she cannot fully understand that she has a *right* not to defer to him. When she says that she freely gives up such a right, she is confused. Her confusion is rather like that of a person who has been persuaded by an unscrupulous lawyer that it is legally incumbent on him to refuse a jury trial but who nevertheless tells the judge that he understands that he has a right to a jury trial and freely waives it. He does not really understand what it is to have and freely give up the right if he thinks that it would be an offense for him to exercise it.

Insofar as servility results from moral ignorance or confusion, it need not be something for which a person is to blame. Even self-reproach may be inappropriate; for at the time a person is in ignorance he cannot feel guilty about his servility, and later he may conclude that his ignorance was unavoidable. In some cases, however, a person might reasonably believe that he should have known better. If, for example, the Deferential Wife's confusion about her rights resulted from a motivated resistance to drawing the implications of her own basic moral principles, then later she might find some ground for self-reproach. Whether blameworthy or not, servility could still be morally objectionable at least in the sense that it ought to be discouraged, that social conditions which nourish it should be reformed, and the like. Not all morally undesirable features of a person are ones for which he is responsible, but that does not mean that they are defects merely from an aesthetic or prudential point of view.

In our paradigm cases, I have suggested, servility is a kind of deferential attitude towards others resulting from ignorance or misunderstanding of one's moral rights. A sufficient remedy, one might think, would be moral enlightenment. Suppose, however, that our servile persons come to know their rights but do not substantially alter their behavior. Are they not still servile in an objectionable way? One might even think that reproach is more appropriate now because they know what they are doing.

The problem, unfortunately, is not as simple as it may appear. Much depends on what they tolerate and why. Let us set aside cases in which a person merely refuses to *fight* for his rights, chooses not to exercise certain rights, or freely waives many rights which he might have insisted upon. Our problem concerns the previously servile person who continues to display the same marks of deference even after he fully knows his rights. Imagine, for example, that even after enlightenment our Uncle Tom persists in his old pattern of behavior, giving all the typical signs of believing that the injustices done to him are not really wrong. Suppose, too, that the newly enlightened Deferential Wife continues to defer to her husband, refusing to disturb the old way of life by introducing her new ideas. She acts as if accepts the idea that she is merely doing her duty though actually she no longer believes it. Let us suppose, further, that the Uncle Tom and the Deferential Wife are not merely generous with their time and property; they also accept without protest, and even appear to sanction, treatment which is humiliating and degrading. That is, they do not simply consent to waive mutually acknowledged rights; they tolerate violations of their rights with apparent approval. They pretend to give their permission for subtle humiliations which they really believe no permission can make legitimate. Are such persons still servile despite their moral knowledge?

The answer, I think, should depend upon why the deferential role is played. If the motive is a morally commendable one, or a desire to avert dire consequences to oneself, or even an ambition to set an oppressor up for a later fall, then I would not count the role player as servile. The Uncle Tom, for instance, is not servile in my sense if he shuffles and bows to keep the Klan from killing his children, to save his own skin, or even to buy time while he plans the revolution. Similarly, the Deferential Wife is not servile if she tolerates an abusive husband because he is so ill that further strain would kill him, because protesting would deprive her of her only means of survival, or because she is collecting atrocity stories for her book against marriage. If there is fault in these situations, it seems inappropriate to call it *servility*. The story is quite different, however, if a person continues in his deferential role just from laziness, timidity, or a desire for some minor advantage. He shows too little concern for his moral status as a person, one is tempted to say, if he is willing to deny it for a small profit or simply because it requires some effort and courage to affirm it openly. A black who plays the Uncle Tom merely to gain an advantage over other blacks is harming them, of course; but he is also displaying disregard for his own moral position as an equal among human beings. Similarly, a woman throws away her rights too lightly if she continues to play the subservient role because she is used to it or is too timid to risk a change. A Self-Deprecator who readily accepts what he knows are violations of his rights may be indulging his peculiar need for punishment at the expense of denying something more valuable. In these cases, I suggest, we have a kind of servility independent of any ignorance or confusion about one's rights. The person who has it may or may not be blameworthy, depending on many factors; and the line between servile and nonservile role-playing will often be hard to draw. Nevertheless, the objectionable feature is perhaps clear enough for present purposes: it is a willingness to disavow one's moral status, publicly and systematically, in the absence of any strong reason to do so.

My proposal, then, is that there are at least two types of servility: one resulting from misunderstanding of one's rights and the other from placing a comparatively low value on them. In either case, servility manifests the absence of a certain kind of self-respect. The respect which is missing is not respect for one's merits but respect for one's rights. The servile person displays this absence of respect not directly by acting contrary to his own rights but indirectly by acting as if his rights were nonexistent or insignificant. An arrogant person ignores the rights of others, thereby arrogating for himself a higher status than he is entitled to; a servile person denies his own rights, thereby assuming a lower position than he is entitled to. Whether rooted in ignorance or simply lack of concern for moral rights, the attitudes in both cases may be incompatible with a proper regard for morality. That this is so is obvious in the case of arrogance; but to see it in the case of servility requires some further argument.

IV

The objectionable feature of the servile person, as I have described him, is his tendency to disavow his own moral rights either because he misunderstands them or because he cares little for them. The question remains: why should anyone regard this as a moral defect? After all, the rights which he denies are his own. He may be unfortunate, foolish, or even distasteful; but why *morally* deficient? One sort of answer, quite different from those reviewed earlier, is suggested by some of Kant's remarks. Kant held that servility is contrary to a perfect nonjuridical duty to oneself.[3] To say that the duty is perfect is roughly to say that it is stringent, never overridden by other considerations (e.g., beneficence). To say that the duty is nonjuridical is to say that a person cannot legitimately be coerced to comply. Although Kant did not develop an explicit argument for this view, an argument can easily be constructed from materials which reflect the spirit, if not the letter, of his moral theory. The argument which I have in mind is prompted by Kant's contention that respect for persons, strictly speaking, is respect for moral law.[4] If taken as a claim about all sorts of respect, this seems quite implausible. If it means that we respect persons only for their moral character, their capacity for moral conduct, or their status as "authors" of the moral law, then it seems unduly moralistic. My strategy is to construe the remark as saying that at least one sort of respect for persons is respect for the rights which the moral law accords them. If one respects the moral law, then one must respect one's own moral rights; and this amounts to having a kind of self-respect incompatible with servility.

The premises for the Kantian argument, which are all admittedly vague, can be sketched as follows:

First, let us assume, as Kant did, that all human beings have equal basic human rights. Specific rights vary with different conditions, but all must be justified from a point of view under which all are equal. Not all rights need to be earned, and some cannot be forfeited. Many rights can be waived but only under certain conditions of knowledge and freedom. These conditions are complex and difficult to state; but they include something like the condition that a person's consent releases others from obligation only if it is autonomously given, and consent resulting from underestimation of one's moral status is not autonomously given. Rights can be objects of knowledge, but also of ignorance, misunderstanding, deception, and the like.

Second, let us assume that my account of servility is correct; or, if one prefers, we can take it as a definition. That is, in brief, a servile person is one who tends to deny or disavow his own moral rights because he does not understand them or has little concern for the status they give him.

Third, we need one formal premise concerning moral duty, namely, that each person ought, as far as possible, to respect the moral law. In less Kantian language, the point is that everyone should approximate, to the extent that he can, the ideal of a person who fully adopts the moral point of view. Roughly, this means not only that each person ought to do what is morally required and refrain from what is morally wrong but also that each person should treat all the provisions of morality as valuable—worth preserving and prizing as well as obeying. One must, so to speak, take up the spirit of morality as well as meet the letter of its requirements. To keep one's promises, avoid hurting others, and the like, is not sufficient; one should also take an attitude of respect towards the principles, ideals, and goals of morality. A respectful attitude towards a system of rights and duties consists of more than a disposition to conform to its definite rules of behavior; it also involves holding the system in esteem, being unwilling to ridicule it, and being reluctant to give up one's place in it. The

essentially Kantian idea here is that morality, as a system of equal fundamental rights and duties, is worthy of respect, and hence a completely
moral person would respect it in word and manner as well as in deed.
And what a completely moral person would do, in Kant's view, is our duty
to do so far as we can.

The assumptions here are, of course, strong ones, and I make no
attempt to justify them. They are, I suspect, widely held though rarely
articulated. In any case, my present purpose is not to evaluate them but
to see how, if granted, they constitute a case against servility. The objection to the servile person, given our premises, is that he does not satisfy the basic requirement to respect morality. A person who fully respected a system of moral rights would be disposed to learn his proper place
in it, to affirm it proudly, and not to tolerate abuses of it lightly. This is
just the sort of disposition that the servile person lacks. If he does not
understand the system, he is in no position to respect it adequately. This
lack of respect may be no fault of his own, but it is still a way in which
he falls short of a moral ideal. If, on the other hand, the servile person
knowingly disavows his moral rights by pretending to approve of violations of them, then, barring special explanations, he shows an indifference to whether the provisions of morality are honored and publicly
acknowledged. This avoidable display of indifference, by our Kantian
premises, is contrary to the duty to respect morality. The disrespect in
this second case is somewhat like the disrespect a religious believer
might show towards his religion if, to avoid embarrassment, he laughed
congenially while nonbelievers were mocking the beliefs which he
secretly held. In any case, the servile person, as such, does not express
disrespect for the system of moral rights in the obvious way by violating
the rights of others. His lack of respect is more subtly manifested by his
acting before others as if he did not know or care about his position of
equality under that system.

The central idea here may be illustrated by an analogy. Imagine a club,
say, an old German dueling fraternity. By the rules of the club, each
member has certain rights and responsibilities. These are the same for
each member regardless of what titles he may hold outside the club.
Each has, for example, a right to be heard at meetings, a right not to be
shouted down by the others. Some rights cannot be forfeited: for example, each may vote regardless of whether he has paid his dues and satisfied other rules. Some rights cannot be waived: for example, the right to
be defended when attacked by several members of the rival fraternity.
The members show respect for each other by respecting the status which

the rules confer on each member. Now one new member is careful always to allow the others to speak at meetings; but when they shout him down, he does nothing. He just shrugs as if to say, "Who am I to complain?" When he fails to stand up in defense of a fellow member, he feels ashamed and refuses to vote. He does not deserve the vote, he says. As the only commoner among illustrious barons, he feels that it is his place to serve them and defer to their decisions. When attackers from the rival fraternity come at him with swords drawn, he tells his companions to run and save themselves. When they defend him, he expresses immense gratitude—as if they had done him a gratuitous favor. Now one might argue that our new member fails to show respect for the fraternity and its rules. He does not actually violate any of the rules by refusing to vote, asking others not to defend him, and deferring to the barons, but he symbolically disavows the equal status which the rules confer on him. If he ought to have respect for the fraternity, he ought to change his attitude. Our servile person, then, is like the new member of the dueling fraternity in having insufficient respect for a system of rules and ideals. The difference is that everyone ought to respect morality whereas there is no comparable moral requirement to respect the fraternity.

The conclusion here is, of course, a limited one. Self-sacrifice is not always a sign of servility. It is not a duty always to press one's rights. Whether a given act is evidence of servility will depend not only on the attitude of the agent but also on the specific nature of his moral rights, a matter not considered here. Moreover, the extent to which a person is responsible, or blameworthy, for his defect remains an open question. Nevertheless, the conclusion should not be minimized. In order to avoid servility, a person who gives up his rights must do so with a full appreciation for what they are. A woman, for example, may devote herself to her husband if she is uncoerced, knows what she is doing, and does not pretend that she has no decent alternative. A self-contemptuous person may decide not to press various unforfeited rights but only if he does not take the attitude that he is too rotten to deserve them. A black may demand less than is due to him provided he is prepared to acknowledge that no one has a right to expect this of him. Sacrifices of this sort, I suspect, are extremely rare. Most people, if they fully acknowledged their rights, would not autonomously refuse to press them.

An even stronger conclusion would emerge if we could assume that some basic rights cannot be waived. That is, if there are some rights that others are bound to respect regardless of what we say, then, barring special explanation, we would be obliged not only to acknowledge these rights but also to avoid any appearance of consenting to give them up. To act as if we could release others from their obligation to grant these rights, apart from special circumstances, would be to fail to respect morality. Rousseau held, for example, that at least a minimal right to liberty cannot be waived. A man who consents to be enslaved, giving up liberty without *quid pro quo*, thereby displays a conditioned slavish mentality that renders his consent worthless. Similarly, a Kantian might argue that a person cannot release others from the obligation to refrain from killing him: consent is no defense against the charge of murder. To accept principles of this sort is to hold that rights to life and liberty are, as Kant believed, rather like a trustee's rights to preserve something valuable entrusted to him: he has not only a right but a duty to preserve it.

Even if there are no specific rights which cannot be waived, there might be at least one formal right of this sort. This is the right to some minimum degree of respect from others. No matter how willing a person is to submit to humiliation by others, they ought to show him some respect as a person. By analogy with self-respect, as presented here, this respect owed by others would consist of a willingness to acknowledge fully, in word as well as action, the person's basically equal moral status as defined by his other rights. To the extent that a person gives tacit consent to humiliations incompatible with this respect, he will be acting as if he waives a right which he cannot in fact give up. To do this, barring special explanations, would mark one as servile.

V

Kant held that the avoidance of servility is a duty to oneself rather than a duty to others. Recent philosophers, however, tend to discard the idea of a duty to oneself as a conceptual confusion. Although admittedly the analogy between a duty to oneself and a duty to others is not perfect, I suggest that something important is reflected in Kant's contention.

Let us consider briefly the function of saying that a duty is *to* someone. *First*, to say that a duty is *to* a given person sometimes merely indicates who is the object of that duty. That is, it tells us that the duty is concerned with how that person is to be treated, how his interests and wishes are to be taken into account, and the like. Here we might as well say that we have a duty *towards*, or *regarding* that person. Typically the person in question is the beneficiary of the fulfillment of the duty. For example, in this sense I have a duty to my children and even a duty to a distant stranger if I promised a third party that I would help that stranger. Clearly a duty to avoid servility would be a duty to oneself at least in this minimal sense, for it is a duty to avoid, so far as possible, the denial of one's own moral status. The duty is concerned with understanding and affirming one's rights, which are, at least as a rule, for one's own benefit.

Second, when we say that a duty is *to* a certain person, we often indicate thereby the person especially entitled to complain in case the duty is not fulfilled. For example, if I fail in my duty to my colleagues, then it is they who can most appropriately reproach me. Others may sometimes speak up on their behalf, but, for the most part, it is not the business of strangers to set me straight. Analogously, to say that the duty to avoid servility is a duty to oneself would indicate that, though sometimes a person may justifiably reproach himself for being servile, others are not generally in the appropriate position to complain. Outside encouragement is sometimes necessary, but, if any blame is called for, it is primarily self-recrimination and not the censure of others.

Third, mention of the person to whom a duty is owed often tells us something about the source of that duty. For example, to say that I have a duty to another person may indicate that the argument to show that I have such a duty turns upon a promise to that person, his authority over me, my having accepted special benefits from him, or, more generally, his rights. Accordingly, to say that the duty to avoid servility is a duty to oneself would at least imply that it is not entirely based upon promises of others, their authority, their beneficence, or an obligation to respect their rights. More positively, the assertion might serve to indicate that the source of the duty is one's own rights rather than the rights of others, etc. That is, one ought not to be servile because, in some broad sense, one ought to respect one's own rights as a person. There is, to be sure, an asymmetry: one has certain duties to others because one ought not to violate their rights, and one has a duty to oneself because one ought to affirm one's own rights. Nevertheless, to dismiss duties to oneself out of hand is to overlook significant similarities.

Some familiar objections to duties to oneself, moreover, seem irrelevant in the case of servility. For example, some place much stock in the idea that a person would have no duties if alone on a desert island. This can be doubted, but in any case is irrelevant here. The duty to avoid servility is a duty to take a certain stance towards others and hence would be inapplicable if one were isolated on a desert island. Again, some suggest that if there were duties to oneself then one could make promises to oneself or owe oneself a debt of gratitude. Their paradigms are familiar ones. Someone remarks, "I promised myself a vacation this year" or "I have been such a good boy I owe myself a treat." Concentration on these facetious cases tends to confuse the issue. In any case the duty to avoid servility, as presented here, does not presuppose promises to oneself or debts of gratitude to oneself. Other objections stem from the intuition that a person has no duty to promote his own happiness. A duty to oneself, it is sometimes assumed, must be a duty to promote one's own happiness. From a utilitarian point of view, in fact, this is what a duty to oneself would most likely be. The problems with such alleged duties, however, are irrelevant to the duty to avoid servility. This is a duty to understand and affirm one's rights, not to promote one's own welfare. While it is usually in the interest of a person to affirm his rights, our Kantian argument against servility was not based upon this premise. Finally, a more subtle line of objection turns on the idea that, given that rights and duties are correlative, a person who acted contrary to a duty to oneself would have to be violating his own rights, which seems absurd.[5] This objection raises issues too complex to examine here. One should note, however, that I have tried to give a sense to saying that servility is contrary to a duty to oneself without presupposing that the servile person violates his own rights. If acts contrary to duties to others are always violations of their rights, then duties to oneself are not parallel with duties to others to that extent. But this does not mean that it is empty or pointless to say that a duty is to oneself.

My argument against servility may prompt some to say that the duty is "to morality" rather than "to oneself." All this means, however, is that the duty is derived from a basic requirement to respect the provisions of morality; and in this sense every duty is a duty "to morality." My duties to my children are also derivative from a general requirement to respect moral principles, but they are still duties *to* them.

Kant suggests that duties to oneself are a precondition of duties to others. On our account of servility, there is at least one sense in which this is so. Insofar as the servile person is ignorant of his own rights, he is not in an adequate position to appreciate the rights of others. Misunderstanding the moral basis for his equal status with others, he is necessarily liable to underestimate the rights of those with whom he classifies himself. On the other hand, if he plays the servile role knowingly, then, barring special explanation, he displays a lack of concern to see the principles of morality acknowledged and respected and thus the absence of one motive which can move a moral person to respect the rights of others. In either case, the servile person's lack of self-respect necessarily puts him in a less than ideal position to respect others. Failure to fulfill one duty to oneself, then, renders a person liable to violate duties of others. This, however, is a consequence of our argument against servility, not a presupposition of it.

Notes

An earlier version of this paper was presented at the meetings of the American Philosophical Association, Pacific Division. A number of revisions have been made as a result of the helpful comments of others, especially Norman Dahl, Sharon Hill, Herbert Morris, and Mary Mothersill.

1. Each of the cases is intended to represent only one possible pattern of servility. I make no claims about how often these patterns are exemplified, nor do I mean to imply that only these patterns could warrant the labels "Deferential Wife," "Uncle Tom," etc. All the more, I do not mean to imply any comparative judgments about the causes or relative magnitude of the problems of racial and sexual discrimination. One person, e.g., a self-contemptuous woman with a sense of racial inferiority, might exemplify features of several patterns at once; and, of course, a person might view her being a woman the way an Uncle Tom views being black, etc.

2. As will become evident, I am also presupposing some form of cognitive or "naturalistic" interpretation of rights. If, to accommodate an emotivist or prescriptivist, we set aside talk of moral knowledge and ignorance, we might construct a somewhat analogous case against servility from the point of view of those who adopt principles ascribing rights to all; but the argument, I suspect, would be more complex and less persuasive.

3. See Immanuel Kant, *The Doctrine of Virtue*, Part II of *The Metaphysic of Morals*, ed. M. J. Gregor (New York: Harper and Row, 1964), pp. 99–103; Prussian Academy edition, vol. 6, pp. 434–37.

4. Immanuel Kant, *Groundwork of the Metaphysic of Morals*, ed. H. J. Paton (New York: Harper and Row, 1964), p. 69; Prussian Academy edition, vol. 4, p. 401; *The Critique of Practical Reason*, ed. Lewis W. Beck (New York: Bobbs-Merrill, 1956), pp. 81, 84; Prussian Academy edition, vol. 5, pp. 78, 81. My purpose here is not to interpret what Kant meant but to give a sense to his remark.

5. This, I take it, is part of M. G. Singer's objection to duties to oneself in *Generalization in Ethics* (New York: Alfred A. Knopf, 1961), pp. 311–18. I have attempted to examine Singer's arguments in detail elsewhere.

4

✢

Self-Respect and Protest

✢

Bernard R. Boxill

Must a person protest his wrongs? Booker T. Washington and W. E. B.
DuBois debated this question at the turn of the century. They did not
disagree over whether protesting injustice was an effective way to right it,
but over whether protesting injustice, when one could do nothing to
right it oneself, was self-respecting. Washington felt that it was not. Thus,
he did not deny that protest could help ameliorate conditions or that it
was sometimes justified; what he did deny was that a person should keep
protesting wrongs committed against him where he could not take decisive steps to end them. By insisting on "advertising his wrongs" in such
cases, he argued, a person betrayed a weakness for relying, not on his
"own efforts" but on the "sympathy" of others. Washington's position was
that if a person felt wronged, he should do something about it; if he
could do nothing he should hold his tongue and wait his opportunity;

This essay was originally published in *Philosophy and Public Affairs* 6 (1976). Copyright ©
1976 by PUP. Reprinted by permission of Princeton University Press.

protest in such cases is only a servile appeal for sympathy; stoicism, by implication, is better. Dubois strongly contested these views. Not only did he deny that protest is an appeal for sympathy, he maintained that if a person failed to express openly his outrage at injustice, however assiduously he worked against it, he would in the long run lose his self-respect. Thus, he asserted that Washington faced a "paradox" by insisting both on "self-respect" and on "a silent submission to civic inferiority,"[1] and he declared that "only in a...persistent demand for essential equality...can any people show...a decent self-respect."[2] Like Frederick Douglass, he concluded that people should protest their wrongs. In this essay I shall expand upon and defend Dubois' side of the debate. I shall argue that persons have reason to protest their wrongs not only to stop injustice but also to show self-respect and to know themselves as self-respecting.

Washington's detractors charge that his depreciation of protest was appeasement; his defenders maintain that it was prudence. Detractors and defenders therefore agree that black protest would have been a provocation to the white South. A provocation arouses an individual's resentment because it challenges his moral claim to a status he enjoys and wants to preserve, thus black protest would have challenged the white South's justification of the superior status it claimed. Washington did not disapprove of every attempt to effect greater justice; he rejected protest in particular. Thus his frequent efforts to urge America to reform were consistent with his position. Since his remonstrations were received considerately, and not at all as provocation or protest, they must have avoided making the kind of challenge protest presumably presents. Therefore, an analysis of them should suggest what protest is.

Washington always failed to press the claim that black people are victims of America's racial injustice. He frequently implied, and sometimes stated explicitly, that the white perpetrators of injustice were economically and, especially, morally the people most hurt and maimed by racial injustice and that, by comparison, the black victims of injustice suffered only "temporary inconvenience."[3] From this kind of reasoning it is easy to conclude that the morally compelling ground for reform is to save, not so much the victims of injustice, but its perpetrators because their "degradation" places them in greatest need.

The notion that because it implies guilt and ultimately moral degradation, inflicting injustice is a greater evil than suffering it is, of course, part of the Christian tradition and before that, the Socratic. Washington seems, however, to be one of the few to use it as an argument for social reform. Whether he really believed it is completely irrelevant. What is pertinent is that this was the consideration he thought prudent to present to America and that he hoped would be efficacious in motivating reform. This consideration, though urged insistently, did not arouse resentment. America apparently did not mind being accused of degradation—as long as its affairs, its advancement and its moral salvation remained the center of moral concern. For, as I have indicated, Washington did explicitly draw the conclusion that the morally compelling ground for reform was the moral salvation of white America.[4]

The idea that being a perpetrator is worse than being a victim is, of course, true in the sense that the person guilty of perpetrating injustice is morally worse than the person who must endure it. But, it does not follow from this that the perpetrator of injustice suffers greater evil than his victim or that the ground for seeking justice is to save the unjust man. As I have argued in another essay, such a position can be maintained only if the victim of injustice has no rights. For if the victim has rights then the perpetrator's duty is not to avoid degrading himself but to respect those rights. To claim that the victim of injustice has rights is thus to challenge the transgressor's arrogant assumption that his own advancement, economic or moral, is the sole legitimate object of social policy. Washington never challenged white America's assumption that its advancement justified the reform he advocated because he never claimed that black Americans had rights. Black protest would have affirmed that they do.

Because protest emphasizes the wrongs of the victim and declares that redress is a matter of the highest urgency, a person who insistently protests against his own condition may seem to be self-centered and self-pitying. He appears to dwell self-indulgently on his grievances and to be seeking the commiseration of others. Washington, for example, criticized Frederick Douglass for constantly reminding black people of "their sufferings"[5] and suspected that persistent protesters relied on "the special sympathy of the world" rather than on "their own efforts."[6] This is an important charge since the self-respecting person is self-reliant and avoids self-pity. It is not answered by the claim that people have rights, for having rights does not necessarily justify constant reiteration that one has them. The charge is answered, however, by a closer consideration of what is involved in claiming a right. The idea that the protester seeks sympathy is unlikely, since in claiming his rights he affirms that he is claiming what he can demand and exact, and sympathy cannot be demanded and exacted. The idea that the protester is self-pitying is likewise implausible, since a person who feels pity for himself typically believes that his condition is deplorable and unavoidable, and this is not what the protester affirms. On the contrary, he affirms that his condition is avoidable, he insists that what he protests is precisely the illegitimate, and hence avoidable, interference by others in the exercise of his rights, and he expresses the sentiment, not of self-pity, but of resentment. Protest could be self-indulgent if it were a demand for help, and it could show a lack of self-reliance if it claimed powerlessness. But, in insisting on his rights, the protester neither demands help nor claims powerlessness. He demands only noninterference. What Frederick Douglass protested against, for example, was interference. He scorned supererogatory help. "Do nothing with us," he exclaimed. "And, if the Negro cannot stand on his own legs, let him fall."[7]

It follows from the above that when a person protests his wrongs, he expresses a righteous and self-respecting concern for himself. If, as we assume, the self-respecting person has such a concern for himself, it follows that he will naturally be inclined to protest his injuries. Would he always have good reason actually to give vent to his indignation? Protest, it seems, is the response of the weak. It is not a warning of retaliation. The strong man does not waste too much time protesting his injuries; he prevents them. Why then should the weak, but self-respecting, person protest his wrongs? Surely if either protest or whining will prevent injury, the self-respecting person will protest rather than whine. For protest is self-respecting. Though it cannot compel the transgressor to reform, it tells him that he should be compelled to reform and that he is being asked no favors. But, if as Washington's defenders aver, protest often provokes persecution, why should a weak and vulnerable people protest? What good could it do? If it will help, why can't a self-respecting people pretend servility? But it seems that people do protest their wrongs, even when it is clear that this will bring no respite and, instead, cause them further injury. W. E. B. Dubois exhorted black people, "even when bending to the inevitable," to "bend with unabated protest."[8] Is this mere bravado? Or does a person with self-respect have a reason to protest over and above the hope that it will bring relief?

It may be argued that he does, that he should protest to make others recognize that he has rights. But, though a person who believes he has a right not to be unjustly injured also believes that others wrong him if they injure him unjustly and that they should be restrained from doing so, it is not clear that he must want them to share his conviction that he has this right. Why should he care what they believe? Why, just because he believes that he has a right, should he desire that others share his belief? There is no reason to suppose that the self-respecting person must want others to believe what he believes. Though he believes that the morally respectable ground for not injuring him is that he has a right not to be injured, it does not follow that he must want others to act on morally respectable grounds. Self-respect is a morally desirable quality but the self-respecting person need not be a saint. He need not want to make others moral. To this it may be objected that he nevertheless has a good reason to convince others of his rights, because the surest and most stable protection from unjust injury is for others to be restrained by solid moral convictions. This may be true. But it does not show that a person will want others to respect him just because he respects himself. Even the person who fails to respect himself may want the surest and most stable protection from unjust injury, and thus may want others to respect him. And, in general, for the protection of his rights, the self-respecting person cannot depend too heavily on the moral restraint of others. His self-reliance impels him to seek the means of self-defense. Secure in the conviction that it is legitimate to defend himself, he is satisfied if others respect him because they fear him.

Alternately, it may be proposed that the self-respecting person will want others to respect him because he wants to remain self-respecting. For unopposed injustice invites its victims to believe that they have no value and are without rights. This confident invitation may make even the self-respecting fear that their sense of their own value is only prejudiced self-love. It may therefore be argued that since protest is an affirmation of the rights of the victim, the self-respecting victim of injustice will protest to make others recognize, and in that way reassure him, that he has rights. Frederick Douglass, for example, once referred to this acknowledgment as the "all important confession."[9] But, though the self-respecting need to reassure themselves that they have rights, they would disdain this kind of reassurance. It is inappropriate because unanimous acknowledgment of a proposition does not imply its truth but only that everyone avows it. It is not self-respecting because it shows a lack of self-reliance. The self-respecting person cannot be satisfied to depend on the opinions of others. This is not to question the proposition that it is difficult to believe what everyone denies and easy to believe what everyone affirms. It is to say that, even while he concedes this, the self-respecting person will want to have his conviction of his worth rationally based.

But it is not clear that the self-respecting person has good reason to protest, even if he does want others to respect him. Washington, for example, understood that social acknowledgment was important but condemned protest. He argued that to be acknowledged as worthy citizens black people would do better to develop the qualities and virtues that would make them economically valuable members of society. Washington was right. For though protest is an uncompromising claim that the victim of some injury has a right not be injured, it does not follow that protest is therefore a likely way of getting others to agree. To affirm something, no matter how sincerely and passionately, may be an indifferent way of persuading others of it. And protest is, essentially, an affirmation that a victim of injury has rights. It is not an argument for that position. Typically, people protest when the time for argument and persuasion is past. They insist, as Dubois put it, that the claim they protest is "an outrageous falsehood,"[10] and that it would be demeaning to argue and cajole for what is so plain. Responding to a newspaper article that claimed "The Negro" was "Not a Man," Frederick Douglass disdainfully declared, "I cannot, however, argue. I must assert."[11]

It may be objected that though protest is not plausibly designed to persuade others that the victim of some injury has value or rights, it is designed to compel them to acknowledge that he is a moral being. This issue is raised by Orlando Patterson in his essay "Toward a Future that Has No Past."[12] Speaking of a slave's stealing as "an assertion of moral worth"—that is, as protest—Patterson points out that by screaming, "You are a thief," the master admits that the slave is a moral being, since it is in the act of punishing him as a thief that the master most emphatically avows the slave to be a moral being. If the slave's stealing is indeed an act of protest then, as I have indicated, protest need not be designed to promote conciliation. Further, since what the slave wants to hear is that he is a thief, his aim is surely not to be acknowledged as an economically valuable asset but as a being who is responsible for his acts. Finally, though this concession is made loudly and publicly and, by all accounts, sincerely, it is nevertheless absurd and paradoxical. For though the master calls the slave a thief, and thus a moral being, he continues to treat him as a piece of property. Still, it may seem that the slave wins a victory. At least, even if it is painful, he enjoys the satisfaction of forcing a most unwilling agent to treat him as a moral being. This argument has considerable force. For a self-respecting person no doubt desires to be treated as a moral being. But it is not clear that a master must, in consistency, deny that a slave is a moral being. If he wants to justify himself, what he must deny is that the slave has rights. And, even if to be consistent he must deny that the slave is a moral being, it is not clear that the slave can always get the master to call him "thief." Or even if he does, it is not clear that the master must admit that he uses the word in any but an analogical sense. And, it is not true that property cannot be punished without absurdity. Animals, for example, are routinely punished without absurdity and with no implication that they are anything but property.

It may finally be argued that affirming one's rights may be necessary to keeping the sense of one's value simply because doing so is an essential part of having self-respect. This must first be qualified. It may be false that one believes that one has rights. Thus, since lying cannot be an essential part of anything valuable, merely affirming that one has rights cannot, without qualification, be essential to keeping the sense of one's value. The argument must therefore be that protest is necessary to keeping the sense of one's value if one believes that one has rights. But why should one affirm what one believes, however deeply and firmly one believes it? To this it may be proposed that the self-respecting person wishes to seem to be what he is; he is, we may say, authentic. But, though authenticity may be a virtue, it is not clear why the self-respecting person must be authentic. To say that someone has self-respect is certainly not to say that he has all the virtues. Further, it is not evident that authenticity is necessarily one of the qualities that the self-respecting person believes to be valuable about himself. Neither is it clear, without further argument, that the self-respecting person's authenticity can be derived from the fact that he is convinced he has rights. Secret convictions seem possible. In the second place, even if the self-respecting person is authentic and wishes to seem to be what he is, it does not follow that he has to say what he is, unless saying what he is, is part of what he is. But this latter proposition is just what is at issue. The self-respecting person may protest because he believes he has rights. He does not believe he has value only if he protests.

Besides meting out injury incommensurate with the victim's worth and rights, uncontested and unopposed injustice invites witnesses to believe that he is injured just because he is wicked or inferior. Oppressors, no doubt, desire to be justified. They want to believe more than that their treatment of others is fitting; they want those they mistreat to condone their mistreatment as proper, and therefore offer inducements and rewards toward that end. Thus, even the self-respecting person may be tempted at least to pretend servility for some relief. But he will find that such pretense has its dangers; it shakes his confidence in his self-respect. I shall argue that the self-respecting person in such straits must, in some way, protest to assure himself that he has self-respect.

Since self-respect is valuable, it contributes to an individual's worth. But a person can have self-respect and few other good qualities. Since all men have inalienable rights, there is always a rational basis for self-respect, but a person may have an inflated and false sense of his worth. He may be utterly convinced, on what he falsely believes to be rational grounds, that he is much better than he really is. He may be mean and cowardly and cut an absurd figure, but insofar as he has faith in himself, he has self-respect. Consequently, when an individual desires to know whether he has self-respect, what he needs is not evidence of his worth in general but evidence of his faith in his worth. I argued earlier that protest is an indifferent way of getting others to acknowledge and thus to confirm that one has worth. But it may be an excellent way of confirming that one has faith in one's worth. For, as the preceding discussion should suggest, evidence of faith in one's worth is different from evidence of one's worth in general.

A person with a secure sense of his value has self-respect. This does not mean that he cannot lose it. It is a contradiction in terms, however, to suppose that anyone with self-respect would want to lose it. A person would want to lose his self-respect only if he feared that his belief in his worth was false or irrational, or, for some other reason, undesirable. But a person cannot be securely convinced of what he fears is false or irrational. And if a person believes that something has worth, he cannot believe that it is desirable to be ignorant of it. Hence, the person with self-respect cannot want to lose it.

Moreover, the self-respecting person cannot be oblivious to, or unconcerned about, the question of his self-respect. He must be aware that he believes he has value and that this is important. A person can have a belief and be unaware of having it, or have a sense of security and be unable to specify what he feels secure about. But the self-respecting person does not merely believe in his worth or have a vague sense of security. He feels secure about his belief in his worth. Thus, since a person cannot feel certain about something and be unaware of what he feels certain about, the self-respecting person must be aware that he believes he has value. And, for reasons already stated, he must believe that this belief is desirable. This does not mean that a person with self-respect must be continuously agitated by the fear of losing it. But it would be a mistake to urge further that only the confident, self-assured person who can take his self-respect for granted really does have self-respect. This would be to confuse self-respect with self-confidence. People do sometimes lose their self-respect. Thus to the extent that he is reflective, the person with self-respect will concede the possibility of losing it. And, though he may be confident of retaining it, he need not be. For, what he is sure of is that he has worth; not that he will always be sure of this. Whether he has this confidence depends on matters other than his self-respect. Though he may not be servile, a person may properly fear that, because of what he is doing or because of what is happening to him, he will become servile.

He may also fear that he is already servile. If he has self-respect he will be aware that he entertains the belief that he has worth and that he should be convinced of it, though he need not be sure that he is convinced of it. For he will probably also know that servile people too can value and persuade themselves that they have the self-respect which they lack. Thus, not only may a person with self-respect fear losing it; he may fear not having it. And this is not untypical. The early Christian may have had faith but doubt that he had it; to abolish his doubt he often sought the test of martyrdom. The courageous man may test his courage in order to know it. Though such tests may incidentally develop qualities they are meant to test, their main function is to discover to the agent a faith he may have, but of which he is not certain.

In sum, a person with self-respect may lose it. He may not be confident of always having it. He may not even be sure that he really has it. But if he does have self-respect, he will never be unconcerned about the question of his self-respect. Necessarily he will want to retain it. But no one will be satisfied that he has something unless he knows that he has it. Hence, the self-respecting person wants to know that he is self-respecting.

To know this he needs evidence. The need for such evidence must be especially poignant to the self-respecting person when, to prevent injury, he pretends servility. Observers often cannot agree on how to interpret such behavior. The "Sambo" personality, for example, is supposed to typify the good humored, ostensibly servile black slave. Sambo was apparently very convincing. In *Slavery: A Problem in American Institutional Life*, Stanley Elkins suggests that Sambo's "docility" and "humility" reflected true servility. On the other hand, other historians suspect that Sambo was a fraud. Patterson, for example, argues that Sambo's fawning laziness and dishonesty was his way of hitting back at the master's system without penalty. Thus, Patterson sees Sambo's "clowning" as a mask, "to salvage his dignity," a "deadly serious game" in which "the perfect stroke of rebellion must ideally appear to the master as the ultimate act of submission." Patterson is persuasive, but true servility is possible. Sambo could have been genuinely servile. Certainly every effort was made to make him so. There is therefore room for uncertainty. Further, it is not clear that Sambo can himself definitively settle the question. The master could have reason to suspect that Sambo's antics were a pretense only if he had evidence that they were. But if he is to know that he is not servile, Sambo too needs such evidence.

It may be pointed out that if Sambo's ostensible servility was his way of "hitting back," he was providing evidence of self-respect all along. But this must be qualified. Unless it is already known to be pretense, apparent servility is evidence of servility. If Sambo gave a perfect imitation of servility, neither he nor his master could have any reason to think he was anything but servile. If his pretense is to provide him with evidence of his self-respect it must, to some discernible extent, betray him. Patterson may be right that the "perfect stroke of rebellion must seem to the master as the ultimate act of submission,"[13] but the deception must succeed, not because it is undetectable, but because the master is so blinded by his own arrogance that he cannot see that what is presented as abasement is really thinly disguised affront.

If the above argument is sound, only consummate artistry can permit a person continuously and elaborately to pretend servility and still know that he is self-respecting. Unless it is executed by a master, the evidence of servility will seem overwhelming and the evidence of self-respect too ambiguous. But, as I have argued, the self-respecting person wants to know he is self-respecting. He hates deception and pretense because he sees them as obstacles to the knowledge of himself as self-respecting. If only occasionally, he must shed his mask.

This may not be so easy. It is not only that shedding the mask of servility may take courage, but that if a person is powerless it will not be easy for him to make others believe that he is taking off a mask. People do not take the powerless seriously. Because he wants to know himself as self-respecting, the powerless but self-respecting person is driven to make others take him seriously. He is driven to make his claim to self-respect unmistakable. Therefore, since nothing as unequivocally expresses what a person thinks he believes as his own emphatic statement, the powerless but self-respecting person will declare his self-respect. He will protest. His protest affirms that he has rights. More important, it tells everyone that he believes he has rights and that he therefore claims self-respect. When he has to endure wrongs he cannot repel and feels his self-respect threatened, he will publicly claim it in order to reassure himself that he has it. His reassurance does not come from persuading others that he has self-respect. It comes from using his claim to self-respect as a challenge.

Thus, even when transgressors will not desist, protest is nevertheless directed at them. For the strongest challenge to a claim to self-respect and one which can consequently most surely establish it as true will most likely come from those most anxious to deny that it has any basis. Protest in such straits is often unaccompanied by argument showing that the protester has rights, for what is relevant to his claim to self-respect is not whether he has rights but whether he believes he has them.[14]

Notes

I am grateful to Tom Hill and Jan Boxill for helpful discussions and to the editors of *Philosophy and Public Affairs* for valuable comments and criticisms.

1. W. E. B. Dubois, "Of Mr. Booker T. Washington and Others," in *Negro Social and Political Thought 1850–1920,* ed. Howard Brotz (New York: Basic Books, 1966), p. 512. Hereafter cited as Brotz.
2. *W. E. B Dubois,* ed. William M. Tuttle, Jr. (Englewood Cliffs, N.J.: Prentice Hall, 1973), p. 48.
3. Booker T. Washington, "Democracy and Education," in Brotz, p. 370.
4. Ibid.
5. Booker T. Washington, "The Intellectuals and the Boston Mob," in Brotz, p. 425.
6. Ibid., p. 429.
7. Frederick Douglass, "What the Black Man Wants," in Brotz, p. 283.
8. *W. E. B. Dubois,* p. 43.
9. Frederick Douglass, "What Are the Colored People Doing for Themselves?" in Brotz, p. 208.
10. W. E. B. Dubois, "The Evolution of the Race Problem," in Brotz, p. 549.
11. Frederick Douglass, "The Claims of the Negro Ethnologically Considered," in Brotz, p. 228.
12. Orlando Patterson, "Toward a Future That Has No Past: Reflections on the Fate of Blacks in the Americas," in *The Public Interest,* no. 27 (Spring 1972), p. 43.
13. Ibid.
14. I have argued that the person with self-respect has a special reason to protest wrongs committed against him. It may be asked whether he also has a special reason to protest wrongs committed against others. As I have indicated, though he possesses one important quality—self-respect itself—he need not possess all or most of the other morally desirable qualities. He need not, for example, be altruistic or care much about others. If he does conceive himself as having duties to aid others, however, he will want to defend his right to be

that sort of person and will accordingly protest interferences with that right. Typically, he will have occasion to do this when his efforts to prevent wrongful injury to others are interfered with.

+

Character,
Agency,
and Shame

+

5

✛

Self-Respect

✛

Elizabeth Telfer

1. Two Aspects of Self-Respect

The first problem concerning self-respect is that of its category: what kind of thing is it? On this will depend the answer to another question: what is the relation between self-respect and the modes of conduct or qualities of character with which it is typically associated, such as self-control, courage, independence?

One view which suggests itself is that self-respect is some kind of favourable opinion of oneself. It might be said that respecting someone is admiring him or thinking highly of him, and so self-respect is having this view of oneself, perhaps with an appropriate emotional accompaniment as with admiration of others. On this view, the modes of conduct and qualities of character would be the *grounds* of one's good opinion of oneself.

This essay was originally published in *The Philosophical Quarterly* 18 (1968). Reprinted by permission from Basil Blackwell Ltd.

Now respect for someone else, in this sense of thinking highly of him, implies that he is above the ordinary, has unusual merits. But *self*-respect does not carry the same implications. A man who has self-respect merely thinks he comes up to scratch. This can be seen by considering loss of self-respect, which does not merely mean ceasing to think well of oneself but rather thinking badly of oneself, regarding oneself as inadequate, below par, and so on. The emotional aspect of loss of self-respect is not merely absence of pride or of pleasure in one's achievements, but disgust, contempt or despair. Self-respect then seems to be a man's belief that he attains at least some minimum standard, and the emotion which goes with this, if any, is something like peace of mind. Loss of self-respect is the loss of this belief, either as a result of conduct judged to fall short of the minimum standard, or because for some other reason a man comes to see himself in a new and unfavourable light. It is often caused by a single action which is such as to alter one's whole view of oneself. Thus people say: "I could never respect myself again if I were to…"

But the account of self-respect we have so far is lop-sided; it deals with only part of the concept, and possibly the less important part. This can be seen if we take into consideration the fact that self-respect can be an explanation of how a man behaves. Consider, for example, expressions like "self-respect made me…" or "self-respect prevented me…" or again "He did it out of self-respect." Or again, we say to someone behaving badly, "Have you no self-respect?" as if to imply that if he had, it would prevent him from behaving in this way.

Now the idea of self-respect as a kind of not-unfavourable opinion of oneself does not square very well with these usages. For one thing the self-respect which we have described earlier is something which is lost as a result of failure; but the usages above suggest that failure shows it to be absent already. Again, if we say to someone, "Have you no self-respect?" we suggest that self-respect is something which everyone ought always to have; whereas it seems quite appropriate that someone who says, "I could never respect myself again if I did that" and then does it, should suffer a loss of self-respect.

Most importantly, it is not clear how self-respect, construed as a belief in one's own adequacy, can explain acting or forbearing to act. It is not clear how a belief that one is already in some way satisfactory can be invoked as an explanation of satisfactory behavior.

I suggest that we have here what amounts to a second sense of the phrase "self-respect." Here it seems to stand for a motive, either a transient desire or one forming the basis of a permanent disposition. Usages such as "out of self-respect" and "self-respect made me" might refer either to a passing desire or permant disposition. Compare "out of vanity" or "jealousy made me." Usages such as "He refused because he has some self-respect" suggest a permanent disposition.

I shall refer to this aspect of self-respect as the *conative* aspect, to distinguish it from the earlier sense, the "favourable opinion" sense, which we may call the *estimative* aspect. These two aspects are closely linked in practice, but it is not at first sight obvious how they are linked. I shall try to show how they are linked presently, but first I shall say a little more about the question I have hitherto slid over—that of the nature and source of the self-respect standard. I think this is most easily investigated from the point of view of *conative* self-respect—by considering, for example, what kinds of shortcomings would provoke us to say: "Have you no self-respect?"

2. The Nature of Conative Self-Respect

If we try to characterize conative self-respect generally, we are inclined to say that it is roughly a desire not to behave in a manner unworthy of oneself, or a disposition which prevents one from behaving in a manner unworthy of oneself. Some things are thought to be unworthy of the man qua man, i.e., unworthy of anyone; other things are unworthy of him in view of some role or status or special quality. One question which suggests itself at once is: what is the difference between acting in a manner unworthy of a man qua man and acting immorally? Surely all immoral conduct is unworthy of man qua man, and vice versa? (There does seem to *be* a difference, in that self-respect is linked more readily with some aspects of morality than with others.) The reply to this question seems to be twofold: (i) On many views of morality, not all types of action which might be called "unworthy of man qua man" fall within the scope of morality. For example, they may concern no one other than the agent, while morality may be held to be by definition interpersonal. (ii) The conception of behaviour worthy of man qua man will not yield the whole range of morality without a good deal of stretching, for example by introducing a Butlerian notion of conscience as the head of man's ideal nature. The basic unstretched conception has mainly to do with the supremacy of reason.

But even where self-respecting conduct is also morally obligatory the motive of a man who acts *out* of self-respect is different in quality from what would normally be thought of as moral motivation. This can be seen if we give a more precise account of conative self-respect. To say merely that it is a desire to act in a manner worthy of oneself covers too many possibilities, since a man might have such a desire for various differing reasons. For example, he might say, "It is man's duty to behave worthily and I desire to do my duty." Here it would be natural to say that his motive is conscientiousness rather than self-respect and that he uses the idea of worthy behaviour as a criterion of his duty. Again, a man may say, "I desire to obey God and I think that behaving worthily is the essence of God's will for us." Here it would be natural to say that his motive is piety, and his idea of worthy behaviour merely his criterion of what piety demands.

Can we then define conative self-respect as the desire to behave worthily for its own sake? This is on the right lines, but we must note that such a desire might take two forms, one egoistic, the other non-egoistic: (i) A man's chief interest may be in his own worthy behaviour, his chief concern may be that he should not be dishonoured. (ii) A man may value worthy behaviour in itself, not merely as being his; this valuation will in practice be manifested mainly by his attempting to behave thus himself. (The former is like Aristotle's proper self-love; the second is like Aristotle's moral motive, the love of what is noble.) I think that when we speak of self-respect we most often have in mind the *egoistically-tinged* motive, and this is what I shall mean by "conative self-respect" from now on. I do not think that actual usage would invariably support such a restriction on the use of the term, but other senses can probably be conveyed as naturally in other words, while the egoistic motive which I am trying to isolate seems to have no other name.

Conative self-respect differs from moral or religious motivation, not only in being egoistic in the above sense, but also in the *light* in which it views unworthy behaviour. The reason why the man with self-respect wishes to shun unworthy behaviour is that he views it as contemptible, despicable and degrading, something to be looked down upon. This is not necessarily our attitude to immorality; for example, we might find it frightening.

Thus in considering in more detail what kinds of conduct show lack of self-respect, we shall expect to find it can be characterized as despicable and/or as sub-human. (It should be noted in passing that whereas people who behave thus show lack of self-respect, it does not follow that those who behave worthily do so *out* of self-respect; as I have tried to show, self-respect is only one possible motive for the types of behaviour characteristically associated with it.)

What types of behaviour are these? First of all, a man is accused of lack of self-respect if he is willing not to be his own master. A man who allows others to "push him around," who refuses to stand up for himself, who lets himself be dependent or dominated, is naturally regarded as despicable, to be looked down upon. He can also be looked upon as less than human, in the sense that a human being is characteristically an autonomous being; Sartre would say that a man who refuses to acknowledge to his autonomy is behaving like a thing.

Whereas the attempt to be in some degree independent of others is an essential part of self-respect, opinions will differ as to the degree to which this is necessary if we are to say that someone has self-respect, and also as to the way in which independence is really manifested. For example, if someone is pushed about by an officious administrator, it is not obvious whether self-respect demands the making of a scene—"Nobody's going to treat *me* like that"—or the *refusal* to be ruffled and "put out," to allow him to matter to that degree. Again, opinions would differ as to whether a man who chooses for some definite idealistic reasons to submit to others is lacking in self-respect—for example, a monk.

It should be noted that it is not the ability to get what one wants which is demanded by self-respect. Very often a man's best method of getting what he wants is to remain dependent on a benefactor (for example, an indulgent parent) who will give him what he wants. But such a man shows lack of self-respect because he is allowing himself to be *passive*, not in control of the situation. We may say: self-respect demands not only the fulfillment of one's purposes, but the exercise of one's purposiveness. A man with self-respect, then, will have the quality of independence; he will also have tenacity, the refusal to be overcome by adverse circumstances.

Secondly, we accuse people of lack of self-respect if they are not "their own masters" in a metaphorical sense—not in control of themselves. We naturally identify the self with the reason and speak of a man as "not his own master" if reason is not in control: reasoned behaviour is characteristic of mankind and so behaviour which is unreasoned is thought of as sub-human. Thus we think of a man who is "enslaved" to drink, or who is swayed from his purposes by emotion, as lacking in self-respect. Thus self-respect demands those virtues which are pre-eminently forms of self-control, such as courage and temperance. A man may also be said to practise so-called "other-regarding" virtues out of self-respect; if so, he is seeing them as forms of self-control or as manifestations of independence of others. Thus, if it is a man's self-respect which makes him generous, he feels that material things must not have too great a hold on him; if he is honest out of self-respect, he feels that he must not be swayed by concern for other men's approval; if self-respect makes him trustworthy, he is a man who feels that he must do what he sets out to do, come what may. It may here be said that whereas a man may perform outwardly generous, honest or trustworthy actions from such a motive, these are not cases of the virtues of generosity, honesty, trustworthiness, because these virtues require an other-regarding *motive*. This raises the whole question of the "right motive"—a question which is more complex than it is sometimes made to seem. I shall discuss this later when I try to assess the value of self-respect.

If a man stresses the self-legislative aspect of duty, and regards it as something to which he has committed *himself*, self-respect and sense of duty will for him be closely related. He will regard lapses from duty in the same light as other failures to carry out purposes or to follow reason, and humiliation will be a powerful element in his remorse.

So far, the standard with which conative self-respect is associated is partly objective and partly subjective. When we say that someone has self-respect, we are attributing to him qualities of independence, tenacity and self-control. A man cannot have conative self-respect if he does not have these; whether he himself values them or not is immaterial. But within this objective framework there is room for subjective standards to play a large part. If a man is to be master of himself and his situation, this will involve meeting standards, attaining goals, fulfilling roles which he has set for *himself*. On the other hand again, the *fulfillment* of some role is to be tested by an objective standard, even if the choice of role is a personal one.

This can be seen by examining the idiom "no *self-respecting x* would..." The "x" here stands for the name of a role which has either been chosen or has at least been accepted and "identified with," so that self-respect, which as we have seen requires the fulfillment of purposes, demands the performance of the role up to some minimum standard. What this standard is will largely be an objective matter. Thus a tutor may say to a student, "No self-respecting student would hand in such work." This suggests both that the work is bad by objective standards for students' work, and that it would not be so bad if it were not for a lack of self-respect as far as his role of student is concerned. Such a person takes no pride in his work, does not make good performance in it a point of honour. And because a person is normally thought to be responsible for having most of the roles he does have, we think of such a person as lacking self-respect in general. Thus if the student in the above example says,

"Well, I never wanted to be a student—people pushed me into it," the tutor might well reply, "No self-respecting boy would allow such a thing to happen."

Of course, there are some roles, such as those of sex, which we cannot be said to choose. Here there can be debate as to whether there is a role at all. Thus a statement like "No self-respecting male would be seen pushing a pram" can be challenged either by questioning the appropriateness of this rule for male behaviour, or by questioning the assumption that there is a special role for men. But it does not seem possible for a male accused of lack of self-respect to rebut the charge by saying, "I didn't choose to be a male"—any more than one can say "I didn't choose to be a human being" when accused of sub-human behaviour. Self-respect demands the adequate enactment of some basic roles, which we find ourselves in rather than choose. This role-fulfillment then is a separate item in the list of types of behaviour demanded by self-respect and cannot entirely be subsumed under "fulfillment of one's own purposes."

The same can be said of the standards demanded by advantages and privileges which some have and not others. One might say, for example: "No self-respecting boy of any intelligence would read that." Again, there is no rebuttal by saying, "I didn't choose to be intelligent." An intelligent person is saddled with standards which do not apply to everyone but which he cannot fall below without degradation, whether or not *he* values his intelligence.

I have suggested that some roles impose standards on us because we adopt them, others because we find ourselves in them. Some roles are a mixture of both: for example, the role of a gentleman. This can be looked on both as a code to which the individual chooses to commit himself—"Do you call yourself a gentleman?"—and also as a position of privilege, like the possession of intelligence, in which a man finds himself.

3. The Connexions Between Conative and Estimative Self-Respect

What are the connexions between conative and estimative self-respect? First, we must distinguish conative self-respect from the desire to preserve one's estimative self-respect. People do say, "I did it to preserve my self-respect" as well as "out of self-respect," and in explanation of why they did not do something they say "I knew that if I did it I would never respect myself again." What deters is the thought of a future unpleasantness. This is like doing one's duty in order to avoid the pain of a nagging conscience. But I think these motives, though they undoubtedly exist,

are derivative and presuppose a primary motive: straightforward conative self-respect in the one case, sense of duty in the other. If these did
not exist, remorse and self-disgust would not *be* painful. Thus the ability
occasionally to lose some estimative self-respect is one sign that one has
some conative self-respect, just as the ability to feel remorse is one manifestation of a sense of duty.

Thus conative self-respect is not equivalent to a desire to preserve estimative self-respect. Indeed, a man might preserve his estimative self-
respect and yet lack conative self-respect. This is because conative
self-respect, like sense of duty, has to do with objective standards in a way
in which estimative self-respect and remorse (or freedom from it) have
not. Thus someone can be accused of lacking self-respect or a sense of
duty even when (because his standards are too low or inept) *he* feels no
self-disgust, or no remorse. We can say to X, "I don't know how you can
respect yourself, behaving as you do" (this is estimative self-respect) and
at the same time say to Y about X, "X completely lacks self-respect" (this
is conative self-respect).

By and large, however, the standards connected with a man's own estimative self-respect will not diverge very much from the standards which
would be attributed to him by others who say he has (conative) self-
respect; the objective framework of conative self-respect leaves scope
within it for subjective standards, as we have seen.

I have said that the ability to lose estimative self-respect is one sign that
conative self-respect is still retained. Two qualifications must be added to
this. (i) If a man too often behaves in a way which causes him to lose his
self-respect (estimative) we shall begin to doubt whether he has much
conative self-respect. If he had, we feel, it would prevent him from behaving thus. (ii) Loss of estimative self-respect may have the effect of undermining a man's conative self-respect by making him despair. Thus a man
who is struggling with temptation and keeps failing may come to feel that
further efforts are useless.

Moreover, failure to retain estimative self-respect may undermine the
basis of conative self-respect in some cases, by destroying the point of
reference, as it were. For example, a person may consider certain conduct beneath him not only because it is unworthy in any case, but
because he "doesn't do that kind of thing" or "is not that kind of person." What is unworthy is what falls below the standard he has hitherto
maintained. Such a person may think of the preservation of the self-
respect standard as like preservation of virginity; once gone it is gone
for ever, and there is nothing to preserve. If he is forced by failure to

acknowledge that he *is* "that kind of person" after all, he loses the basis of his self-respect standard.

A somewhat similar case is where failure to maintain the self-respect standard may destroy a man's belief in his *ideal* self. This self is what a man *wants* to be like, rather than what he *is* like; but it bears a relation to his actual character, because he thinks of it as representing his highest potentialities or the best of which he is capable, and also because his actual character sets the style, as it were, in which the ideal is cast. Moreover, he tends to think of it as existing in some sense all the time, as when he considers actions to be unworthy of his *real* or *true* self, or says to himself, "I'm not really like that."

Now, for many people, self-respect is seen in terms of an ideal self— "This is beneath me" means "This is unworthy of my idea self, even though my actual self may stoop to it." But repeated failure to attain the standard may make a man doubt whether belief in an ideal self makes sense, doubt whether he has any good points or high potentialities, doubt whether he is worth anything. And if he is worth nothing, he may feel, there is no conduct which can be said to be beneath him. This is an illogical feeling, for conduct can be beneath a man simply because he is a man; but it is a powerful and common one, and indicates very clearly how loss of estimative self-respect can undermine conative self-respect.

4. The Value of Self-Respect

People sometimes ask whether self-respect is entirely a good thing. I want finally to suggest how we might answer this in the light of what I have been saying. In order to do this, I think we need to consider the two aspects separately.

First, estimative self-respect. Notice that we cannot in evaluating estimative self-respect ask whether it is a virtue; a virtue is a permanent trait or disposition, whereas estimative self-respect is an attitude to oneself, which a man may have in different degrees at different times. Whether we think it a good attitude or not will depend on whether we think it justified in a particular case. If we think a man behaves in the way in which objective standards demand, and is not merely complacent, we approve of his having the appropriate attitude.

What then is humility? Humility does not consist in thinking one is a failure when one is not. Indeed, a man who does this may be guilty of pride, if it indicates that he feels he ought to be judged on higher standards than other people for no good reason. Humility is rather the recognition that there is infinite room for improvement and that the minimum standard which is connected with self-respect is no great achievement. Thus it is perfectly compatible with estimative self-respect.

Next, conative self-respect. This *is* of the right category to be a virtue. I shall not try to establish whether or not it is to be called one, but simply point out one or two pros and cons. It is a quality which is at least very useful in the moral life, providing very powerful incentives to virtue. An appeal to it is a good piece of moral strategy which can be applied to others or oneself. But in the end it seems too egoistic to be an appropriate basis for other-regarding conduct. If A is treated rightly by B "out of self-respect," A may feel thankful that this safety-net motive worked on B *faute de mieux*, but may also feel (rightly, I think) that B, in treating him well for this reason only, shows a lack of respect for others.

Notes

This discussion is a development of part of a paper read to the Scots Philosophical Club in December, 1965. I am very grateful to my fellow-symposiast on that occasion, Mr. R. S. Downie, whose ideas on self-respect formed the starting-point for my own; and to Professor W. G. Maclagan, who read a first draft of this paper and made many valuable criticisms.

6

✛

Self-Respect Reconsidered

✛

Thomas E. Hill, Jr.

When thinking about the servility of an Uncle Tom, an overly deferential wife, and an extremely self-deprecating person, I once suggested that one way persons can lack self-respect is to fail to appreciate their
equal basic rights as human beings.[1] The failure, I thought, could stem
either from unawareness of one's status as an equal or from valuing that
status less than one should. The servile person, it seemed, let others violate his rights at will or too readily declined to exercise his rights.

One appealing feature of this idea was that it corresponded with the
intuitive feeling that everyone ought to be respected in some ways,
regardless of talent, social position, accomplishment, etc. Basic respect
as a human being, one feels, does not need to be earned; and if respect is
having proper regard for rights, then at least some respect is due each
person without his needing to earn it. A person may lack self-respect not

This essay was originally published in *Respect for Persons, Tulane Studies in Philosophy*, vol. 31,
edited by O. H. Green (1985). Copyright © 1985 by Tulane University Press. Reprinted by
permission.

merely by underestimating his merits and achievements but also by misunderstanding and undervaluing his equal rights as a human being.

Although this account may still explain the instances of servility I considered, it does not fit all cases in which a person fails to respect himself. Just as one may respect others for their special merits and achievements, one may respect oneself for exceptional qualities. One who lacks this sort of respect for himself, perhaps because he does not have any special merit, does not necessarily misunderstand or undervalue his *rights*. More importantly, there are ways in which we feel everyone should respect himself which have little to do with either acknowledging one's merits or appreciating one's rights.

Consider some examples.

Suppose an artist of genius and originality paints a masterwork unappreciated by his contemporaries. Cynically, for money and social status, he alters the painting to please the tasteless public and then turns out copies in machine-like fashion. He does it deliberately, with full awareness of his reasons, but not without some sense of disgust at himself.[2]

Again, consider the talented, aspiring actress who has been supporting herself largely by waiting on tables. After comparing the hourly wages and other costs and benefits, she decides to take up prostitution as an interim means of support. This decision is not impulsive or from dire need, nor is it the only means to her desired career. Sometimes, she says, she hates herself for what she is doing, but at least she has some pride that she never puts up with any abuse from her patrons.

Another example comes from the classic film, *The Blue Angel*. Here a respected schoolmaster gives up his position to follow a burlesque dancer and ends up playing the clown before his former students. His choices, it seems, were not impulsive, and no one forced him to do anything.

In each case a person seems not to respect himself as he should. This is not to say, however, that what they did (self-respect aside) was immoral. It is at least arguable that altering one's own painting, selling sexual services, and changing jobs from schoolmaster to clown were within their rights;[3] and, unlike my servile persons, they are not obviously guilty of letting others ignore their own rights. (The prostitute, recall, refused to accept abuse from her customers; the schoolmaster voluntarily gave up his right to be treated as a teacher instead of a clown, etc.) Their problem is also not that they have a low opinion of their merits and achievements: each may in fact give himself high marks in this regard. They may suspect and fear the low opinion of others, and so feel ashamed, but their lack of *self*-respect is more than this. Although each, in a sense, acts contrary to his values, the problem is not really weakness of will.[4] They knew what they were doing, and they made a deliberate decision, involving a change of life-plan, not a momentary aberration. It was not that their wills were weak, for they willed to do just what they did. The sign that they fail to respect themselves fully is in how they feel (self-disgust, self-hate, etc.); but the feeling is a sign, not the whole story.

These points seem confirmed when we imagine what a friend might say when he saw them and wished that they had more respect for themselves. The appropriate response is hardly, "You should feel that way because, after all, you are within your rights." Nor would it be, "You are doing something immoral; reform your ways." It seems beside the point to say, "You have many talents and achievements, and others acknowledge them." And it would show lack of understanding to call for more strength against impulse: "You are too weak; stick to your decisions." The question is, what more could one say?

A clue may be found by considering ways in which we respect others. Sometimes we respect a person as an office holder (the President, one's father, etc.), but this seems largely a matter of acknowledging their special rights. We also respect people as human beings, which again seems to be respect for rights. We respect extraordinary people for their exceptional abilities and achievements: e.g., I respect Isaac Stern as a violinist, my colleagues as philosophers, etc. But none of these examples provides the sort of analogue we want. What is needed is a case of respecting someone independently of rights and special merits.

Suppose I have two neighbors who are quite ordinary in their abilities and aspirations. I respect both the human and special rights of each, and yet, in another sense, I respect one much more than the other. Neither is doing anything illegal or morally wrong, but one, unlike the other, has a clear sense of what he values and counts important and he lives accordingly. It is not that he has exceptionally high ideals. Rather, he has a sense, quite aside from matters of moral right and wrong, that certain ways of behaving are beneath him, and his acts, both deliberate and impulsive, never go past this line. He will not, for example, let his house fall into disarray or his debts increase beyond a certain point; he refuses to hide or apologize for his unpopular political opinions, and he will not see films he regards tasteless or obscene even though he admits that they arouse his interest. He is not, however, a person of extraordinary strength of will; for he over-eats and over-drinks even after he decides not to. Moderation and will-power in such matters are not among his fundamental values. Though he holds them deeply, he does not universalize his basic non-moral standards (except in a trivial sense).[5] That is, apart from certain moral principles (respect for life, honesty, some contribution to charity, etc.), he feels that others may live as they choose. He does not criticize others for their debts, their house-keeping or preference in films. He says that he just has certain standards for himself and would lower himself in his own eyes if he did not stick by them. Even those who disagree with him, I imagine, tend to respect him.

The other neighbor, let us say, lives equally well within the bounds of the law and basic moral requirements (respect for life, etc.) but otherwise seems to have no personal standards. Not only does he lack high ideals of self-improvement, style, aesthetic taste, etc., he also lacks a sense of a minimum non-moral standard. So long as he satisfies basic moral requirements, he does whatever he feels like doing without ever looking down on himself for it. He generally avoids what is against his interest and often does good things for others, but this is never a matter of pride or principle with him. He would feel *regret* if he acted, impulsively or deliberately, in ways that failed to have the consequences he wanted; but he would never feel *self-contempt*. Basic morality aside, he does not put his sense of self-worth on the line. He is, so to speak, tolerant and non-judgmental about himself in the way the other neighbor is about others. Even those who find what he actually does quite agreeable, do not respect him as they do the other neighbor.[6]

These examples suggest a way in which a person can respect himself quite aside from acknowledging his merits and appreciating his rights. This form of self-respect would require that one develop and live by a set of personal standards by which one is prepared to judge oneself even if they are not extended to others. The standards might be ideals for which one strives or merely a minimum below which one cannot go without losing face with oneself.[7] The sort of standards I have in mind need not be moral ones; but they are also not identical with what one most wants. A person might find that what he most wants, all considered, is a life that conflicts with much of what he really values, sees as admirable for himself, or at least ensures his good opinion of himself. Weighing the pain of self-contempt against potential pleasures of another sort, he might quite reflectively choose what he regards as a lower way of life for himself. The peace of mind that comes from congruence between one's values and one's behavior is doubtless always seen as desirable; but one can deliberately sacrifice it for other things one wants more. Though a person need not believe that his values for himself are "objective" or irrational to deny, he cannot simply make anything, arbitrarily, one of his values. One who claimed it as his ideal, or minimum value, to get as fat as he could, or avoid exerting himself, or to tear bits of paper all day, would hardly be convincing, barring very peculiar background beliefs. The sort of personal standards and ideals on which one's self-respect depends are typically seen as inescapably a part of oneself. Whether one sees them as objective or not, one genuinely takes the attitude that one is, in one's own view, better or worse according to how one measures up to them.

Returning to our initial examples, we can see how the artist, the prostitute, and the schoolmaster failed to respect themselves. Unlike my second neighbor, they had personal standards but they did not live by them. The artist's self-disgust reveals that he regards altering his masterpiece for money and popularity as contrary to his own ideals. In admitting that she sometimes hates herself, the actress/prostitute shows that she feels that, at least for her, prostitution is a lower way of life. The schoolmaster's self-contempt drives him insane, leaving no doubt that, rightly or wrongly, he felt he had cheapened himself. Had each lacked standards for themselves, they would not feel self-contempt; but, assuming the absence was complete, they would also have no way to treat themselves with respect. As it was, they had ideals but chose instead to pursue other wants. What they failed to respect was not their rights or merits but their own personal standards. What they lacked was not simply a certain feeling but behavior in accord with a self-imposed standard.

Those who have self respect are often said to have a "sense of their own worth." While often moving and doubtless important, this idea is also puzzling. What sort of worth, one wonders, is in question? Not simply worth *to* others; for a person who is useful to others, is loved by others, and knows it, can lack this sense of self-worth. Also a person who is neither useful nor loved sometimes has a strong sense of self-worth. This sense is also not identical with a belief that one has, despite others' opinion, an equal status in a system of moral rights; for unfortunately not everyone who appreciates his *moral* equality feels that self-worth which parents, and then psychotherapists, try to foster in their children. One can be aware that he is morally equal to others but still feel depressed and worthless in another way. It is as if one's interests, projects, and plans seem worthless even *to oneself*. Though often couched in objectivist language, the attitude is hardly to be explained as belief that one lacks an objective, inexplicable, intuitable property, "worthiness." Though the topic remains a difficult one, one conjecture emerges from our examples: at least part of a sense of one's own worth is having, and living by, personal standards or ideals that one sees, whether objective or not, as an important part of oneself.

In the paper mentioned earlier, I tried to isolate a type of self-respect which it seemed plausible to say everyone should, morally, try to have. *That* self-respect, however, involved appreciating one's own *moral* rights. Since the form of self-respect discussed above is not respect for any moral standard, the question naturally arises whether it is any moral fault not to have such self-respect. The question is too large for more than a brief comment, but one preliminary thought may be in order. Philosophers have often thought that we have duties to ourselves as well as to others; but others have rejected the idea partly, it seems, because they find it intuitively implausible that we have a moral duty to promote our own happiness. After all (as Kant noted) we are usually all too ready to seek our own happiness. An ideal moral legislator, aware of the burden of imposing duties, would see little reason to make such pursuit a matter of duty (as with restraint from killing) even though he counted the happiness of all an ideal end. The most intuitively plausible cases, however, in which one feels a person has a duty to himself seem to be cases in which a person is not respecting himself, not cases in which he is curtailing his happiness. It is tempting to say to the artist, the actress, and the schoolmaster in our examples, "You owe it *to yourself* to change." This is not just an estimate that a change will bring greater happiness, though we may believe that, too. It is as if we take a moral interest in persons' setting and living by their own values, even when the values are not required for all. We care for their having the satisfaction of a good opinion of themselves, but not just for the pleasure of it. Perhaps the moral interest is in each person living as an *autonomous* agent, where "autonomy" implies both personal integration and forming values beyond comfort, least resistance, etc.

Thinking of self-respect in the previous way (appreciation of rights), I argued that one should respect oneself as well as every other human being. And, in that sense, absence of self-respect tends to undermine respect for others. But, given the conception of self-respect I have discussed here, one cannot say the same. Perhaps we do believe that everyone should try to respect himself in this sense, but we cannot reasonably ask that everyone respect all others. For respect of the sort we have been considering requires seeing that the respected person has personal standards or ideals and believing that he lives by them. But, unfortunately, not everyone seems to have such standards, and, even more obviously, not everyone lives by the standards he has. The respect in question need not be merited by special talent, achievement, or even ambition; but one must qualify for it by setting and sticking to some personal values. Again, it is not clear that those who lack self-respect of this sort cannot respect others. But what does follow is that one who does not respect himself in this way cannot expect that others will. To ask them to respect him would be to ask them to acknowledge what he himself cannot, namely, that he has and lives by his own (morally permissible) values. As Kant remarked, perhaps too harshly, "One who makes himself a worm cannot complain if people step on him."[8]

Notes

1. "Servility and Self-Respect," *The Monist*, Vol. 57 no.1 (January 1973) [chapter 3, this volume].

2. This example, I think, comes from Daniel Wikler, whose correspondence has especially stimulated my second thoughts on this subject.

3. Many, I know, will argue that prostitution is wrong aside from any question of self-respect; but it should be sufficient for the point if they will agree that the particular prostitute in our example shows inadequate self-respect quite aside from how one resolves the controversy about the morality of prostitution in general.

4. Here I realize that I am taking a position contrary to the usual view of weakness of will; but I would argue that it is a mistake to see weakness of will, in general, as failure to do what one believes right or best. One can, I think, quite deliberately will a plan which one believes base and even immoral, and then when one carries it out with firm resolution one is not suffering from weakness of will.

5. It is no doubt true that one who says "I would be better if I did x" is committed to something like "Anyone in exactly similar or relevantly similar circumstances would be better if he did x"; but unless "relevantly similar" is specified broadly enough to be, for practical purposes, applicable to others, the speaker may still be without any commitment to judgments about the people he knows or is likely to meet. My first neighbor either professes to know too little of others to judge them or else construes the "relevantly similar" circumstances to include such special features about himself that his judgment about himself does not extend to them.

6. An exception might be a person who lived the same sort of life as my second neighbor *on principle*. That is, he sees it as a defect to be "judgmental" about himself (basic morality aside), admires and strives to emulate those who seem

free from liability to self-contempt. Such a person has, as it were, a second-order ideal to live without the sort of personal standards the first neighbor subjects himself to. For simplicity, let us imagine that the second neighbor lacks this sophisticated second-order ideal. He is not *proud* of living without personal standards, as one might be who has struggled his way out of neurotic attachments to such standards; he simply lacks them.

7. The standards in question need not be to do what is morally ideal or supererogatory, for two reasons. First, they need not be standards which everyone morally ought to pursue or even ones which anyone would be morally admirable for pursuing. They might include, for example, artistic achievement, stylish dress, a comic personality, etc. Second, they need not be remote stars for which one reaches or goals one would be pleased to achieve but which one does not see as required. Some of the personal standards may be seen as (nonmorally) "required"; one is not particularly pleased, merely satisfied, to meet the standards, but failure to live up to them lowers oneself in one's own eyes. Of course, many, perhaps most, people make it a personal standard to live by moral principles and to do what is morally supererogatory; but then, I think, their lack of self-respect when they act immorally is due, not simply to violating moral standards, but to violating personal standards which they happen to believe morally required.

8. *The Doctrine of Virtue*, Part II of the *Metaphysics of Morals*, ed. Mary Gregor (New York: Harper Torchbooks, 1964), p. 103; p. 437 Academy edition. Kant's remark lends itself to my point, but I do not want to argue that it is just what he meant.

7

✛

Self-Respect, Excellences, and Shame

✛

John Rawls

On several occasions I have mentioned that perhaps the most important primary good is that of self-respect. We must make sure that the conception of goodness as rationality explains why this should be so. We may define self-respect (or self-esteem) as having two aspects. First of all, as we noted earlier,[1] it includes a person's sense of his own value, his secure conviction that his conception of his good, his plan of life, is worth carrying out. And second, self-respect implies a confidence in one's ability, so far as it is within one's power, to fulfill one's intentions. When we feel that our plans are of little value, we cannot pursue them with pleasure or take delight in their execution. Nor plagued by failure and self-doubt can we continue in our endeavors. It is clear then why self-respect is a primary good. Without it nothing may seem worth doing, or if some things have value for us, we lack the will to strive for them. All

Reprinted by permission of the publishers from *A Theory of Justice* by John Rawls, Cambridge Mass.: Harvard University Press, Copyright © 1971 by the President and Fellows of Harvard College. This essay appears as chapter 67 in *A Theory of Justice.*

desire and activity becomes empty and vain, and we sink into apathy and cynicism. Therefore the parties in the original position would wish to avoid at almost any cost the social conditions that undermine self-respect. The fact that justice as fairness gives more support to self-esteem than other principles is a strong reason for them to adopt it.

The conception of goodness as rationality allows us to characterize more fully the circumstances that support the first aspect of self-esteem, the sense of our own worth. These are essentially two: (1) having a rational plan of life, and in particular one that satisfies the Aristotelian Principle;[2] and (2) finding our person and deeds appreciated and confirmed by others who are likewise esteemed and their association enjoyed. I assume then that someone's plan of life will lack a certain attraction for him if it fails to call upon his natural capacities in an interesting fashion. When activities fail to satisfy the Aristotelian Principle, they are likely to seem dull and flat, and to give us no feeling of competence or a sense that they are worth doing. A person tends to be more confident of his value when his abilities are both fully realized and organized in ways of suitable complexity and refinement.

But the companion effect of the Aristotelian Principle influences the extent to which others confirm and take pleasure in what we do. For while it is true that unless our endeavors are appreciated by our associates it is impossible for us to maintain the conviction that they are worthwhile, it is also true that others tend to value them only if what we do elicits their admiration or gives them pleasure. Thus activities that display intricate and subtle talents, and manifest discrimination and refinement, are valued by both the person himself and those around him. Moreover the more someone experiences his own way of life as worth fulfilling, the more likely he is to welcome our attainments. One who is confident in himself is not grudging in the appreciation of others. Putting these remarks together, the conditions for persons respecting themselves and one another would seem to require that their common plans be both rational and complementary: they call upon their educated endowments and arouse in each a sense of mastery, and they fit together into one scheme of activity that all can appreciate and enjoy.

Now it may be thought that these stipulations cannot be generally satisfied. One might suppose that only in a limited association of highly gifted individuals united in the pursuit of common artistic, scientific, or social ends is anything of this sort possible. There would seem to be no way to establish an enduring basis of self-respect throughout society. Yet this surmise is mistaken. The application of the Aristotelian Principle is always relative to the individual and therefore to his natural assets and particular situation. It normally suffices that for each person there is some association (one or more) to which he belongs and within which the activities that are rational for him are publicly affirmed by others. In this way we acquire a sense that what we do in everyday life is worthwhile. Moreover, associative ties strengthen the second aspect of self-esteem, since they tend to reduce the likelihood of failure and to provide support against the sense of self-doubt when mishaps occur. To be sure, men have varying capacities and abilities, and what seems interesting and challenging to some will not seem so to others. Yet in a well-ordered society anyway, there are a variety of communities and associations, and the members of each have their own ideals appropriately matched to their aspirations and talents. Judged by the doctrine of perfectionism, the activities of many groups may not display a high degree of excellence. But no matter. What counts is that the internal life of these associations is suitably adjusted to the abilities and wants of those belonging to them, and provides a secure basis for the sense of worth of their members. The absolute level of achievement, even if it could be defined, is irrelevant. But in any case, as citizens we are to reject the standard of perfection as a political principle, and for the purposes of justice avoid any assessment of the relative value of one another's way of life.[3] Thus what is necessary is that there should be for each person at least one community of shared interests to which he belongs and where he finds his endeavors confirmed by his associates. And for the most part this assurance is sufficient whenever in public life citizens respect one another's ends and adjudicate their political claims in ways that also support their self-esteem. It is precisely this background condition that is maintained by the principles of justice. The parties in the original position do not adopt the principle of perfection, for rejecting this criterion prepares the way to recognize the good of all activities that fulfill the Aristotelian Principle (and are compatible with the principles of justice). This democracy in judging each other's aims is the foundation of self-respect in a well-ordered society.

Later on I shall relate these matters to the idea of social union and the place of the principles of justice in human good.[4] Here I wish to discuss the connections between the primary good of self-respect, the excellences, and shame, and consider when shame is a moral as opposed to a natural emotion. Now we may characterize shame as the feeling that someone has when he experiences an injury to his self-respect or suffers a blow to his self-esteem. Shame is painful since it is the loss of a prized good. There is a distinction however between shame and regret that should be noted. The latter is a feeling occasioned by the loss of most any sort of good, as when we regret having done something either imprudently or inadvertently that resulted in harm to ourselves. In explaining regret we focus say on the opportunities missed or the means squandered. Yet we may also regret having done something that put us to shame, or even having failed to carry out a plan of life that established a basis for our self-esteem. Thus we may regret the lack of a sense of our own worth. Regret is the general feeling aroused by the loss or absence of what we think good for us, whereas shame is the emotion evoked by shocks to our self-respect, a special kind of good.

Now both regret and shame are self-regarding, but shame implies an especially intimate connection with our person and with those upon whom we depend to confirm the sense of our own worth.[5] Also, shame is sometimes a moral feeling, a principle of right being cited to account for it. We must find an explanation of these facts. Let us distinguish between things that are good primarily for us (for the one who possesses them) and attributes of our person that are good both for us and for others as well. These two classes are not exhaustive but they indicate the relevant contrast. Thus commodities and items of property (exclusive goods) are goods mainly for those who own them and have use of them, and for others only indirectly. On the other hand, imagination and wit, beauty and grace, and other natural assets and abilities of the person are goods for others too: they are enjoyed by our associates as well as ourselves when properly displayed and rightly exercised. They form the human means for complementary activities in which persons join together and take pleasure in their own and one another's realization of their nature. This class of goods constitutes the excellences: they are the characteristics and abilities of the person that it is rational for everyone (including ourselves) to want us to have. From our standpoint, the excellences are goods since they enable us to carry out a more satisfying plan of life enhancing our sense of mastery. At the same time these attributes are appreciated by those with whom we associate, and the pleasure they take in our person and in what we do supports our self-esteem. Thus the excellences are a condition of human flourishing; they are goods from everyone's point of view. These facts relate them to the conditions of self-respect, and account for their connection with our confidence in our own value.

Considering first natural shame, it arises not from a loss or absence of exclusive goods, or at least not directly, but from the injury to our self-esteem owing to our not having or failing to exercise certain excellences.

The lack of things primarily good for us would be an occasion for regret but not for shame. Thus one may be ashamed of his appearance or slow-wittedness. Normally these attributes are not voluntary and so they do not render us blameworthy; yet given the tie between shame and self-respect, the reason for being downcast by them is straightforward. With these defects our way of life is often less fulfilling and we receive less appreciative support from others. Thus natural shame is aroused by blemishes in our person, or by acts and attributes indicative thereof, that manifest the loss or lack of properties that others as well as ourselves would find it rational for us to have. However, a qualification is necessary. It is our plan of life that determines what we feel ashamed of, and so feelings of shame are relative to our aspirations, to what we try to do and with whom we wish to associate.[6] Those with no musical ability do not strive to be musicians and feel no shame for this lack. Indeed it is no lack at all, not at least if satisfying associations can be formed by doing other things. Thus we should say that given our plan of life, we tend to be ashamed of those defects in our person and failures in our actions that indicate a loss or absence of the excellences essential to our carrying out our more important associative aims.

Turning now to moral shame, we have only to put together the account of the notion of a good person (in the previous section[7]) and the remarks above concerning the nature of shame. Thus someone is liable to moral shame when he prizes as excellences of his person those virtues that his plan of life requires and is framed to encourage. He regards the virtues, or some of them anyway, as properties that his associates want in him and that he wants in himself. To possess these excellences and to express them in his actions are among his regulative aims and are felt to be a condition of his being valued and esteemed by those with whom he cares to associate. Actions and traits that manifest or betray the absence of these attributes in his person are likely then to occasion shame, and so is the awareness or recollection of these defects. Since shame springs from a feeling of the diminishment of self, we must explain how moral shame can be so regarded. First of all, the Kantian interpretation of the original position means that the desire to do what is right and just is the main way for persons to express their nature as free and equal rational beings. And from the Aristotelian Principle it follows that this expression of their nature is a fundamental element of their good. Combined with the account of moral worth, we have, then, that the virtues are excellences. They are good from the standpoint of ourselves as well as from that of others. The lack of them will tend to undermine both our self-esteem and the esteem that our associates have for us. Therefore indications of these faults will wound one's self-respect with accompanying feelings of shame.

It is instructive to observe the differences between the feelings of moral shame and guilt. Although both may be occasioned by the same action, they do not have the same explanation.[8] Imagine for example someone who cheats or gives in to cowardice and then feels guilty and ashamed. He feels guilty because he has acted contrary to his sense of right and justice. By wrongly advancing his interests he has transgressed the rights of others, and his feelings of guilt will be more intense if he has ties of friendship and association to the injured parties. He expects others to be resentful and indignant at his conduct, and he fears their righteous anger and the possibility of reprisal. Yet he also feels ashamed because his conduct shows that he has failed to achieve the good of self-command, and he has been found unworthy of his associates upon whom he depends to confirm his sense of his own worth. He is apprehensive lest they reject him and find him contemptible, an object of ridicule. In his behavior he has betrayed a lack of the moral excellences he prizes and to which he aspires.

We see, then, that being excellences of our person which we bring to the affairs of social life, all of the virtues may be sought and their absence may render us liable to shame. But some virtues are joined to shame in a special way, since they are peculiarly indicative of the failure to achieve self-command and its attendant excellences of strength, courage, and self-control. Wrongs manifesting the absence of these qualities are especially likely to subject us to painful feelings of shame. Thus while the principles of right and justice are used to describe the actions disposing us to feel both moral shame and guilt, the perspective is different in each case. In the one we focus on the infringement of the just claims of others and the injury we have done to them, and on their probable resentment or indignation should they discover our deed. Whereas in the other we are struck by the loss to our self-esteem and our inability to carry out our aims: we sense the diminishment of self from our anxiety about the lesser respect that others may have for us and from our disappointment with ourself for failing to live up to our ideals. Moral shame and guilt, it is clear, both involve our relations to others, and each is an expression of our acceptance of the first principles of right and justice. Nevertheless, these emotions occur within different points of view, our circumstances being seen in contrasting ways.

Notes

1. [Editor's Note: *A Theory of Justice*, §29 ("Some Main Grounds for the Principles of Justice"). In that section Rawls argues that considerations of self-respect give the parties in the original position good reason to adopt the two principles of justice as fairness rather than the principle of utility, for the former principles but not the latter "publicly express men's respect for one another" (p. 179). This is important, for "In this way, they insure a sense of their own value" (p. 179), since "our self-respect normally depends on the respect of others" (p. 178). Moreover, "It is clearly rational for men to secure their self-respect. A sense of their own worth is necessary if they are to pursue their conception of the good with zest and to delight in its fulfillment. Self-respect is not so much a part of any plan of life as the sense that one's plan is worth carrying out" (p. 178).]

2. [Editor's Note: The Aristotelian Principle states that "other things equal, human beings enjoy the exercise of their realized capacities (their innate or trained abilities), and this enjoyment increases the more the capacity is realized, or the greater the complexity"(*A Theory of Justice*, p. 426) There is also what Rawls calls "the companion effect": "As we witness the exercise of well-trained abilities by others, these displays are enjoyed by us and arouse a desire that we should be able to do the same things ourselves. We want to be like those persons who can exercise the abilities we find latent in our nature" (p. 428).]

3. [Editor's Note: *A Theory of Justice*, § 50 ("The Principle of Perfection").]

4. [Editor's Note: Ibid, §§ 79–82.]

5. My definition of shame is close to William McDougall, *An Introduction to Social Psychology* (London: Methuen, 1908), pp. 124-128. On the connection between self-esteem and what I have called the Aristotelian Principle, I have followed [Robert] White, "Ego and Reality in Psychoanalytic Theory," [*Psychological Issues*, vol. 3 (1963)], chapter 7. On the relation of shame to guilt, I am indebted to Gerhart Piers and Milton Singer, *Shame and Guilt* (Springfield, Ill.: Charles C. Thomas, 1953), though the setting of my discussion is quite different. See also Erik Erikson, "Identity and the Life Cycle," *Psychological Issues*, vol. 1 (1959), pp. 39–41, 65–70. For the intimacy of shame, see Stanley Cavell, "The Avoidance of Love," in *Must We Mean What We Say?* (New York: Charles Scribner's Sons, 1969), pp. 278, 286f.

6. See William James, *The Principles of Psychology*, vol. 1 (New York: [Henry Holt & Co.,] 1890), pp. 309f.

7. [Editor's Note: This concept is discussed in *A Theory of Justice*, § 66 ("Good Applied to Persons"): "a good person, then, or a person of moral worth, is someone who has to a higher degree than average the broadly based fea-

tures of moral character that it is rational for the persons in the original position to want in one another" (p. 437).]

8. [Editor's Note: *A Theory of Justice*, § 73 ("Features of the Moral Sentiment").]

8

✣

Shame and Self-Esteem: A Critique

✣

John Deigh

Twenty-five years ago the psychoanalyst Gerhart Piers offered what remains the most influential way of distinguishing shame from guilt. Reformulated without terms special to psychoanalytic theory, Piers's distinction is that shame is occasioned when one fails to achieve a goal or an ideal that is integral to one's self-conception whereas guilt is occasioned when one transgresses a boundary or limit on one's conduct set by an authority under whose governance one lives. Succinctly, shame goes to failure, guilt to transgression. Shame is felt over shortcomings, guilt over wrongdoings.[1]

More recently, writers who have addressed themselves to the way shame differs from guilt, notably, among philosophers, John Rawls, have characterized shame as an emotion one feels upon loss of self-esteem and have analyzed self-esteem and its loss in a way that bears out Piers's influence.[2] Rawls plainly is in Piers's debt. He explains self-esteem in terms of the goals and ideals one incorporates into one's life plans, and he makes this explanation central to his account of our moral personality, in particular, our capacity to feel shame.

A characterization of shame like Rawls's, when set in the context of distinguishing shame from guilt, we are likely to find intuitively appealing. And we may feel a further pull in its direction when we think of shame in comparison with other emotions to which it is thought similar—for instance, embarrassment. For we associate both shame and embarrassment with an experience of discomfiture, a sudden shock that short-circuits one's composure and self-possession; yet we would agree, I think, that embarrassment is an experience of discomfiture that, unlike shame, does not include a diminishment in one's sense of worth. An experience of shame, by contrast, strikes at one's sense of worth. Here we may be reminded of times when things were going well and we were somewhat inflated by the good opinion we had of ourselves, when suddenly, quite unexpectedly, we did something that gave the lie to our favorable self-assessment, and we were shocked to see ourselves in far less flattering light. Such are the circumstances for shame, and the positive self-image that disappears in these circumstances and is replaced by a negative one spells loss of self-esteem.

These contrasts between shame and guilt and shame and embarrassment present the bare outlines of a characterization of shame, which, when filled out, appears rather attractive. It is the topic of this article. My thesis is that this characterization, though attractive at first appearance, is unsatisfactory. It represents, I contend, a dubious conception of shame. In particular, I mean to call into question its central idea that shame signifies loss of self-esteem.

The paper is divided into three parts. In the first I lay out what I shall call the Rawlsian characterization of shame, Rawlsian in that I retain the controlling thesis and overall structure of Rawls's account but do not concern myself with its specifics, an exact rendering of Rawls being unnecessary for my purposes. Though my approach here is largely uncritical, my aim is to set up a well-defined target for subsequent criticism. In the second, then, I begin that criticism. I set forth a case of loss of self-esteem and some cases of shame that pose problems for the characterization. By themselves these cases stand as counterexamples to it, but my hope is that they will have a more illuminating effect, that they will produce a sense or spark an intuition that its central idea is problematic. Accordingly, in the third part I complete the criticism. I draw from the cases two lessons about shame intended to give definition to the intuition I hope will already have been sparked. Each lesson points to a key feature of shame that the characterization leaves out or misrepresents, its central idea being implicated as the source of these failures. Thus, while the criticism of this third part is aimed at the target set up in the first, the force of the criticism should lead us to consider rejecting the idea at the target's center.

I

We need at the start to fix our understanding of self-esteem, since the concept is at the base of the Rawlsian characterization. To this end I shall present some considerations leading up to a definition of self-esteem, from which an explanation of its loss will follow directly. This will then yield the characterization of shame we seek. Let us begin with the general idea that self-esteem relates to what one makes of oneself or does with one's life. One has self-esteem if one's spirits are high because one believes that one has made or will make something of oneself, that one has been or will be successful in one's life pursuits. Conversely, one lacks self-esteem if one is downcast because of a judgment that one has failed to make or never will make something of oneself, that one doesn't or won't ever amount to much. Something of this idea is suggested in William James's equation that sets self-esteem equal to the ratio of one's successes to one's pretensions.[3]

The first thing to note in this general idea is that self-esteem connects up with the condition of one's spirits. We speak of vicissitudes of self-esteem: highs and lows. One's self-esteem can plummet. It can also be boosted or bolstered. Indolence and languishing in doldrums are signs that one's self-esteem is at a low ebb. Enthusiasm for and vigorous engagement in activities in which one chooses to participate are signs of an opposite condition. We also describe persons in these conditions as having or lacking self-esteem. And though subtle differences may exist between a person's having self-esteem and his self-esteem's being high and between his lacking self-esteem and his self-esteem's being low, I shall treat the two in each pair as equivalent.

A second point to note, which is corollary to the first, is that self-esteem goes with activity. But to assert that having self-esteem requires that one be active would be an overstatement. We should allow that the esteem a person has for himself is relative to that period in his life with which he identifies for the purpose of self-assessment. Thus, a person may retain his self-esteem after having retired from active life if he looks back on his endeavors and accomplishments with pride while content to take it easy. He maintains a high opinion of himself while leading a rather leisurely and unproductive life because his self-assessment proceeds from recollections of an earlier period when he was active and successful. Or, to take the viewpoint of a youth looking forward in time, he may have esteem for himself in view of the life he aspires to lead if he believes in the accuracy of the picture he has of his future. He identifies, for the purpose of self-assessment, with the person he believes he will become, his present self having little bearing. Consequently, he may even at the time be leading an altogether easygoing and frivolous life while exuding self-esteem. I mention these possibilities only to set them aside. We simplify our task of explaining self-esteem if we restrict the discussion to self-esteem had in view of one's current doings and development.

Besides this simplifying restriction, we must also add a qualification to the statement that being active is a condition of having self-esteem. As a third point, then, one's actions, if they are signs of self-esteem, must have direction. They must be channeled into pursuits or projects and reflect one's goals and ideals. A wayward vagabond does not present a picture of someone who has self-esteem. Nor do we ascribe self-esteem to someone who, having no settled conception of himself, tries on this and that trait of personality, as he would sunglasses of different styles, to see which gives him the most comfortable look. Self-esteem is had by persons whose lives have a fairly definite direction and some fairly well-defined shape, which is to say that self-esteem requires that one have values and organize one's life around them.

One's values translate into one's aims and ideals, and a settled constellation of these is necessary for self-esteem. Specifically, we may take this as a precondition of self-esteem. For, arguably, someone who had no aims or ideals in life, whose life lacked the direction and coherence that such aims and ideals would bring, would be neither an appropriate object of our esteem nor of our disesteem. We would understand his behavior as the product of primitive urges and desires that impelled him at the time of action. Having given no order or design to his life, he would act more or less at random or for short-lived purposes. We should recognize in him a figure who frequents recent philosophic literature on human freedom: the man assailed by a battery of desires and urges, who is helpless to overpower them because he lacks a clear definition of himself.[4] Such a man is impelled in many directions at once but moves in no particular one for any great distance. Frustrated and disoriented by inner turmoil, he lapses into nonaction. He would, were we ever to encounter his like, properly evoke in us pathos indicating abeyance of judgment rather than scorn indicating low esteem for him.

By contrast, when a person has aims and ideals that give order and direction to his life, counterpoint between primitive forces that impel him and his wanting to fulfill those aims and ideals becomes possible. Thus, at those times when he acts in conflict with his aims and ideals, he may declare that he was caught in the grip of some emotion or was overpowered by some urge or desire. He would then convey the idea that he had been acted upon or compelled to act as opposed to doing the act or choosing the act. Undeniably, the emotion, urge, or desire is attributable to him; but by such declaration he disowns it and so disclaims authorship of the act it prompted. Authorship, not ownership, is the key notion here, that is, authorship in the general sense of being the originator or creator of something. When one has a settled constellation of aims and ideals, then one distinguishes between the acts of which one is the author and those in which one serves as an instrument of alien forces.[5] Without any such constellation, one is never the author of one's actions, though many times the instrument of alien forces that act on one, triggered by external events.

It is in view of this contrast that I suggest we take one's having a settled constellation of aims and ideals as a precondition of self-esteem: when one is the author of one's actions, one is an appropriate object for esteem or disesteem; when one is only an instrument of alien forces, one is not. We can then look to this precondition for the defining conditions of self-esteem. So while we would have said, loosely speaking, that self-esteem came from one's having a good opinion of oneself, we may now say more strictly that it comes from a good opinion of oneself as the author of one's actions, more generally, one's life. Accordingly, this opinion comprises a favorable regard for one's aims and ideals in life and a favorable assessment of one's suitability for pursuing them. Lacking self-esteem, one would either regard one's aims and ideals as shoddy or believe that one hadn't the talent, ability, or other attributes necessary for achieving them. Either would mean that one lacked the good opinion of oneself that makes for self-esteem, and either would explain the dispirited condition that goes with one's lacking self-esteem.

These considerations then yield an understanding of self-esteem as requiring that two conditions jointly obtain. This we can formulate as a definition. Specifically, one *has self-esteem* if, first, one regards one's aims and ideals as worthy and, second, one believes that one is well suited to pursue them.[6] With reference to the first we say one has a sense that one's life has meaning. With reference to the second we speak of a confidence one has in the excellence of one's person. And this combination of a sense that one's life has meaning and a confidence in one's ability to achieve one's ends gives one impetus to go forward.

Turning then to loss of self-esteem and, in particular, the sudden loss taken on the Rawlsian characterization to be explicative of shame, we obtain immediately from the foregoing definition an account of this experience. One loses self-esteem if, because of a change in either one's regard for the worthiness of one's aims and ideals or one's belief in one's ability to achieve them, a once favorable self-assessment is overturned and supplanted by an unfavorable one. The loss here is the loss of a certain view of oneself. One had self-esteem and correspondingly a good opinion of oneself: one viewed oneself as having the attributes necessary for successfully pursuing worthy ends around which one had organized one's life. The change in judgment about the worthiness of one's ends or the excellence of one's person destroys that view. One's good opinion of oneself gives way to a poor one. This constitutes loss of self-esteem.

The Rawlsian characterization has it that shame is the emotion one feels when such loss occurs. Moreover, shame is to be understood as signifying such loss. Shame on this characterization is the shock to our sense of worth that comes either from realizing that our values are shoddy or from discovering that we are deficient in a way that had added to the confidence we had in our excellence. Either is a discovery of something false in the good opinion we had of ourselves, and such self-discovery spells loss of self-esteem.

Of course, self-discovery of this sort does not figure in every experience of shame, for a person who has a poor opinion of himself is nonetheless liable to feel shame when the very defect that is his reason for the poor opinion is brought to his notice. Thus, as a last point, we must say something about shame felt by someone whose self-esteem is already low. While a schoolboy, Philip Carey, in Maugham's novel *Of Human Bondage*, feels shame innumerable times over his clubfoot. His feelings do not involve loss of self-esteem, since his self-esteem is low to begin with, nor, obviously, do they reflect any act of self-discovery. But it would be uncharitable to object to the Rawlsian characterization on the ground that it does not cover such cases, for they can be treated on analogy with cases it does cover. Philip does not always have his crippled foot on his mind; there are plenty of times when he is forgetful of it. On these occasions, especially when he is comfortable with himself, he is liable to feel shame when made conscious of his "freakish" condition, when, as it were, he rediscovers it. Then, while he does not lose any self-esteem, his being comfortable with himself is certainly lost to him.

II

In this section I shall set forth a case of loss of self-esteem and some cases of shame that present real problems for the Rawlsian characterization. I begin with the former. The case itself is quite straightforward. We have only to think of someone who suddenly loses self-esteem because he discovers that he lacks the ability to achieve some aim he has set for himself, who is crestfallen, dispirited, and deeply disappointed with himself, but owing to circumstances or a philosophical temperament, does not feel shame. And such a case is not hard to construct.[7]

Imagine, for example, some youth who is indisputably the best tennis player in his community. He defeats all challengers; he wins every local tournament; and he has recently led his high school team to a first-place finish in a league consisting of teams from the high schools of his and the neighboring towns. His coach rates him the most promising player. to come along in a decade, and he is highly touted by other tennis enthusiasts in the area. Quite naturally, he comes to have a high opinion of his ability and visions of winning tournaments on the professional tour. At some point in his high school years, he makes professional tennis a career goal and devotes much time to improving his game. In truth, though, the grounds for his high opinion of his ability and for his decision to make tennis a career are shaky. The competition in his and the neighboring towns is rather poor, these being rural and isolated from urban centers. And the aging coach's hopes have distorted his judgment of his star player's talents. Thus, when this young player enters his first state tournament, he quickly discovers that his skills are below those of the top seeded players. His first defeat need not be humiliating, just convincing. And though he will surely lose some self-esteem, we need not suppose that he feels any shame.

One explanation of his losing self-esteem but not feeling shame is this. The first defeat is sufficiently convincing that it alters his view of himself as a tennis player, and given his aims, this means loss of self-esteem. But just as others close to him would respond that his defeat is nothing to be ashamed of, so his own attitude toward it may reflect such judgment. Accordingly, he would be deeply disappointed with himself but not ashamed. This possibility becomes even more vivid if we suppose that he has gone to the tournament alone or with friends who, unlike him, have only a passing rather than an abiding interest in tennis. For then he does not find himself having to face someone like his coach before whom feeling some shame would be natural, though even here the presence of the coach does not necessitate the emotion. This case thus broaches the question what distinguishes those cases of loss of self-esteem whose subjects feel shame from those whose subjects feel disappointment but no shame. The inability of the Rawlsian characterization to answer this question implies that the understanding of shame it gives is, at best, incomplete.

Let us take up cases of shame. The first comes from an observation, made by several writers, that shame is commonly felt over trivial things. One writer instances experiences of shame had on account of "one's accent, one's ignorance, one's clothes, one's legs or teeth."[8] Another, to illustrate the same point, mentions shame felt over "an awkward gesture, a gaucherie in dress or table manners, ...a mispronounced word."[9] To be sure, none of these examples poses a threat to the Rawlsian characterization, since each of the things mentioned could be for someone a shortcoming the apprehension of which would undercut the confidence he had in the excellence of his person. This would certainly be true of someone who consciously subscribed to ideals the achievement of which required that he not have the shortcomings. For then, though others would disparage these ideals as superficial or vulgar and accordingly think the shortcoming trivial, to him it would still appear as a serious flaw in himself. Naturally, the more interesting case is that in which the subject also thinks the shortcoming trivial and is surprised at having felt shame on its account. This case too can be understood as coming under the Rawlsian characterization. For one need not fully realize the extent to which one places value on certain things, and one may even deceive oneself about one's not being attached to certain ideals. We need, then, to distinguish between, on the one hand, what one would declare were one's aims and ideals and would list as one's important attributes if one were asked to describe oneself and, on the other, one's self-conception as it is reflected by one's behavior apart from or in addition to any explicit self-description. By one's self-conception I mean the aims and ideals around which one has organized one's life together with the beliefs one has about one's ability to pursue them. And what we understand is that these aims, ideals, and beliefs can guide one's behavior without one's being conscious of having subscribed to them. Consequently, a person who feels shame over crooked teeth or the slurping of soup, though he would have thought himself unconcerned with appearance and proper form, shows by his emotion that a pleasant-looking face or good table manners are important to him, that he subscribes to ideals of comeliness or social grace. Hence, we can easily understand his shame as signifying loss of self-esteem.

At the same time, such examples invite us to look for things over which someone might feel shame though he did not believe they made him ill suited to pursue his ends. Shame one feels over something one could not believe affected one's excellence, say, because one could not regard it as a fault in oneself, would present a problem for the Rawlsian characterization. Thus, consider shame felt over a humorous surname. The example comes from Gide. He describes to us the experience of a young French girl on her first day of school, who had been sheltered at home for the first ten years of her life, and in whose name, Mlle Péterat, something ridiculous is connoted, which might be rendered in English by calling her Miss Fartwell. "Arnica Péterat—guileless and helpless—had never until that moment suspected that there might be anything laughable in her name; on her first day of school its ridicule came upon her as a sudden revelation; she bowed her head, like some sluggish waterweed, to the jeers that flowed over her; she turned red; she turned pale; she wept."[10]

With this example we move from attributes that one can regard as minor flaws and insignificant defects to things about a person that leave him open to ridicule, though they do not add to or detract from his excellence. The morphemes of one's surname do not make one better or worse suited for pursuing the aims and ideals around which one has organized one's life. Hence, shame in this example, because it is felt over something that lies outside its subject's self-conception, opposes the Rawlsian characterization.

The second case of shame is cousin to the first. One finds oneself in a situation in which others scorn or ridicule one or express some deprecatory judgment of one, and apprehending this, one feels shame. Given only this general description, such a case presents no real problem for the Rawlsian characterization. It serves to remind us that one's self-esteem depends to some extent on the esteem others accord one— certain others, anyway—and the greater that dependency the more readily one will feel shame in response to any deprecatory judgments they express. This can be understood by way of the amount of confidence one has in one's own independent judgments about the worthiness of one's aims and one's ability to fulfill them, for this, we might say, varies inversely with the strength of the dependency of one's self-esteem on the esteem of others. That is, the greater that dependency, the less one's confidence will be in independent judgments one makes about oneself and, concomitantly, the more accepting one will be of the judgments others make about one. Consequently, given a strong enough dependency, if they criticize or ridicule one for some fault, one accepts their criticism and thus makes the same judgment about oneself, where before one did not notice the fault or it did not much matter to one. This arouses shame inasmuch as the judgment issues in an unfavorable self-assessment that replaces a favorable one, that is, in loss of self-esteem. We have then an account of the case that is fully in line with the Rawlsian characterization.

But we must also admit cases of shame felt in response to another's criticism or ridicule in which the subjects do not accept the other person's judgment of them and so do not make the same judgment of themselves. And these cases do present a problem for the Rawlsian characterization. Consider Crito and his great concern for what the good citizens of Athens will think of him for failing to deter Socrates from meeting his demise. "I am ashamed," he says in vainly trying to argue Socrates out of accepting his fate, "both on your account and on ours your friends'; it will look as though we had played something like a coward's part all through this affair of yours."[11] And though Crito is in the end convinced that Socrates' course is the right one and knows all along that he has done everything one can expect of a friend, we still have, I think, no trouble picturing this good-hearted but thoroughly conventional man feeling ashamed when before some respectable Athenian, who reproaches him for what he believes was cowardice on Crito's part. Examples like this one demonstrate that shame is often more, when it is not exclusively, a response to the evident deprecatory opinion others have of one than an emotion aroused upon judgment that one's aims are shoddy or that one is deficient in talent or ability necessary to achieve them.

The third problematic case of shame is this. We commonly ascribe shame to small children. Shaming is a familiar practice in their upbringing; "Shame on you" and "You ought to be ashamed of yourself" are familiar admonishments. And, setting aside the question of the advisability of such responses to a child's misdemeanors, we do not think them nonsensical or incongruous in view of the child's emotional capacities. Furthermore, close observers of small children do not hesitate to ascribe shame to them. Erik Erikson, writing about human development, observed that children acquired a sense of shame at the stage when they began to develop muscular control and coordination.[12] Charles Darwin, writing about blushing, noted that small children began to blush around the age of three and later remarked that he had "noticed on occasion that shyness or shamefacedness and real shame are exhibited in the eyes of young children before they have acquired the power of blushing."[13]

But it would certainly be a precocious child who at the age of four or five had a well-defined self-conception, who organized his life around the pursuit of certain discrete and relatively stable aims and ideals and measured himself by standards of what is necessary to achieve them. In other words, a child at this age, though capable of feeling shame, does not have self-esteem. Hence, the shame he experiences does not signify loss of self-esteem.

Finally, a fourth problematic case of shame emerges once we juxtapose the orientation of an aristocratic ethic and that of an achievement ethic. The Rawlsian characterization with its emphasis on making something of oneself, being successful in one's life pursuits, is tied to the latter. The experiences of shame it describes are at home in a meritocratic society, one in which social mobility is widespread, or, at any rate, the belief that it is constitutes a major article of faith. On the other hand, some experiences of shame reflect an aristocratic ethic; one feels shame over conduct unbecoming a person of one's rank or station. The experiences are better suited to a society with a rigidly stratified social structure like a caste society. And, as we shall see, they stand in marked contrast to experiences the Rawlsian characterization is designed to fit.

The contrast is this. With shame reflective of an achievement ethic, the subject is concerned with achieving his life's aims and ideals, and he measures himself against standards of excellence he believes he must meet to achieve them. So long as he regards his aims and ideals as worthy, they define for him a successful life, and accordingly he uses the standards to judge whether he has the excellence in ability or of character necessary for success. He is then liable to shame if he realizes that some of his aims and ideas are shoddy or that he has a defect portending failure where previously he had ascribed to himself an excellence indicating success. And this fits nicely the idea that shame signifies loss of self-esteem. On the other hand, with shame reflective of an aristocratic ethic, the subject's concern is with maintaining the deportment of his class and not necessarily with achieving aims and ideals that define success in life. He is concerned with conforming to the norms of propriety distinctive of his class, and conformity to these is neither a mark of achievement nor an excellence that forecasts achievements. In the usual case one is born into one's class and conforms to its norms as a matter of course. Failure to conform, that is, failure to deport oneself as becomes a member of one's class, invites comparison to persons of lower classes on whom the members of one's class look down. Thus, someone from a social class beneath which there are other classes may be liable to shame over such failure: someone wellborn may be liable to shame if he behaves like the vulgar. And such shame does not fit the Rawlsian characterization. For the subject neither realizes that his aims and ideals are shoddy nor discovers a defect in himself that makes him ill suited to pursue them. In other words, given the analysis we have laid out, he does not lose self-esteem.

But, one might ask, can't we say of someone who feels shame over conduct unbecoming a member of his class that he too has ideals that regulate his actions and emotions? After all, with his class we associate a way of life, and this implies an ideal or set of ideals. To feel constrained to act as becomes a member of one's class is to feel pressed to conform to its ideals, and conduct unbecoming a member is, in other words, conduct that falls short of an ideal. Granted, one doesn't so much achieve these ideals as conform to them, which shows perhaps that the conception of self-esteem on which the Rawlsian characterization is built must be modified. But supposing we make whatever modification is needed, isn't it sufficient to bring the experience under the Rawlsian characterization that we can redescribe it as shame felt over one's falling short of an ideal?

Something, however, gets lost in this redescription. When we redescribe the experience as shame felt over falling short of ideals around which one's life is organized, our focus shifts from who one is to how one conducts one's life. The subject's identity as a member of a certain class recedes into the background. We see it as the source of his ideals but do not assign it any further part. This, I think, is a mistake. In this experience the subject has a sense of having disgraced himself, which means he has an acute sense of who he is. We do not have an understanding of shame otherwise.

It is revealing that on the Rawlsian characterization this shift in focus does not register. For the characterization recognizes no distinction between questions of identity and questions of life pursuits, between who one is and how one conducts one's life. From its viewpoint, a person says who he is by telling what his aims in life are and what ideals guide him through life.[14] This makes it an attractive characterization of the shame felt by persons who are relatively free of constraints on their choice of life pursuits owing to class, race, ethnic origins, and the like. For such persons tend more to regard their aims and ideals as constituting their identity and their ancestry, race, class, and so forth as extrinsic facts about themselves. So the characterization explains the shame they feel as including an acute sense of who they are. But because it restricts a person's identity to his aims and ideals in life, it fails to explain as including this sense the shame someone, living in a rigidly stratified society, feels when he does not act as befits a member of his class or the shame someone, living in a multiethnic society, feels when he acts beneath the dignity of his people. Granted, such a person recognizes that his conduct falls short of ideals members of his class or culture are expected to follow, but these ideals do not constitute his identity. Another, a pretender for instance, could have the same ideals as he but not the same identity, just as a tomboy has the ideals of a boy but not the identity of one. Hence we fail to account for such shame if we describe it as being felt over one's having fallen short of ideals that regulate one's life.

Thus, about the following experience, which Earl Mills, a Mashpee Indian, relates, a defender of the Rawlsian characterization will insist that sometime during the episode Mills must have embraced the ideals of an Indian way of life, or, alternatively, that he must have realized, though he nowhere suggests this, that the ideals he was then pursuing were shoddy. But ignoring the Rawlsian characterization, we can explain Mills's feeling shame without importing either of these assumptions: his having, in the circumstances he describes, to acknowledge his ignorance of Mashpee traditions disgraced him as an Indian, made him betray, as it were, his Indian identity, and this aroused shame. This explanation accepted, his experience directly opposes the Rawlsian characterization, for it suggests that, despite the aims and ideals around which a man organizes his life, circumstances may arise that make him, because of an identity he has that is independent of those aims and ideals, liable to experience shame.

When I was a kid, I and the young fellows I ran around with couldn't have cared less about our Indian background. We never participated in any of the tribal ceremonies, we didn't know how to dance, and we wouldn't have been caught dead in regalia. We thought anyone who made a fuss about our heritage was old-fashioned, and we even used to make fun of the people who did. Well, when I came back from the Army in 1948, I had a different outlook on such matters. You see, there happened to be two other Indians in my basic training company at Fort Dix. One of them was an Iroquois from Upper New York State, and the other was a Chippewa from Montana. I was nineteen years old, away from Mashpee for the first time in my life, and, like most soldiers, I was lonely. Then, one night, the Iroquois fellow got up and did an Indian dance in front of everyone in the barracks.

The Chippewa got up and joined him, and when I had to admit I didn't know how, I felt terribly ashamed.[15]

III

Before drawing any lessons about shame from the discussion of Part II, I should say something to allay doubts about the import of the cases of shame presented there. Such doubts naturally arise because one might think that some, if not all, of those cases exemplify experiences of the emotion the subjects of which one could criticize for being irrational or unreasonable. That is, while agreeing that many persons are liable to such experiences, one might wonder whether they ought to be so liable and then note that a case's force as a counterexample lessens if it only describes an experience of irrational or unreasonable emotion. The first and last cases of shame are especially in point. To feel shame over one's surname and because of conduct unbecoming a person of one's class seem good examples of shame one ought not to experience. For one is not responsible for one's parentage and thus ought not to judge oneself according to facts wholly determined by it. Inasmuch as shame in these cases reflects such judgment, they exemplify experiences to which one ought not to be liable.

These doubts arise under the assumption that, in giving a characterization of an emotion, one specifies those conditions in which the emotion is experienced reasonably or rationally. Such an approach to characterizing an emotion requires that one regard as its standard cases those in which the subjects are fully rational individuals and not at the time of the experience in any irrational frame of mind. But we ought to question this requirement. Why should we restrict the class of standard cases to these? While there is, for instance, something absurd in the familiar picture of an elephant terrified at the sight of a mouse, why should this absurdity lead us to regard the elephant's terror as any less important a case to be considered in characterizing that emotion than the terror a lynch mob strikes in the person on whom it takes revenge? To be sure, the elephant is not a creature capable of bringing its emotions under rational control, whereas a human being, if sufficiently mature, is. And for this reason there is a point in criticizing the emotional experiences of human beings, whereas making similar criticism of an elephant's emotional experiences is altogether idle. But this provides no reason to regard the class of rational or reasonable experiences of a given emotion as privileged for the purposes of conceptual inquiry. To have brought one's emotions under rational control means that the range of one's emotional experiences has been modified through development of one's rational capacities: one no longer responds with, say fear, to certain sensory stimuli that before the development provoked fear, and conversely. But far from instructing us to discount the elephant's or the toddler's emotions in our conceptual inquiries, this bids us to examine emotional experiences had in response to sensory stimuli unmediated by rational thought as well as experiences the occurrence of which we explain by reference to rational thought.

Similar points then apply to characterizing shame. To focus primarily on cases the subjects of which one would not criticize for being irrational or unreasonable is to risk introducing distortion into the characterization. Indeed, one might be well advised to examine closely those cases in which such criticism is forthcoming on the grounds that they may display more prominently than others certain characteristic features of the emotion. Thus, one might be well advised to examine closely the shame typical of *homo hierarchicus*, even though one thought that rigid, hierarchial social structures lacked rational foundations (i.e., even though one thought that the emotion indicated an irrational attachment to social class), on the grounds that in such shame one sees more clearly than in shame typical of persons living in an egalitarian society those parts of the subject's self-conception in virtue of which he is liable to the emotion. Moreover, though the resultant characterization rendered shame an emotion that, from the perspective of an egalitarian or meritocratic ethic, one never had good reason to feel, this would not in itself show the characterization to be faulty: no more than that gentlefolk like the Amish, because of certain theistic beliefs, regard resentment as an emotion one never has good reason to feel shows that they harbor misconceptions about resentment. Since we are capable of bringing our emotions under rational control, we may regard our feeling a specific emotion as incompatible with our moral principles and so try to make ourselves no longer liable to it. Alternatively, we may regard this emotion as essential to our humanity and so revise our principles. The conflict makes evident the importance of having a correct understanding of such emotions; at the same time we should see that altering the understanding one has in order simply to avoid such conflict or the criticism of irrationality would be misguided.

Turning then to lessons that come out of our discussion of the problematic cases, I shall draw two. The first is that a satisfactory characterization must include in a central role one's concern for the opinions of others. This is really a lesson in recall. From Aristotle onward, discussions of shame have focused attention on the subject's concern for the opinions others have of him.[16] Aquinas, Descartes, and Spinoza each incorporated this concern into his definition of shame.[17] And latter-day writers, Darwin and Sartre in particular, took the experience of shame before another as key to an understanding of the emotion.[18] Thus, we should not be surprised to find that the Rawlsian characterization founders, since it regards such concern as not internally related to shame.

Its failure, however, is not due to neglect. The characterization, through emphasis on the dependency of one's self-esteem on the esteem of others, can accord the concern an important role in an overall understanding of shame.[19] But this makes the concern part of a mechanism that induces shame rather than part of our conception of shame. A mechanism exists which, when put into operation, transforms high self-esteem into low; part of that mechanism is the concern one has for the opinions of others; and one way in which the mechanism gets going is when others on whose good opinion one's self-esteem depends depreciate one and one apprehends this. In this way, the characterization gives one's concern for the opinion of others an important role. But it is only a supporting role and not the central one I think it deserves. And this is one reason for its failure.

Each of the first three problematic cases bears out this last point. It is evident in the second and third cases, where the subjects feel shame but do not lose self-esteem. In the third case shame is felt directly in response to another's scorn or reproach. Thus, an expressed low opinion of the subject induces in him shame without affecting his self-esteem. In other words, the mechanism is not engaged, though the subject's concern for the opinion of another is clearly operative. In the second, Mlle Péterat, even apart from the context in which she feels shame, jeering classmates, feels the emotion because of something about herself that is laughable. It invites deprecatory responses. Thus, she may feel ashamed because of it, even though it is not a deficiency. It is not a ground for reassessing her excellence, though, of course, the whole experience could cause her to think less of herself. Here, too, there is shame reflecting a concern for the opinion of others without the mechanism's being engaged.

We can also mine the first case to bring out the point that the Rawlsian characterization has misconstrued the role one's concern for the opinion of others has in shame. Consider again our young tennis phenom. In the circumstances described, he loses self-esteem, is disappointed with himself, but does not feel shame. On the other hand, as we noted, if the circumstances had been different, if he had had, say, to face his coach after the defeat, then his feeling shame would have been well imaginable. There would then have been someone at courtside whose look he could not meet. He would have averted his eyes, lowered his head, gulped to fight back tears. That the coach's presence could spell the difference between disappointment and shame cannot be explained by reference to the player's losing self-esteem, for the loss occurs in either case. The mechanism would be in operation whether or not the subject felt shame, so it would not account for the role his concern for the coach's opinion would have had in his experiencing shame. We can thus conclude from these three cases that one's concern for the opinion of others has a role in shame apart from the way in which their opinion can support or bring down one's self-esteem.

The second lesson is about our sense of worth. The Rawlsian characterization yields an understanding of a person's sense of worth according to which it has two sources. One is the person's conviction that he has given meaning to his life. The other is the confidence he has in his own excellence as a person. The first comes from his regarding his aims and ideals in life as worthy. The second comes from his belief that he is well suited to pursue them. Thus, according to the Rawlsian characterization, shame, since it is felt either upon a judgment that one's aims or ideals are shoddy or upon a judgment that one is deficient in a way that makes one ill suited to pursue them, is aptly described as a shock to one's sense of worth. One experiences a diminishment in one's sense of worth since either one's sense of having given meaning to one's life or one's confidence in one's excellence has been struck down.

There is difficulty in this, however, because, while the description of shame as a shock to one's sense of worth is apt, the account of the various ways in which the sense gets shocked is, at best, too meager. The reason for this is that the characterization omits important sources of our sense of worth. The point is directly evident in our last two cases. The child of four who feels shame over some misdemeanor has not given meaning to his life and does not have confidence in his excellence as a person. Hence, he has a sense of worth the source of which the characterization does not acknowledge. Similarly, we recognize in an aristocrat who feels shame over behaving like a plebian or in an American Indian who feels shame over betraying his Indian identity a sense of worth the source of which is neither a conviction about the worthiness of his ends nor a belief about his suitability to pursue them. A sense of worth that comes from knowledge that one is a member of the upper class or a noble people also lies beyond the sight of the Rawlsian characterization.

To put the point generally, the Rawlsian characterization fails to recognize aspects of our identity that contribute to our sense of worth independently of the aims and ideals around which we organize our lives.

We should note here the structural, as well as the substantive, difference between the sense of worth the Rawlsian characterization recognizes and the one it excludes. We can get at this structural difference by looking at the theory of worth that underlies the characterization. That theory is based on a conception of us as the authors of our actions. We are authors in the sense discussed in Part I, that is, in virtue of having a constellation of aims and ideals according to which we live our lives. We have worth on this theory in accordance with the value of our lives, such as they are and such as they promise to be. An author has worth in view of his work, completed or in progress, and our lives, so to speak, are our work. This analogy can be pressed. Our work has value to the degree that it is the kind of thing that when well made has value and is itself well made. So we have worth to the degree that we produce such things or have directed our energies toward producing them and possess the talents and skills that augur successful production. Our lives, conceived as our work, thus have value to the degree that the ends that give them order and direction define a kind of life that has value and those ends have been realized. And we have worth as authors of our lives to the degree that we live lives of value or have directed our energies toward living such lives and possess the attributes that promise success.

In capsule form, what might be called the auteur theory of worth is that what a person does with his life, how well he directs it, determines his worth. On this theory, then, we attribute different degrees of worth to someone depending on how valuable we deem the kind of life he lives and how successful we think he has been in living it or how suitable we think he is for it. In other words, we attribute to him more or less worth according to how well or badly he conducts his life. Contrast this with attributions of worth made because of one's class or culture. Judging from these attributions, we might say that a person's worth is determined by his status in the context of some social hierarchy. The salient feature here is that one's status, and so one's worth, is fixed independently of one's conduct. To be sure, one can change classes through marriage or cultures through immigration, but short of this the general conduct of one's life, that is, however well or badly one conducts it, does not increase or decrease the worth that is attributed to one because of one's status. And pretty much the same holds of worth that is attributed to human beings because of their species or to persons because of the kind of beings they are conceived to be: rational ones, say, spiritual ones, or autonomous ones. That is, worth attributed to one because of one's essential nature is, like worth attributed to one because of one's status, fixed independently of how one conducts one's life.

Consequently,the dynamics of the sense of worth that comes from knowing the worth that goes with one's status or essential nature, that is, the understanding we give to augmentations and diminishments in that sense, are altogether different from those of the sense of worth the auteur theory recognizes. Statically, both kinds of sense correspond to the degree of worth one attributes to oneself. But an augmentation in one's sense of worth, as is experienced in pride, or a diminishment in it, as is experienced in shame, is not, if this sense originates in a recognition of one's status or essential nature, to be understood in terms of an attribution to oneself of greater or lesser worth than one attributed to oneself before the experience.[20] A college boy who wears his fraternity pin with pride does not regard himself as having greater worth for having worn it, and a man who feels ashamed of having eaten like a pig does not regard himself as having less worth than is attributed to human beings as such. This contrasts with the way the auteur theory would have us understand augmentations and diminishments in one's sense of worth. In particular, it would have us understand a diminishment in one's sense of worth, as is experienced in shame, as amounting to loss of self-esteem and so corresponding to an assessment of oneself as having less worth.

On the auteur theory, a sense of worth reflects concern with one's real worth, and one takes one's conduct and appearance as evidence of or, more strongly, as the grounds for attributing to oneself that worth. By contrast, a sense of worth that comes from knowing one's status or essential nature reflects concern with the congruency between one's conduct or appearance and one's real worth. Here, we could say, one's concern is with the relation between appearance and reality. If one's status is high relative to that of others or one's nature is noble, then behavior that is congruent with one's worth and so displays it is occasion for pride, and behavior that is at variance with it and so gives appearance of lesser worth is occasion for shame.

This model better accommodates the idea that to have a sensibility to shame means that one is prepared to restrain oneself when one verges on the shameful and to cover up the shameful when it comes into the open. We speak in this regard of having shame as opposed to having no shame, and we connect this with modesty, particularly sexual modesty, which involves a sensibility to shame in matters of decorum. Having shame, that is, having a sensibility to shame, can be understood here as self-control that works to restrain one from giving the appearance of lesser worth and self-respect that works to cover up shameful things that, having come to light, give one such appearance.[21]

This suggests that we should conceive shame, not as a reaction to a loss, but as a reaction to a threat, specifically, the threat of demeaning treatment one would invite in giving the appearance of someone of lesser worth. Its analogues then are, not grief and sorrow, but fear and shyness.[22] Like fear, shame serves to protect one against and save one from unwanted exposure. Both are in this way self-protective emotions. Fear is self-protective in that it moves one to protect oneself against the danger one senses is present or approaching. From fear one draws back, shields oneself, or flees. Of course, it may also render one immobile, thereby putting one in greater danger, so the point does not hold without qualification.[23] Still, the general idea is clear. Shame too, is self-protective in that it moves one to protect one's worth.[24] Here the general idea is not so clear, though a trope may be useful. Shame inhibits one from doing things that would tarnish one's worth, and it moves one to cover up that which through continued exposure would tarnish one's worth. Less figuratively, we might say that the doing or exposure of something that makes one appear to have less worth than one has leaves one open to treatment appropriate only to persons or things that lack the worth one has, and shame in inhibiting one from such things and in moving one to cover them up thus protects one from appearing to be an unworthy creature and so from the degrading treatment such appearance would invite.

This idea that shame is a self-protective emotion brings together and explains two important features: first, that a liability to shame regulates conduct in that it inhibits one from doing certain things and, second, that experiences of shame are expressed by acts of concealment. The second is crucial. Covering one's face, covering up what one thinks is shameful, and hiding from others are, along with blushing, the most characteristic expressions of shame. Students of shame commonly note them. A quote from Darwin is representative, "Under a keen sense of shame there is a strong desire for concealment."[25] Moreover, etymology reinforces the point. According to many etymologists, a pre-Teutonic word meaning "to cover" is the root of our word *shame*.[26]

Now the Rawlsian characterization, since it conceives shame as a reaction to loss, can explain, on the model of fear of loss, how one's liability to shame regulates one's conduct. Where it has trouble is in explaining shame's moving one to cover up and hide. For it does not have in itself the materials needed to construct such an explanation. Because it conceives shame as a reaction to the loss of something one prizes, it yields an account of the emotion as at first giving way to low spirits and dejection and eventually moving one to attempt to recover what one lost, that is, to regain through self-improvement one's good opinion of oneself and so one's self-esteem.[27] Acts of concealment, however, are nowhere implicated in this account. Hence, if one adheres to the characterization, one must make use of supplementary materials to explain them. One must go outside the characterization by, say, citing certain fears associated with shame: fear of ridicule or rejection by those upon whose good opinion of one one's self-esteem depends.[28] But such an explanation would not be adequate, for it fails to explains acts of concealment as expressions of shame. Instead, it takes these as expressions of fears associated with shame. And the same objection would hold for any explanation one constructed from materials found outside the characterization. The characterization, in other words, is unable to explain, as expressions of shame, these acts. And this should tell us that something has gone wrong.

The adherent to the Rawlsian characterization thus appears to be in an untenable position. We would dismiss any suggestion that covering up and hiding were not really among shame's natural expressions. Reflection on shame, particularly shame concerning sexual improprieties, alone suffices to rule this out. And we should reject any characterization of an emotion that misrepresents its natural expressions. Faced with these objections, the adherent might retreat to a weaker thesis by proposing that the characterization gives an adequate account of some, but not all, experiences of shame. But this thesis is no more defensible than the original. For our adherent, as we saw from the first problematic case of Part II, has the burden of showing how the emotion the characterization describes is distinguishable from disappointment with oneself. Since he admits on this weaker thesis that some experiences of shame elude the characterization, he has, in other words, the burden of showing that the experiences of emotion the characterization captures are classifiable with these as shame. What reason could he give to show this? That they have the same feeling-tone is itself questionable, insistence on the point being question begging. That they involve a shock to one's sense of worth is insufficient. For the characterization identifies this shock with one's suffering loss of self-esteem, and this by itself does not qualify an experience as one of shame. The trouble with this proposal, I think, is that it would, in effect, divide shame into disparate kinds, one kind having fear as its analogue, the other grief. That is, we should suspect of any conception of shame the proposal spawned that it covered a mismatched set of experiences.

We can trace the characterization's problems back to the understanding it gives to the sense of worth that makes one liable to shame and ultimately to the auteur theory of worth, which grounds that understanding. On that theory one attributes to oneself worth according to how one conducts one's life, and so perceptions of that conduct determine one's sense of worth. Shame then, since it is felt upon discovery of shortcomings in oneself that falsify the worth one thought one had, includes a sense that one lacks worth. And this proves problematic because it leaves unexplained how shame motivates acts of concealment. By contrast, when we conceive shame as including a sense that one has worth, we can readily explain its motivating such acts: one covers up because one senses that the worth one has is threatened. This speaks in favor of the understanding of the sense of worth the idea that shame is a self-protective emotion entails, which understanding is grounded on a conception of worth that opposes the one the auteur theory yields. Consequently, we should suspect that the conception of worth the auteur theory yields is the wrong one for explaining the sense of worth that makes one liable to shame, and, because the Rawlsian characterization presupposes that conception, we should give up the view of the emotion it represents.

Notes

I am indebted to Herbert Morris for helpful comments on a earlier draft of this article.

1. Gerhart Piers and Milton B. Singer, *Shame and Guilt: A Psychoanalytic and a Cultural Study* (Springfield, Ill.: Charles C. Thomas, 1953), pp. 11–12.
2. John Rawls, *A Theory of Justice* (Cambridge, Mass.: Harvard University Press, 1971), pp. 440–46 [chapter 7, this volume]. For similar views see Helen Merrell Lynd, *On Shame and the Search for Identity* (New York: Harcourt Brace & Co., 1958), pp. 23–24; Robert W. White, "Competence and the Psychosexual Stages of Development," in *Nebraska Symposium on Motivation 1960*, ed. Marshall Jones (Lincoln: University of Nebraska Press, 1960), pp. 125–27; and David A. J. Richards, *A Theory of Reasons for Action* (Oxford: Oxford University Press, 1971), pp. 250–59.

3. William James, *The Principles of Psychology*, 2 vols. (1890; reprint ed., New York: Dover Publications, 1950), vol. 1, p. 310.

4. See Joel Feinberg, "The Idea of a Free Man," in *Educational Judgments: Papers in the Philosophy of Education*, ed. James Doyle (London: Routledge & Kegan Paul, 1975), pp. 148-49; Harry Frankfurt, "Freedom of the Will and the Concept of a Person," *Journal of Philosophy* 68 (1971): 5-20; Wright Neely, "Freedom and Desire," *Philosophical Review* 83 (1974): 32-54; and Gary Watson, "Free Agency," *Journal of Philosophy* 72 (1975): 205-20.

5. I have drawn here from Harry Frankfurt, "Identification and Externality," in *The Identities of Persons*, ed. Amélie Rorty (Berkeley: University of California Press, 1976), pp. 239-51.

6. The definition matches Rawls's (see *A Theory of Justice*, p. 440 [p. 125, this volume].

7. Examples similar to this first case were suggested to me by Herbert Morris and Rogers Albritton.

8. Stanley Cavell, *Must We Mean What We Say?* (Cambridge: Cambridge University Press, 1976), p. 286.

9. Lynd, *On Shame*, p. 40.

10. André Gide, *Lafcadio's Adventures*, trans. Dorothy Bussy (New York: Alfred A. Knopf, 1953), p. 100. The rendering of her name in English is suggested by the translator.

11. Plato, *Crito* 45d-e. Quoted from the Hugh Trednick translation, *The Collected Dialogues of Plato*, ed. Edith Hamilton and Huntington Cairns (Princeton, N.J.: Princeton University Press, 1961), p. 30.

12. Erik Erikson, *Childhood and Society*, 2d ed. (New York: W.W. Norton & Co., 1963), pp. 251-54.

13. Charles Darwin, *The Expression of the Emotions in Man and Animal* (1872; reprint ed., Chicago: University of Chicago Press, 1965), p. 331.

14. See Rawls, *A Theory of Justice*, p. 408.

15. Paul Brodeur, "A Reporter at Large: The Mashpees," *New Yorker* 54 (November 6, 1978): 62-150, p. 103.

16. For Aristotle's view see *Rhetoric*, bk. 2, chap. 6.

17. For Aquinas's definition see *Summa Theologiae* 1a2ae, 41, 4. For Descartes's see *The Passions of the Soul*, pt. 2, art. 66. For Spinoza's see *The Ethics*, pt. 3, definition 31.

18. See last chap. of Darwin. Sartre's view is found in *Being and Nothingness*, trans. Hazel E. Barnes (New York: Philosophical Library, Inc., 1956), pp. 252-302.

19. See, e.g., Rawls's discussion of the companion effect to the Aristotelian Principle, *A Theory of Justice*, pp. 440-41 [p. 126, this volume].

20. Of course there are exceptions to this, e.g., the white supremacist who dis-

covers he has a black ancestor.

21. On these points, see Carl D. Schneider, *Shame, Exposure and Privacy* (Boston: Beacon Press, 1977), pp. 24–27.

22. Whether to pattern shame after grief and sorrow or after fear and shyness is an issue a review of the literature reveals. One often finds in the writings of those offering definitions of shame use of one or the other of these emotions as analogues, sometimes even as a generic emotion of which shame is defined as a specific type. For definitions of shame as a type of grief or sorrow see Hobbes (*Leviathan*, chap. 6) and Descartes (*The Passions of the Soul*, pt. 3, art. 205) (though the passage is equivocal since he also says there that shame is a species of modesty). For a definition of shame as a type of fear see Aquinas; it is also suggested in Plato's *Euthyphro* 12a–d. In connection with this issue see Havelock Ellis's "The Evolution of Modesty," in *Studies in the Psychology of Sex*, 2 vols. 3d ed. (New York: Random House, 1942), vol. 1, p. 36, n. 1. Ellis himself appears to hold that shame is a kind of fear (see pp. 36–52, 72).

23. I owe this point to John T. MacCurdy, "The Biological Significance of Blushing and Shame," *British Journal of Psychology* 21 (1930): 174–82.

24. The idea is one of the central themes of Max Scheler's essay "Über Scham und Schamgefühl," in *Gesammelte Werke*, ed. Maria Scheler and M. S. Frings, 11 vols. (Berne: Franke Verlag, 1954), vol. 10, pp. 65–154.

25. Darwin, *The Expressions of the Emotions*, p. 320.

26. See *Oxford English Dictionary*, s.v. "shame"; also Ernest Klein, *A Comprehensive Etymological Dictionary of the English Language* (Amsterdam: Elsevier, 1967).

27. See Rawls, *A Theory of Justice*, p. 484; Lynd, *On Shame*, pp. 50–51; and Richards, *A Theory of Reasons*, p. 256.

28. See Piers and Singer, *Shame and Guilt*, p. 16; and Rawls, *A Theory of Justice*, p. 445 [p. 129–130, this volume]. White, however, expresses reservations against connecting shame to such fears ("Competence," pp. 125–27).

9

✛

Shame, Integrity, and Self-Respect

✛

Gabriele Taylor

I. Shame, Self-Respect, and Self-Esteem

[S]ome philosophers speak of different kinds of shame, and pick out
only one of these kinds as a moral emotion, in the sense that in this case,
but in this case only, feeling shame involves an appeal to some moral
standard in the light of which the person is judged, or judges himself. My
own claim was that this division into kinds is mistaken, for all cases of
shame share the same structure, and what they refer to as "kinds" are
merely specific sets of cases covered by the present analysis.[1] In rejecting
the division into kinds I also reject the labelling of just one kind as
"moral." There is no reason to deny that shame in all its occurrences is a
moral emotion, provided that morality is not thought of just in terms of
adhering to or breaking certain moral rules, but is taken to include personal morality, a person's own view of how he ought to live and what he

ought to be. The final self-directed adverse judgement in shame is always the same: that he is a lesser person than he should be, for an in some way better person would not find himself in a position where he can be seen as he is or may be seen. What is different in the different cases of shame is just that which in the agent's view has made his position so vulnerable. The possible variety here is immense, and, just as in the case of pride, it is impossible to set objective limits to possible objects of shame. Only sometimes is the reason why his position is so vulnerable that he has done something morally disgraceful. To speak of certain cases only as being cases of moral shame is to emphasize the means by which the agent has arrived at the position in which he now finds himself. This is what for instance Rawls has in mind when he says:

> Consider first natural shame…natural shame is aroused by blemishes in our person, or by acts and attributes indicative thereof…Turning now to moral shame…someone is liable to moral shame when he prizes as excellences of his person those virtues that his plan of life requires… (*A Theory of Justice*, p. 444 [p. 128–129, this volume]).

According to him shame is a moral emotion on those and only those occasions when the agent's explanatory beliefs refer to some failure to act virtuously on his part. But shame may also be thought of as a moral emotion because of the nature of his final self-directed judgement. Rawls himself points to this possibility when he suggests that shame is the feeling someone has when he experiences an injury to his self-respect or suffers a blow to his self-esteem (442 [127]). He does not distinguish between self-respect and self-esteem and seems to think that they amount to the same thing (440 [125]). But this is not so. They are distinguishable from one another and there is a case for regarding shame as primarily linked with self-respect rather than with self-esteem. They are, however, so interrelated with each other that a neat pigeon-holing of the different phenomena is hardly possible.

The person who has self-esteem takes a favourable view of himself, while he who lacks it will think of himself in unfavourable terms: he is not worth much. If possession and lack of self-esteem consist in these contrasting attitudes a person has towards himself then there is also a third possibility, namely that a person neither possesses nor lacks self-esteem. He has no particular attitude towards himself; he does not give much thought to the matter and takes himself as he comes. There is a connection between self-esteem and emotional pride: the person who is proud of this or that enjoys, at the time of feeling proud, an increase in his self-esteem; he can now take a more favourable view of himself (in some respect). Conversely, a person experiencing shame is forced to think that he is less admirable than he had supposed and this is indeed a blow to his self-esteem. So, as Rawls suggests, shame may well be felt by someone who suffers a blow to his self-esteem. It seems to me, nevertheless, that self-esteem is linked primarily with humiliation rather than with shame, for these two reasons: to suffer a blow to one's self-esteem is to modify one's favourable attitude towards oneself. Hence to suffer such a blow one has to have a favourable attitude towards oneself in the first place. But a person may not have such an attitude. In that case he could not modify it, and so could not experience a blow to his self-esteem, but he could still feel shame under certain circumstances. And secondly, a blow to one's self-esteem may be experienced if the person concerned believes that he does not get the recognition he ought to have, he deserves better than he gets. This is an occasion primarily for humiliation rather than for shame, for he may not therefore also think that he is worth less than he thought.

For a person to have self-respect does not mean that he has a favourable attitude towards himself, or that he has any particular attitude towards himself at all. Nor is self-respect connected with emotional pride. Its connection with pride is different in that the person who respects himself will "have his pride," he will be too proud to do this or suffer that. Certain kinds of behaviour and certain kinds of treatment will seem intolerable to the person of self-respect, and to pursue or suffer them would mean loss of self-respect to a certain extent. It is true that his expectations concerning his behaviour and treatment may be fulfilled and yet he may not have much self-respect: to respect oneself is to have a sense of one's own value, and this requires also a degree of self-confidence, a belief that he has got his expectations right. But a person who has such confidence in himself and whose relevant expectations are fulfilled need not therefore have a favourable attitude towards himself, for if he thinks of the matter at all he may just think that to behave in such ways or to be so treated is the least a person can expect, and so is not something to be proud of. But while the one does not necessarily lead to the other, it may well be that keeping one's self-respect is often seen as grounds for feeling proud. It has recently been suggested[2] that there is a conceptual connection between self-respect and self-esteem which consists in this: retaining one's self-respect always supplies a ground of reason for self-esteem, and lack or loss of self-respect always supplies a ground for disesteem. This is true, and it is also true that, conversely, retaining one's self-esteem may be a reason for retaining one's self-respect, and loss of self-esteem may involve loss of self-respect. The reason for this is the already familiar point that norms of expectations are pitched at different levels.[3] The implication of this point in the present context is that what people regard as an injury to their self-respect will differ according to what form of behaviour and treatment they expect of and for themselves. Maintaining one's self-respect is then a reason for self-esteem if one thinks that one's norm is a cut above that of others, or that one is better at living up to it than others are. In that case, although in the person's view living up to that norm is only to be expected from a person such as he, it is, against the foil of others, also a reason for self-esteem, or (which comes to the same thing) a reason for being proud of himself. It follows that in such a case not living up to one's norm would at one and the same time be a blow to one's self-esteem and an injury to one's self-respect.

Given these interrelations between self-respect and self-esteem it seems churlish to quarrel with Rawls's view as to what shame is about. But the point is that the occasions for loss of self-respect and the occasions for feeling shame coincide as neither does with the occasion for experiencing a blow to one's self-esteem. The self-respecting person has certain views of what is due to him and from him, though of course these views may not be very articulate or may formulate themselves only when he is confronted by certain types of action or certain forms of treatment. He will lack self-respect if he has no such views, and he will lose his self-respect if the relevant expectations are not fulfilled. But the frustration of his expectations in this area is precisely the occasion for feeling shame: he will feel shame if he becomes aware that his expectations are being frustrated. This is so because of the nature of these expectations: they relate to the status of the person concerned, and their frustration will, for the agent, amount to a lowering of his status. This is not to say that whenever injury to self-respect then also the experience of shame. For it is conceivable that such injury or loss may not be noticed by the agent. It is the converse which is always true: whenever a person experiences shame then he experiences an injury to his self-respect.

The only possible general point that can be made about the nature of the relevant expectations is that they must be based on something which the agent thinks of great importance, of great value to himself and to the life he envisages himself as leading. What is thought to be of such value will obviously be different for differing agents, and consequently what they see as occasions for shame will differ, too. Some of these values the agent may think of such importance to just his individual life, others he may think are crucial for the life of any human being. But in whatever terms, a person must be able to evaluate himself, his treatment and his actions, if he is to have any self-respect at all.

In the light of this conceptual link between shame and self-respect it does not come as a surprise that we can characterize self-respect by reference to shame: if someone has self-respect then under certain specifiable conditions he will be feeling shame. A person has no self-respect if he regards no circumstances as shame-producing. Loss of self-respect and loss of the capacity for feeling shame go hand in hand. The close connection between these two makes it clear why shame is often thought to be so valuable. It is, firstly, that a sense of value is necessary for self-respect and so for shame, so that whatever else may be wrong about the person feeling shame he will at least have retained a sense of value. And secondly, it is a sense of value which protects the self from what in the agent's own eyes is corruption and ultimately extinction.

The individual member of an honour-group in the setting of a shame-culture can be used to illustrate this point: the relevant values are provided by the honour-code, and his survival as the person he is—which is determined by his membership of the group—depends on his accepting and living by these values. His doing so is therefore protective of the person he is. If on the occasion of his acting against the code he feels shame, then he will at least have retained a sense of what protects that endangered self. He still has some hold on the person he was, so that it is (in theory) still possible for him to regain his old position. But if he feels no shame then he will have abandoned totally the values he lived by, and will have discarded with it the person he once was.[4]

To respect the self, then, is not to think either favourably or unfavourably of the self, but is rather to do that which protects the self from injury or destruction, just as to respect others is not to think well or badly of them, but is at least to abstain from injuring or destroying them, whether physically or morally. And shame is the emotion of self-protection: it may prevent the person concerned from putting himself into a certain position, or make him aware that he ought not to be in the position in which he finds himself. Of course, he may or may not be right in his view of what needs protecting, he may be muddled and misguided in this matter, and so concentrate his energies on protecting a part of himself which is not worth protecting. It is for this reason that in the literature we meet two conflicting views: on the one hand we are told that shame is a good thing, and even that it is the supreme virtue;[5] on the other, shame is regarded as an emotion which it is bad to feel, at least on most occasions when it tends to be felt.

The reasons for these opposing views differ, but on the present account the value of shame must lie in its role as self-protective emotion and its disvalue in the possibility of the protection being wholly misplaced. Of course, feelings of shame may be short-lived and non-recurrent if the agent himself recognizes that that which in his view placed him in the vulnerable position should not in fact be seen as bringing about a lowered status.[6] So when in Bunyan's *Pilgrim's Progress* Faithful is told by Shame that few of the powerful and rich would agree with Faithful's view that a tender conscience is a thing of value but would regard it as unmanly, he only briefly accepts the adverse view on a tender conscience and can quickly be made to see that Shame was "a bold Villain," i.e., be made to recognize that he suffered from false shame. But such recognition may be long delayed or may not happen at all. It is from this point of view that Stanley Cavell discusses the case of Gloucester:

> For Gloucester has a fault... He has revealed his fault in the opening speeches of the play, in which he tells Kent of his shame... He says that now he is "braz'd to it," that is, used to admitting that he has fathered a bastard... He recognizes the moral claim upon himself, as he says twice, to "acknowledge" his bastard...but all this means to him is that he acknowledges that he has a bastard for a son. He does not acknowledge *him,* as a son or a person, with *his* feelings of illegitimacy and being cast out. *That* is something Gloucester ought to be ashamed of; his shame is itself more shameful than his one piece of licentiousness. This is one of the inconveniences of shame, that it is generally inaccurate, attaches to the wrong thing.[7]

As father of a bastard, Gloucester, in his own view, is in a vulnerable position, for this is an aspect of himself which does not fit the sort of person he thinks he ought to be, or wants to be. Revelation of this position (which may be just the recollection that he is in this position) will cause him to experience shame unless he can take certain measures to prevent this occurrence. He takes in fact two steps in this direction. The first (as Cavell later points out) is a very common one under the circumstances: he avoids that which will serve as a reminder to himself and others of what he regards as a flaw in himself, which in this case is achieved by keeping Edmund abroad for long periods of time. The other more daring and interesting move is that he "brazens it out," that is, he draws attention to the fact that Edmund is illegitimate and so makes it appear that having a bastard son is a less weighty matter than might be supposed. In other words, he tries to turn himself into someone who is shameless: he pretends not to recognize the importance of the value involved and makes light of such a value. Now one may well, like Cavell, believe that Gloucester has got his values all wrong, and that what he should really feel shame about is his treatment of his son, rather than the son's existence. But this of course does not mean that it can be right for Gloucester to make light of his values and thus avoid shame. For in doing so he denies what is in fact of great importance to him. If it were not so important he would not have to take such elaborate steps to avoid exposure. There are therefore two ways of looking at the value of the occurrence of shame in cases like that of Gloucester. The first is Cavell's way in the passage quoted: Gloucester's shame attaches to the wrong object because he has not got his values right. In this sense his shame is misplaced and so unjustified, it is an emotion he ought not to be experiencing. But (and this is the other way of looking at the matter) for the agent it is the experiencing of the emotion which is in this sense justified, and the avoidance of it which is not. Avoidance of shame is one way of losing self-respect, for it is one way of blurring the values the person is committed to. From this point of view genuine shame is always justified, where "genuine" is to be opposed to the "false" shame felt by Faithful when for a brief period he let an alien standard be imposed on him. Gloucester, on the contrary, lets an alien standard be imposed on him when he tries to avoid shame, and the one is as much a form of corruption as the other.

Shame can be seen as a moral emotion, then, not because sometimes or even often it is felt when the person believes himself to have done something morally wrong, but rather because the capacity for feeling shame is so closely related to the possession of self-respect and thereby to the agent's values. The implications of this relationship are deeper than has so far been indicated, and can be done justice to only when the notion of integrity has been discussed....

II. Integrity and Self-Respect

The thoughts which are constitutive of the emotions of self-assessment are directed towards the self and its status. A person, to be able to experience these emotions, needs a form of self-consciousness which is not just the capacity to ascribe experiences to himself, though this is of course a minimum requirement. The person concerned must be capable of being self-conscious also in the sense that he can see himself as a being that can be seen by others, that can be assessed and judged.

If there is self-consciousness there is a self to be conscious of. This does not imply that there is one unchanging entity, the self, which is the object of such consciousness. The self is not unchanging, and it cannot be the object of consciousness in the way in which a physical object or event can be an object of consciousness. The "perceiver" is part of that self and so contributes to what it is. He can affect and shape what he perceives as the observer of the physical event cannot affect and shape what he perceives.

The person capable of experiencing the emotions of self-assessment sees himself from the point of view of being an agent in the world, who tries and succeeds or fails to bring about certain states of affairs; he sees himself as affected by others, and he takes a view of his own effectiveness and the value of what he has achieved. He sees himself as a moral agent, at least in the minimal sense that he thinks about himself and his life evaluatively. As such an agent he has an identity. Necessarily, the identity of the moral agent depends on other criteria for self-identity being fulfilled; in particular, for it to be possible for an agent to assess himself, there must be a degree of connectedness between his states of consciousness. But the dependence is one way only: a being's identity as moral agent may be lost without this affecting any identity he may have in mental or physical terms.[8] The problem concerning the identity of a moral agent is not how to re-identify the same individual in different situations; this point is assumed to be settled. It is rather the question of what identifies the person as essentially the person he is. For what he thinks very worthwhile doing, and what he thinks very important not to do, contributes essentially to his being one sort of person rather than another. Whether or not a moral agent preserves his identity depends on whether or not he possesses integrity.

The person of integrity is sometimes seen as the person who possesses certain moral virtues. Most obviously, she will be honest in various ways: she does not systematically deceive, she does not cheat or break her word. She will, it seems, possess those virtues which may be labelled "forms of conscientiousness," viz., honesty, fairness, truthfulness, and being a person of one's word.[9] But there is also what seems to be quite a different aspect of integrity, and one more closely linked to the etymology of the term (*integritas*: wholeness): the person of integrity is not corrupt, she is autonomous and takes responsibility for her choices and actions. What she does or chooses is truly hers.[10] If such considerations are centrally relevant to the question of whether or not a person possesses integrity then it is not enough to think of "integrity" as simply a label for a set of virtues, and the question arises how these different or seemingly different, aspects of integrity can be reconciled....

[L]ack of control over what a person does is the crucial factor responsible for lack or loss of integrity. In order to remain in control it is necessary for the agent to be clear about her evaluations, and this in turn implies that there cannot be unacknowledged desires which seriously interfere with these evaluations. She has to be honest with herself. She will also be honest with others in that she will express in her actions what she values most and thereby take responsibility for it. Failure to do so is always a threat to her evaluations, at least if it is at all frequent or prolonged. It will tend to weaken and confuse them. If failing to act according to her evauations is not to be a case of loss of integrity she must at least be quite clear why she acts as she does. From this point of view the not fully conscious deception of others perpetrated by the self-deceived is worse than the calculated deception of the hypocrite, just because the self-deceived does not know that she is doing.

Bruno Bettelheim, in an essay about life in a concentration camp, seems to have in mind the notion of integrity as it is here outlined. He writes:

To survive as a man, not a walking corpse, as a debased and degraded but still human being, one had first and foremost to remain informed and aware of what made up one's personal point of no return beyond which one would never, under any circumstances, give in to the oppressor, even if it meant risking and losing one's life. It meant being aware that if one survived at the price of overreaching this point one would be holding on to a life that had lost all meaning. It would mean surviving—not with lower self-respect, but without any...

Second in importance was keeping oneself informed of how one felt about complying when the ultimate decision as to where to stand firm was not called in question...One had to comply with debasing and amoral commands if one wished to survive; but one had to remain cognizant that one's reason for complying was "to remain alive and unchanged as a person." Therefore, one had to decide, for any given action, whether it was truly necessary for one's safety or that of others, and whether committing it was good, neutral or bad. This keeping informed and aware of one's actions—though it could not alter the required act—this minimal distance from one's own behaviour, and the freedom to feel differently about it depending on its character, this too was what permitted the prisoner to remain a human being....[11]

In contrast to those who are not at all clear about their personal point of no return, the prisoner who, while forced to do what he thinks degrading, knows what he is doing and why, saves his integrity. He is not corrupted by the treatment he receives or by the sort of behaviour forced upon him. Even though he has no control over what he actually does, he at least retains control over his evaluations in the sense of being sure which sorts of desires he would consistently want to be effective in any circumstances other than these extreme ones. He is very different from someone who has lost the degree of control he still possesses and just acts from that desire which at the time is the strongest.[12] To maintain that much control under such circumstances is of course a considerable achievement, and there must always be the threat of its being undermined. Public acknowledgement of one's evaluations is the only safeguard against such threats. But while such acknowledgement is therefore very important for integrity, the lack of it on some occasions is not by itself sufficient for integrity to be lost.

An account of integrity as being primarily a matter of the agent's control over what she is doing explains the type of behaviour we expect of a person we regard as having integrity. To be a candidate for possession of integrity the person's choices and evaluations must be her own: her identifications with her desires must be neither subject to unconsidered change nor be distorted or confused. Her reasons for action must be genuine. Such integrity cannot be maintained without a degree of courage: she cannot fail to do or say what she thinks she should even on those occasions when she finds it difficult to do so. This is so because, by and large, her actions must accord with her evaluations. She will stand by her values and not be bribed to act against them, whether the source of the bribe is in herself or in others. In publicly acknowledging her evaluations she accepts responsibility for what she does. For to explain away her actions, or find excuses for them, is to disown what she sets store by. It is then not surprising that honesty and uprightness should be seen as the mark of a person of integrity....

If it is a person's evaluations and her ordering of these evaluations which are crucial to integrity then there is of course no guarantee that these are widely shared and acceptable, or that the values in question are particularly moral. The person of integrity need not be a morally good person, she may not be much, or possibly not be at all, moved by other-regarding reasons. But at least she cannot wholly ignore others. This point is connected with the requirement that she must be clear about her evaluations. She must get her practical reasoning right and act on that reason which, all things considered, she thinks best. But to have any thought about what might or might not be important to pursue in her life she cannot treat herself as if she were an isolated being. If she is to have a sane view of herself and the life she wants to lead she cannot ignore the evidence of her impact on others and their reactions to her. She must therefore give some recognition to others as persons who have views and interests and intentions of their own. Nor can she see others simply as providers of evidence about herself. For it is not possible that her impact on others could be understood by her were she to abstract their reactions to her from the context of general social communication. The evidence about herself which she could gather under such circumstances would be bound to be distorted. Her recognition of others cannot, therefore, be a wholly superficial one. She cannot be indiscriminate about the evidence that comes her way, either, for not everything will be equally worth having. So she will have to assess the views of others, and their evaluations. But this again cannot leave altogether untouched her own evaluations. It may be that these are now shown up as being shallow or shortsighted. The suppression of or turning away from such evidence about herself and her values would be a threat to her integrity. Unless she is open to such evidence her pattern of reasoning is likely to remain unexamined and static, and is unlikely to reflect as it should the wider and more varied experiences of a person capable of change and development.

If it is true that the person of integrity must be aware of others to the extent described then there is perhaps a closer link between integrity and morality than was earlier suggested. At least the person of integrity cannot be a moral solipsist, for she will recognize that others, too, are evaluators who, in so far as they act with integrity, act on reasons which they regard as justificatory. It is a reasonable assumption (and one to which I shall return) that her self-respect is not independent of her integrity: she respects herself in so far as she acts with integrity. If so, then it would seem unreasonable and even inconsistent of her to withhold respect from others who also act according to their evaluations. But to respect others, if it is not to remain an empty phrase, must mean that to some extent at least consideration of their rights and interests will figure in that person's practical reasoning....[13]

A moral agent's evaluation will range from the (in her view) centrally important to the quite trivial. Given sound practical reasoning, more or less trivial evaluations will be expressed in action only if they do not conflict with more important ones; whether this happens rarely or frequently will depend on the circumstances of the agent's life. Being on the periphery of her sets of values any change in them will not have particularly far-reaching consequences on the nature and order of her other evaluations. They therefore do not contribute to her identity and have nothing to do with her possession or lack of integrity. Only those evaluations have bearing on this question which figure prominently as overriding reasons in the agent's practical reasoning. I shall refer to these as the agent's "commitments."

Of the emotions of self-assessment discussed, shame and guilt are essentially connected with a person's integrity, though the details of the connection are different in the two cases. In the case of shame the connection is through self-respect. A person can have self-respect, or a sense of her own value, only if she believes some form of life is worth living, and believes that by and large she is capable of leading such a life. Self-respect must be based on what she takes to be her commitments, for it must be based on that in virtue of which she thinks herself worthy of respect, and she cannot think herself worthy of respect in virtue of something which she herself regards as relatively trivial. That is, to have self-respect she must have a degree of integrity; without some integrity there would be no self to respect.[14] And further, if integrity is the identity of the person in terms of her commitments then self-respect protects this identity by protecting the relevant values: the person who has self-respect will not tolerate certain types of behaviour on her own part, nor certain types of treatment offered her by others. As a person's commitments are normally varied and cover different areas of activity, it is possible to maintain self-respect with regard to some areas and not with regard to others. She may believe that some of her evaluations have implications which she feebly ignores, or that some areas of her life are not governed by the sorts of values by which they ought to be governed.

Shame is felt about injury to, or loss, or lack of self-respect. At the moment of experiencing shame the person believes that some of her important expectations concerning what is due to or from her have been frustrated. She thinks, possibly only briefly, that her commitments are not the right ones, or that she does not live up to them, or that she lacks commitments altogether in an area where she ought to have them. If, broadly, every case of feeling shame is a case of perceived injury to self-respect, and if self-respect is connected with integrity in the way just described, then there should be some connection also between shame and integrity. This connection is not hard to see: those occasions where the perceived injury to my self-respect is due to my thinking my evaluations shoddy or my actions contrary to their dictates are also occasions of my perceiving a threat to my integrity—whether or not I myself describe my awareness in these terms. That is to say, whenever I feel shame about something I have done or have omitted to do then I will see a threat to my integrity; for shame is about my shortcomings with respect to formulating or living up to my commitments. But not all cases of shame are of this sort. I may feel shame not about something I have done, but feel it rather about the deed or state of somebody else to whom I see myself as so related that his defects reflect on my worth. My father has done something disgraceful, and the sense of my value based on the conception of being the daughter of this father is now underminded. But this does not seem to constitute a threat to my integrity. Whether or not there is such a threat depends rather on how I cope with the new situation. I may (or may not) react in a way which amounts to a betrayal of what I value, and then of course loss of integrity is involved. But the feeling of shame occasioned by my father's doings is as such unrelated to my integrity as there is here no conflict of identifications. Such cases of shame seem to fall outside the area of integrity, except that they put the person concerned in a position where her reactions have some bearing on her integrity....

To say that when feeling shame the agent's view of the situation can be described (over the range of cases indicated) as "constituting a threat to her integrity" is not to say that her view is necessarily correct; what is perceived as a threat need not in fact be one. This is so where the person suffers from "false" shame, the shame which is occasioned by the temporary acceptance of an alien standard, or by momentarily attaching a degree of importance to a piece of behavior which the agent comes to see it does not deserve. Not living according to such a standard, or behaving in that way, does not in fact threaten the agent's integrity. But there is a threat here none the less, though not as perceived by her at the time, for she lets herself be muddled about her values. The threat may be quite minor, as it was in Faithful's case. But the more often a person suffers from false shame, the more serious the threat to her integrity, or the more indicative, perhaps, of confusion or uncertainty about her values.[15] It is the experiencing of shame itself which here constitutes the threat. There is a parallel between this case and that where a person does not feel shame although her integrity is threatened, for she is not aware of that fact. Here her lack of shame is an indication that the corruption is serious indeed: not even to perceive an injury to self-respect must mean that the agent has lost grip on her evaluations. It was for this reason, I suggested earlier, that shame is regarded sometimes as a virtue.

While a perceived threat to integrity may or may not be an actual threat, it is always the case that a perceived injury to self-respect is in fact such an injury, even if what the person experiences is false shame. This is so because self-respect may be lost although there is nothing wrong with the person's evaluations. In rightly or wrongly believing something to be wrong she loses her confidence in her evaluations and so in her own worth. She is no longer sure that this is how she ought to behave or be treated, and such lack of certainty affects her respect for herself. It is therefore possible that a person of integrity may have little or even no self-respect just because that person lacks confidence in her evaluations. But her integrity cannot under such circumstances be very secure, for her lack of confidence makes her the sort of person who is a likely prey to false shame. The relation of shame to integrity is therefore not always straightforward. It may be that what is perceived as constituting a threat to integrity is just that. In that case her shame is justified, in the sense that it relates to her genuine evaluations. (Whether or not it is objectively justified is of course a different question.) Where shame is in this sense unjustified the threat to integrity is still there, but it is not what in the agent's own view constitutes the threat. It is however still the injury to self-respect which makes integrity insecure, for lack of confidence in her commitments increases the chances of her practical reasoning being confused.

It is its relation to integrity which makes shame such a potentially devastating emotion. Guilt can be equally devastating. It, too, is related to integrity, though the perceived threat to integrity takes here a different form. In shame the self is seen as less worthy than the agent thought, assumed, or hoped he was or might become; such thoughts, hopes or assumptions have now turned out to be unfounded. When feeling guilt, on the other hand, the agent sees himself as the doer of a wicked deed and so as alien to himself; he sees another self emerging. The "wicked deed" refers to his action (or omission) seen as violating some taboo, and the emerging self is the self capable of violating the taboo. In many ordinary cases of guilt, of course, the particular action or omission may not be thought by the agent to be a very serious violation, or not thought to be the violation of a very serious taboo. In such a case the second self does not have much substance; its appearance is only fleeting and so is not much of a threat. As in shame there is here a range of cases vastly differing in degrees of severity. But if in feeling guilt the agent thinks of himself as having done something he regards as alien to himself and which yet has been brought about by him, then there is here the danger of a split, however fleeting that danger might be. Once there is this danger then there is also the possibility that the alien self, the doer of the forbidden deed, might assume control, and so what is important to the person feeling guilt is to purge himself of that self and thereby to regain his (degree of) integrity. Guilt, then, is different from shame in that it is not felt at the recognition of the failure of the worthy self, but is felt rather at the recognition of the emergence of a worse self. It is therefore also differently related to integrity. The person feeling guilt does not perceive an injury to his self-respect, it is not his worth which is primarily his concern. The self he is aware of is alien precisely because its deed expresses an evaluation which is not his own. Such a self is unrelated to his self-respect, or becomes a candidate for self-respect only if, like Macbeth, he tries to realign himself. It is because the alien evaluation interferes with his own that the person feeling guilt sees a threat to his integrity.

These differences between the two emotions explain other contrasting features. They explain why guilt but not shame is rightly connected with fear and anxiety:[16] an alien self whose doings conflict with the agent's evaluations is indeed something to fear and feel anxious about. In shame the agent sees himself diminished, and a diminished self need not be feared; it is just something to be despised. The emerging alien self, on the other hand, is not despicable, it has after all not been a failure but has on the contrary made its mark. So a person feeling guilty may not be without a feeling of pride in what he has done. Although what he did was wrong, in breaking a command (it may seem to him) he has at least done something positive, and in this he may conceivably see cause for self-admiration. Of course feelings of pride would be quite incompatible with feeling shame. A person cannot despise and admire himself at the same time. He has, in his view, failed to have the right values, or failed to be clear about them, or failed to act in such a manner that his behaviour unambiguously expresses his values. Shame is always felt about some failure of this kind, and so the self always appears weak and ineffectual. For this reason there is in cases of shame a loss of confidence in either his values or in his capacity to live up to them which is not to be found in cases of guilt.

There are consequently types of behaviour which seem more appropriate occasions for shame than for guilt, and the other way about. The response to an obviously aggressive and violent deed, such as murder, would perhaps more naturally be expected to be guilt rather than shame, and that to what are plainly failures, such as avoidance of discomfort, ridicule, or danger, to be shame and not guilt. But of course it all depends on how the agent himself sees the situation. The killer may be struck not by the violence of his action but by its failure to comply with his code of conduct, and the coward may be impressed not by his failure but by his acting against his obligations as he sees them.

The same type of behaviour, such as telling a lie, may be an occasion for guilt, or for shame, or both. If it is an occasion for guilt the agent will see telling the lie as something he must not do. Telling the truth is obligatory and remains obligatory however good the reasons may be for on this occasion acting otherwise. If it is an occasion for shame then it is out of respect for himself that he tells the truth. He owes it to himself to do so, it is beneath him, he is too proud to tell a lie. In each case the motivation differs from the motives that prompt either prudential or other-regarding actions. In that case the agent's reasons for action can be stated in terms of the aim he has in mind in acting as he does: he tells the truth to serve his own best interests or those of another. This is not so in the former case: the agent does not act in order to do what is obligatory, or in order to preserve his self-respect. At most the reference to obligation and self-respect indicates that there are such reasons, which would be reasons for his evaluations being what they are. In particular, a person acting out of self-respect does not act in order to preserve his integrity, or to keep himself morally pure. As Bernard Williams has pointed out, such desires can hardly be a person's primary motive for action, for to have such a desire the agent first needs something to be pure about.[17] If, then, the charge that acting with integrity may be acting self-indulgently is based on the thought that self-respect (or for that matter, integrity) generates the kind of reason the description of which completes an "in order to..." formulation, then this charge is indeed misplaced. The mistake would not just be in turning "acting out of self-respect" into the sort of reason which it is not; it would lie also in trying to find at all an isolated reason for the action which will explain just it. A person acts out of self-respect when he does what he feels himself committed to, and the reasons for the action are those which have played a part in determining his commitments. But commitments are deeply rooted and have implications which are likely to be far-reaching. To pick out just one reason as giving the aim of this particular action would hardly be adequate as either an explanation or justification of what he is doing.

Acting out of self-respect, while it is not acting in order to protect the person's integrity, nevertheless does protect it, and so is a bonus for the agent. Whether or not this particular action is generally beneficial is quite a different question and depends partly on the nature of the agent's evaluations. In acting out of self-respect his thoughts are on his commitments rather than on himself, the focus is primarily on the action and not on the actor. But of course they are *his* commitments, they embody the values he thinks make his life worthwhile. So the self is obliquely involved. By contrast, self-esteem is more directly centred on the self.

The two emotions concerned with self-esteem are pride and humiliation. In contrast to guilt and shame, emotional pride is not essentially connected with integrity. This is not to say that a person may not be proud of having acted with integrity, or of being a person of integrity. He may well see reason for self-esteem in the fact that his commitments are of a certain kind and that he acts accordingly on relevant occasions. But pride need not take this direction. The person who feels proud experiences a boost to his self-esteem. He sees his position as in some respect comparatively better and so can take a more favourable view of himself. But he may think the respect in which his position is now better a quite unimportant one in his general scheme of values. He may, for instance, be proud of his precious snuff-box although being a snuff-box owner does not strike him as a matter of much moment. A person may be proud of something which he regards as relatively trivial and as having nothing to do with his commitments. What makes a person, if only temporarily, take a more favourable view of himself is wide-ranging and need not touch on his integrity. I said earlier that pride in all its forms concerns the status of the self. But what is included here under "status" goes beyond his identity in terms of his commitments. "Status" was explained in terms of a persons's norm of expectations, and these expectations cover areas of, to him, varying degrees of importance. In this respect pride and shame are not polar opposites: if "status" includes but is not exhausted by expectations relating to the agent's commitments then the occasion for pride may be found anywhere in that area, whereas occasions for shame are restricted to what is seen at the time as centrally important.

It may seem that the contrast just drawn is not soundly based: it may be that as the emphasis in the discussion of shame has been on the moment of its occurrence while pride has been seen as primarily dispositional, the comparison is between features which are not analogous. It may be that on those occasions when pride wells up in a person, whatever he is proud of will at that moment also strike him as centrally important, and it is only later, when he thinks about the matter, that he recognizes its relative triviality. But whether or not this is the case, the difference between shame and pride in their respective relation to integrity rests ultimately not on this but on the difference in the way self-respect and self-esteem are related to integrity. Whether or not a person thinks favourably of himself has nothing to do with his integrity, whereas whether or not he can respect himself has. This is so because a person need not be conscious of his possessing or acting with integrity, he need pay no particular attention to himself and have no particular attitude towards himself.

Self-respect required both that the person had certain commmitments and that he was confident that by and large he had got his commitments right and was capable of living accordingly. It seemed possible that a person could have integrity and yet lack self-respect because he lacked the required self-confidence. It may be that he cannot have confidence in himself unless he can think well of himself. Self-esteem may be necessary for him to have self-respect. In that case, of course, self-esteem and self-respect are interconnected. But the interconnection between them is in an area which does not touch that person's integrity. Self-esteem may be connected with self-respect in that it contributes to his having a sense of his own value. But this aspect of self-respect is itself independent of the agent's integrity, or is related to it only to the extent that a more secure sense of one's own value is a better protector of one's integrity.

Humiliation, like pride, is also not directly connected with integrity, and that for the same reason. When feeling humiliated a person realizes either that her good opinion of herself is unfounded, or that her belief that she commands the good opinion of others is mistaken. Her belief that she is not, or is no longer, esteemed by others as she had supposed may affect her own self-esteem. But she may also retain her self-esteem if she believes these others to be mistaken. They do not give her what she deserves. Either experience may also affect her self-respect, whether it does or not will depend on what she needs to maintain her sense of her own value. Just as increased self-esteem may have a favourable effect on a person's self-respect, so a blow to her self-esteem may undermine her self-respect. But the fact that it is here a matter of loss and not, as in pride, a matter of gain in self-esteem will make the impact on the person's integrity a more serious one. If the occasion of her humiliation is the shattering of the favourable view she had been taking of herself as having certain commitments and acting in certain ways, then confidence in her values may be shaken to such a degree that it may well constitute a threat to her integrity.

It is after all not surprising that it should be the "negative" emotions like shame and guilt and possibly humiliation which are more importantly connected with a person's integrity than is a "positive" emotion like pride. The self in terms of a web of commitments, though not static, may still be thought of as being in a state of equilibrium, if all is well with these commitments. Such an equilibrium can be affected only by something going wrong; it can be upset, but it cannot be improved. So pride has here no role to play. Guilt and shame, however, have: the beliefs which identify these emotions are concerned with a disturbance in the equilibrium. But this does not mean that in experiencing them the agent just takes a certain view of herself. The experience is not wholly cognitive. She is not related to her integrity as a detached observer is to some independent state of affairs. The occurrence of the thoughts and the feeling-reactions which constitute guilt or shame itself has an effect on the self.

The experiencing of these emotions affects the self in that it operates as a pressure to maintain or return to the equilibrium. In feeling guilt or shame the agent sees the equilibrium being disturbed or threatened in different ways, and the painfulness of the emotions is occasioned by the perceived contrast between what the agent has done and ought to have done, or by what she is and ought to be. Within the person's scheme of evaluations the pressure exercised by them may or may not be properly channelled. False shame, for example, or irrational guilt, exert pressures to be a self which is not the agent's genuine self. A person experienced false shame on an occasion when she (perhaps only momentarily) accepted a standard that was alien to her. The pressure here is therefore destructive of the equilibrium which consists of her genuine commitments. Feelings of guilt may similarly be misdirected. Guilt is not false in the sense in which shame may be false, for what is thought to be forbidden will not be alien to the person concerned: it is part of a scheme of values which the agent accepted at any rate at some point, even if she now thinks differently. But guilt (like shame) may be irrational, i.e., it may be felt about something which the agent now judges not to be wrong at all, or which in the light of her general commitments she would so judge if she thought about the matter. The pressure of irrational guilt is as misplaced as is that of false shame: in implying an evaluation which is contrary to the agent's genuine commitments its pressure is a threat to the equilibrium rather than a push towards maintaining it.

From the agent's own point of view, then, genuine guilt and shame have a useful function to fulfill, whereas, as one might expect, these emotions are merely destructive if, given the person's evaluations, they are ill-founded. Although genuine shame or guilt are always constructive in the sense of being a pressure towards maintaining or returning to the equilibrium, they need not therefore be of equal value to the agent. Sometimes they may simply be frustrating, viz., if their occasion is a state of affairs the agent cannot do anything about, as when she feels shame at the circumstances of her birth. In such cases, perhaps, they may be taken as a reminder that evaluations are not data to be accepted as given but may themselves be in need of reassessment.

Notes

1. [Editor's Note: In chapter 3 of *Pride, Shame, and Guilt* Taylor gives the following analysis of shame:

   There are basically two elements in each case of shame. There is firstly the self-directed adverse judgement of the person feeling shame: she feels herself degraded, not the sort of person she believed, assumed, or hoped she was or anyway should be. This judgement is constitutive of the emotion, it is the person's identificatory belief. Secondly, there is the notion of the audience...[which] has a role to play in the explanation of the self-directed judgment.... It consists of two distinguishable points of view. The first point of view audience sees the agent under some description...the second point of view audience...concerns the relation between the agent and the first audience. It views the different forms of seeing, and always views them critically: to be so seen is to be exposed, for the agent should not be seen in this way.... To speak of an audience is of course to speak metaphorically...the metaphors of an audience and of being seen...reflect the structural features of the agent's becoming aware of the discrepancy between her own assumption about her state or action and a possible detached observer-description of this state or action, and of her further being aware that she ought not to be in a position where she could so be seen, where such a description at least appears to fit. (pp. 64–66).]

2. By David Sachs in *Philosophy and Public Affairs*, Vol. x (1981), pp. 346–60.

3. [Editor's Note: Taylor defines a person's "norm of expectations" as what that

person expects as a matter of course or is accustomed to taking for granted (*Pride, Shame, and Guilt*, pp. 37–40).]

4. For an example of the importance of shame for members of an honour-group see, e.g., Wolfram von Eschenbach's *Parzival* (trans. H. M. Mustard and C. E. Passage). Gurnemanz is advising the young and inexperienced Parzival on the proper conduct of life for one of high birth and breeding:

    Follow my advice: it will keep you from wrongdoing. I will begin thus: See that you never lose your sense of shame. A man with-out a sense of shame, what good is he? He lives in a molting state, shedding his honor, and with steps directed towards hell....
    (p. 93)

    And later, after Parzival has failed in one of his tests, the narrator reassures the reader: "Still another virtue was his, a sense of shame. Real falsity he had shunned..." (p. 172).

5. Plato in the *Laws* (Bk. 2, 671c) praises shame as that which will prevent a man from doing what is dishonourable. Aristotle in the *Nicomachean Ethics* suggests that while feeling shame is all right for children it is not a suitable emotion for an adult (Bk. 4 Ch. IX), but he also acknowledges its value in *Rhetoric* 1367a10. Both Bollnow (*Die Ehrfurcht*) and Scheler (*Schriften aus dem Nachlass)* emphasize the value of shame.

6. This is not the only case, of course, where shame may not have much effect. The agent may not think his position so very vulnerable and he may be able to forget with relative ease the occasion for shame.

7. From Cavell, "The Avoidance of Love: A Reading of *King Lear*" in *Must We Mean What We Say?* (Cambridge: Cambridge University Press, 1976), p. 276.

8. This is only roughly true: changes in the identity of a person in so far as he is a moral agent may have repercussions; they may for example lead to the suppression or overemphasis of certain memories.

9. The term is borrowed from James D. Wallace, *Virtues and Vices*, Contemporary Philosophy Series (Ithaca: Cornell University Press, 1978), ch. 4.

10. For this sort of view on integrity see Bernard Williams in "A Critique of Utilitarianism," in Williams and J. J. C. Smart, *Utilitarianism For and Against* (Cambridge: Cambridge University Press, 1973); and in "Persons, Character and Morality," in Williams, *Moral Luck* (Cambridge: Cambridge University Press, 1981); and also Peter Winch, "Moral Integrity" in *Ethics and Action* (London: Routledge and Kegan Paul, 1972).

11. Bruno Bettelheim, [*The Informed Heart: Autonomy in a Mass Age* (Glencoe, Ill.: Free Press, 1961), p. 157.]

12. Contrast the case of Bettelheim's prisoner with that of Winston in Orwell's *1984*. The latter loses his integrity when, under threat of unbearable torture,

he betrays his love for Julia. He loses his ability to discriminate and so loses all control over his action.

13. It may be possible to establish other links between integrity and morality: e.g., Mary Midgley argues that a lasting divorce between the inner and outer life is a denial of reason and sanity; in "The Objection to Systematic Humbug," *Philosophy* 53 (1978). See also Bernard Mayo's paper "Moral Integrity," where he wants to show that "personal" integrity is much the same thing as "moral" integrity: *Human Values*, Royal Institute of Philosophy Lectures, vol. 11 (1976–7).

14. She must *have* some integrity, rather than merely *think* she has. If she only thinks she more or less consistently acts according to her evaluations when in fact she does not she would obviously be self-deceived to a considerable extent. But the point of such self-deception would be to persuade herself that she can (still) respect herself, an exercise which would be unnecessary if she had self-respect anyway.

15. "False shame" covers a range of cases. Faithful's shame is one type, Fanny Thornton's another:

> "Mr. Thorton! Does he really find time to read with a tutor, in the midst of all his business,—and this abominable strike in hand as well?"
>
> Fanny was not sure, from Mrs. Slickson's manner, whether she ought to be proud or ashamed of her brother's conduct; and, like all people who try and take other people's "ought" for the rule of their feelings, she was inclined to blush for any singularity of action. Her shame was interrupted by the dispersion of the guests. (Elizabeth Gaskell, *North and South*, Ch. 20.)

16. E.g. Freud, *Civilization and Its Discontents*, trans. James Strachey (New York: W. W. Norton, 1961), sec. 7.

17. Bernard Williams, "Utilitarianism and Moral Self Indulgence," in *Moral Luck*, pp. 48–9.

+

Are There Different Kinds of Self-Respect?

+

10

✛

Two Kinds of Respect

✛

Stephen L. Darwall

I

An appeal to respect as something to which all persons are entitled marks
much recent thought on moral topics. The appeal is common both in
writings on general moral theory and in work on particular moral problems. For example, such writers as John Rawls, Bernard Williams, David
Gauthier, R.S. Downie, and Elizabeth Telfer refer to the respect which is
due all persons, either in arguing for or in articulating various moral
principles.[1] The idea is not particularly new, since one of the keystones
of Kant's ethics is the view that respect for the moral law entails treating
persons (oneself included) always as ends in themselves and never simply as means. Precisely what Kant meant, or should have meant, by this
is a matter of some controversy, but it is generally thought that the same
claim is expressed in saying that one must respect persons as such.[2]

The appeal to respect also figures in much recent discussion of more specific moral problems such as racism or sexism. For example, it is argued that various ways of regarding and behaving toward others, and social arrangements which encourage those ways, are inconsistent with the respect to which all persons are entitled.

The claim that all persons are entitled to respect just by virtue of being persons may not seem wholly unproblematic, however. How could respect be something which is due to all persons? Do we not also think that persons can either deserve or fail to deserve our respect? Is the moralist who claims that all persons are entitled to respect advocating that we give up this idea? Questions of this sort should call into question just what respect itself is.

Other questions about respect appear as soon as one starts to press. Is respect a single kind of attitude? Is it primarily, or even solely, a moral attitude? Are persons the only sort of thing to which respect is appropriate? Everyone at least understands the coach who says that his team must respect the rebounding strength of the opposing team's front line. No moral attitude is involved here. Nor may persons be respected only as persons. Frank may be highly respected as a weaver, Sarah as a doctor.

II

Several writers have in fact given explicit attention to what constitutes respect for persons. On most such accounts it is a willingness to take into consideration one or another aspect of persons when one's actions affect them. Candidates for the relevant aspects of persons which are owed our consideration are their wants,[3] their point of view on a particular situation,[4] and the like. These accounts are not intended as general accounts of respect. They are only meant to give some more specific content to what it is that persons are entitled to by virtue of being persons.

One notable exception to such accounts is a recent attempt by Carl Cranor to give a general account of respect.[5] Cranor holds respect to be a complex relationship which obtains between two persons (the respecter and the respected), some characteristic (the basis of respect), and some evaluative point of view (from which the person is respected). This relationship consists, roughly, in the respecter's judging that the person's having the characteristic is a good thing (from the relevant point of view), his appreciating why it is a good thing, and his being disposed to do what is appropriate to the person's having that characteristic.

III

One problem that infects each of the accounts mentioned as a general theory of respect is that each fails to distinguish two rather different ways in which persons may be the object of respect. Or, as I am inclined to say, two rather different kinds of attitude which are both referred to by the term "respect."[6] The two different ways in which a person may be respected provide but one instance of a more general difference between two attitudes which are both termed respect. Crudely put the difference is this.

There is a kind of respect which can have any of a number of different sorts of things as its object and which consists, most generally, in a disposition to weigh appropriately in one's deliberations some feature of the thing in question and to act accordingly. The law, someone's feelings, and social institutions with their positions and roles are examples of things which can be the object of this sort of respect. Since this kind of respect consists in giving appropriate consideration or recognition to some feature of its object in deliberating about what to do, I shall call it *recognition respect.*

Persons can be the object of recognition respect. Indeed, it is just this sort of respect which is said to be owed to all persons. To say that persons as such are entitled to respect is to say that they are entitled to have other persons take seriously and weigh appropriately the fact that they are persons in deliberating about what to do. Such respect is recognition respect; but what it requires as appropriate is not a matter of general agreement, for this is just the question of what our moral obligations or duties to other persons consist in. The crucial point is that to conceive of all persons as entitled to respect is to have some conception of what sort of consideration the fact of being a person requires.

A person may not only be the object of recognition respect as a person. As Erving Goffman has shown in great detail, human beings play various roles, or present various "selves," both in their interactions with others and in private before imagined audiences.[7] Others may or may not respond appropriately to the presented self. To fail to take seriously the person as the presented self in one's responses to the person is to fail to give the person recognition respect as that presented self or in that role. It is this sort of respect to which Rodney Dangerfield refers when he bemoans the fact that neither his son nor his wife takes him seriously as a father or a husband with the complaint, "I can't get no respect."

There is another attitude which differs importantly from recognition respect but which we likewise refer to by the term "respect." Unlike recognition respect, its exclusive objects are persons or features which are held to manifest their excellence as persons or as engaged in some specific pursuit. For example, one may have such respect for someone's integrity, for someone's good qualities on the whole, or for someone as a musician. Such respect, then, consists in an attitude of positive appraisal of that person either as a person or as engaged in some particular pursuit. Accordingly the appropriate ground for such respect is that the person has manifested characteristics which make him deserving of such positive appraisal. I shall later argue that the appropriate characteristics are those which are, or are based on, features of a person which we attribute to his *character*.

Because this sort of respect consists in a positive appraisal of a person, or his qualities, I shall call it *appraisal respect*. Unlike recognition respect, one may have appraisal respect for someone without having any particular conception of just what behavior *from oneself* would be required or made appropriate by that person's having the features meriting such respect. Appraisal respect is the positive appraisal itself. It is like esteem or a high regard for someone, although, as I shall argue later, the appropriate grounds for appraisal respect are not so broadly based as those of these latter attitudes.

Typically, when we speak of someone as meriting or deserving our respect, it is appraisal respect that we have in mind. We mean that the person is such as to merit our positive appraisal on the appropriate grounds. It is true that in order to indicate or express such respect, certain behavior from us will be appropriate. But unlike recognition respect, appraisal respect does not itself consist in that behavior or in the judgment that it is appropriate. Rather, it consists in the appraisal itself.

In giving this characterization of appraisal respect, it would seem that I am giving no role to *feelings* of respect. Just as one may be said to have feelings of admiration so one may be said to feel respect for another. Although I won't pursue this point further, I suggest that such feelings may be understood as feelings which a person would explain by referring to his or her positive appraisal of their object. Just as we understand the feeling of fear to be that which is explained by one's belief in the presence of danger, so the feeling of respect for a person is the one which is occasioned by the positive appraisal which constitutes appraisal respect for that person.[8]

My project in this paper is to develop the initial distinction which I have drawn between recognition and appraisal respect into a more detailed and specific account of each. These accounts will not merely be of intrinsic interest. Ultimately I will use them to illuminate the puzzles with which this paper began and to understand the idea of self-respect.

IV

The most general characterization which I have given of recognition respect is that it is a disposition to weigh appropriately some feature or fact in one's deliberations. Strictly speaking, the object of recognition respect is a fact. And recognition respect for that fact consists in giving it the proper weight in deliberation. Thus to have recognition respect for persons is to give proper weight to the fact that they are persons.

One can have recognition respect for someone's feelings, for the law, for the judge (in a legal proceeding), for nature, and so on. In each case such respect consists in giving the appropriate recognition to a fact in one's deliberations about how to act. It is to consider appropriately, respectively, the fact that a person feels a certain way, that such and such is the law, that the person one is addressing is the judge, that the object one is confronting is part of nature, and so forth. To respect something in this way is just to regard it as something to be reckoned with (in the appropriate way) and to act accordingly.

On this very general notion of recognition respect, any fact which is something that one ought to take into account in deliberations is an appropriate object. As it stands, then, the notion has somewhat wider application than what we would ordinarily understand as respect, even of the recognition sort.

One rather narrower notion of recognition respect conceives of it as essentially a moral attitude. That is, some fact or feature is an appropriate object of respect if inappropriate consideration or weighing of that fact or feature would result in behavior that is morally wrong. To respect something is thus to regard it as requiring restrictions on the moral acceptability of actions connected with it. And crucially, it is to regard such a restriction as not incidental, but as arising because of the feature or fact itself. One is not free, from a moral point of view, to act as one pleases in matters which concern something which is an appropriate object of moral recognition respect. To have such respect for the law, say, is to be disposed to regard the fact that something is the law as restricting the class of actions that would be morally permissible. It is plainly this notion which we have in mind when we speak of respect for persons as a moral requirement. Accordingly, when I speak of recognition respect below, I shall be referring specifically to moral recognition respect.

There are attitudes similar to moral recognition respect, and referred to as respect, but which differ importantly. A boxer talks of having respect for his opponent's left hook and an adventurer of respecting the rapids of the Colorado. Neither regards the range of morally permissible actions as restricted by the things in question. Rather each refers to something which he fails to consider appropriately at his peril. What is restricted here is the class of prudent actions. Thus a careful crook who has no moral recognition respect for the law per se may still be said to have this sort of respect for the power that the law can wield. Here again we have the idea that the object of respect (or some feature or fact regarding it) is such that the class of "eligible" actions is restricted. But in this case the restriction is not a moral but a prudential one. Some people hesitate to use the word "respect" when speaking of such cases. That makes no difference. All that matters is that we understand what the attitude comes to and thus how it is like and unlike moral recognition respect.

As we are understanding recognition respect it includes a component of regard. To have recognition respect for something is to regard that fact as itself placing restrictions on what it is permissible for one to do. It is of course true that one can "be respectful" of something without having any respect for it (even of a recognitional sort). This will be the case if one behaves as one who does have respect would have behaved, but out of motives other than respect. For example, a person participating in a legal proceeding who in fact has no respect for the judge (i.e., for the position he occupies) may take great pains to be respectful in order to avoid a citation for contempt. Such a person will restrict his behavior toward the judge in ways appropriate to the role that he plays. But his reason for so doing is not that the mere fact of being the judge is itself deserving of consideration, but that the possibility of a contempt citation calls for caution.

Importantly, the sort of regard involved in recognition respect is a regard for a fact or feature as having some weight in deliberations about how one is to act. This is rather different from the sort of regard involved in appraisal respect.

V

The latter sort of respect is a positive appraisal of a person or his character-related features. As such it does not essentially involve any conception of how one's behavior toward that person is appropriately restricted.

I have distinguished appraisal respect for persons judged as persons from appraisal respect for persons assessed in more specific pursuits. As I shall later argue in more detail, those excellences of persons which are the appropriate grounds for appraisal respect are those which we delimit as constituting character. I shall also have something more specific to say by way of a rudimentary account of character.

Appraisal respect for a person as such is perhaps a paradigm of what people have in mind when they speak of moral attitudes. On the other hand, appraisal respect for persons judged in more particular pursuits need not be. The particular virtues or excellences of a particular pursuit may either be irrelevant or even bear negatively on an overall appraisal of the person judged as a person. To be highly respected as a tennis player, for example, one must demonstrate excellence in tennis playing which is not primarily excellence of character. At the very least one must be a good tennis player and that will involve having abilities which are in themselves irrelevant to an appraisal of the tennis player as a person. Even in such cases, however, respect for a person assessed in a particular pursuit seems to depend on features of his character (or his excellence as a person) in at least two ways.

To begin with, somebody may be an excellent tennis player without being a highly respected one. He may be widely acclaimed as one of the best players in the world and not be widely respected by his fellows— though they may (in the extended recognition sense) respect his return of serve, his vicious backhand, and so on. Human pursuits within which a person may earn respect seem to involve some set of standards for appropriate and inappropriate behavior within that pursuit. In some professions this may be expressly articulated in a "code of ethics." In others it will be a more or less informal understanding, such as that of "honor among thieves." To earn more respect within such a pursuit it is not enough to exercise the skills which define the pursuit. One must also demonstrate some commitment to the (evolving) standards of the profession or pursuit.

Even in a game like tennis one can lose the respect of other players by paying no attention to such standards of behavior. If a player constantly heckles his opponent, disputes every close call to throw off his opponent's concentration, or laughs when his opponent misses shots, then even if his skill is such that he would be capable of beating everyone else without such tactics, he is not likely to be respected as a tennis player. Thus, insofar as respect within such a pursuit will depend on an appraisal of the participant from the perspective of whatever standards are held to be appropriate to the pursuit, such respect will depend on a judgment to which excellences of character are thought relevant.

Note that exactly what aspect of the person's character is thought to be relevant in this instance is his recognition respect (or lack of it) for the standards of the pursuit.

Second, even when we attend to those features of a person which are the appropriate excellences of a particular pursuit and involve no explicit reference to features of character, the excellences must be thought to depend in some way or other on features of character. The point here is that purely "natural" capacities and behavior manifesting them are not appropriate objects of appraisal respect, although perhaps of recognition respect, even in the context of a fairly narrowly defined human pursuit.[9] If someone is capable of some feat (which may be widely admired) solely by virtue of, say, his height, then neither this feat nor the person's ability to perform it are appropriate objects of respect—just as one cannot respect an ant for its ability to carry comparatively large objects long distances to the anthill, though one may be appropriately amazed.

This is because it is almost never the case that human accomplishments are a result of simple natural ability. Talents and capacities of various sorts are prerequisites for various accomplishments, but almost invariably talents must be developed, disciplined, and exercised in the face of various obstacles, and this will call into play features of persons which we identify as a part of their character.

Which features of persons are properly regarded as features of their characters and hence as appropriate grounds for appraisal respect? Being resolute and being honest are character traits. Being prone to sneeze in the presence of pepper is not. But there are difficult cases as well. How about being irascible? Or being good natured? Or prudent? Discerning? Sensitive?

The notion of character (whether of persons or other things) seems to involve the idea of relatively long-term dispositions. But not all long-term dispositions of persons are held to be parts of their characters. The question then becomes, which such dispositions constitute character?

I have suggested that those features of persons which we delimit as constituting character are those which we think relevant in appraising them as persons. Furthermore, those features of persons which form the basis of appraisal respect seem to be those which belong to them as moral *agents*. This much Kantianism is, I think, at the core of the conception of the person which we generally hold to be relevant to appraisal respect. If this is true, then there may be other features of human beings, for example their capacity for affective sympathy, which are not encapsulated in the conception of the person which is relevant to appraisal respect. As Kant wrote, "Rational beings are designated 'persons' because their nature indicates that they are ends in themselves."[10] Those features of persons which are appropriate grounds for appraisal are their features as agents—as beings capable of acting on maxims, and hence, for reasons.[11] Thus, there may well be characteristics of human beings which are regarded as *human* excellences but which are not appropriate grounds for appraisal respect. For example, warmth in one's dealings with other human beings is regarded as an excellence of humanity, but may be irrelevant in the appraisal of persons which constitutes appraisal respect. Compare lack of warmth or being stiff in one's relations to others to deliberate cruelty as a ground for failing to have appraisal respect for someone. Of course, lack of personal warmth is an appropriate ground for failing to have appraisal respect for someone to the extent that we conceive such a lack to be the result of insufficient effort on the person's part. But insofar as we so conceive it, we regard it as a lack in the person's agency: an unwillingness to do what is necessary to treat others warmly.

If the appropriate conception of the person which is relevant to appraisal respect is that of a moral *agent*, then one would expect our notion of character to be likewise tied to such a conception. I think that this is indeed the case. Those dispositions which constitute character (at least as it is relevant to appraisal respect) are dispositions to act for certain reasons, that is, to act, and in acting to have certain reasons for acting. For example, honesty is a disposition to do what one takes to be honest at least partly for the reason that it is what honesty requires. Aristotle's theory of virtue and Kant's theory of the moral worth of actions both stress that what is appropriate to the assessment of persons is not merely what they do, but as importantly, their reasons for doing it.[12]

As it stands the conception of character as constituted by our dispositions to act for *particular* reasons is inadequate. This account captures such particular character traits as honesty, fairness, kindness, and the like. But there are other dispositions of persons which we hold to be part of their character, and thus relevant to appraisal respect, but which are not best thought of as dispositions to act for particular reasons. For example, we may fail to have appraisal respect for someone because we regard him to be weak of will or not sufficiently resolute. What is referred to here is not a disposition to act for any particular reason, but rather the higher-level disposition to act on what one takes to be the best reasons whatever they may be. Thus, the conception of character which is relevant to appraisal respect includes both rather more specific dispositions to act for certain reasons and the higher-level disposition to do that which one takes to be supported by the best reasons.

Two final points need to be made about appraisal respect. First, not every positive attitude toward a person on the ground of his or her character amounts to appraisal respect for that person. If I want to pull a bank heist and am looking for partners, I may look for someone who has no reservations about stealing (at least from banks) and who can be counted on to threaten violent action and, if need be, carry it out. Thus, I may have a favorable attitude toward such a person on the ground that he has those particular character traits. But my having that attitude toward such a person is not the same thing as my having appraisal respect for him for having those traits. This attitude fails of being appraisal respect in that my having it toward the person is *conditional* on those traits being such as to make him serve a particular purpose that I happen to have—heisting the bank. In order for the attitude toward the trait, or toward the person for having it, to constitute appraisal respect it must not be thus conditional on such an interest or purpose. We may employ some Kantian terminology here and say that it must be a *categorical* attitude, one which is unconditional on the fact that the traits in question happen to serve some particular purpose or interest *of mine.*[13]

The second point is that appraisal respect is something which one may have or fail to have for someone, *and* it is an attitude which admits of degree. One may respect someone more than someone else. When we speak of having or not having respect for someone what is implied is an appraisal of him as satisfactory with respect to the appropriate grounds. Many attitudes have this sort of structure. We speak alternatively of liking and not liking things as well as of liking something more than something else.

To sum up: Appraisal respect is an attitude of positive appraisal of a person either judged as a person or as engaged in some more specific pursuit. In the first case, the appropriate grounds are features of the person's character: dispositions to act for particular reasons or a higher-level disposition to act for the best reasons. In the second case, though features of character do not exhaust the appropriate grounds for appraisal respect, some such character traits will be relevant (recognition respect for the standards of a particular pursuit). Also, the other features which constitute the appropriate excellences of the pursuit must be related to traits of character in the way specified. In both cases, the positive appraisal of the person, and of his traits, must be categorical. It cannot depend on the fact that the person, because of his traits, serves an interest or purpose of one's own.

Appraisal brings into focus the idea of virtue. Much of recent moral philosophy has been exclusively concerned with the assessment of actions or social institutions. However, an account of the appropriate grounds for appraising persons, the virtues, is also a proper concern of moral philosophers.

VI

Since appraisal respect and recognition respect may both have persons, conceived of as such, as their objects, it is important to distinguish them as attitudes.

To have recognition respect for someone as a person is to give appropriate weight to the fact that he or she is a person by being willing to constrain one's behavior in ways required by that fact. Thus, it is to recognition respect for persons that Kant refers when he writes, "Such a being is thus an object of respect *and, so far, restricts all (arbitrary) choice.*"[14] Recognition respect for persons, then, is identical with recognition respect for the moral requirements that are placed on one by the existence of other persons.

This is rather different from having an attitude of appraisal respect for someone as a person. The latter is a positive appraisal of an individual made with regard to those features which are excellences of persons. As such, it is not owed to everyone, for it may or may not be merited. When it is, what is merited is just the positive appraisal itself.

To bring out the difference between recognition respect and appraisal respect for persons as such, consider the different ways in which the two attitudes may be said to admit of degree. When one person is said to be more highly respected as a person than someone else, the attitude involved is appraisal respect. One's appraisal of a person, considered as a person, may be higher than of someone else. Consider the instruction to order a list of persons according to one's respect for them. The natural way to respond would be to rank the persons in the light of one's appraisal of them as persons.

What sense can be given, however, to degrees of recognition respect? For example, a person might think that we should have more respect for people's feelings than for social conventions. Presumably what such a person thinks is that we ought to weigh other people's feelings more heavily than we do considerations of social convention. Insofar as we can give a sense to having more recognition respect for one thing than another it involves a disposition to take certain considerations as more weighty than others in deciding how to act. There is, of course, a kind of appraisal involved here. But it is not an appraisal of a person as such, but of the weight that some fact or feature ought to have in one's deliberations about what to do, and if all persons as such should be treated equally, there can be no degrees of recognition respect for them, although one may be a greater or lesser respecter of persons.

The confusion between appraisal respect and recognition respect for persons as such infects the account of respect for persons given by Cranor. He intends his account to capture the sort of respect that it is claimed persons are entitled to by virtue of being persons. Part of his account is the claim that for one person to have respect for another there must be some characteristic that the respected person is believed to have, and the possession of which is held to be a good thing from some point of view. Cranor fleshes this out with the following remarks: "In respecting a person we are giving him credit for having some trait or characteristic...the believed characteristic in virtue of which one respects a person must be believed to be a good-making characteristic of persons or contingently connected to a good-making characteristic of them."[15]

These remarks apply only to appraisal respect for persons. When one is appraising an individual as a person, those features which merit a positive appraisal are good-making characteristics of persons. Or to use the language of Cranor's other remark, they are to his credit as a person. On the other hand, to have recognition respect for a person as such is not necessarily to give him *credit* for anything in particular, for in having recognition respect for a person as such we are not appraising him or her as a person at all. Rather we are judging that the fact that he or she is a person places moral constraints on our behavior.

The distinction between appraisal respect and recognition respect for persons enables us to see that there is no puzzle at all in thinking both that all persons are entitled to respect just by virtue of their being persons and that persons are deserving of more or less respect by virtue of their personal characteristics.

Though it is important to distinguish between these two kinds of respect, there are connections between them. I will mention two in particular. First, there will be connections between the grounds of one's appraisal respect, or lack of it, for particular persons and the considerations which one takes as appropriate objects of recognition respect. For example, if one judges that someone is not worthy of (appraisal) respect because he is dishonest, one is committed to recognition respect for considerations of honesty. Our appraisal of persons depends on whether they show the appropriate recognition respect for considerations which merit it. The account of character brings this out. Second, the only beings who are appropriate objects of appraisal respect are those who are capable of acting for reasons and hence capable of conceiving of various facts as meriting more or less consideration in deliberation. Once again, so much is entailed by the account of character. Because of the particular sorts of reasons which are relevant to our assessment of character, we may say that the only beings who are appropriate objects of appraisal respect are those who are themselves capable of recognition respect, that is, of acting deliberately.

VII

Both recognition respect for persons as such and appraisal respect for an individual as a person are attitudes which one can bear to oneself. Accordingly, these two kinds of self-respect must be distinguished.

Consider the following remark of Virginia Held's: "For persons to acquiesce in the avoidable denial of their own rights is to lack self-respect."[16] What "self-respect" refers to here is recognition respect for oneself as a person. The passage is obviously false when we take it to refer to appraisal respect for oneself as a person. To acquiesce in the avoidable denial of one's rights is to fail to respect one's rights as a person. Exactly what such self-respect requires depends on what moral requirements are placed on one by the fact that one is a person.

It is recognition self-respect to which we appeal in such phrases as "have you no self-respect?" hoping thereby to guide behavior. This is not a matter of self-appraisal but a call to recognize the rights and responsibilities of being a person. As a person capable of recognition respect, one is liable to reflective appraisal of one's own behavior, and as such has a *stake* in it—that stake being appraisal self-respect or self-contempt.

One's behavior can express a lack of recognition self-respect in different ways. It may have a negative effect on one's ability to continue to function as a person. Such behavior is self-destructive, and therefore manifests a lack of appropriate regard for oneself as a person. If not actually self-destructive, behavior may be degrading in expressing a conception of oneself as something less than a person, a being with a certain moral status or dignity. Submitting to indignities, playing the fool, not caring about whether one is taken seriously and being content to be treated as the plaything of others may or may not be actually self-destructive but nevertheless manifests lack of self-respect.[17] Exactly what behavior is so regarded depends both on the appropriate conception of persons and on what behaviors are taken to express this conception or the lack of it. Certainly the latter is something which can vary with society, convention, and context.

One may give adequate recognition to the fact that one is a person and still have a rather low opinion of oneself as a person. People appraise themselves as persons, and the attitude which results from a positive appraisal is appraisal self-respect. Like appraisal respect generally, the appropriate grounds for appraisal self-respect are those excellences of persons which we delimit as constituting character.

It is important, therefore, to distinguish appraisal self-respect from other attitudes of appraisal which one can bear to oneself. One such attitude is that which we normally refer to as *self-esteem*.[18] Those features of a person which form the basis for his self-esteem or lack of it are by no means limited to character traits, but include any feature such that one is pleased or downcast by a belief that one has or lacks it. One's self-esteem may suffer from a low of opinion of, for example, one's appearance, temperament, wit, physical capacities, and so forth. One cannot always be what one would wish to be, and one's opinion of oneself may suffer. Such a failing by itself does not give rise to lack of appraisal self-respect, although it might suffer if one attributed the failing to a lack of will, an inability to bring oneself to do what one wanted most to do. So far forth the failing would be regarded as arising from a defect in one's character and not solely from, for example, a lack of physical ability.

The self-appraisal which constitutes self-respect is of oneself as a person, a being with a will who acts for reasons. The connection between respect and agency is striking. Recognition respect consists in being disposed to take certain considerations seriously as reasons for acting or forbearing to act. On the other hand, appraisal respect consists in an appraisal of a person on the basis of features which are a part of, or are based on, his or her character. And we conceive a person's character to consist in dispositions to act for certain sorts of reasons together with the higher order disposition to act for what one takes to be the weightiest reasons. Thus, the appropriate conception under which a person is appraised as worthy of respect is as a being capable of recognition respect for those things which are entitled to it. This is what connects the two kinds of respect. The one is the attitude which is appropriate for a person to bear, as an agent, toward those things which deserve his or her consideration in deliberation about what to do. The other is an attitude of appraisal of that person as just that sort of being, a being capable of expressing such consideration in action.

Notes

I am indebted to several of my colleagues at Chapel Hill, to Lawrence Crocker and Stephen Hudson, and to the editor of *Ethics* for help with this essay.

1. John Rawls, *A Theory of Justice* (Cambridge, Mass.: Harvard University Press, 1971); Bernard Williams, "The Idea of Equality," in *Moral Concepts*, ed. Joel Feinberg (Oxford: Oxford University Press, 1970), pp. 158–61; David Gauthier, *Practical Reasoning* (Oxford: Oxford University Press, 1963), pp. 119–20; R. S. Downie and Elizabeth Telfer, *Respect for Persons* (London: Allen & Unwin, 1969).
2. Kant, *Foundations of the Metaphysics of Morals*, trans. L. W. Beck (Indianapolis: Bobbs-Merrill Co., 1959), hereinafter FMM. See especially p. 46 (Ak. p. 428), where Kant claims that "rational beings are designated persons because their nature indicates that they are ends in themselves." See also *The Metaphysical Principles of Virtue*, trans. James Ellington (Indianapolis: Bobbs-Merrill Co., 1964), pp. 96–98, 112–14, 130–33. It is interesting to observe in this connection the rather different uses that various writers have made of the Kantian principle. Both Rawls and Robert Nozick invoke it in support of quite different substantive concedptions of justice; see Rawls, passim; and Nozick, *Anarchy, State, and Utopia* (New York: Basic Books, 1974), p. 32.
3. Gauthier, *Practical Reasoning*, p. 119; and Downie and Telfer, *Respect for Persons*, p. 29.
4. Williams, "Idea of Equality," p. 159; and Rawls, *A Theory of Justice*, p. 337.
5. Carl Cranor, "Toward a Theory of Respect for Persons," *American Philosophical Quarterly* 12 (October 1975): 303–19.
6. Though I prefer to put the point in this way, nothing crucial hangs on it. I could as well speak throughout of two different ways in which persons may be the object of respect.
7. Erving Goffman, *The Presentation of Self in Everyday Life* (Garden City, N.Y.: Doubleday & Co., 1959).
8. For a similar account of the moral sentiments see Rawls, *A Theory of Justice*, pp. 481–82.
9. On this point see Cranor, "Toward a Theory of Respect," p. 312.
10. FMM, p. 46.
11. Thus Kant: "Only a rational being has the capacity of acting according to the conception of laws, i.e., according to principles" (FMM, p. 29).
12. Aristotle argues that character is constituted by our dispositions to *choose*, where the notion of choice is held to involve the idea of picking an alternative on some grounds or other (see, e.g., *Nicomachean Ethics*, 1112a15, and Book VI, chaps. 12–13). Especially relevant here is Aristotle's distinction between a

"natural disposition" to virtuous qualities and virtue "in the strict sense" which involves a self-reflective habit of acting on the "right rule" (*Nicomachean Ethics*, 1144b1–28). Kant's famous discussion of the good will and the moral worth of actions as grounded in the "principle of the will," i.e., the agent's reason for acting, is in the first section of FMM.

13. See Kant's distinction between hypothetical and categorical imperatives in FMM, sec. 2. This idea of unconditionality on one's interests (i.e., on the fact that they are one's interests) is involved in Hume's notion of "moral sense" and Butler's notion of the "principle of reflection." David Hume, *A Treatise of Human Nature*, ed. L. A. Selby-Bigge (Oxford: Oxford University Press, 1967), p. 472; Joseph Butler, *Sermons* (New York: Liberal Arts Press, 1950), p. 27.

14. FMM, p. 428, emphasis added. Cranor is by no means alone in confusing recognition respect with appraisal respect. Hardy Jones faults Kant's identification of respect for persons with being disposed to treat persons as ends in themselves on the grounds that: "To respect a judge or a parent is not merely to behave in specific deferential (and thus 'respectful') ways. It is also to have a certain attitude toward them and to regard them in certain ways. 'To respect a person' is often properly used to mean 'to think well of him'" (Hardy Jones, *Kant's Principle of Personality* [Madison: University of Wisconsin Press, 1971], p. 75). If we interpret Kant as identifying recognition respect for persons as such with a willingness to treat persons as ends in themselves no such problem arises. See also Downie and Telfer, *Respect for Persons*, p. 18, for another instance of this confusion.

15. Cranor, "Toward a Theory of Respect," p. 312.

16. Virginia Held, "Reasonable Progress and Self-Respect," *Monist* 57 (January 1973).

17. Kant's writings on self-respect are especially useful here; see *Lectures on Ethics* (New York: Harper & Row, 1963), pp. 118–19. The place of respecting one's own autonomy is especially important in the Kantian idea of self-respect. For some illuminating comments about servility and its relation to a recognition of oneself as a person, see Thomas E. Hill, Jr., "Servility and Self-Respect," *Monist* 57 (January 1973): 87–104 [chapter 3 of this volume].

18. To some degree Rawls's remarks on self-respect in *A Theory of Justice* suffer from a confusion between self-respect and self-esteem. (This point is developed in Larry L. Thomas, "Morality and Our Self-Concept," *Journal of Value Inquiry* [12 (1978): 258–268].) Rawls's explicit account of self-respect (p. 440 [p. 125, this volume]) is very close to my notion of appraisal self-respect. In other places, however, it seems to be the more broadly based attitude of self-esteem that he has in mind. This is especially clear in his remarks on the

connection between natural shame and self-respect (p. 444 [p. 128, this volume]). It is an interesting qustion to what extent this conflation affects his account of self-respect as a primary good and his argument for the proposed principles of justice.

11

+

Is Self-Respect a Moral or a Psychological Concept?

+

Stephen J. Massey

Many people regard self-respect as important and worth investigating. For example, we can read George Bernard Shaw's play, *Mrs. Warren's Profession*, as an inquiry into the sources and nature of self-respect. Most people are likely to share the sentiment Mrs. Warren expresses when she replies to her daughter Vivie's query whether she might not (had she to do it over again) go to work at the Waterloo bar, or marry a laborer, or even go to work in a factory:

> (Indignantly) Of course not. What sort of mother do you take me for! How could you keep your self-respect in such starvation and slavery? And what's a woman worth? What's life worth? Without self-respect! [Act 2]

This essay was originally published in *Ethics* 93 (1983) by The University of Chicago Press. Copyright © 1983 by The University of Chicago. Reprinted by permission of the author and The University of Chicago Press.

Philosophers have recently focused on self-respect in the belief that it plays a crucial role in moral and political theory. For example, self-respect has an important place in the revived interest in the virtues. James Wallace claims that we can understand why character traits such as benevolence or generosity are virtues by seeing their importance for self-respect.[1] Self-respect might also be thought of as a virtue similar to courage or temperance.

Even more important is the widely accepted connection between self-respect and rights. In the past two decades, many philosophers have argued that rights are the central concept in political theory and have maintained that we can best understand their nature and value in terms of their contribution to self-respect.[2] Hugo Adam Bedau suggests that human rights are those rights which are central to people's being "free and self-respecting."[3] In *A Theory of Justice*, self-respect plays a crucial role in the argument for one of Rawls's most important conclusions, the priority of basic rights and liberties over the claims to distributive shares conferred by the difference principle.[4]

Despite the importance attributed to self-respect, philosophers have failed to face squarely and adequately a central question: is self-respect a psychological (or, as I shall say, subjective) or a moral (objective) notion? If it is a subjective notion, it is both necessary and sufficient for respecting oneself that one have a certain kind of favorable self-attitude, which can be adequately defined in psychological terms.[5] If it is an objective notion, then a self-respecting person must not simply value himself, but properly value himself, however the notion of "properly" valuing oneself is defined.

In the first two sections, I argue that there are two concepts of self-respect: subjective and objective. I begin in Section I by showing the plausibility of the view that self-respect is a subjective concept. Philosophers, however, have generally insisted that it is an objective concept, requiring that a person properly value himself. In Section II, I consider two arguments that seem to support the claim that self-respect is an objective concept. Though these arguments do not establish this claim, they direct our attention to the phenomenon of properly valuing oneself, which is distinct from, though related to, the phenomenon of valuing oneself referred to by the subjective concept. Since each concept points our attention to a distinct phenomenon, I speak of *two* concepts of self-respect. Their contents and relation justify calling them both concepts of self-respect, since each captures different features of our thought and discourse about respecting oneself.[6]

We can see the importance of determining whether self-respect is a subjective or an objective concept if we consider its philosophical role. In Section III, I describe two roles that philosophers have attributed to it: (1) self-respect can be used to explain the importance of moral notions such as rights and virtues, and (2) self-respect is the most important primary good. I argue that the subjective concept is well suited to meeting the first role, but ill suited for the second, while the objective concept may be well suited for the second role, but is ill suited for the first.

My argument that each concept of self-respect can meet only one of the roles assigned to self-respect parallels criticism of Rawls's theory of the good. Michael Teitelman, for example, argues that the thin theory of the good, which satisfies Rawls's desire for an Archimedean vantage point, may be inadequate to yield our judgments of the justice of institutions. Similarly, the "thin" psychological account of self-respect is inadequate to support the claim that self-respect is the most important primary good. According to Teitelman, however, the thicker theory of the good necessary to yield those judgments would violate Rawls's desire for a morally neutral starting point. Analogously, I argue that if we use self-respect to explain the importance of moral notions such as rights and virtues, we may have to reject the morally "thicker" objective account in favor of the morally neutral subjective account.[7] A proper understanding of the role of self-respect in moral and political philosophy therefore requires that we determine which concept is being used when a philosopher claims that self-respect is central to an argument.

I

According to the subjective account, a person who respects himself believes that he acts in accord with his conception of worthy behavior and has confidence that he will continue to do so. Since the subjective account is made plausible by examples of people who act in a particular way because they respect themselves, I begin by discussing such an example.

Consider Professor Andersen, who has spent her life studying and teaching Elizabethan literature, and is proud of her scholarship and the love of literature she has engendered in her students. The producers of "Whiz-Bang" quiz show, a midday extravaganza, make Professor Andersen a lucrative offer to appear as a guest, for they think that she will help to establish that their show is superior to its competitors. Out of respect for herself (and her profession), Professor Andersen refuses the offer. She is not adverse to the money. Rather, she believes that to use a reputation based on the pursuit and dissemination of learning to legitimate a television quiz show would demean herself and prostitute her values.

Professor Andersen's refusal involves her self-respect because she identifies with the activities of teaching and serving the university, and believes that there is value in meeting the obligations she regards as associated with these activities. For one of her colleagues, being a teacher might simply be a way of earning a living, and meeting the criteria that this person believes are associated with being a teacher may have no special significance for his self-respect. This person may have dissociated himself from the role of teacher and derive his self-respect from acting in accord with the standards he believes are provided by other features that he regards as of worth about himself. However, since Professor Andersen identifies with being a teacher, accepting the offer to appear on television would involve acting in a way which she believes is unworthy of her, and would therefore diminish her self-respect.[8]

This example suggests the following criteria of self-respect.

1. A person who respects himself identifies with a project, activity, or status which he regards as having value. Identification is important, since a person who does not identify with his projects or status may fail to respect himself, even if others regard them as having worth.

2. Identification with a project, activity, or status provides both a standard of worthy or appropriate conduct and a desire to act in accordance with it. This desire is central to the attitude involved when we speak of self-respect, since to respect oneself is to have certain attitudes and desires, especially the desire to act in a manner that one believes is worthy of oneself, and not simply to have certain beliefs about one's worth.

3. A person with self-respect believes that he has acted in accordance with his conception of what is worthy. For example, Professor Andersen's self-respect is grounded in her commitment to teaching and the university, and in her belief that she has acted consistently with what she regards as worthy about those projects.

4. A self-respecting person is confident that he will continue to act in accordance with his standards of worthy behavior. Were Professor Andersen, for example, to doubt her ability to refuse future quiz-show offers, she might suffer a loss of self-respect, despite having refused the "Whiz-Bang" offer.

These four criteria constitute an analysis of what I call the subjective concept of self-respect. They share one crucial feature with similar analyses that differ in the particular list of criteria or in the emphasis given to items on the list. This feature involves the claim that it is both necessary and sufficient that a self-respecting person have a certain kind of favorable attitude toward himself, an attitude that can be adequately described in psychological terms. According to this account, a self-respecting person's beliefs about and attitude toward himself need not have any particular content, nor must his actions meet any independent standards of worthiness or appropriateness. For example, we may disagree with Professor Andersen's claims that (1) there is something of worth about teaching and service to the university, or (2) appearing on a television game show is inconsistent with commitment to teaching and the university. Yet we can accept that she respects herself, provided we see that *she* believes her claims. This concept is subjective in the sense that respecting oneself simply involves having certain beliefs about and attitudes toward oneself, without reference to any independent standard.

Thinking of self-respect as a subjective concept requires that we separate two questions: (1) does a person respect himself? and (2) is the person's basis of self-respect appropriate (or morally good)? It is possible to give an affirmative answer to question 1, yet insist that a person's current bases of self-respect are morally unacceptable, and that he ought not to respect himself on those bases.

Some important philosophers and most psychologists who have written on self-respect (or self-esteem) accept the adequacy of this subjective account. The shorthand description that Rawls uses throughout *A Theory of Justice*—that a person with self-respect has a "sense of worth"—suggests that he holds a subjective account.[9] Rawls's definition of self-respect provides further evidence that he regards self-respect as a subjective phenomenon; he states: "We may define self-respect (or self-esteem) as having two aspects. First of all, as we noted earlier (§ 29), it includes a person's sense of his own value, his secure conviction that his conception of his good, his plan of life, is worth carrying out. And second, self-respect implies a confidence in one's ability, so far as it is within one's power, to fulfill one's intentions."[10]

Psychologists have explicitly endorsed a subjective account of self-esteem (self-respect). Morris Rosenberg defines self-esteem as "a positive or negative attitude toward...the self."[11] Stanley Coopersmith states that self-esteem "is a *personal* judgment of worthiness that is expressed in the attitudes the individual holds toward himself. It is a subjective experience which the individual conveys to others by verbal reports and other overt expressive behavior."[12]

Despite the intrinsic plausibility of the claim that self-respect is a subjective concept, and the support given to this claim by some philosophers and psychologists, most philosophers who have written about self-respect have denied that it can be adequately characterized in terms of a person's beliefs about and attitudes toward himself. These philosophers regard self-respect as an objective concept, and insist that a self-respecting person's attitudes and actions must satisfy independent standards of worthiness. Unlike defenders of the subjective account, proponents of this view insist that we cannot give an affirmative answer to the question whether a person respects himself until we have determined that the basis of the person's favorable attitude toward himself is appropriate (or morally good).

The philosophical roots of this view are in Kant, who maintains that a person shows respect for himself only by treating himself (and others) as an end in himself, that is, by determining his will in accordance with the moral law. According to Kant, the self-respecting person has the attitudes and performs the actions characteristic of the fully virtuous person.[13]

In recent writings on self-respect, there are many variants of the claim that self-respect is an objective concept. Elizabeth Telfer expresses one version when she states: "When we say that someone has self-respect, we are attributing to him qualities of independence, tenacity and self-control. A man cannot have conative self-respect if he does not have these; whether he himself values them or not is immaterial."[14] The most frequent version of objectivism involves the requirement that a self-respecting person believe himself to have equal basic rights and properly value his rights.[15] The rejection of a subjective account, by those authors who accept this version of objectivism, is most evident in the claim that whatever favorable attitudes toward himself a person may have, he does not have self-respect if he fails to recognize or properly value his equal basic rights.[16]

Objectivism regarding self-respect, and especially that version requiring that a self-respecting person properly value his equal basic rights has, however, been more often asserted than argued for. In the next section, I consider two arguments which might be used to support the claim that self-respect is an objective concept.

II

One way of supporting the claim that self-respect is an objective concept would be to describe examples of people who have the favorable attitude that defines self-respect according to the subjective account. If we hesitate to say that such people respect themselves, and if this hesitancy can only be explained on the grounds that self-respect is an objective concept, then we would have a basis for accepting that self-respect is an objective concept. We can begin by describing two such examples.

Consider a black person whom I will call an Uncle Tom, who accepts benefits such as basic decent treatment by others, which are his by right, as if they were a favor. His overly deferential and respectful behavior toward whites displays his conviction that he does not have the same moral rights as they do.[17]

Though this Uncle Tom does not believe that he has equal basic rights, there may be grounds for maintaining that he respects himself. Suppose he is an honest and trustworthy man, deeply concerned for the welfare and happiness of his family, friends, and others in his community. He may not regard his values and the fulfillment of his desires as having an importance equal to his master's, but he thinks they have some importance and respects himself for meeting what he regards as his obligations. Since he meets the criteria of the subjective account (mentioned above), we can say that he respects himself.[18]

Some people may doubt whether an Uncle Tom respects himself, despite the fact that he acts in accordance with his own conception of worthy behavior. Consider how the Uncle Tom would respond in various situations. When his qualifications for a job are as good as any white person's, but he cannot apply because the job is reserved for whites, he will not resent this unequal treatment. In other situations, he may accept as appropriate that the white population have rights, for example, to interrogate blacks at will, that no member of the black population possesses. Such an individual accepts a situation in which he, simply in virtue of being black, is thought worthy of less respect than others, simply in virtue of their not being black. Whatever attitudes toward himself the Uncle Tom may have as a result of acting worthily in other spheres, in his relations with whites he shows that he believes himself worthy of less respect than they.

As a second example, consider Skip, whose favorable attitude toward himself is based on having built the largest and most profitable hamburger chain in the country. In building this empire, Skip has relied on bribery of public officials, fraudulent land deals, and misrepresentation of his product. Even on the assumption that Skip satisfies the criteria of the subjective account, some people may hesitate to accept that someone whose life displays a gross disregard for morality and for basic principles of integrity respects himself.

A defender of the objective account may claim that what underlies the intuitions that the Uncle Tom and Skip fail to respect themselves are the beliefs that they have incorrect views about what is worthy of them, and that they act in ways that are unworthy. According to the objective account, it is necessary but not sufficient for self-respect that a person believe he acts in ways that he believes are worthy. In addition, the person must have correct views about his worth, and act in ways that are objectively worthy.[19] Regardless of the particular version of objectivism, a proponent of the view that self-respect is an objective concept must claim that, although people such as the Uncle Tom and Skip think that they respect themselves, in fact they do not, since their attitudes toward themselves, or their actions, fail to satisfy the appropriate objective standards.

Intuitions concerning examples such as the Uncle Tom and Skip do not, however, provide a sound basis for concluding that self-respect is an objective concept. Some people may accept without hesitation that the Uncle Tom and Skip respect themselves, or believe that the question whether they respect themselves is not pertinent. If so, there is simply nothing to be explained in terms that support the claim that self-respect is an objective concept. If there is hesitancy, it can be explained in terms that are consistent with self-respect's being a subjective concept. Hesitancy because of the Uncle Tom's failure to recognize and properly value his equal basic rights, for example, might plausibly be explained on the ground that the Uncle Tom's self-respect lacks certain morally desirable bases, and should therefore not be encouraged on its present bases. We can explain any uncertainty over whether Skip respects himself on the ground that his self-respect is not of a morally good sort, since it is based on acting in a morally objectionable way. These alternative explanations show that we do not have to accept the objectivist account of why we may hesitate to say that the people in these examples respect themselves.

A second way of defending the claim that self-respect is an objective concept involves establishing that *respect* is an objective concept, coupled with the claim that this creates a presumption that *self*-respect is also objective. To determine whether someone respects another person, we seem to consider whether he properly values the other person, and not simply whether he values him. If the condition that the respected person be properly valued is included in all accounts of respect, the asymmetry between respect and the subjective account of self-respect calls for an explanation.

Consider an example which seems to support the view that respect is an objective concept. The leaders of a community like Walden II believe that what is of worth about the people living there is their capacity for pleasure and pain. Since they regard freedom (or autonomy) as a myth, decisions about the majority are formulated by a few people, who have the power to implement them. Moreover, this small group manipulates the majority so that they believe that they are acting on their own unmanipulated choices.

A proponent of the subjective account of respect can accept that the leaders respect the other people in the community, since they believe that there is something of worth about them and treat them accordingly. We may, however, hesitate to accept that these leaders respect the other people.

A proponent of the view that respect is an objective concept must explain this hesitancy on the ground that the leaders do not respect the other members, since they fail to value their autonomy. According to an objective account, people (e.g., the leaders of my hypothetical community) respect others only if they properly value them. If autonomy is a feature of great worth about people, then someone who claims to respect people must properly value it. Though the leaders of the Walden II-like community think that they respect the other members, in fact they do not, since they fail to value their autonomy.

Just as with the examples involving self-respect, our intuitions concerning this example can be explained on grounds favorable to a subjective account of respect. There is a basis for claiming that the leaders respect the other people, since they hold appropriately favorable attitudes toward these members and treat them accordingly. However, since they fail to value their autonomy, their attitudes toward the other members are morally objectionable and should not be encouraged. From a moral viewpoint, their respect should be reestablished on grounds that include valuing the autonomy of these other members. According to a subjective account of respect, hesitancy concerning this example derives from the belief that the leaders' attitudes are morally unacceptable, rather than from the intuition that the leaders do not respect the other members.

This alternative explanation does not warrant the conclusion that the objective account fails to capture important features of our thought and discourse about respect. Indeed, it is these features that have most interested philosophers.[20] This alternative explanation does, however, defeat the presumption that, since respect is an objective concept, self-respect must also be objective.

Though the two arguments just considered are insufficient to establish that self-respect is an objective concept, they point to a phenomenon that is different from, though related to, the phenomenon referred to by the concept of self-respect developed in Section I. The phenomenon involved in a person's respecting himself, according to the subjective account, concerns having a favorable self-attitude (believing that he acts in accordance with his own conception of worthy behavior, etc.). The phenomenon suggested by the discussion in this section concerns properly valuing oneself.[21] In whatever way this latter phenomenon is to be analyzed, for example, in terms of belief in rights or in valuing the capacity to act morally, *properly* valuing oneself differs from valuing oneself *simpliciter*. Because these two phenomena are distinct, I speak of two concepts of self-respect. However, since both are commonly called self-respect, they are both concepts of self-respect.

The existence of these two concepts, each capturing part of our thought and discourse about self-respect, has not been sufficiently appreciated by philosophers. As a result, their arguments are flawed by attempting to use one concept of self-respect in a role that only a different concept could fulfill. In the final section, I will consider some examples of confusion about the role of self-respect resulting from failure to distinguish the two concepts.[22]

III

Philosophers have made two claims about the role of self-respect. (1) Self-respect can be used to explain the importance of moral notions such as rights and virtues (or to justify certain courses of action); and (2) self-respect is the most important primary good. I begin by discussing an example of the first role and showing why the objective concept is ill suited to fulfill this role.

In the past two decades, many philosophers have argued that rights are fundamental in moral and political theory. The importance they attribute to rights is evident from what Ronald Dworkin says concerning having a right. According to Dworkin, rights are so important that significant utilitarian advantages must be forgone when they can be obtained only by denying someone that to which he has a right. The claim that rights have this importance requires defense, for the question naturally arises why these utilitarian advantages should be forgone. Why should people have rights that act as trumps against such policies and institutions?[23] To answer questions such as these, philosophers have turned to self-respect, since it seemed that the importance of rights could be explained in terms of their contribution to self-respect. Joel Feinberg's "The Nature and Value of Rights" is one of the most important and prominent attempts to make this connection between self-respect and rights.

Feinberg argues that in a hypothetical community, "Nowheresville," in which people do not think of themselves (or others) as having rights, there would be no self-respect (or respect for others). Understanding the importance of rights requires appreciating the way in which they contribute to (or make possible) self-respect. Feinberg states:

> To think of oneself as the holder of rights is not to be unduly but properly proud, to have that minimal self-respect that is necessary to be worthy of the love and esteem of others. Indeed, respect for persons (this is an intriguing idea) may simply be respect for their rights, so that there cannot be the one without the other; and what is called "human dignity" may simply be the recognizable capacity to assert claims. To respect a person then, or to think of him as possessed of human dignity, simply *is* to think of him as a potential maker of claims.... More than anything else I am going to say, these facts explain what is wrong with Nowheresville.[24]

While Feinberg wants to explain the value of rights in terms of their contribution to self-respect, his account of self-respect presupposes the importance of rights. The difficulty in the argument is precisely the circularity of attempting to explain the importance of rights on the basis of an account of self-respect that presupposes their importance. We can see this more clearly by considering what Feinberg's argument requires and what he suggests as an analysis of self-respect.

Feinberg's thought experiment succeeds in explaining the importance of rights only if, prior to the introduction of rights into their community, the Nowheresvillians lack something that is essential to their respecting themselves. Two possibilities deserve consideration. The first consists in claiming that self-respect involves an attitude toward oneself other than simply believing oneself to have rights, but maintaining that belief in rights is necessary ("causally necessary") for having this attitude. On this possibility, the Nowheresvillians lack self-respect prior to the introduction of rights, even though self-respect is not itself defined in terms of beliefs in rights. Although this possibility is interesting and deserves consideration, it does not seem to be Feinberg's way of understanding the connection between self-respect and belief in rights.

Feinberg suggests that the reason the Nowheresvillians lack self-respect is that belief in rights is a conceptually (not causally) necessary condition of respecting oneself. Although he never explicitly says that a conceptually necessary condition of respecting oneself is that one believe oneself to have rights, he makes claims that strongly support this interpretation of his argument. We have seen that he says, for example, that "respect for persons…may simply be respect for their rights, so that there cannot be the one without the other." He shortly thereafter makes the stronger claim that "To respect a person…simply *is* to think of him as a potential maker of claims [i.e., as someone who has rights]." These statements about what is involved in respecting others strongly suggest that respecting oneself simply is thinking of oneself as a potential maker of claims, that is, thinking of oneself as having rights. Once we see how Feinberg understands self-respect, we can appreciate why he thinks the Nowheresvillians lack self-respect and why he regards the thought experiment involving Nowheresville as an appropriate device for explaining the importance of rights.

If, as Feinberg suggests, respecting oneself simply is believing oneself to have rights, then the importance of respecting oneself must derive from the prior importance of having rights. One cannot then use the importance of self-respect (understood in the terms Feinberg suggests) to explain the importance of rights. Circles of concepts may be virtuous when the circle is large enough and the concepts may consequently mutually illuminate each other. The tightness of the circle between self-respect (understood as requiring belief in rights) and rights ensures that the circularity to which I have drawn attention is of the nonvirtuous variety. Someone who knows that he values self-respect might be convinced of the value of rights by being shown their analytic connection to self-respect. This psychological fact, however, differs from explaining the importance of rights in terms of a concept of self-respect that is itself analytically connected to rights.

Given the possibility of circularity, the discussion of Feinberg's argument shows that, if we use the objective concept to explain the importance of a particular moral notion, then the concept must be independent of that moral notion. This example does not preclude the possibility that some non-rights version of the objective concept might avoid the charge of circularity and have a role in explaining rights. It is not obvious, however, that any of the other versions of an objective concept of self-respect (mentioned above) could perform the role that Feinberg requires. The argument also does not show that the rights version of objectivism might not have a role in explaining moral notions other than rights or in justifying a course of action. In "Reasonable Progress and Self-Respect," for example, Virginia Held uses, in a noncircular manner, a rights version of the objective concept in an argument concerning what constitutes reasonable progress toward equality for women.

No one use of self-respect, then, is sufficient to show the necessity of a concept of self-respect that is independent of all moral notions. Nevertheless, the fact that philosophers have thought that self-respect provides a basis for understanding many different moral notions—rights, virtues, and so on—shows why it might be desirable that the concept of self-respect used in this kind of argument be independent of all moral notions, that is, not be a version of the objective concept. If the concept used is independent of all moral notions, then we avoid the risk that the concept of self-respect used on one occasion, to explain the importance of one moral notion, presupposes another moral notion, the importance of which, on another occasion, we might also want to explain in terms of its contribution to self-respect.

The subjective concept of self-respect is independent of all moral notions in just this way. Since a person's respecting himself, according to the subjective concept, is entirely a psychological phenomenon, the importance of self-respect (on the subjective account) does not presuppose the importance of any moral notion. The attempt to use self-respect to explain, in a noncircular manner, the importance of moral notions such as rights and virtues therefore points us toward the subjective concept. In the remainder of this section, I will show that the subjective concept, though especially suited for the first role attributed to self-respect, cannot meet the conditions of the other role, that of being the most important primary good.

We first need to know what is involved in the claim that self-respect is the most important primary good. According to Rawls, primary goods "...are things which it is supposed a rational man wants whatever else he wants."[25] Rawls also suggests some grounds for thinking that self-respect is a primary good: "Without it nothing may seem worth doing or if some things have value for us, we lack the will to strive for them. All desire and activity becomes empty and vain, and we sink into apathy and cynicism."[26] Considerations such as these may incline us to the view that self-respect is a primary good.[27] But the claim is not that self-respect is *a* primary good, but that it is *the most important* primary good.

Self-respect might be the most important primary good were it true that without it other goods have no value, or that one could enjoy nothing else without self-respect. Yet, neither of these claims is true. It is false that Rawls's other primary goods, for example income and opportunities, have no value for a person who has little or no self-respect. It is sure-ly an excess of rationalism to claim that a person cannot enjoy going to the beach or to a baseball game unless he respects himself.

We might try a weaker version of the claim that self-respect is the most important primary good, according to which it is that good without which other goods diminish in value. This weaker version may be true.[28] No matter how much wealth and income, or how many opportunities a person has, his enjoyment of these goods is likely to be diminished if he lacks self-respect. Even if the claim is true, we cannot base the primacy of self-respect on the claim that without it other goods diminish in value, since this is equally true of goods other than self-respect. Consider health, which is plausibly regarded as a primary good despite its not being included on Rawls's list. Just as in the case of self-respect, the value of a person's wealth, income, and opportunities is likely to be diminished if he lacks health, since medical problems impair his ability to enjoy these other goods.[29]

Whereas on the first way of understanding the claim that self-respect is the most important primary good, the claim is false, on a weaker inter-pretation, it is not the only good without which one's enjoyment of other goods diminishes. We therefore have reason to suspect the truth of the claim that self-respect is the most important primary good. We can, how-ever, approach the problem by considering the implications of this claim. We can then see more clearly why the subjective concept is inadequate to meet the requirements of the second role.

If self-respect is the most important primary good, this fact would have important implications for our assessment of social, political, and eco-nomic institutions. There are many ways of interpreting these implica-tions, some of which make the claim too weak, while others make it too strong.[30] A plausible interpretation is that a society promoting self-respect (on the subjective account) to a greater extent than another soci-ety is to be preferred, even when the gains in terms of self-respect are achieved at the cost of a significant loss of other important goods. Moreover, gains in terms of other primary goods cannot, to the same extent, outweigh losses in terms of self-respect. The following compari-son of two societies suggests that the subjective concept cannot support this implication.

In society A, people are born into an established social hierarchy and receive an education that encourages them to accept their position and to believe that there is worth in carrying out the obligations attached to it. The positions in the hierarchy are well differentiated and circumscribed, in the sense that occupants of particular slots develop only a few of their capacities. The members of this society nevertheless have high self-respect, subjectively conceived, since they believe that what they are doing is worthwhile, and they have been raised to have the competencies necessary to carry out successfully their tasks. This high self-respect is achieved at the cost of their not autonomously choosing the course of their own development, and of their being able to experience only a very limited range of possibilities.

In society B, people are free to determine their own course of life and have the opportunity to develop as many possibilities as they choose and are capable of pursuing. Among the consequences of this freedom are a greater likelihood of failure in what they have chosen to do and a greater sense of responsibility for having determined their own plan of life. The net effect is that the members of society B have, on average, a lower respect for themselves than the members of society A.

If self-respect (on the subjective account) is the most important primary good, then society A must be morally preferable. Yet it is not clear that this is true. We may believe that the gains, in terms of autonomy and opportunities for development, that occur in society B outweigh the decline in self-respect. If so, then even if gains in self-respect sometimes outweigh losses in terms of other goods (as perhaps in society A), self-respect is not the most important primary good. For the truth of this claim requires that it not be the case that gains in primary goods other than self-respect be capable of outweighing significant declines of self-respect. This example therefore suggests that even if self-respect, conceived as a psychological phenomenon along the lines sketched in Section I, is a primary good, it is not the most important primary good.

The claim that self-respect is the most important primary good might be salvaged by arguing that it is respecting oneself, according to one of the versions of an objective account, that is the most important primary good. Suppose we accept the version of objectivism requiring that a self-respecting person properly value his capacity to act morally and act in ways characteristic of the virtuous person. We might then conclude that a society promoting self-respect (on this understanding) to a greater degree than another society is preferable, even if the society with high self-respect has significantly less of other primary goods, for example, income or health. Moreover, we might conclude that gains in terms of these other primary goods were not, to the same extent, capable of compensating for a decline in self-respect (on the objective account we are now considering). I am not proposing that these conclusions are acceptable. My point is rather that even if they are, they show the necessity of acknowledging that it is not self-respect according to the subjective account that is the most important primary good. The objective concept may be adequate to satisfy this second role. However, we saw that this concept cannot meet the first role assigned to self-respect when we established the desirability of a concept that is completely independent of moral notions.

While using a version of the objective account to explain moral notions exposes us to danger of circularity in argumentation, the conclusion here is that the subjective concept cannot be the most important primary good. These examples of the problems that arise from attempting to use one concept of self-respect in a role that only the other concept could fulfill show the importance of distinguishing the objective and the subjective concepts if we are to achieve a proper understanding of the role of self-respect in moral and political theory.

Notes

Versions of this article were read at SUNY Stony Brook, Colgate University, Marquette University, and at a conference on self-respect and sex roles at St. Olaf College. I am grateful for comments I received at these presentations, as well as for the support of my colleagues at Case Western Reserve University, where I wrote the article during my tenure as a Mellon Fellow. I would especially like to thank Christopher S. Hill, T. H. Irwin, David Lyons, Richard Miller, and Martha Ratnoff for their suggestions.

1. James Wallace, *Virtues and Vices* (Ithaca, N.Y.: Cornell University Press, 1978), pp. 152–58.
2. See Joel Feinberg, "The Nature and Value of Rights," *Journal of Value Inquiry* 4 (1970): 243–57.
3. Hugo Adam Bedau, "The Right to Life," *Monist* 52 (1968): 550–72, p. 571.
4. John Rawls, *A Theory of Justice* (Cambridge, Mass.: Belknap Press, 1971), esp. sec. 82.
5. Rawls, e.g., speaks of this self-attitude as involving a "sense of one's worth" (ibid, pp. 178, 440 [p. 126, this volume]).
6. The two concepts do not represent two conceptions of the same concept, in the sense that there is agreement about what the concept of respect involves, but differing conceptions of when respect ought to be conferred. In the first place, there is disagreement over what respect involves. More important,

unless we accept relativism, only one of the conceptions of a concept can be correct. (In our case, only one of the theories about when respect ought to be conferred can be correct.) (For a discussion of the concept/conception distinction, cf. Rawls, pp. 9–10, and Ronald Dworkin, *Taking Rights Seriously* [Cambridge, Mass.: Harvard University Press, 1977], pp. 134–36.) Nor can these two concepts be adequately described as involving two analyses of the same concept. Were there only one phenomenon, then the concept referring to this one phenomenon would have only one correct analysis. Since there are two phenomena, both commonly called self-respect, it is appropriate that there are two concepts of self-respect, each of which reflects different aspects of ordinary usage.

7. See "The Limits of Individualism," *Journal of Philosophy* 69 (1972): 545–56, esp. sec. IV; cf. Adina Schwartz, "Moral Neutrality and Primary Goods," *Ethics* 83 (1973): 294–307.

8. For an interesting discussion of identification and roles, cf. Bernard Williams, *Morality* (New York: Harper & Row Publishers, 1972), pp. 51–58.

9. Cf. Rawls, *A Theory of Justice*, pp. 178, 545.

10. Ibid., p. 440 [p. 125, this volume].

11. Morris Rosenberg, *Society and the Adolescent Self-Image* (Princeton, N.J.: Princeton University Press, 1965), p. 30.

12. Stanley Coopersmith, *The Antecedents of Self-Esteem* (San Francisco: W. H. Freeman & Co., 1967), p. 5. Philosophers may object to Rawls's identification of self-respect and self-esteem, and to my use of definitions of self-*esteem* to support the subjective account of self-*respect*. (Cf. Edward Kent, "Respect for Persons and Social Protest," in *Social Ends and Political Means*, ed. Ted Honderich [London: Routledge & Kegan Paul, 1976], pp. 29–47; and Larry Thomas, "Morality and Our Self-Concept," *Journal of Value Inquiry* 12 [1978]: 268–78.) Unless the arguments of these philosophers be understood as stipulating different definitions for self-respect and self-esteem, they seem insufficient to establish that much of philosophical importance hinges on rigorously distinguishing them. In a recent article, David Sachs notes some differences between self-respect and self-esteem. Had his article appeared earlier, I would have discussed it at greater length. For now I will confine myself to the observation that the title of Sach's article suggests that something of philosophical (or moral) importance turns on distinguishing self-esteem and self-respect. Sachs, however, provides no hint as to what hinges on making the distinction for which he argues. David Sachs, "How To Distinguish Self-Respect from Self-Esteem," *Philosophy and Public Affairs* 10 (1981): 346–60.

13. Cf "Concerning Duties to Oneself," pp. 77–81 of Immanuel Kant's *The*

Metaphysical Principles of Virtue, pt. 2 of *The Metaphysics of Morals*, trans. James Ellington (Indianapolis:Bobbs-Merrill Co., 1964). I discuss Kant's views more fully in "Kant on Self-Respect," *Journal of the History of Philosophy* 21 (1983): 57–73.

14. "Self-Respect," *Philosophical Quarterly* 18 (1968): 114–21, p. 118 [chapter 5 of this volume, p. 112]. Telfer's rejection of a subjective account of self-respect, evident in the last clause of the above quotation, is also displayed when she maintains: "An intelligent person is saddled with standards which do not apply to everyone but which he cannot fall below without degradation [i.e., losing self-respect], whether or not *he* values his intelligence" (ibid, p. 119 [p. 113, this volume]).

15. Virginia Held, "Reasonable Progress and Self-Respect," *Monist* 57 (1973): 12–27, p. 22; Feinberg, "The Nature and Value of Rights," p. 252; Bernard Boxill, "Self-Respect and Protest," *Philosophy and Public Affairs* 6 (Fall 1977): 58–69, p. 69 [chapter 4, this volume]; and Thomas Hill, Jr., "Servility and Self-Respect," *Monist* 57 (1973): 87–104 [chapter 3, this volume].

16. Cf. Thomas, "Morality," p. 273 and Hill, "Servility and Self-Respect," sec. 1.

17. I take this example, with considerable modification, from Hill.

18. We can also make sense of the Uncle Tom's doing something that would diminish his self-respect. Were he to betray a friend or relative, or breach an important trust with another person, he might suffer a loss of self-respect.

19. The variants of the view that self-respect is an objective concept (mentioned above) can be understood as attempts to specify what is required to properly value oneself, or to act worthily in the objective sense. More needs to be said about this objective notion of worthiness. It is not clear, for example, that every failure to act worthily (in the objective sense) involves a moral failing. We might think that the Uncle Tom acts unworthily (and thereby displays a lack of self-respect) without regarding his so acting as displaying a moral defect. See in this regard Elizabeth Telfer, who states: "On many views of morality, not all types of action which might be called 'unworthy of a man *qua* man' fall within the scope of morality. For example, they may concern no one other than the agent, while morality may be held to be by definition interpersonal" (Telfer, "Self-Respect," pp. 115–16 [p. 110, this volume]). For an argument that the Uncle Tom actions do display a moral defect, cf. Hill, "Servility and Self-Respect."

20. Cf. Ronald Dworkin, "Reverse Discrimination," in *Taking Rights Seriously*.

21. In speaking of "properly valuing oneself," I do not intend to commit myself to any claims about the existence and nature of this phenomenon. I only draw attention to the fact that certain ways of thinking and talking about

self-respect presuppose the existence of the phenomenon of properly valuing oneself.

22. My argument in the final section does not strictly depend on accepting that there are two concepts of self-respect. The argument could be reformulated in terms acceptable to someone who thought there was only a subjective concept of self-respect; such a person need only substitute "properly valuing oneself" wherever I speak of self-respect's being an objective concept.

23. Cf. Dworkin, introduction to *Taking Rights Seriously*.

24. Feinberg, pp. 252–53. I cannot consider all the interesting and controversial claims that Feinberg makes in this article. However, one apparent gap in the argument deserves notice. Feinberg wants to explain the moral superiority of a society which has rights in the following way: a society with rights is one in which people believe that they have rights (are in a position to make claims against each other, etc.), and therefore one in which people have self-respect. Strictly speaking, the argument from the importance of self-respect explains the significance of people's believing that they have rights and not the significance of rights *simpliciter*. This gap would be filled if it were a necessary condition of people's believing that they have rights that they actually have them. This claim may be true, but it certainly needs to be argued for. An alternative strategy would be to maintain that self-respect requires the justified belief that one has rights. Although this may be true, we again need an argument to show that it is. Moreover, if it is true, it only makes more apparent the circularity of Feinberg's argument.

25. Rawls, *A Theory of Justice*, p. 92.

26. Ibid.

27. Religious views which regard self-abnegation in a favorable light may call into question the claim that self-respect is a primary good. A more complete discussion of this claim would require a response to such views.

28. The claim may not seem true in all cases, since a person's lack of self-respect may provide a reason for his caring even more about other primary goods, e.g., income and wealth. This psychological fact is compatible with the claim that without self-respect other goods diminish in value, since goods may increase in significance (or concern) to a person, without a compensating increase in their value to him, in the sense of providing more enjoyment. (This difficulty was suggested by Richard Wasserstrom at the St. Olaf conference on self-respect and sex roles.)

29. A similar argument can be made for income and wealth. In a society in which the worth of one's rights and liberties depends on economic position, a person who lacks significant income and wealth will find his enjoyment of his rights and liberties diminished.

30. One possibility is that, in determining a society's moral acceptability, it is necessary to consider the consequences for people's self-respect of its major institutions. This interpretation of the implication of self-respect's being the most important primary good seems too weak. In determining a society's moral acceptability, we might also think it necessary to consider its consequences for other goods, e.g., health and opportunities for access to political and economic power, not claimed to be the most important primary good. The claim that, since self-respect is the most important primary good, a society that promotes self-respect to a greater degree would, ceteris paribus, be preferred, is similarly too weak. It is possible to claim that, ceteris paribus, a society promoting its members' health to a greater extent should be preferred, without accepting that health is the most important primary good. Other attempts to explain the implications of self-respect's being the most important primary good are too strong. It might be claimed that since self-respect is the most important primary good, a society promoting self-respect to a greater extent than another society is to be preferred, no matter what the costs in terms of other goods. As opposed to this, self-respect might be the most important primary good, even if gains in terms of self-respect did not outweigh losses of all other goods in determining a society's moral acceptability.

12

✛

Self-Respect and Autonomy

✛

Diana T. Meyers

I. A Portrait of Self-Respect

On a steamy July afternoon at a bus stop in downtown Manhattan, a homeless woman approached each person who came to wait for the bus. In her hand, she clutched a transfer which she offered to sell for fifty cents. Bus transfers are given out gratis as one boards New York City buses and pays the one dollar fare. They entitle passengers to a free ride on any bus on an adjoining, perpendicular line. To enable the bus drivers to quickly identify cheaters trying to pass transfers from distant or parallel routes, the transfers are coded. But no one except the drivers bothers to study the system of codes. So no one standing at the bus stop, losing patience in the summer heat, had any idea what transfer the drivers on the Sixth Avenue line would accept.

The woman who was trying to sell her transfer for fifty cents was offering her prospective customers a ride at half price. However, one person after another turned her down. Some of them said they doubted that the transfer was any good on the Sixth Avenue line. To these accusations, she replied, "It's good. I wouldn't be selling it if it wasn't good." But no one was persuaded until a young man dressed in a plaid shirt, well-worn jeans, and penny loafers appeared. When she offered him the transfer, he not only said he would buy it, but he also insisted on paying her the dollar it was worth to him. At first, she refused the additional money, but finally, she took it and left.

At that, a woman standing near the youth crowed, "She finally found a sucker!" Disingenuously, she added, "I hope it's good." "It doesn't matter," the youth quietly replied. Several more passengers gathered before the bus came. When at last we all boarded the bus, the youth handed his transfer to the driver and took a seat.

I have related this story because I think it illustrates the concept of self-respect in action. Both the homeless woman and the youth seem to me exemplars of self-respect, and I shall use them to explicate this concept in a preliminary fashion.

In different ways, the homeless woman and the youth displayed a fine sense of proportion in regard to their own desires and those of other people. When people declined to purchase her transfer, the homeless woman did not persist. She moved away and waited for another customer to arrive. She did not make a pest of herself. The youth, I am sure, preferred not to lose a dollar, but he balanced the urgency of the homeless woman's need against his desire and saw that her need was more pressing. Maybe he was taking a gamble on her good faith, but the fact that he refused to buy the transfer at the bargain rate she proposed suggests to me that he simply wanted her to have a little money. Self-respecting people are capable of putting other people ahead of themselves.[1]

Self-respect by no means requires overbearing self-assertion, but neither are human doormats paragons of self-respect. The homeless woman and the youth would not stand for such insults. She proclaimed her honesty, and he rejected the label "sucker." A number of philosophers have contended that the hallmark of self-respect is the self-respecting person's refusal to submit passively to victimization. People who sheepishly acquiesce in violations of their rights lack self-respect, as do people who do not resent others' gratuitous indifference to their concerns.[2]

But self-respect is not solely a defensive posture. The homeless woman had found a way to ease her poverty, and the work she had improvised for herself showed self-respect. She retained her dignity through an open and aboveboard enterprise that enabled her to give people something in return for their assistance. Likewise, the youth acted on his compassion and, despite the jeer of his neighbor, showed no sign of embarrassment. Indeed, his very lack of self-importance coupled with his undramatic, yet decisive conduct was a reproach to everyone who had thought him a fool. Needlessly secretive or dissimulating people are deficient in self-respect, for they conceal or betray themselves.[3] Put positively, satisfying one's desires and pursuing one's plans evidence self-respect, for such conduct affords the individual's capacity for agency its rightful scope.[4] Engaging in one's preferred activities furnishes an outlet for one's attributes and an affirmation of the worth of one's self.

Closely related to the self-respecting person's commitment to his or her projects is the link between maintaining personal standards and self-respect. In my story, both the figures uphold moral values—honesty, on the part of the homeless woman; charity, on the part of the youth. Although moral standards are central to self-respect, non-moral standards are by no means peripheral. The homeless woman, though plainly destitute, was remarkably clean compared to most of the other homeless people one encounters on the streets of New York. What might seem to those of us who take baths for granted a small defiance of the street person's plight may well, in her eyes, have been essential to preserve her dignity. People may have settled convictions about what sorts of behavior are debasing to them as persons—for example, they might regard the titillation of pornography as beneath them.[5] Or they may identify with enterprises which in turn set standards for those associated with them—for example, a scholar might consider displaying her knowledge on a television quiz show a desecration.[6] These need not be moral standards. The people who embrace them may not think less of those who do not share their views; however, they would feel themselves diminished if they abrogated these strictures.

Adopting and upholding principles of this kind brings the complexity of human agency to prominence. Human agency is not merely a matter of choosing actions; it also comprises self-chosen constraints on choice. To make only first-order decisions to do this or that, then, is to neglect an important potentiality inherent in personhood, hence to show disrespect for the fact that one is a person. But, perhaps more importantly, the possibility of establishing and adhering to personal standards explains one way in which self-respect shields people from others' adverse opinions. Both the homeless woman and the youth had ready answers to others' taunts. Although the difficulty of retaining one's self-respect in the face of other people's manifest contempt is evident, one of the most compelling reasons to think self-respect good is that it can protect the individual from others' scorn—from derision as well as from icy avoidance. Though an unreasoned affirmative attitude toward oneself could conceivably stand one in good stead, a reflective commitment to a set of values or projects should prove more reliable. For such convictions enable one to justify oneself—alone in the mirror, as well as in the company of others.

I have described only the outward signs of self-respect, which I could observe as I watched the events at the bus stop unfold. Still, the sine qua non of self-respect is what is unobservable, the basic attitude one bears to oneself. It is tempting to characterize this attitude by negation. Self-respecting people are not dissatisfied with their self-images and disheartened by their inability to improve them; they do not have major qualms about their personalities, they do not constantly regret their conduct. All of this is true. Yet, self-respect is not simply the absence of self-contempt.

Self-respect is a standing favorable attitude toward oneself predicated upon a sense of one's own worth as a person.... There was nothing in the conduct of the homeless woman or the youth that would have led me to suspect that either of them lacked a favorable reflexive attitude nor that this attitude was anchored in anything other than their sense of their worth as agents. To some extent, this positive view of oneself seems to take the form of an emotional primitive—one simply feels this way about oneself, and, like a happy disposition, this feeling can override reasons to the contrary. But, in addition, self-respect is amenable to rationally grounded support and sabotage. One may consider one's failings more or less grievous, and one may consider oneself more or less deserving of respect. Still, self-respect is not so sensitive to the individual's reflexive approval or disapproval as to be like the barometric pressure, rising and falling with the weather. Since self-respect reflects a cumulative assessment of one's worth as a person, trivial pratfalls and exceptional misadventures are discounted. Thus, self-respect is stable.[7] If the homeless woman were permanently reduced to begging or stealing, she might gradually lose her self-respect, but she could retain her self-respect, one would hope, if she occasionally had to resort to these practices.

Self-respecting people have due regard for their dignity as agents. Not obsequious, not imperious, they neither belittle nor overrate the importance of their own inclinations. They take their own desires to be worthy of consideration, but they give these desires only their proper weight in deliberation. Conscious of their powers of choice and of the significance of choosing well, self-respecting people adhere to personal as well as moral standards. Neither their own momentary impulses nor faddish social currents buffet them about. Though self-respecting people are not rigid, their sense of their own identity precludes chameleon-like change.

Self-respect is not volatile. For the most part, it endures. Yet, it is clear that self-respect can be strengthened or weakened. People can find themselves improving, stagnating, or degenerating; they can discover that they are better or worse than they had realized. Though steady, then, self-respect is not fixed.

This observation points to the question of how autonomy is related to fluctuations in self-respect. After providing a structural analysis of the concept of respect, I shall urge that autonomy is related to self-respect in two main ways. First, low proficiency in the skills of autonomy can attenuate self-respect. Though virtually all people have sufficient autonomy competency to form a base for self-respect, the self-respect of minimally autonomous people is compromised, and it is less intrinsically good than that of more autonomous individuals. Second, the exercise of autonomy competency stabilizes self-respect on a secure psychological foundation. But inasmuch as compromised self-respect is psychologically precarious, it is not as instrumentally good for the individual as uncompromised self-respect. Whereas nonautonomous people have trouble keeping serious disappointments in perspective, autonomous people are not prone to the self-recrimination and prolonged despair that unfavorable outcomes or other people's disapproval can precipitate. Since the remedy for compromised self-respect is proficiency in autonomy skills, socializing some people to be minimally autonomous inflicts a serious injury on them.

II. Compromised and Uncompromised Respect

Recent philosophical discussions of self-respect divide into two competing camps—one advocating a moral view of self-respect, the other advocating a psychological view. The former approach construes self-respect as a moral duty to uphold one's dignity, a duty one owes to oneself in virtue of one's personhood. This duty is a complex one that requires people to resist affronts to their dignity or attacks on their rights and to adhere to moral standards in their own conduct. Thus focusing on the moral propriety of self-respect, this view denies that self-respect can be excessive, unjustified, or undesirable.[8] The alternative view treats self-respect as a psychological phenomenon that gains support from whatever behavior one engages in that one happens to deem worthy of oneself. Although this psychological variant of self-respect requires fulfilling one's plans and measuring up to one's ideals, one's plans and ideals are relative to individual beliefs and desires. In this view, self-respect has no special moral import, for it is compatible with patently immoral conduct.[9] Furthermore, since one can be deluded about one's success, one can respect oneself more than one should.

Supporters of the moral view dismiss the alternative account by banishing anomalous forms of self-respect—those that violate moral imperatives—to the purportedly psychological category of self-esteem. What appears to be respect for vice is really misguided esteem.[10] Meanwhile, supporters of the psychological view explain away intuitions that support the moral view by denying that these intuitions stem from the internal logic of the concept. When we seem to question the self-respect of a vicious person, we are really questioning the goodness of this person's self-respect.[11]

Though the moral account and the psychological account conflict, neither of them is unattractive. Yet, since neither of them is compelling alone, I blended elements from both in my "portrait" of self-respect. On the one hand, the moral account captures our recognition that there can be something disturbing about some forms of self-respect, but it does so at the cost of denying that these degenerate forms of self-respect can correctly be called self-respect. The latter claim seems merely stipulative. In the hands of this theory, self-respect withers into a dry little knot of ethical fastidiousness. On the other hand, the psychological account excludes nothing that people ordinarily classify as self-respect, but in so doing, it denies that self-respect is intrinsically desirable. The latter conclusion is counter-intuitive. Here, the healthy self-regard that is the juice of self-respect is scrutinized and found morally dubious. Each of these accounts seems rather artificial, for neither is faithful to the whole range of phenomena associated with self-respect.

In what follows, I shall present a unified account of self-respect. An advantage of the account that I shall offer is that it explains why neither the moral nor the psychological view of self-respect can be dismissed and also why neither of these accounts is altogether satisfying. I shall urge that respect is a triadic relation, but that there are forms of respect in which one component of the triad is defective. Proponents of the moral view of self-respect deny the latter claim, and proponents of the psychological view discount the significance of the defective component in the latter forms of self-respect.

In general, respect can be a mystifying phenomenon because it comprises a subjective component—an attitude—and two objective components—conduct and the object it is aimed at—and because these three components can be at odds. One's respectful attitude may fail to find expression in one's conduct; one may act respectfully despite an indifferent or disrespectful attitude; one's respectful conduct may be addressed to an object unworthy of respect. An unexpressed respectful attitude is *suppressed* respect. Respectful conduct that is not grounded in a respectful attitude is *insincere* respect. Respectful feelings and conduct that are aimed at an unworthy object is *unwarranted* respect. Any one of these discrepancies, I shall argue, *qualifies* respect. Thus, a respectful attitude must converge with respecting conduct vis-à-vis a respectable object if a person is to respect so-and-so without qualification. Moreover, I shall urge that none of these qualified forms of respect is intrinsically good, but that unqualified respect is intrinsically good. To convey the thought that qualified respect is not intrinsically good, I shall say that qualified respect is *compromised*....

The category to which respect belongs is a class of concepts that apply unequivocally only when attitudes or feelings find expression in actions addressed to worthy objects.... Respect is qualified unless all three components obtain. Two familiar members of this class are sympathy and resentment. Sympathetic conduct devoid of sympathetic feelings is not straightfowardly sympathizing, and commiseration backed by sympathetic feelings also raises questions if it is addressed to someone who acts gloriously happy and is in fact entirely care-free. Resentment works the same way. We are reluctant to say that an agent resents someone else when the agent harbors no complaint against the person but perversely treats that person resentfully. Likewise, we hesitate to say that someone resents an associate whose conduct is above reproach, despite the fact that the agent feels slighted and acts resentfully. Whatever the explanation of these peculiar behaviors, they fall short of standard cases of sympathizing and resenting.

Of course, it must be acknowledged that sympathetic or resentful conduct that is unhinged from sympathetic or resentful attitudes is, in a sense, sympathy or resentment. It is insincere sympathy or resentment. Also, it is evident that sincere, but misdirected sympathizing or resenting is, in a sense, sympathy or resentment. Still, where one of the elements—the appropriate attitude, the appropriate conduct, or an appropriate object—is missing, the concept pertains only in a qualified sense.... The logic of respect is similar.... Millicent can listen attentively to her aging parents' advice and take care of their every need, but, if she secretly despises them and bridles at their demands, her filial respect is vitiated. Without feelings of respect or a respectful attitude, respectful behavior is insincere, if not calculating or hypocritical....

Moreover, the assertion that one respects so-and-so is undermined if one's conduct expressive of a respectful state of mind is not directed at a worthy object. There is a spectrum of cases in which respectful attitudes and respectful conduct are misdirected. Consider a naive, but concerned citizen, Harry. Harry respects a political candidate who is a mere figurehead—a politician who has no principles or ideas of his own. Still, his admirable staff of researchers and writers instructs him to support sensible and fair positions; he appears knowledgeable and candid in interviews thanks to professional coaching in the art of public appearances; and he has gained a reputation for effective management thanks to the ingenuity of his public relations firm's television spots. Though the candidate's emptiness is abundantly evident to more sophisticated voters, Harry shows his respect by contributing to the candidate's campaign and voting for him. Now consider a star-struck teenager, Barbara. Barbara respects the svelte sensuality of a glamorous movie actress, and she expresses her feelings of respect for the actress by trying to emulate her and by bringing her films to the attention of friends. More sensitive film buffs regard the actress's physical charms as minor attractions and dismiss her movies as trite vehicles. Finally, consider a callow youth, Andrew, who respects a famous real estate developer for his ruthless greed. By purchasing the developer's best-selling autobiography and by justifying the developer's conduct in conversations with others, Andrew demonstrates his respect. Yet, more acute observers of the real estate scene are appalled by the developer's indifference to environmental and aesthetic considerations, not to mention the developer's preying on poor tenants whom he wants to evict to make way for profitable luxury condominiums.

Although Harry, Barbara, and Andrew feel respectful and act respectfully, I would urge that their respect is problematic. Less naive people and people who have more cultivated taste and higher standards do not share Harry's, Barbara's, and Andrew's views. One cannot deny that, in a sense, they respect the politician, the actress, and the developer. Yet, one is prompted to add that each of them has been taken in, and therefore that the respect of each is misplaced....

No doubt, it is generally desirable that one have good reasons for trust, anger, delight, and like states of mind, yet trusting, angry, and delighted behavior are fully intelligible in the absence of good reasons. Whereas people can be indiscriminately trusting, a person does not understand what respect is if that person is indiscriminately respectful. Thus,…one *needs* good reasons for respect, as well as for sympathy and resentment. As we have seen, one can believe that such reasons obtain; one can be wholeheartedly moved by these ostensible reasons; and one can take action to express one's attitude. Still, if there are in fact no good reasons, …one's subjective respectfulness has failed to make contact with respectable reality, and, when this happens, one's respectful behavior is unwarranted.

Millicent's, Harry's, Barbara's and Andrew's respect share a common defect. None expresses a correspondence between the individual's subjective state and an instantiation of value. But it is the unity of one's subjective state with an instantiation of value, I submit, that makes respect intrinsically good. Needless to say, respectful behavior typically brings about good consequences. But it need not always do so, and it might on balance bring about detrimental results. Still, there would remain something good about the respect itself provided that it was heartfelt and provided that it was directed at a worthy object. If it were unwarranted, it would seem lame or worse. If it were insincere, this falsity would contaminate it. Neither form of qualified respect could counterbalance harmful consequences of any weight. But unqualified respect would remain valuable—though not necessarily of paramount value—regardless of whether it contributed to bad consequences. Only the desideratum of conforming one's subjective state and one's behavior to an instantiation of value can account for this residual, intrinsic goodness.

Here, it is worth noting that this unity is presupposed by the further claims that respect is due regard for some object and that respect is stable. If one's subjective state inflates or deflates something's value, one's respect is disproportionate, and one is apt to be disillusioned or enlightened about the real value of the object. Undue respect is liable to abrupt change. Thus, it can only be unqualified respect—the intrinsically good congruence between the self and value—that people have in mind when they affirm the fittingness and the persistence of respect.

Contrariwise, respecting things that are unworthy of respect is intrinsically bad when a unity of one's self with disvalue is effected. Likewise, respecting things that are unworthy of respect is intrinsically bad when the agent sees value in what is negligible, though obviously this sort of misplaced respect is not as intrinsically bad as respect for what is evil or base. Not only is the agent deluded about the true value of what he or she respects, but also, as a result, the self is more attached to this object than it should be. In either case, respect is compromised.

Still, it is important to appreciate that respect can be unwarranted for different kinds of reasons. Harry, Barbara, and Andrew fasten their respect on inappropriate objects. The difference between Barbara and Andrew, on the one hand, and Harry, on the other, is that Barbara and Andrew falsely believe that certain types of things deserve respect and accurately aim their respect at targets their beliefs prescribe, whereas Harry knows what deserves respect but mistakenly directs his respect at a target his beliefs exclude. Harry's unwarranted respect for the empty politician is innocent, albeit unfortunate. If he were disabused of his illusions about the candidate, his respect would presumably dissolve. In contrast, Barbara's respect for the starlet is misguided, and Andrew's respect for the real estate tycoon is corrupt. Since their respect is based on deficient values, it is intrinsically more pernicious, and it is harder to dislodge. Nonetheless, unlike Andrew's respect for the real estate developer, Barbara's respect for the movie actress is unwarranted, but not indecent.

Perhaps, proponents of the moral conception of self-respect focus on respect that is both indecent and unwarranted while overlooking respect that is unwarranted, but innocent or misguided. As a result, they suppose that all unwarranted respect is reprehensible and conclude that reprehensible respect is not respect at all. It is undeniable that odious respect compounds the error of unwarranted respect. Yet, once one realizes that unwarranted respect can be morally innocuous, it becomes implausible to maintain that only morally mandated respect can count as respect. That someone feels respect for something and acts accordingly does not make it worthy of respect. But the unworthiness of the object need not extinguish the feelings or halt the behavior, and it may not justify moral condemnation.

Those who defend an independent psychological account of self-respect also neglect the complexity of the logic of respect. Consequently, they affirm that unwarranted self-respect is a second kind of unqualified self-respect. But once the three different ways in which respect can be qualified have been laid out, it becomes clear that psychological self-respect differs from moral self-respect in quality, not in kind. Sometimes psychological respect is not intrinsically good, for it may not evidence the requisite correspondence between one's subjective state and an instantiation of value. But psychological respect is not a discrete phenomenon. Moreover, to deny that some forms of self-respect that are certified by the psychological account, but not by the moral account, can be intrinsically good is to affirm that moral worth is the sole type of value that people instantiate. However, I shall argue below that this view is unduly restrictive.

III. Uncompromised Self-Respect and Autonomy

The second point of contention between the moral account of self-respect and the psychological account concerns the sort of self that can be the object of self-respect. Whereas the moral view insists that only the morally autonomous self and its good qualities can be respected, the psychological theory counters that any self together with its traits can be respected. For the purposes of this discussion, I shall assume, with Kant and his followers, that the morally autonomous self is a worthy object of self-respect, though I shall depart from this view by acknowledging that people can respect themselves in a compromised way for immoral conduct. The question I wish to raise is whether the personally autonomous self is also a proper object of respect and whether failure to exercise autonomy competency in personal decisions compromises self-respect.[12]

I shall urge that the moral account of self-respect is too narrowly discriminating—that is, it should not exclude the personally autonomous self as an object of respect; but I shall also urge that the psychological account is too indiscriminate—that is, it should exclude the nonautonomous self. A further advantage of my unified account of self-respect, then, is that it exposes the relation between self-respect and both moral and personal autonomy. Kant furnished a persuasive account of the link between moral autonomy and self-respect, but he simultaneously obscured the link between personal autonomy and self-respect. In order to appreciate the importance of the contribution the psychological view makes to our understanding of self-respect, it is necessary to recover the role of personal autonomy in self-respect.

Since self-respect requires a worthy object, it seems natural to suppose that there are standards that any self-respecting person must meet along with failings that are sure to engender self-contempt. The most obvious candidates to serve as objective standards for self-respect are moral requirements. A common strategy used to persuade people not to behave immorally is to appeal to their self-respect: "Have you *no* self-respect?" or "No self-respecting person could do *that*!" However, these very same exclamations can be used to enforce societal norms that have assumed a quasi-moral status under the sway of nearly unanimous opinion. Strict, yet nonmoral imperatives continue to govern sexuality in many cultural groups, and it is not uncommon for people to aver that they could not respect themselves if they violated these norms. When female chastity was enforced and publicly revered in the United States and Europe, many women considered promiscuity a reason for self-contempt. As I shall argue, failure to fulfill one's moral duties does compromise self-respect. Nevertheless, it is important to see, on the one hand, how people can violate core moral requirements and give every appearance of unimpaired self-respect and, on the other hand, how people can abrogate immoral and nonmoral social norms and maintain their self-respect.

Since people readily embrace prevalent standards, social tradition can protect the self-respect of people who engage in immoral behavior. A prime example of self-respect shielded in this way from moral scrutiny is the unregenerate macho male. Expected to exert absolute power over his wife and, in some groups, expected to beat her once in awhile to remind her of her place, the macho male respects himself for categorically immoral conduct. Imbued from childhood with the masculine stereotype and egged on by his pals, this individual undoubtedly believes that he could not forgo his prerogatives—which, of course, he does not deem immoral—without losing face and self-respect. Thus, the good of self-respect can help to conceal the evil of entrenched social conventions. When customary social practices conflict with morality, the former typically take precedence in people's assessments of their self-worth, since all too often people lack the intellectual and emotional independence necessary to embrace unconventional views.[13] To the extent that self-respect is widely founded on morally defective conventions, then, autonomy competency not only provides the only hope of relief for the victims of these conventions until social practices finally change for the better, but also it provides the only hope of establishing a worthy object of self-respect.[14] Thus, the moral view of self-respect denies that the proper object of reflexive respect is merely the socially condoned self, for the socially condoned self too often proves to be morally wanting.

But the moral account has a further reason for resting self-respect on the autonomous self. In this connection, Stephen Darwall has observed that respect for an ant's ability to heft enormous loads relative to its body weight is suspect, though amazement at this capacity is not.[15] Since the ant's feats result from the natural capabilities its species has gained over the course of evolution, they are not suitable objects of respect. Whoever warrants respect does so in virtue of his or her dignity as an agent or, in other words, in virtue of capacities to choose reflectively and to cultivate desirable dispositions to choose as opposed to natural endowments.[16] Thus, taking precautions to avoid stepping on the ants parading around one's kitchen because they are carrying gigantic crumbs seems a misplaced expression of respect.

Similarly, absorbing and following a socially enforced code manifests a natural capacity comparable to the ant's ability to transport heavy loads. When self-respect is based on this sort of adaptability rather than on a capacity for reflection and choice, self-respect is directed at a natural capability rather than at one's distinctive capacities as an agent. Thus, this respect is unwarranted, and uncompromised self-respect requires the exercise of the complete range of one's moral faculties.

Moreover, if people realize that they are observing immoral conventions and understand that they should be doing otherwise, their self-respect is compromised is two additional ways. Not only is this respect insincere inasmuch as these people do not feel respect for themselves for acting in these ways, but also their respectful feelings are suppressed inasmuch as they refrain from acting in a manner for which they do feel respect. Thus, conformity to morally deficient norms can tarnish people's self-respect, despite other people's admirations for them. Not all conduct that looks self-respecting is. Conversely, defying such norms in the name of a higher law, thereby eschewing standards that had been the bulwark of one's self-respect and also losing the respect of one's peers, need not undermine one's self-respect. Not all conduct that looks self-contemptuous is.

There is some truth, then, in the doctrine that immorality is incompatible with self-respect. The macho male I mentioned above stakes his self-respect on a nonautonomously adopted and immoral role. Thus, his self-respect is doubly misdirected. Social expectations have so shaped his mentality that he is blind to the cruelty of his behavior. Thus, he aims his respect at a social fabrication, not at a self-governing agent. In addition, by unconsciously guarding himself against recognizing the error of his ways, he obviates the possibility of discerning any antagonism between his true self and his violence against women. Still, the immorality of people's lives cannot be counted on to erode their favorable opinions of themselves, and it is futile to maintain that people cannot feel good about themselves, however contemptible their conduct may be. What is wrong with these people's self-respect is that it lacks a worthy object. To the extent that their self-respect is based on conduct that no morally autonomous agent could adopt, it is compromised.

Now, it is important to notice that people's everyday attributions of self-respect and self-contempt extend to nonmoral norms, too. To see this, let us turn the macho male's opposite number—the henpecked husband.

Many people would accept the latter as a humble, retiring figure of fun—a paradigm of self-contempt. If he testified that he could not respect himself if he ever spent an evening playing poker with the boys, most people would scoff. Why does the self-respect of the henpecked husband provoke such skepticism? First, he violates conventions of masculinity—he does not dominate his wife. Since he must realize that he is not a "real man," he must be contemptuous of himself. Second, simply because he is a man, he is assumed to be capable of resisting his wife's demands. If he does not do so, it must be because he has no respect for his dignity. He must not care if he looks pathetic and ridiculous. Not only does the henpecked husband fail to meet relevant standards, he is not properly chagrined by his inadequacy. Though no one would accuse the henpecked husband of immorality—at most, he might be snidely accused of betraying his sex—he is seen as lacking self-respect.

We have already established that not being henpecked does not guarantee unqualified self-respect. Though by no means henpecked, the macho male's self-respect is unwarranted since he lacks moral autonomy. Can the henpecked husband be self-respecting?

If there is anything that would convince us that the henpecked husband has not sacrificed his self-respect on the altar of his marriage, it would be evidence that he really considers poker a waste of time, really believes that men should share domestic chores, really loves and admires his wife, and so forth—that is, evidence that this man is not playing the patsy to his wife; evidence that he himself spurns certain prevalent masculine modalities. If the man whom others laughingly call "henpecked" describes himself in terms of autonomously adopted desiderata that belie the subservience implicit in the popular epithet, there is no reason to doubt his self-respect. Just as a morally autonomous, reformed macho male can be self-respecting despite others' scorn, a personally autonomous violator of gender norms can be self-respecting. Indeed, once a man has become disenchanted with these norms, he will need to violate them in order to preserve his self-respect. Under these circumstances, autonomy skills are indispensable, for they not only assure individuals that they are not giving up others' respect in vain, but they also give individuals the strength to withstand others' ridicule. An unorthodox life plan can support self-respect, provided that it is a projection of the individual's authentic self.

There are four salient parallels between moral and personal autonomy. First, both involve the deployment of the complete repertory of the person's faculties of reflective choice. The difference is that moral autonomy turns these skills outward while personal autonomy turns them inward. Second, people gain knowledge of their authentic selves through both forms of autonomy. Both moral autonomy and personal autonomy ensure that people do what they, as individuals, really want to do. Third, moral autonomy enables the individual to benefit other people and to contribute to society. Similarly, personal autonomy gives individuals the satisfaction of acting on their own beliefs, desires, and the like. Fourth, moral autonomy protects other people from wrongful harm, and personal autonomy protects the individual from needless frustration.

These parallels militate in favor of accepting the everyday assumption that, like moral autonomy, personal autonomy supports self-respect. Thus, they call into question the narrow construal of the grounds for self-respect that the moral account of self-respect stipulates, and they buttress the psychological account's less restrictive view of the possible grounds for self-respect. However, I did not merely argue that moral autonomy supports self-respect; I maintained that moral autonomy is necessary to uncompromised self-respect. Yet, people do not usually think that someone who heteronomously complies with prevailing nonmoral social norms lacks self-respect, and the psychological account concurs with this inclusive assessment. Thus, it is necessary to inquire whether this view of nonautonomous, conventional people mistakes compromised self-respect for uncompromised self-respect—that is, whether personal autonomy is also necessary for uncompromised self-respect.

It is easy to understand why conventional people are presumed to have their self-respect intact. Since they have been socialized to assume their roles, they slide smoothly into these assigned positions. They do not grudgingly go through the motions of conformity. Nor do they report ambivalence or self-betrayal. In addition, conventional people may have a meta-rationale for striving to perform their roles well. If they believe in the value of the social order, conventional people can be satisfied that they are acting in a worthwhile way insofar as living up to the standards implicit in their roles helps to maintain the social order. Though society molds nonautonomous conventional people, they see themselves as mature, upstanding members of the community. Moreover, they give every appearance of caring about their dignity because they act in ways that others regard as commendable.

Only when we have evidence that someone conforms to customary practices unwillingly are we moved to deny that conventionality invariably supports self-respect. As I remarked earlier, some behavior that looks self-respecting is not, and one way to live a lie is to carry off a conventional life plan superbly while inwardly deploring it. To bow to convention against one's better judgment is not to show due regard for oneself. Still, there is no reason to believe that autonomous conventionality is incompatible with self-respect. In this case, the individual and society concur about what befits the dignity of human agents. Furthermore, nonautonomous, but willing conformity to nonmoral norms seems sufficient for self-respect, too.

Still, self-respect founded on nonautonomous, though willing conventionality is troublesome. When a person has a life plan that is not that person's own life plan, a gap opens between the person's fulfilling the life plan and the person's authentic self. Since the life plan is alien to the person, however estimable the plan may be and however impressively it may be carried out, undertaking it does not seem to evidence *self-respect*. Just as a person who nonautonomously pursues typical human interests may not be promoting what is distinctively in his or her own self-interest, a person who carries out a conventional life plan may not be demonstrating self-respect. From this vantage, personal autonomy seems more crucial to self-respect than it otherwise might.

Defense mechanisms and cognitive filters represent the most treacherous and pervasive threat to the self-respect of nonautonomous individuals.... Although social psychologists have found that nearly everyone uses the same socially approved standards to assess their worth, these investigators have also discovered that this common fund of standards does not commit people to objectivity in appraising themselves.[17] People limit their aspirations to levels they can sensibly expect to achieve, and they unconsciously exaggerate their own success on seemingly inflexible scales.[18] Moreover, since they measure themselves within the framework set by their immediate social environment, and since they have some control over which environments they enter, the puny swimmers in small ponds often class themselves as big fish.[19] Though people seldom adopt idiosyncratic standards to preserve their self-worth, they are by no means at the mercy of a stern, incontrovertible metric.

People may regard themselves as inferior in many ways and mediocre in many others; they may be afflicted by grave doubts about their merits; but, if worst comes to worst, virtually everyone has a system of defense mechanisms and cognitive filters that ensures at least a modicum of positive self-regard in the face of damaging experience.[20] Indeed, most people would find a life altogether bereft of the salve of these protective devices unendurable.[21] Among other benefits, defense mechanisms and cognitive filters ensure that people have enough positive self-regard to sustain a respectful attitude toward themselves when they occasionally behave abominably or when they suffer a grave set-back. Defense mechanisms and cognitive filters function as a tonic against self-contempt.[22]

But when these devices conceal serious and remediable faults from agents, or when they grossly mislead agents about the nature of their projects or the degree of their success, they interfere with self-respect. For, when people are mistaken about their attributes, they are open to charges that they are misdirecting their respect. They respect themselves for good qualities they do not have or for projects they do not realize are undesirable, and their self-respect is reinforced by their obliviousness to unpleasant truths about their shortcomings. Of course, on the assumption that these people are sane and therefore are not totally deluded about themselves, their self-respect is not entirely compromised. Yet, the social psychological evidence suggests that many people's self-portraits bear scant resemblance to their actual personalities and achievements and that their self-respect is extensively compromised.

Not only do defense mechanisms and cognitive filters compromise self-respect by blinding people to the realities of their lives, but they also compromise self-respect by preempting self-definition. Promiscuously self-affirming people are not self-respecting. To be self-respecting, one may have to reform oneself by disavowing discredited beliefs, harmful habits, demeaning associations, trivial goals, and so on. Self-respect may require change, but defense mechanisms and cognitive filters often prevent minimally autonomous people from noticing that change is called for. Moreover, change that is imposed from without or unconsciously insinuated from within may again defeat self-respect.

Harry Frankfurt has termed the nonautonomous person a wanton.[23] Wantons do what they want, but they have no autonomously accepted personal standards with which they identify and which curb their impulses. They epitomize self-indulgence. This does not prevent them from taking the initiative on many projects, nor from being very exasperated when they are opposed. As a result, they may seem self-respecting, and it is altogether possible that some of them would not describe themselves as indifferent to themselves, let alone self-contemptuous. But since nothing is beneath them, however moving and appealing they sometimes appear to be, they cannot be said to respect themselves without qualification. Accordingly, the need for autonomy as an underpinning for self-respect seems inescapable.

At this point, it might be countered that people who have not autonomously chosen the overall direction of their lives can respect themselves for performing the duties incumbent on them well or for exercising autonomy competency in the performance of these duties. While I do not deny that people can obtain a measure of self-respect in these ways, I would note that these bases for self-respect do not guarantee that a person's self-respect is uncompromised.

People who measure up to standards or fulfill plans that they do not autonomously embrace are less wanton than thoroughly self-indulgent people, but only slightly so. Though the former individuals discipline themselves to play delegated roles, and though they may respect themselves for the willpower they exert in order to comply with these strictures, nothing precludes the standards being inferior, if not contemptible. If they are, living up to them may demonstrate respect for the established social order or for some authority figure, but it hardly demonstrates unalloyed self-respect. Similarly, exercising autonomy competency to handle some situations—that is, episodic autonomy—or to set some policies—that is, narrowly programmatic autonomy—while fulfilling a pre-ordained role gives the individual some control over the values his or her life expresses. Nonetheless, the general life plan that subsumes these activities may be inferior, if not contemptible. If it is, fulfilling it does not evidence unqualified self-respect.

Still, it might seem that socialization could bypass autonomy by inserting people into benign social roles. As basic human interests constitute a default conception of self-interest in the absence of autonomous choice, so conventional life plans may constitute a default basis for self-respect in the absence of autonomous choice. Yet, however redoubtable one's cultural heritage may be, no one could confidently assume that it only endows people with incontrovertible beliefs, justifiable practices, and elevated goals. Moreover, it is well known that cultures often fail to assign people roles that are calibrated to their abilities and inclinations. Caste systems notoriously oblige the so-called lower orders to limit themselves to menial enterprises and to cede social responsibility to their purported superiors. Just as no self-respecting person would cling desperately to a position that was beyond his or her capacities, so self-respecting people do not repress potentialities that they regard as good and that they want to fulfill. Suppressed respect, it must be remembered, is another form of qualified respect. Although nonautonomous conventionality can immunize people against feelings of self-contempt, such people may nonetheless be behaving in a self-contemptuous way, and their self-respect may be compromised.

Though developed autonomy skills are not infallible, they do enable people to generate more accurate self-portraits, to alter undesirable characteristics, and to pursue plans that comport with their authentic selves. People who exercise these skills can correct their misconceptions about themselves and can change as needed. Also, whether by fitting into the existing social system or by working to change it, they can devise ways to join in social life without betraying their own desires, values, and the like. Accordingly, autonomy enables people to confront themselves honestly without undue risk of collapsing into despair and self-contempt, and autonomy provides the remedy for self-respect that defense mechanisms and cognitive filters compromise.

There is no assurance that self-respect is intrinsically good, as the proponents of the moral account maintain it is, unless it is grounded in autonomy. However, personal autonomy is as necessary to self-respect as moral autonomy. Moral autonomy ensures that people's moral decisions are as wise as is humanly possible. Personal autonomy ensures that people's personal ideals and life plans befit their individual strengths and needs and that their lives match their personal ideals and life plans. Moreover, both modes of autonomy exhibit respect for human agency by utilizing the full range of people's deliberate and volitional capabilities.

However, self-respect can be compromised. Self-respect that is unwarranted because people have execrable traits and plans which they regard as splendid is intrinsically bad, for these agents are doubly bonded to evil. They are bad, and they respect that very badness. Such self-respect is corrupt, and, when people's autonomy competency is well developed, corrupt self-respect is morally blameworthy. People endowed with autonomy competency have no excuse for endorsing such defective values. But neither is self-respect that is predicated on jejune or trivial values intrinsically good. In this case, self-respect is disproportionate, for these agents are overinvested in their traits and plans. Such self-respect is misguided.... Misguided self-respect is not immoral, but neither is there any reason to applaud it. Still, it is important to recognize that unwarranted self-respect can be innocent. If the agent's autonomy skills are weak, the agent is at the mercy of defense mechanisms and cognitive filters. Such people's values are in order. Nevertheless, they have vile or mediocre traits and plans which they do not notice at all or which they take for admirable ones, or they have good traits which they perceive as wonderful. Such people can hardly be held accountable for the compromised nature of their self-respect, yet their self-respect is not intrinsically good. Whereas corrupt and misguided self-respect are deplorable (though, of course, not equally so), innocent, yet compromised self-respect is pitiable.

Since personal autonomy together with moral autonomy brings into play the individual's complete repertory of powers as an agent, human dignity is most fully realized in the autonomous self. Thus, it is not surprising that, the moral account of self-respect notwithstanding, the proper object of self-respect proves to be the personally and morally autonomous self—the authentic self as it emerges through the exercise of autonomy competency. Still, I have argued that people possess self-respect in varying degrees and that their respect for themselves can be more or less well-grounded. Lack of autonomy compromises self-respect by depriving self-respecting attitudes and conduct of a worthy object. The trouble with the psychological view is that it neglects the possibility that self-respect can be unwarranted; that is, it refuses to acknowledge that anything is amiss when respect is aimed at an unworthy object. In specifying what sort of self is worthy of self-respect, the moral account of self-respect is underinclusive, but the psychological account is over-inclusive.

Now, it is important to recognize that, since few people live completely heteronomous lives, hardly anyone's self-respect is altogether compromised. Accordingly, to maintain that autonomy is necessary for uncompromised self-respect is not to deny that most people have self-respect. It is only to contend that the self-respect of many people is to a significant degree compromised. Insofar as their self-respect is compromised, it is not intrinsically good. Still, it could be objected that warranted self-respect may be no better than unwarranted self-respect from an instrumental standpoint. In people's psychological economy, that is, unwarranted self-respect may feel just as ennobling and may motivate dignified conduct just as assuredly as warranted self-respect. In the discussion to follow, I shall focus on the fragility of this sort of compromised self-respect and the psychological problems it poses.... Specifically, I shall urge that uncompromised self-respect shields self-respecting people from suffering by protecting them from the self-condemnation that disillusionment and disappointment with oneself can bring.

IV. The Psychological Liabilities of Compromised Self-Respect

By calling upon the full range of one's capacities as an agent, autonomy secures uncompromised self-respect. Still, we have seen that people who are far from maximally autonomous often feel perfectly respectful and behave respectfully towards themselves. In light of this fact, the claim that minimally autonomous people do not show unqualified respect for themselves seems dubious. To still this doubt, it is necessary to probe the psychological burden compromised self-respect imposes. Preliminary to doing so, I shall suggest that there is no reason to accept the appearance of unqualified self-respect as the reality. Since self-respect is part of an integrated psychological system, independent psychological factors can bolster compromised self-respect and can prevent it from being exposed. Thus, people may not feel as much respect for themselves as they suppose they do. Then I shall describe the traps that compromised self-respect sets. Though people whose self-respect is compromised are often unaware of it, their psychological equilibrium is needlessly imperiled.

As I noted earlier, people can behave respectfully yet have no respect. That people object to dismissive or demeaning treatment while routinely pursuing their interests and proceeding with their plans does not entail that they respect themselves. Instead, they may act assertively because they are obstinate, proud, domineering, irascible, compulsive, or insensitive to others. They may even produce a simulacrum of self-respect because they are eager to please someone who is known to place a high value on personal dignity.... Likewise, people's subjective experience can mimic self-respect. They can feel offended by dismissive or demeaning treatment, and they can care about their interests and their plans without respecting themselves. Among the less noble explanations of these responses, apart from self-respect, are importunity, rapacity, and conceitedness, but notice that excessively self-effacing dedication to a wholly admirable cause could foster these same responses. Furthermore, since people often worry that they will be excluded from social groups or shunned by particular individuals unless they make themselves interesting and attractive, a normal desire for affiliation probably contributes to many people's feelings of self-concern.

Many of the motives I have mentioned can coexist with self-respect. Self-respect does not exist in isolation from other psychological forces; it is one factor in a complex psychological economy. But extraneous motives can mask deficient self-respect. Though some of these motives are liable to mushroom into bloated regard for oneself while others are liable to devolve into slavish obsequiousness, in a wide range of circumstances they subjectively and behaviorally resemble self-respect. For this reason, I would question the credibility of testimony from minimally autonomous people affirming that their self-respect is unqualified. Especially when people's self-reading skills are weak, this putative evidence does not inspire confidence.

Now the considerations I have adduced might be dismissed as experientially vacuous and practically trivial. Since people whose self-respect is only partially warranted are not aware that other psychological forces are camouflaging their compromised self-respect, compromised self-respect does not bother them. They do not suffer from dejection and despair. Quite the contrary, they are often happy. Since they feel good about themselves, it may seem presumptuous and counterproductive to pronounce their self-respect compromised.

Of course, self-respect normally blends with other attitudes and motives in the human psyche. Since few situations isolate self-respect and put it to the test, it is rarely possible to dissect the sources of an action or of a self-referential response with any precision. Nevertheless, it does not follow that the question of compromised self-respect can be safely ignored. When self-respect is compromised, I shall urge, people are needlessly exposed to the withdrawal of others' approval and other reversals. Thus, it seems to me that there are two reasons why it would be cynical not to take the problem of compromised self-respect seriously. First, this cavalier view of the matter is indifferent to the relative fragility of many people's positive feelings about themselves and therefore to the potential for misery they conceal. Second, it justifies refusing to implement the social reforms necessary to promote autonomy and uncompromised self-respect. I shall close this section by considering the first of these rejoinders, but I shall reserve the question of justice for [another discussion[24]].

The trouble with compromised self-respect is that people can take pride in their self-control or in the quality of their performances, and they can go about some of their tasks independently; yet they can, at the same time, have compelling reasons to dislike, if not to despise, themselves for lending their talents to the broader enterprise in question. The most casual acquaintance with human history amply demonstrates that no one can justifiably assume that conventional life plans are necessarily unobjectionable. Moreover, that a life plan is not wicked does not entail that there is no compelling reason to reject it. An individual's personal standards and preferences may rule out life plans that are morally unexceptionable.

Let us consider the predicament of a person whose self-respect is compromised. There are three main sources of compromised self-respect: illusions about the goodness of one's attributes, compliance with standards of which one would disapprove if one were to scrutinize them, and adherence to a life plan that does not comport with one's authentic self.

In each case, the object of self-respect is unworthy of the individual, and, plainly, the respectful person would cease to feel respect if only this individual realized how wrongheaded his or her beliefs or actions were. Since compromised self-respect is susceptible to reversal in this way, it is tenuous. Though it is undeniable that supportive social arrangements or powerful psychological defenses can shelter people from disillusionment, compromised self-respect is perilous.

When compromised self-respect rests on fairly unimportant misconceptions about one's self or one's conduct, the exposure of these misconceptions is ordinarily not terribly discomfiting. Indeed, Shelley Taylor and Jonathan Brown argue that social and cognitive filters typically render most negative information about one's self as benign as possible.[25] People with positive self-concepts tend to dismiss negative feedback as inaccurate.[26] Moreover if they accept the accuracy of such feedback, their self-concepts are temporarily adjusted to compass it but soon drift back in a positive direction.[27] One might feel foolish for one's lack of discernment or irritated with oneself for missing some opportunity, but one is hardly plunged into despair.

Nevertheless, people's discovery that their self-respect is compromised can precipitate reactions much more serious than embarrassment or annoyance. When compromised self-respect rests on momentous choices or on abiding features of one's personality—as all too often it does when people's autonomy skills are poorly developed—the revelation of the fatuousness or the odiousness of one's decisions or one's attributes can be deeply disturbing....

The plight of women whose automatic submission to the role of housewife-mother has recently been called into question provides a broad-based test case for my claims regarding the fragility of compromised self-respect. What traditional women had regarded as a natural and inevitable division of labor—wife as domestic caretaker and husband as provider—feminists and, to a large extent, federal and state law have declared an option. Thus, a possible rejoinder to my account of the harm minimal autonomy can do to self-respect stems from the popular belief that housewife-mothers have lost self-respect as alternative roles have become available to them. The anecdotal evidence for this view is certainly worrisome. For if the prognosis for self-respect is improved by a social climate hospitable to autonomy, the shift over the last two decades away from compulsory marriage, motherhood, and homemaking should have been accompanied by commensurate advances in self-respect among women. Yet, it seems that creating a social environment more conducive to autonomy need not augment self-respect, indeed, that the reverse has occurred.

The traditional woman's battle for self-respect manifests a number of the principles I have developed in my discussion of compromised self-respect. Larry Blum, Marcia Homiak, Judy Housman, and Naomi Scheman have persuasively argued that the traditional woman's dependency and lack of individual identity undermine her altruism, that is, her "feminine virtue." For example, the traditional woman is inclined to conflate providing emotional support, which is beneficial to her husband, with providing uncritical emotional support, which is potentially harmful to him.[28] Thus, the traditional woman's self-respect rests on an inflated conception of the help she is giving her family and a correspondingly suspect self-image.

In addition, as I have urged, people whose overall life plans are not autonomous can to some degree compensate for this lack by setting standards for themselves within their assigned roles. Ann Oakley has found that the housewife's main strategy for obtaining satisfaction from her work is to invent stiff criteria of hygiene and efficiency that she can commend herself for satisfying.[29] Confirming their devotion to their families in this way, these women demonstrate to themselves that they are "good women," women who deserve respect.

Yet, these tactics are not altogether successful. A recent study contends that one third of the women in an urban population were borderline depressives, if they were not clinically depressed.[30] ...Since Oakley has found that not having paid employment outside the home is positively correlated with the onset of depression, and since depression is associated with self-denigration, it is evident that whatever self-respect women obtain from their domestic wizardry is commonly offset by the contempt they feel for themselves as homemakers....

Yet, women are by no means unanimous in their hostility to housewifery. The least educated women in America were as satisfied with housework in 1976 as they were in 1956, and the numbers of these women who acknowledged that they once wanted a career declined during this period.[31] ...Further, many educated housewives have remained at home and kept their self-respect. Moreover, Sarah Usher and Mort Fels have determined that support for feminist ideas is positively correlated with self-respect among both working and nonworking, university educated, middle-aged, married mothers.[32] That is, educated housewife-mothers who have come to grips with the recent undermining of assumptions about women's proper role and who have remained committed to the traditional feminine role have retained their self-respect. Educated housewife-mothers who cannot accept the greater freedom and equality that feminists advocate for women have been less able to preserve their self-respect.

Although housewife-mothers taken as a group have not lost as much self-respect as is commonly thought, recent social and economic developments have created a new category of women—the part-time workers—who do seem to be in turmoil. Douglas Hall and Francine Gordon's data show that the latter women are least satisfied with their lives. In view of the fact that part-time jobs are rarely challenging or prestigious, it is not surprising that these women find life less rewarding than others. What is surprising is that, despite their greater dissatisfaction, part-time working women are less willing to change roles than any other group.[33] Hall and Gordon suggest that these women have struck a compromise between traditional femininity and contemporary careerism, but that their dissatisfaction indicates incomplete identity resolution.[34] Part-time employment may be the refuge of many of the least autonomous women. They have been raised to be housewife-mothers, but new social forces are pressuring them to work outside the home. Pulled in opposing directions but unable to choose between them, these women undertake to do both and suffer from this attempt to straddle two roles. That their unhappiness with this arrangement fails to subvert their allegiance to it points to an underlying problem with poorly developed autonomy skills.

Jane Mansbridge holds that women who are oriented to traditional feminine values and functions and who have recently lost self-respect have suffered in this way because high status women have entered the world of paid employment.[35] Yet, it is unlikely that these women have simply internalized other people's newly critical attitudes towards their occupation and thereby lost self-respect. Since public opinion remains divided on the question of women's proper role, there are no unambiguous social norms that can account for these women's downcast feelings about themselves. Moreover, social-psychological studies do not confirm the oft-repeated claim that self-respect and self-contempt merely mirror the respect or contempt in which other people hold a person. Though there is some correlation between people's self-referential attitudes and their beliefs about others' attitudes toward them, there is little correlation between these beliefs and their associates' actual attitudes.[36] Since people communicate ambiguous information about their views of their fellows, individuals must interpret the cues they receive, and their interpretations rarely supply accurate pictures of the way others see them.[37] The process of self-scrutiny that leads to self-respect or self-contempt does not take place in a social vacuum, but self-respect and self-contempt are not reducible to the internalization of others' favorable or unfavorable attitudes.

Though some traditional women may have come to believe that many people no longer hold housewifery in the same esteem they once did, and though this belief may figure in some of these women's diminished self-respect, the question remains as to why these women are so adversely affected by shifting social mores. Why do they not dismiss women who have embraced careers as dupes of a misguided fad? Why do they not remind themselves of the gratification they obtain from their own work, instead of taking on tedious part-time jobs? If economic need obliges them to work, why do they profess an unassailable loyalty to their dual role, instead of acknowledging that they would prefer not to work at all?

I would contend that the best explanation of the drop in their self-respect is that socioeconomic developments have brought the compromised nature of these women's self-respect to the surface. As their commitment to the feminine role was never anchored in their true selves, so their self-respect was never founded on an autonomous life plan. Since they are most probably minimally autonomous, they lack the skills to assimilate their transformed self-perception, as well as the skills to generate an alternative course of action. Having relied on compromised self-respect, many women were vulnerable to feminist criticism of gender stereotypes, and they are now condemned to self-contempt. Once people relinquish the assumption that they have no choice about some matter, their self-respect comes to hinge in part on making wise choices. In the face of expanding opportunities, some women sank into depression or adopted conflict-ridden stopgap measures; however, many others took the opportunity to renew their previous commitments or to reorient their lives.

Women who were receptive to the feminist challenge despite long-standing traditional marriages often discovered that their major life choices had been made unreflectively and acquiescently. Some of these women then went on to accuse themselves of self-betrayal and cowardice while others became convinced that they had settled upon satisfying and worthwhile plans. Though it appears that many housewives lost self-respect, I would maintain that they never really had the self-respect they thought they had. Without their realizing it, their self-respect was compromised; social and economic changes merely opened their eyes to this compromise and, in many cases, spurred them to take steps to put their self-respect on a solid basis. Whatever the outcome, these individuals moved from viewing self-respect as a superficial question about how well one does a predetermined task to viewing it also as a profound question about whether one's life is worthy of and congruent with one's self.

These observations highlight the integral relationship between autonomy and uncompromised self-respect. Autonomous people have a realistic understanding of their capacities as well as the limits of their ability to control their circumstances, and self-respecting people are not disposed to degrading self-flagellation. Thus, autonomy and uncompromised self-respect together provide a bulwark against adverse circumstances and against others' disdain. Yet, autonomy and uncompromised self-respect both entail accepting responsibility for one's conduct. Autonomy prevents people both from evading responsibility and from inflating their responsibility and thus sustains self-respect, while uncompromised self-respect preserves people's sense of their worthiness as agents and thus prevents people from confounding their capacity for self-governance by giving in to social pressure or undesirable impulses. Thus, autonomy and uncompromised self-respect reciprocally reinforce one another.

But people whose self-respect is compromised respect themselves for good characteristics they do not have but believe they have; they respect themselves despite bad characteristics they have but do not acknowledge; or they respect themselves for carrying out life plans they believe to be their own but that are socially imposed. Since minimal autonomy is widespread, compromised self-respect that depends on nonautonomous, yet major elements of people's self-portraits or that depends on nonautonomous, yet major life choices is all too common. But the disclosure of such distorted self-concepts can lead to devastating condemnation of one's own character or the overall course of one's life. Thus, compromised self-respect threatens people's emotional stability.

It is clear, then, that whatever self-respect people obtain from disciplining themselves to fulfill standards implicit in social roles that have been imposed on them or from making episodically autonomous choices once in awhile is comparatively precarious. When people's self-regard is confined to their level of achievement or occasional self-expression within an assigned activity and does not penetrate to the overall shape of their lives, they are vulnerable to the most profound form of self-contempt.... Of course, luck, social approbation, or self-deception can save minimally autonomous people from this fate. However, such cosseting does not so much ensure self-respect as it obviates the need for self-respect, thereby allowing individuals to rest content with compromised self-respect.[38]

To be self-respecting, people must chart their own courses. Discovering a mismatch between one's self and one's life plan which one is powerless to remedy detracts from self-respect. But, as we have seen, uncompromised self-respect is both intrinsically and instrumentally valuable.... Accordingly, insofar as official social policy and entrenched cultural norms subject people to a contracted sense of self-worth, society owes these individuals a reappraisal of the options it countenances. Of course, nothing I have said entails that societies are obligated to ensure that everyone's dreams can come true. Mature people modulate their aspirations and expectations in accordance with a realistic assessment of what should be possible. However, if socially enforced deficiencies in autonomy competency leave some people minimally autonomous and ill-equipped to respect themselves, there is a powerful reason to condemn those practices that constrain people to minimal autonomy and to implement reforms designed to enhance autonomy. Likewise, if obdurate prejudice forces some individuals to classify reasonable projects as idle fantasies, the society sponsoring these restrictions wrongs some of its members. It compels them either to distort their personalities or to become pariahs. Both options put self-respect in jeopardy. Though this risk may be supportable for people who have a high degree of autonomy but who have less than full autonomy, it can be tragic for marginally autonomous people.

Notes

1. Marilyn Friedman, "Moral Integrity and the Deferential Wife," *Philosophical Studies* 47 (1985): 141–150, pp. 144–46.
2. Thomas E. Hill, Jr., "Servility and Self-Respect," *The Monist* 57 (1973): 87–104 [chapter 3, this volume,]; Larry Thomas, "Morality and Our Self-Concept," *Journal of Value Inquiry* 12 (1978): 258–268, p. 264; David Sachs, "How To Distinguish Self-Respect from Self-Esteem," *Philosophy and Public Affairs* 10 (1981): 346–360, p. 352.
3. Bernard R. Boxill, "Self-Respect and Protest," *Philosophy and Public Affairs* 6 (1976): 58–69, p. 69 [chapter 4, this volume, p. 102].
4. David Sachs, "Self-Respect and Respect for Others," in O. H. Green, ed., *Respect for Persons, Tulane Studies in Philosophy*, vol. 31 (New Orleans: Tulane University Press, 1983), pp. 109–128, pp. 122–123.

5. Thomas E. Hill, Jr., "Self-Respect Reconsidered," in *Respect for Persons, Tulane Studies in Philosophy*, pp. 128–137, p. 132 [chapter 6, this volume, p. 119].

6. Stephen J. Massey, "Is Self-Respect a Moral or a Psychological Concept?" *Ethics* 93 (1983): 246–261, p. 249 [chapter 11, this volume, p. 201].

7. Compare Stephen Darwall, *Impartial Reason* (Ithaca, N. Y.: Cornell University Press, 1983), p. 154.

8. Sachs, "How To Distinguish Self-Respect", pp. 350–357. Stephen Darwall complicates this picture by distinguishing recognition self-respect from appraisal self-respect (Darwall, "Two Kinds of Respect," *Ethics* 88 (1977): 36–49, pp. 38–39 [chapter 10, this volume, p. 184]). However, in view of my present purposes, I shall ignore this distinction.

9. Massey, "Is Self-Respect a Moral Concept?" pp. 249, 252–254 [pp. 202. 204–207, this volume].

10. Darwall, "Two Kinds," p. 48 [p. 194, this volume].

11. Massey, "Is Self-Respect a Moral Concept?" p. 253 [p. 205, this volume].

12. [Editor's Note: In *Self, Society, and Personal Choice*, Meyers understands personal autonomy as the exercise of a competency—a repertory of introspective, imaginative, communicative, reasoning, and volitional skills that enables one to engage in self-discovery, self-definition, and self-direction. According to Meyers, no authentic or "true" self exists apart from the exercise of autonomy competency; the traits, values, goals, etc., that are embraced as a result of exercising these skills constitute the authentic or "true" self. Moreover, on this view, personal autonomy is a matter of degree. Fully autonomous people have well developed, well coordinated autonomy skills that they bring to bear on all of their decisions, but people who use these skills less proficiently or less frequently are partially autonomous.]

13. Stanley Coopersmith, *The Antecedents of Self-Esteem* (New York: Consulting Psychologists Press, Inc., 1981), p. 140.

14. For discussion of moral autonomy as a form of autonomy competency, see Diana T. Meyers, "The Socialized Individual and Individual Autonomy: An Intersection between Philosophy and Psychology," in Eva Feder Kittay and Diana T. Meyers, eds., *Women and Moral Theory* (Totowa, N.J.: Rowman and Littlefield, 1987), pp. 147–152.

15. Darwall, "Two Kinds," p. 42 [p. 188, this volume].

16. Ibid, p. 47 [p. 193, this volume].

17. Coopersmith, *Antecedents*, p. 140; see also Meyers, *Self, Society, and Personal Choice* pt. 3, sec. 4.

18. Coopersmith, *Antecedents*, pp. 141, 245–246.

19. Ibid, p. 243.

20. Ibid, pp. 42–43.

21. *The New York Times*, 26 November 1987, sec. B12.

22. At this point, it might be tempting to conclude that building effective defense mechanisms provides the prime remedy for self-contempt. However, this suggestion runs afoul of two insuperable problems. First, since defense mechanisms operate unconsciously, it is not possible to instruct self-contemptuous people in the subtleties of denying their failings. Second, even if it were possible to instill effective defense mechanisms in the self-contemptuous, they would not necessarily be better off from the standpoint of self-respect, for their respect would be misdirected and therefore compromised. Though the salubrious effects of defense mechanisms are undeniable, autonomy is the only reliable remedy for self-contempt.

23. Harry G. Frankfurt, "Freedom of the Will and the Concept of the Person," *The Journal of Philosophy* 68 (1971): 5–20, p. 11.

24. [Editor's Note: See Meyers, *Self, Society, and Personal Choice*, pt. 4, sec. 3.]

25. Shelley E. Taylor and Jonathan D. Brown, "Illusion and Well-Being: A Social Psychological Perspective on Mental Health," *Psychological Bulletin* 103 (1988): 193–210, p. 201.

26. Ibid, p. 202.

27. Ibid.

28. Larry Blum, Marcia Homiak, Judy Housman, and Naomi Scheman, "Altruism and Women's Oppression," *The Philosophical Forum* 5 (1973–1974): 222–247, p. 234; for a similar view, see Friedman, "Moral Integrity," pp. 147–148.

29. Ann Oakley, *Subject Women* (New York, Pantheon Books, 1981), p. 174.

30. Ibid, p. 80.

31. Jane Mansbridge, *Why We Lost the ERA* (Chicago: University of Chicago Press, 1986), p. 106.

32. Sarah Usher and Mort Fels, "The Challenge of Feminism and Career for the Middle-Aged Woman," *International Journal of Women's Studies* 8 (1985): 47–57, p. 51.

33. Douglas T. Hall and Francine E. Gordon, "Career Choices of Married Women: Effects on Conflict, Role Behavior, and Satisfaction," *Journal of Applied Psychology* 58 (1973): 42–48, p. 47.

34. Ibid.

35. Mansbridge, *ERA*, p. 105.

36. J. Sidney Shrauger and Thomas J. Schoenman, "Symbolic Interactionist View of Self-Concept: Through the Looking Glass Darkly," *Psychological Bulletin* 86 (1979): 549–565, p. 558.

37. Ibid, p. 565.

38. In this connection, it is worth adding that people's economic circumstances can compromise self-respect by severely restricting their autonomy. Recalling

my tale of the homeless woman and the youth in section I, it is evident that the homeless woman's hold on her self-respect is tenuous because her material circumstances are extremely uncertain and largely beyond her control. In telling her story, I mentioned that her self-respect would probably suffer if she were forced to turn to begging or stealing. People's circumstances may become intractable; that is, no matter how ingenious and determined they are, severe deprivation can prevent them from pursuing life plans that are minimally acceptable to them. When this happens, self-respect is undermined, if not converted into self-contempt.

+

Politics

+

13

✛

Self-Respect: Theory and Practice

✛

Laurence Thomas

We begin life as rather frail creatures who are quite unable to do much of anything for ourselves. If all goes well we end up as healthy adults with a secure sense of worth. At the outset of our lives, there are two things that are generally thought to enhance significantly the likelihood of our turning out to be adults of this sort: (i) our being a continuous object of parental love (or, of course, a permanent parental surrogate) and (ii) the acquisition of a strong sense of competence with respect to our ability to interact effectively with our social and physical environment.[1] It is obvious that whereas the latter continues to be important throughout our lives, the former does not. Of course, we may continue to value the love of our parents; the point, rather, is that as adults our sense of worth is not, if we develop normally, tied to our being loved by our parents. Does this mean, then, that the only important sense of worth to be counte-

This essay was originally published in *Philosophy Born of Struggle: Anthology of Afro-American Philosophy from 1917*, edited by Leonard Harris, Kendall/Hunt Publishing Company, 1983. Copyright © Laurence Thomas. Reprinted by permission of the author.

nanced among adults is that which turns upon their having a sense of competence? One reason to be skeptical that this is so is just that love, and therefore parental love, has very little to do with a person's performances. I believe that self-respect can be seen as the social analogue, for adults, to the sense of worth that is generated by parental love. My aim in this essay is to show the importance which this line of reasoning has for both moral theory and social philosophy.

I

It will be instructive to begin this section with a brief look at the role that parental love, as opposed to parental praise, plays in the life of the child. Indeed, what I shall have to say will be all too brief; however, I believe it will be enough to at least give one a feel for why I take self-respect to be the social analogue for adults to the sense of worth that is generated by parental love.

Praise, being a form of approval, is conceptually tied to a person's performances. There can be no such thing as serious praise for behavior of which we disapprove. Insincere praise is empty and sometimes cruel. Love, on the other hand, has precious little to do with a person's performance. It constitutes both an acceptance of a person and a concern for his well being, which is not tied to what he does. It is unconditional, not because one may never cease to love an individual, but because there is nothing which a person can do that constitutes a conceptual bar to loving him. Thus, one can have the most genuine love for a person whose behavior one disapproves of in every way. The person can even be one's enemy. (The Christian commandment to this effect is thought to be difficult, not conceptually impossible.)

Now, whereas both parental love and praise play a most important role in the child's life, the very fact that the child is very dependent upon his parents for food, shelter, and protection should make it obvious why parental love plays yet a more significant role in the child's life than parental praise. A child would be in an awful way if his being provided with these things were conditional upon his doing what his parents deemed praiseworthy. Because learning how to do as one's parent have instructed one is precisely what one does as a child, the fear of parental rejection would loom large in the life of a child for whom receiving these benefits was contingent upon his doing what his parents deemed praiseworthy; for he would be constantly fearful of failing to behave in this way. Moreover, if a child's receiving parental protection were made contingent upon this sort of thing, then out of fear he would be more reluctant to engage in exploratory behavior. This is because he would lack the assurance that his parents would protect him when things got out of hand for him. This would be unfortunate for the child, since engaging in exploratory behavior is one of the chief means by which the child acquires a strong sense of competence.[2]

As no doubt one has already surmised, the significance of parental love lies in the fact that, first of all, it allays, if not precludes entirely, the child's fear of parental rejection; second, it minimizes the child's fear of engaging in exploratory behavior. For, as a result of being the continuous object of parental love, the child comes to have the conviction that the reason why he matters to his parents is just that they love him, and not that he has this or that set of talents or that he behaves in this or that way. Parental praise, as important as it is,[3] could never instill in the child a conviction such as this. As a result of parental love, the child then comes to have a sense of worth that does not turn upon either his abilities or his behavior. This sense of worth is, I want to say, the precursor to self-respect.

To the fact that there are many ways in which persons can be treated is added morality, a conception of how persons ought to be treated. The primary way in which a rights-based moral theory does this is by postulating a set of basic rights, which each person has simply in virtue of being a person. Creatures other than persons may have a subset of these rights; and some creatures, as well as other things, may have none of these rights. (For the purposes of this essay, I shall be concerned with only a rights-based moral theory.[4]) Persons, then, have full moral status; some creatures other than persons have partial moral status; and still others, along with other things, have no moral status at all.[5] While I shall offer an illustration of these points below (in section III), we can, on the basis of these remarks alone, say what self-respect comes to. A person has self-respect, I shall say, if and only if he has the conviction that he is deserving of full moral status, and so the basic rights of that status, simply in virtue of the fact that he is a person. Having self-respect, then, is not so much a matter of being able to give a run-down of what one's basic rights happen to be as it is a way of viewing oneself vis-à-vis others from the moral point of view. Everyone, including oneself, is equally deserving of full moral status and so of being treated in accordance with the basic rights that come with that status. And the reason for this is just that one is a person.

It is clear that, understood in this way, self-respect makes no reference at all to the abilities of persons, since a person is no less that in view of what her abilities are. If it is one of our considered moral judgments that a person's moral status ought not to be a function of what her natural endowments are or how she behaves, then this judgment is captured by the view of self-respect that I am putting forth. What is more, it follows, on my view, that in order to have self-respect, a person need not have a morally acceptable character. For the belief that one is deserving of full moral status is certainly compatible with the belief that one's moral character is not up to par. And this underscores the fact that self-respect, as I conceive it, does not turn upon a person's abilities. For there can be no question but that having a morally accepted character calls for abilities and capacities that we do not all possess equally. Consider, for example, such moral virtues as honesty and kindness. The former calls for a considerable measure of resoluteness, a strong will one might say; the latter is intimately connected with the capacity for the sympathetic understanding. And it is a brute fact about this world that individuals differ with respect to these capacities.[6] As one might surmise from the fact that I do not take self-respect to be tied to having an acceptable moral character, I am not offering a Kantian account of this notion.[7] This, I believe, is a strength rather than a weakness of the account that I offer, though I shall make no attempt to defend this claim here. (But see the next section's concluding paragraph.)

Thus far, I have merely offered an account of self-respect; I have not argued for its soundness. The argument that I shall offer will draw upon two examples from the black experience in the United States (section III); however, that argument will presuppose an appreciation for the difference between self-respect and self-esteem. So, before I begin it, a brief discussion about this latter concept is in order.

II

William James defined self-esteem as the ratio of a person's successes to his aspirations:[8]

$$\text{SELF-ESTEEM} = \frac{\text{SUCCESSES}}{\text{ASPIRATIONS}}$$

Contemporary psychologists have made no theoretical advance over James's notion of self-esteem.[9] They consider it to be the sense of worth that an individual has, which turns upon his evaluation of his ability to interact effectively with his environment, especially his social environment. It is of utmost importance to note that self-esteem is quite neutral between ends in that the successful pursuit of any end towards which a person aspires can contribute to his self-esteem. If a person has the appropriate aspirations, then being any one of the following can be a significant source of self-esteem for her or him: being a good parent, the first woman to sit on the United States Supreme Court, a gigolo, a call girl, a highly regarded academician, a highly regarded member of one's religious faith, a racist or a sexist.[10] Of course, it may be that we are more likely to value some ends rather than others; indeed, this may be so precisely because the society in which we live encourages the pursuit of some ends rather than others. None of this, though, militates against the point that self-esteem is neutral between ends.

Now, as James's formula makes clear, the more (or less) in line our successes are with our aspirations, the higher (or lower) our self-esteem will be. From this it straightforwardly follows that, other things equal, the well-endowed are favored to have high self-esteem, since the well-endowed, in comparison to those whose natural assets are minimal, have fewer ends that are beyond their reach. There are more things that the well-endowed can do successfully. Given the premise that people differ with respect to their natural assets, it seems implausible to suppose that everyone can have (equally) high self-esteem. For, if anything like what Rawls calls the Aristotelian Principle and its companion effect are sound,[11] the displays of complex talents and skills by others will cause some to aspire beyond their reach. After all, any and every person could be a great janitor or typist, say, if only he should try, whereas it is far from obvious that any and every person could be a great physicist or artist, if only he should try. In any society where people are free to attempt to pursue the ends of their choosing, it is virtually inevitable that the talents of some will fail to match their aspirations and, therefore, that some will have low self-esteem. If I am right in this, then, although it may be that social institutions are unjustly arranged, if undermining the self-esteem of persons is the very point of the arrangement, it would be a mistake to suppose that this is so simply because such institutions do not guarantee that each member of society will have (equally) high self-esteem. As we shall see (section V), this is a very important respect in which self-esteem differs from self-respect.

I have said that if a person has the appropriate aspirations, then the successful pursuit of any end can contribute significantly to his self-esteem. I want to conclude this section with the observation that the aim to lead a morally good life is no exception to this claim. A person's high self-esteem can turn just as much upon his moral accomplishments as it can upon his accomplishments in sports or the academy. Naturally enough, we may think of self-esteem that turns upon the former as moral self-esteem. And just as the failure to measure up to our non-moral aspirations occasions nonmoral shame, the failure to measure up to our moral aspirations occasions moral shame. I have bothered to make this point explicit in order to show that we can capture an important Kantian insight in the absence of a Kantian conception of self-respect. If we assume that everyone morally ought to aspire to lead a minimally decent moral life, then we can rightly say that there is a sense of shame—indeed, moral shame—that a person rightly feels in failing to do so. This we can say without saying that such a person must view herself or himself as not being deserving of full moral status. Thus, in order to experience moral shame a person need not lack self-respect. Self-respect, as I conceive of it, cannot be the source of moral shame; but, as these remarks make clear, the account of self-respect offered leaves room for such shame. I have not taken it out of the picture; rather, I have merely shifted its location.

III

I have offered an account of self-respect, which I have argued is distinct from self-esteem. I turn now to argue for the soundness of the account offered. As I remarked, I shall do this by drawing upon two examples from the black experience.

By definition (or so it seems) an Uncle Tom is a black who lacks self-respect. I do not know whether or not Booker T. Washington was an Uncle Tom; nor shall I be concerned to take a stand on the matter. I do know, however, that he has often been called an Uncle Tom.[12] What has been the force behind this epithet? Well, it is obvious that no one familiar with his life could have ever meant that he was lacking in talent or, in any case, that he set his sights too high. For this was a man who, though he was born a slave, went on to found an academic institution, the Tuskegee Institute. This is not something that a minimally talented person is apt to do; and he did as much as any black could have reasonably hoped to do, life being what it was for blacks then. What is more, Washington was held in high esteem, for both his accomplishments and his views, by a great many blacks and whites, which undoubtedly served to enhance his self-esteem. (This point is compatible with the view of self-esteem presented, since our conviction that we are performing well the tasks that we have set out to perform is secured or, at the very least, supported by the admiration and esteem that we receive from others. And holding the right views is one of the many aims that a person may have.[13]) Washington was most surely a man of considerable self-esteem, as defined here; and it is rather implausible to suppose that, in calling him an Uncle Tom, people have meant to deny this.

Nor is it plausible to suppose that, in calling him an Uncle Tom, people have meant to cast aspersions upon his moral character. At any rate, not even W. E. B. DuBois, his staunchest contemporary critic,[14] took Washington's flaw to be that he had a morally corrupt character. On the contrary, what had made him seem so vulnerable to the charge of being an Uncle Tom is that he appeared to be too accepting of the status quo. It was the prevailing view of whites back then that blacks were not socially prepared for full-fledged citizenship and, therefore, that social intercourse between blacks and whites, political participation on the part of the blacks, and rights given to them should be kept to a minimum. It has seemed to a great many that, in his "Atlanta Exposition Address,"[15] it is precisely this view that Washington, himself, endorsed. If he did endorse this view, then the charge that he was an Uncle Tom seems fair enough. But, for all we know, and it is certainly not implausible to suppose this, Washington may have been a very shrewd and calculating black whose public stance was designed to appease the status quo in order to assure continued financial support from whites for the educational endeavors of blacks. If so, then I should think that a great deal more has to be said before one has a convincing case that he was an Uncle Tom. For, even if one should find fault with his strategy, the fact that it was a strategy, which did not reflect Washington's actual beliefs about how blacks should be treated, designed to advance the cause of blacks would be reason enough to resist labeling him an Uncle Tom.

But, now, suppose that Washington did subscribe to the prevailing view about blacks then; why would this warrant the charge that he was an Uncle Tom and so lacked self-respect? Before answering this question, I should first like to say a word about the sort of rights that come with having full moral status.

Both animals and persons have a right not to be treated cruelly. Only the latter, however, have a right to be treated fairly; hence, animals have only partial moral status, whereas persons have full moral status. Inanimate things have no moral status at all. They have nothing resembling a right nor are there any duties owed them; though, to be sure, what one does to or with an inanimate thing may constitute a moral wrong in that one is thereby violating some right or duty.[16] In any event, what is clear is that possession of the rights mentioned has absolutely nothing to do with having a morally good character. This is most obvious in the case of animals, since they lack the capacity for such. And to see that this is so in the case of persons, observe that if the right to be treated fairly were grounded in having a morally good character, then we could not, contrary to what we presently hold, treat a criminal unfairly by punishing him more harshly than he deserves nor could we treat one criminal more (or less) fairly than another, since, by hypothesis, criminals lack a morally good character. But, needless to say, we can do both of these things. Mutatis mutandis, the argument holds for the right that persons have not to be treated cruelly. Now, I take it to be equally clear that possession of the rights mentioned also has absolutely nothing to do with the talents or abilities of persons. This view has general acceptance, so I shall not bother to argue the case. Whether or not there are other rights that persons have in virtue of having full moral status, the two that I have mentioned, especially the right to be treated fairly, will suffice for our purposes.

The right to be treated fairly is a very powerful right in that it ranges over other rights, institutional ones, in particular, in the following way: First, fairness rules out irrelevant grounds for having institutional rights such as the right to vote. Thus, the grandfather clause,[17] to take an example, is ruled out by considerations of fairness as a requirement for having the right to vote. Second, fairness requires (a) that with respect to the same rights, the grounds for having them be the same and (b) that equal protection be given to the same rights. So, as I indicated, the right to fair treatment applies to rights that persons do not have simply in virtue of the fact that they have full moral status. To have the conviction that one is deserving of fair treatment in virtue of the fact that one is a person is to have a fundamentally important conviction and a tremendous sense of worth; accordingly, I shall assume that a person who has this conviction has self-respect.

It should be easy enough to see how what has just been said applies to Booker T. Washington. If, in fact, he believed that blacks were not deserving of full-fledged citizenship; if, in particular, he believed that the franchise was something of which blacks should have to prove themselves worthy, then he is quite vulnerable to the charge that he was an Uncle Tom. As is the case now, the right to vote was not, during Washington's time, something that had to be earned: one needed only to be born in this country and to reach the age of majority. This is how whites were treated then; and Washington should have believed, regardless of what he maintained publicly, that considerations of fairness required blacks be treated in the same way. If he, or anyone else, did not see that it was unfair that blacks should have to earn this fundamentally important right, when whites did not have to do so, then he failed to see that, even in the case of institutional rights, a person's claim to fair treatment is not secured by either his social standing as determined, say, by his wealth and mastery of the social graces or the hue of his skin. If so, then the charge that he was an Uncle Tom, and so lacked self-respect, would appear to be warranted. This claim holds even if Washington himself had earned the right to vote, since he was mistaken in thinking that he had to earn it.

If, indeed, Washington did lack self-respect, and I have not maintained that he did, I suspect it is because he did not allow the law to be subject to any significant moral criticism. He was an extreme legal positivist, one might say.[18] I say this because a person might argue, with some plausibility, that Washington viewed the equality of the races as a moral ideal, but thought that social institutions were at liberty to determine how this moral ideal would be realized. There is no surer sign, however, that a person lacks self-respect than that he should hold this view. For, at the very minimum, morality is about how persons should treat one another; and this is done primarily in the context of and, therefore, is largely influenced by the social institutions of society. Anyone who subscribes to extreme legal positivism has so little appreciation for this fact that it would seem that the very point of morality itself escapes him. As these remarks suggest, I do not take extreme legal positivism to be a very coherent view at all. It is an unfortunate fact, and a testimony to the tremendous power of social institutions, though, that incoherence is no bar to what people can be socialized to believe. Still, if the charge that Washington lacked self-respect can be made to stick, saddling him with this incoherent view would be preferable to saddling him with the view that equality for blacks was not even a moral ideal. To my mind, at any rate, it is not very likely that Washington believed the latter; nor is it very likely that he lacked self-respect. For he was far too determined and labored far too hard to better the conditions of blacks during his time. I seriously doubt that this could be said of a person who lacked self-respect.

The civil rights movement of the 1960s provide us with another illustration from the black experience that supports the account of self-respect presented in this essay. At the outset, I should acknowledge that as a result of the civil rights movement, the self-esteem of many blacks was enhanced as business and social institutions in the United States opened their more privileged positions to blacks in increasingly greater numbers and as various aspects of black culture and history gained greater appreciation in the American mainstream. And it is clear that both the collective pride and self-esteem of blacks was enhanced.[19] I take as evidence of this the change in hairstyles and, most importantly, the fact that the term "black," which hitherto had been considered a most disparaging term, replaced "coloured" and "Negro" as the accepted term for referring to persons of African descent.

Now, as significant as the changes that I have just described were, the civil rights movement wrought yet a more fundamental change in the lives of blacks. It enhanced their self-respect. It secured or, in any event, made more secure the conviction on the part of blacks that they are deserving of full moral status and, therefore, of the right to fair treatment. One must remember, after all, that the civil rights movement did not straightaway result in the vast majority of blacks going on to pursue careers that greatly enhanced their self-esteem. Nor did it result in each black discovering in himself talents that hitherto had gone unnoticed by him. And although it is certainly true that the physical features of whites came to be a less important yardstick by which blacks measured their own physical attractiveness, the end result was not that all blacks got to be beautiful. Thus, if the success of the civil rights movement were to be judged along these lines only, then it would have to be deemed a failure. But, in at least one very important respect a failure it was not.

A person did not need to acquire a new career, to discover new talents in himself, or to consider his physical appearance improved in order to feel the effects of the civil rights movement. For, the raison d'etre of this movement was not to secure these things as such. Rather, it was to stir the conscience of the American people, to arouse their sense of justice, and to move them to end the injustices that blacks have suffered.[20] *The* goal of the civil rights movement was to secure the conviction on the part of both blacks and whites that blacks were deserving of full moral status and, therefore, of just and fair treatment. In order for blacks to see themselves in this light, a new career, or whatever, was far from necessary. Of course, given what the unjust treatment of blacks came to, the just treatment of blacks could not help but have a positive effect upon their self-esteem. (I take justice to be subsumable under fairness.[21] Nothing of substance turns on the talk about justice here.)

However, it would be a mistake to generalize from the civil rights movement to the conclusion that whenever a group of people who have been treated unjustly are treated justly, their self-esteem, as well as their self-respect, will be enhanced. For the unjust treatment of people does not, as a matter of logic, involve denying the fact that they have the talents and abilities to pursue, with hope of success, and to appreciate the ends of the academy and the other professions. If it did, then we would be logically committed to the absurd view that we could not treat unjustly those who lack the natural endowment to pursue such ends. This last remark points to why self-respect is a more fundamental sense of worth than self-esteem. It could turn out, given our abilities, that so few ends are within our reach that our having low self-esteem is all but inevitable. But not so with self-respect, since it is not, in the first place, a sense of worth that turns upon what our abilities happen to be. Thus, observe that in the 1960s what blacks demanded, in the name of justice and fairness, is that they be allowed the freedoms, opportunities, and privileges to which others had been so long accustomed. What they did not demand, and rightly so, is that they be given the natural assets to do as others do. It is because blacks had a claim to the enhancement of their self-respect that they had a claim to the enhancement of their self-esteem. Sometimes the importance of the latter, as in the case at hand, is derivative upon the importance of the former; the importance of self-respect, however, is never derivative upon the importance of self-esteem.

In this section, I have drawn upon two examples from the black experience in the United States to support the account of self-respect offered in this essay. Using the life of Booker T. Washington and the lives of blacks during the civil rights movement, I have tried to show, respectively, that the sense of worth that the former lacked, purportedly, and the latter gained could not have been simply self-esteem. For, what the former lacked, if anything, was a proper conception of himself from the moral point of view; and what the latter gained or had enhanced was just such a conception of themselves. In the wake of this the self-esteem of the latter was also enhanced. To lose sight of this fact is not only to fail to understand the significance of the civil rights movement, but also to fail to grasp the importance of distinguishing between two important, but very different senses of worth, namely, self-respect and self-esteem.

IV

Since self-esteem has to do with the assessment that persons make of their abilities, there are some rather reliable indicators of whether or not a person has (high) self-esteem or lacks it (has low self-esteem). For example, the former tend to be more self-confident and independent than the latter, and they are more inclined to believe that what they do will be well received by others.[22] Since, on the other hand, self-respect has nothing at all to do with the assessment that persons make of their abilities, one naturally wonders whether or not there are any reliable indicators of whether or not a person has this sense of worth. I believe that there are.

It will be remembered that those who have self-respect have the conviction that they are deserving of fair treatment simply by virtue of the fact that they are persons. However, there can be both good and bad reasons for tolerating unfair treatment, for not insisting upon being treated fairly, as I shall illustrate in what follows.

In 1955, Mrs. Rosa Parks became a hero to the people of Montgomery, Alabama, when she refused to follow one of the Jim Crow practices insisted upon by the driver of the bus on which she was riding, namely that of moving to the back of the bus in order to accommodate white passengers.[23] The three other blacks who were on the bus at the time followed the bus driver's command, but Mrs. Parks remained seated. Her arrest was the catalyst of the black civil rights movement.

In retrospect, we might be inclined to say that Mrs. Parks had self-respect, but not the three blacks who followed the bus driver's command. But this is not as obvious as all that. When she first boarded the bus, which was nearly empty, she took the first seat behind the section reserved for whites. The bus driver's command to move to the rear of the bus came after all of the seats had been taken, which meant that Mrs. Parks would have had to stand had she moved. That she did not want to stand seems clear, that she was insisting on her rights out of self-respect is not so clear. We do not know the reason why she did not move; we do not know the reason why the other three did move. But supposing that she refused to move out of considerations of self-respect, it does not follow that she alone had self-respect. For each had a self-interested justificatory reason for obeying the bus driver's command, given the way blacks were treated in the South back then for standing up to whites. That a person has self-respect does not mean that he has to put his life on the line.

As I remarked, when Mrs. Parks first boarded the bus, she sat in the black section of the bus (the other three blacks did as well). What was her reason for doing this? (1) Is it that she did not mind this Jim Crow practice so long as she did not have to stand? Or, (2) is it that she did not want to invoke an outbreak of hostility towards her? Or, (3) is it rather that her income was a major part of the family income and she was concerned not to do anything that would result in a major loss in the family's income?

It is conceivable that the answer to all three of these questions is an affirmative one. If, though, the answer to (1) is affirmative, whereas the answer to (2) and (3) is negative, then there would be a strong presumption that she lacked self-respect. If, on the other hand, the answer is affirmative to the second question, but negative to the others, then she acted out of self-interested reasons, and justifiably so. And if the answer is affirmative to (3) only, then her action, although not a self-interested one, was nonetheless justified. Finally, suppose, though it seems rather unlikely, that Mrs. Parks's reason for sitting in the black section when she first boarded the bus was that she is a "good" black who knows her place in a public setting, and that one of her aims was to continue to convey this impression to whites. Well, although we have here a self-interested reason why Mrs. Parks took the black section of the bus, this self-interested reason, far from rebutting the presumption that she lacked self-respect, would seem to confirm just this lack on her part.

The case of Mrs. Parks illustrates quite clearly the important place that reasons have in determining whether or not a person has or lacks self-respect. And by way of our embellishment of the case, we hit upon the extremely significant point that acting out of self-interested reasons does not always suffice to rebut the presumption that a person lacks self-respect. This is as it should be, surely; for we should hardly want to say that lacking self-respect precludes having self-interested reasons for acting.

Self-interested and other-regarding reasons, then, may suffice to rebut the presumption that a person lacks self-respect, though she tolerates unfair treatment. Reasons of this sort are justificatory ones. They are reasons that recommend this or that course of action. However, there can be good nonjustificatory reasons why a person fails to insist upon being treated fairly. Consider the case of accommodating slaves in the Old South. It may have been futile for them to insist upon being treated fairly; and they may have not done so for just this reason. Or, they may have grown weary from insisting upon such treatment either because previous efforts along this line were so futile or because doing so had brought them so much suffering. Unfortunately, it is so easy for excuses of this sort to mask the fact that a person no longer has the conviction that he is deserving of fair treatment. Thus, in spite of the fact that they will gain nothing and bring nothing but suffering to themselves, sometimes an oppressed people must protest the injustices visited upon them just to convince themselves that this conviction has not slipped away.[24] The ideal may have it that we fight for what we believe. To this, reality demurely adds: But if we fight first, then we will surely come to believe.[25]

V

It is obvious that the social institutions among which we live have a most profound affect upon the way in which we view ourselves. This essay would be incomplete if I said nothing about what ought to be the connection between having self-respect and living amongst social institutions. In view of the fact that having self-respect calls for having the conviction that one is deserving of fair treatment and that the social institutions of society ought to be fairly arranged, it is almost too obvious for words that I want to say that the social institutions of society are fairly arranged if and only if they are conducive to every member of society having self-respect. But this needs to be explained.

To have self-respect is to have certain beliefs. However, it clearly will not do to maintain that the social institutions of society are fairly arranged if and only if every member of society has the appropriate beliefs. There are too many things which might prevent a person from having the appropriate beliefs that have nothing to do with any social institutions being unfairly arranged. Let us say, then, that the social institutions of society are fairly arranged and, therefore, conducive to everyone having self-respect if and only if from the standpoint of such institutions everyone is justified in having the beliefs for which self-respect calls, since to be justified in believing a proposition does not entail believing that proposition. This much alone enables us to say when there is a strong presumption that the social institutions of society are not conducive to some of its members having self-respect and so are not fairly arranged, as the following argument will show.

Let L represent the class of persons in a given society who lack self-respect. And let K represent any class of persons that is identifiable by the fact that all of its members share the same biological or social characteristics, for example, all are of the same sex, or share the same ethnic or religious background. If the social institutions of society are fairly arranged, and so conducive to everyone having self-respect, then barring some special explanation, no K-like *class* should turn out to be a subclass of the L-class.[26] This, of course, is not to say that no *member* of the K-class will be a member of L, but rather that not all of the members of any such class will be members of L. If there is a K-class that is a subclass of L, then there is the presumption that the social institutions of society are not conducive to members of that class having self-respect and, therefore, that the members of that class are not being fairly treated by such institutions. Hence, there is the presumption that society is to blame for the lack of self-respect on the part of the members of that class. Observe that these remarks do not apply, mutatis mutandis, to self-esteem, since social institutions that are fairly arranged are not thereby conducive to persons having (high) self-esteem. In any event, the idea here is a very straightforward one. If all the members of a heterogeneous class are justified in believing a proposition to be true, then, barring some special explanation, the class of persons who fail to believe the proposition to be true should not be identifiable on grounds other than that its members fail to believe that the proposition is true.

The mark of a sexist or racist society is that its social institutions target people on the basis of either their gender or skin color.[27] The remarks in the preceding paragraph bring into sharper relief the reason why that targeting is so morally repugnant.

A final comment. I believe that the arguments of this section bring into sharper focus the difference between self-respect and self-esteem. For observe that it would be most implausible to suppose that the social institutions of a society are fairly arranged if and only if they are conducive to everyone having (high) self-esteem. One of the things that political theorists differ about is the latitude that justice or fairness gives society in the arrangements of its social institutions. I have a hunch that one reason why there is so often an impasse between political theorists is that they fail to distinguish between self-respect and self-esteem. Liberals cannot really mean that the social institutions of a society are fairly arranged only if the members of society have (high) self-esteem, though they can mean this about self-respect. And libertarians cannot really be indifferent to whether or not the social institutions of society are conducive to the members of society having self-respect, though they can be about self-esteem.

Indeed, I believe that the failure to take seriously this distinction is one reason why Marx's critique of capitalism founders somewhat. A capitalist society, to be sure, is compatible with persons having low self-esteem. But, I see no reason to suppose that a communist society is not. Any economic system that is compatible with persons valuing ends that are beyond their reach is compatible with persons having low self-esteem. Both capitalism and Marx's communism are compatible with this. And if we suppose, for the sake of argument, that the social institutions of Marxist society would be conducive to everyone having self-respect, suffice it to say there is no conceptual bar to a capitalist society being conducive to everyone having self-respect.

After all, the United States, which is unquestionably (thought to be) a capitalist society, could have had a different history, surely. American slavery need not ever have existed, nor the Jim Crow practices of the Old South. Educational practices need not ever have required the Supreme Court's *Brown v. Board of Education* decision in 1954, and so on. If racism had never existed in this country, it would not follow that all blacks would have led fulfilling lives, and so all would have had high self-esteem. However, it would follow that their moral status would never have been called into question; indeed, it would have been affirmed. If these remarks, sketchy though they may be, are sound, then, as I have claimed, the social institutions of a capitalistic society can be conducive to persons having self-respect.

VI

In the introduction to this essay, I made the claim that self-respect is the social analogue to the sense of worth engendered by parental love. That must have seemed to be a quite controversial claim those many pages ago. I hope it is less so now. Self-respect, I have tried to show, is a sense of worth that is not in any way tied to a person's abilities. It is a moral sense of worth. It is among social institutions that we live, and these institutions can be conducive to our having self-respect. Not only that, it is of the utmost importance that social institutions are conducive to persons having self-respect, just as it is of the utmost importance that parents love their children. The reasons why both of these claims are true has nothing whatsoever to do with the talents and abilities of persons. Now, if drawing upon the black experience has made it easier to see that self-respect is the social analogue to the sense of worth that is engendered by parental love, then our indebtedness to that experience may very well be greater than many have been inclined to suppose.

Notes

This essay develops and refines a view I have developed in a number of essays: "Morality and Our Self-Concept," *The Journal of Value Inquiry* 12 (1978); "Rawlsian Self-Respect and the Black Consciousness Movement," *The Philosophical Forum* 9 (1978); and "Capitalism versus Marx's Communism," *Studies in Soviet Thought* 20 (1979). Permission from the editors of these journals to draw upon these essays is gratefully acknowledged.

1. In connection with (i) see, e.g., John Bowlby, *Child Care and the Growth of Love* (Baltimore: Penguin Books, 1953); with (ii) see, e.g., Robert W. White, *Ego*

and Reality in Psychoanalytic Theory (New York: International Universities Press, Inc., 1963). For arguments that support both (i) and (ii) see, among others, H. Rudolf Schaffer and Charles K. Cook, "The Role of the Mother in Early Social Development," in Harry McGurk, ed., *Issues in Childhood Social Development* (London: Metheun and Co., 1978), and M. Rutter, "Early Sources of Security and Competence," in Jerome Bruner and Alison Garton, eds., *Human Growth and Development* (Oxford: Oxford University Press, 1978).

2. See White, *Ego and Reality*, ch. 3.

3. For the way in which I have unpacked the difference between parental love and parental praise, I am much indebted to Gregory Vlastos, "Justice and Equality," in Richard Brandt, ed., *Social Justice* (Englewood Cliffs, N.J.: Prentice-Hall, 1962). See section II especially. I have also benefited from the following essays: Ann Swidler, "Love and Adulthood in American Culture" and Leonard I. Pearlin, "Life Strains and Psychological Distress Among Adults." Both are in Neil J. Smelser and Erik H. Erikson, eds., *Themes of Work and Love in Adulthood* (Cambridge, Mass.: Harvard University Press, 1980).

4. For two excellent discussions regarding the difference between a rights-based moral theory and a duty-based moral theory, see Ronald Dworkin, *Taking Rights Seriously* (Cambridge, Mass.: Harvard University Press, 1977), ch. 6, and W. L. Sumner, *Abortion and Moral Theory* (Princeton, N.J.: Princeton University Press, 1980), chs. 3, 5. The notion of self-respect, as I understand it, can be accommodated in a utilitarian framework; however, it would seem that it would only have derivative importance in that framework.

5. As far as I can tell, my use of the term "moral status" exactly parallels Sumner's use of the term "moral standing." See chs. 1 and 4 of *Abortion and Moral Theory*.

6. For an eloquent statement of this point, see Bernard Williams's essay "The Idea of Equality" in his *Problems of the Self* (Cambridge: Cambridge University Press, 1973).

7. I am guided here by what Kant says in the *Lectures on Ethics* in the section "Proper Self-Respect" and his second formulation of the Categorical Imperative: "Always act so that you treat humanity, whether in your own person or in another, as an end, never merely as a means."

8. William James, *Principles of Psychology*, vol. 1 (New York: Dover Publications, 1950), "The Consciousness of Self."

9. Roger Brown in *Social Psychology* (New York: The Free Press, 1965) writes that James has "written, with unequaled sensitivity and wisdom, of the self as an object of knowledge, as a mental construction of the human organism" (p. 648). Stanley Coopersmith, in *The Antecedents of Self-Esteem* (San Francisco, Calif.: W.H. Freeman and Company, 1967), writes, "Earlier psy-

chologist and sociologists such as William James...provided major insights and guidelines for the study of self-esteem. Their formulations remain among the most cogent on the topic, particularly their discussions of the sources of high and low esteem" (p. 27).

10. On the relevance of self-esteem to being a sexist or racist, see my "Sexism and Racism: Some Conceptual Differences," *Ethics* 90 (1980), and my "Sexism, Racism, and the Business World," *Business Horizons* 24 (1981).

11. *A Theory of Justice* (Cambridge, Mass.: Harvard University Press, 1971), p. 426.

12. For a discussion of the life of Booker T. Washington, see, among others, John Hope Franklin, *From Slavery to Freedom*, 3rd ed. (New York: Random House, 1967), ch. 21, and Charles E. Silberman, *Crises in Black and White* (New York: Random House, 1964), ch. 5. And for the story of his life, see, of course, Washington's autobiography *Up From Slavery* (Boston, Mass.: Houghton, Mifflin, 1901).

13. Cf. Coopersmith, *Antecedents*, ch. 3.

14. *The Souls of Black Folk* (Chicago, Ill.: A. C. McClurg, 1903).

15. Consider the following passages from the address, which is to be found in Washington's autobiography, *Up From Slavery*, ch. 14:

    —No race can prosper till it learns that there is as much dignity in tilling a field as in writing a poem. It is at the bottom of life we must begin, and not at the top.

    —In all things that are purely social we can be as separate as the fingers, yet be one as the hand in all things essential to mutual progress.

    —It is important and right that all privileges of the law be ours, but it is vastly more important that we be prepared for exercising these privileges.

16. A great many creatures are capable of having expectations about how others will treat them or behave. See, e.g., Daniel C. Dennett, *Brainstorms* (Cambridge, Mass.: The MIT Press, Bradford Books, 1978), pp. 274–5. But only persons, or so it seems, are capable of having a conception of how others ought to treat them or behave; only persons are capable of having a conception of how they ought to treat others or behave. This capacity, it seems to me, is the mark of moral agency. And a being has full moral status, I want to say, if and only if it is a moral agent. Along with moral agency comes the capacity for moral character, a capacity that animals unequivocally lack.

17. Cf. William A. Mably, "Louisiana Politics and the Grandfather Clause," *The North Carolina Historical Review* 13 (1936).

18. On legal positivism, see H. L. A. Hart, *The Concept of Law* (Oxford: Oxford

University Press, 1961) and Martin P. Golding, *Philosophy of Law* (Englewood Cliffs, N.J.: Prentice-Hall, 1975).

19. I cannot stop here to distinguish fully between pride and self-esteem. I trust that the following marks will suffice. Suppose that I have just learned that one of my ancestors of long ago was an African king. This is very likely to enhance my pride, but not my self-esteem, since I will not come to think, nor will I expect that anyone else will or should do so, that I am better able to accomplish the tasks I set for myself. A person's self-esteem may be out of proportion to his actual accomplishments, but this does not mean that he has foolish pride. For this a person has when he puts himself on the line in a reckless way: either there is no need to prove himself or it is obviously not worth doing so. Although an unexpected accomplishment in a fun and casual game of sports is likely to swell my pride, it will do little for my self-esteem, since I do not really aspire to do well in sports. Finally, there is what I would pefer to call derivative self-esteem (collective self-esteem). If Ø is an end that is valued by society at large and, as it happens, persons of kind K tend to be the most successful at pursuing Ø; and if the association between end Ø and people of kind K becomes strong enough, then being of kind K can itself suffice to enhance a person's self-esteem. The self-esteem that comes with being a member of a high socio-economic class is perhaps the most striking example of this. The temptation to suppose that collective pride and self-esteem must come to the same thing should be resisted. To see this, one need only to let the example with which I began this discussion hold for an entire group.

   In any event, I should mention in connection with the self-esteem of blacks the work of Morris Rosenberg, *Conceiving the Self* (New York: Basic Books, 1979). It turns out that the integration of lower-class black children into predominantly white middle-class schools has had the undesirable effect of lowering the self-esteem of black children, whereas lower-class black children who attend predominantly black schools prove to have very high self-esteem. The explanation for this, of course, is that such black children are made more aware of their lower-class status. See Rosenberg, ch. 4.

20. See Rawls's discussion on the role of civil disobedience in *A Theory of Justice*, pp. 382–391.

21. This is Rawls's insight, which is first stated in his "Justice as Fairness," *The Philosophical Review* 68 (1958). To put it most intuitively, justice is simply fairness backed up by rules of enforcement, especially legal ones. We speak of the sword of justice, not the sword of fairness. Talk about the virtue of justice, as exhibited in the just man, is not all that much at odds with this point, if one supposes that the mark of the just man is that he does what should be

required of him whether or not this is so. He does not treat others *unfairly* although he could easily get away with doing so. I owe this point to Paul Ziff.

22. Coopersmith, *Antecedents*, ch. 3.

23. The story of Mrs. Rosa Parks is to be found in Martin Luther King, Jr., *Stride Toward Freedom* (New York: Harper & Row, 1958), pp. 43–46, 48–54.

24. This point is nicely developed by Bernard R. Boxill, "Self-Respect and Protest," *Philosophy and Public Affairs* 6 (1976) [chapter 4, this volume].

25. This point is most cogently developed in Daryl J. Bem, *Beliefs, Attitudes, and Human Affairs* (Belmont, Calif.: Brooks/Cole Publishing Company, 1970), ch. 6.

26. Thus, suppose that a society is homogeneous in its makeup. Or, suppose that all the members of a K-class are new to society, and that the effects of unfair treatment that they received in their former society have yet to wear off. Explanations of this sort are what I have in mind.

27. It is generally supposed that gravely unjust societies target some identifiable group in this way. But as I have tried to show this surmise is mistaken. See my "Law, Morality, and Our Psychology Nature," in *Social Justice*, Michael Brodie and David Braybrooke, eds., (Bowling Green, Ohio: Bowling Green Studies in Applied Philosophy, 1982), pp. 111–123.

14

✛

Race, Class, and the Social Construction of Self-Respect

✛

Michele M. Moody-Adams

Introduction

In the mid-1950s, when Kenneth Clark first investigated the influence of racial prejudice on children, discrimination appeared to pose a serious threat to the self-conception of many Black American children.[1] Clark's famous "doll study" of racial preferences in children tested black and white children in several age groups to determine which of two dolls—black or white—they preferred. A majority of Black children in every age group studied expressed a preference for the white doll and rejected the black doll. Of course, not every child who grew up during this period would have displayed such a response, but the self-conceptions of those who did seemed to have been distorted by the complex consequences of discrimination. Many social theorists hoped that social reforms of the 1960s might help remedy the problem. Yet when the study was recently

This essay was originally published in *The Philosophical Forum* 24 (1992–1993). Copyright © 1992 by the Philosophical Forum, Inc. Reprinted by permission of the Philosophical Forum, Inc.

repeated, the results were surprisingly similar to Clark's original findings: a majority of the Black children studied expressed the same kind of racial preferences as those of similar children in the 1950s.[2]

Anecdotal accounts suggest that the increasing economic isolation of some Black children in American cities may compound the effects of discrimination. A public teacher in a major American city recently reported a disturbing conversation with a ten-year-old Black child who was asked to explain his disruptive classroom behavior. When this student was cautioned that he was preventing his classmates (all of whom were Black) from learning, he replied that it didn't matter, since they were "nothing." Reminding him that he was disrupting his own education, he answered that he, too, was "nothing," and added "my mother told me I ain't nothing."[3]

This article describes and defends a new way of understanding the notion of self-respect, as a contribution to philosophical psychology and as an attempt to understand why the relevant social reforms seem to have failed the child in my example—and others like him. The first section defines and describes the two distinct components of self-respect and discusses the influences of social conditions on each component. I also distinguish self-respect from self-esteem and discuss the complicated relation between the two phenomena. The second section shows how socially developed expectations about persons and their capacities help shape self-conceptions and ultimately influence the ability to have and affirm self-respect and self-esteem. I show, further, how socially developed expectations—especially those bound up with class and race— sometimes undermine the capacity to develop a *robust* sense of self-respect. Finally, the third section discusses the most important social bases of self-respect. Social reforms may be a necessary component of any effort to ensure the socially widespread emergence of robust self-respect. Yet we can restore the social bases of self-respect only if we also seek to revise destructive expectations about persons and their characteristics—including many self-regarding expectations—that have supported unreformed social practices.

What Is Self-Respect?

Self-respect, or due respect for one's own worth, has two fundamental components. The first, more fundamental, component involves the conviction that one best affirms one's own value by using one's abilities and talents to contribute to one's survival. One who fails to act on this conviction fails to affirm self-respect, while one who lacks the conviction fails to have self-respect. Yet the conviction and the readiness, together, are just the minimum content of self-respect; a *robust* sense of self-respect is far more than simply a concern to use one's talents in the interest of self-preservation. Further, even the minimum content of self-respect is itself more than simply a concern for one's survival. A person might care about her own survival and yet be unwilling to try to contribute to it: such a person places some value on her own existence but lacks the attitude properly called self-respect. A person has self-respect only when the value she places on her own survival is sufficient to make her willing to contribute to it.

What constitutes contributing to one's survival will always be relative to the specific circumstances of an individual life. For instance, what might be a significant affirmation of the minimum content of self-respect for a hostage bound and gagged in a dark cell would be relatively insignificant for a person not confined in this way.[4] But virtually no human beings who are capable of consciousness and reflection are incapable of having and actively affirming the minimum content of self-respect. A mentally handicapped person who seeks employment, a young child who wants to be allowed to choose what to wear to school, even a person wishing to end some addictive behavior by first acknowledging a need for the assistance of others—all of these people affirm their possession of the minimum content of self-respect. Finally, most people have a tenacious and regularly observable tendency to seek, and to try to protect, the minimum content of self-respect. As I suggest below, even people who have suffered severe economic and social deprivation typically bear out this observation.

The second component of self-respect is a willingness to do whatever is within one's power to enhance or develop one's abilities and talents. A person who must travel long distances to work, for instance, might need to learn to drive if she cannot take public transport to work. The willingness to develop one's talents initially emerges because, usually, one can best exercise one's abilities when these abilities have been adequately developed.

The relation between the two aspects of self-respect is typically unproblematic—it is generally easy to reconcile concerns that might be generated by the two aspects of self-respect. However, certain circumstances may complicate the relation between the two components of self-respect, making it difficult to reconcile their demands. The first complication arises because human beings have the capacity to place intrinsic value on the development and exercise of some kinds of abilities—such as artistic abilities and moral capacities. Concerns generated by the development and exercise of such abilities may even take priority over concerns associated with the minimum content of self-respect. When this happens, self-forgetfulness or even self-sacrifice can be transformed into manifestations of self-respect.[5] A great writer who works to exhaustion to complete her book, or a lifeguard who risks his life to save a child from drowning, both illustrate this kind of transformation.

But a second, very different kind of complication arises when a person is consistently thwarted in her efforts to develop or exercise her talents and abilities. Such a person may begin to distrust her abilities; severe frustration and disappointment can make the exercise of one's talents and abilities seem antithetical to self-preservation. One may even come to believe that one's misfortune and unhappiness actually result from the exercise of one's talents and abilities—even when, as a matter of fact, one is not responsible for the unhappiness suffered. Thus children who suffer extreme abuse, for example, can come to hate the exercise of their distinctive talents and abilities—with dire consequences for their sense of self-respect.

Of course, the relation between the two components of self-respect can be more harmonious: indeed, a robust sense of self-respect must comfortably combine the two components (to some degree) over a lifetime. Moreover, a robust sense of self-respect is a central ingredient of a satisfying life. To see why, we must understand, first, that the two components of self-respect are often mutually reinforcing. The satisfaction that often accompanies the development of one's distinctive talents and abilities typically increases one's enjoyment of life. This increase may in turn strengthen one's conviction of the importance to one's self-respect of using and developing those abilities. Second, a robust sense of self-respect typically generates a wish to formulate and pursue an effective life plan rather than to seek self-preservation merely by means of ad hoc reactions to circumstances. One is likely to lead a better life in virtue of having and acting upon such a wish than if one never developed, or acted upon, such a wish. Thus John Rawls is right to view self-respect as a good that any rational person will want, whatever else she might want.[6] Finally, a robust sense of self-respect generally makes one better able, and more willing, to engage in the social cooperation that makes possible the rational pursuit of life plans. Since it is in general rational to want to encourage such cooperation, it is also rational to want every member of one's society to be given the fullest possible chance to develop a robust sense of self-respect.[7]

I distinguish self-respect from self-esteem. My account thus departs substantially from Rawls's claims about the content of self-respect. Rawls contends that "a person's sense of his own value" is equivalent to that person's "secure conviction that his conception of the good, his plan of life, is worth carrying out" (TJ 440). Rawls also claims that "self-respect implies a confidence in one's ability, so far as it is within one's power, to fulfill one's intentions" (TJ 440). Like other critics of this claim, I think that what Rawls describes here is not self-respect but self-esteem.[8] Moreover, the distinction between self-esteem and self-respect is crucial. How else can we understand that a person might lose confidence in the worth of some particular life plan without at the same time questioning her value as a person?[9] People can sometimes refine, revise, or relinquish a life plan (or some portion of it) should circumstances require them to do so. This is because self-respect is more fundamental, and less fragile, than self-esteem.

But while self-esteem—confidence in one's life plan—is distinct from self-respect—a due sense of one's worth—severe diminutions in self-esteem may nonetheless have devastating effects on self-respect. Such effects are most likely when a loss of confidence in one's plans causes a further loss of confidence in one's abilities to attend to one's own preservation. For instance, a person might attribute some drastic failure of his plans to his own mistakes (correctly or incorrectly) rather than to bad fortune or human malevolence. Should such a belief diminish his confidence in his abilities—and, especially if the failure is extreme enough—his self-respect will be severely diminished. In a very different sort of case, a person's response to misfortune (rather than to her own mistakes) might diminish her self-esteem so severely as eventually to diminish her confidence in her abilities and talents. Repeated or extreme bad fortune forges a particularly close link between the fragility of self-esteem and the fragility of self-respect. To be sure, we can neither insulate people from all imaginable misfortune nor prevent them from making mistakes. Yet we can support a socially sanctioned scheme of education that teaches people how to avoid those mistakes most likely to undermine self-respect. We can also try to remedy at least some accidents of fortune that pose the gravest danger to self-esteem and hence to self-respect. But once we have sought the appropriate remedies, we must leave people free to make mistakes. A robust sense of self-respect develops only if one is allowed to learn the extent and limits of one's own powers; here, experience is the best teacher.

While some circumstances threaten self-respect indirectly through self-esteem, a variety of circumstances can pose a *direct* threat to self-respect. Every society gradually develops a set of mechanisms—social, political, and economic institutions and practices—through which its members typically learn to seek constructive affirmations of self-respect. Yet one's access to mechanisms for the constructive affirmation of self-respect can be artificially limited. For instance, societies with a tradition of discrimination (de jure or de facto) against some group of people may effectively exclude those people from the typical mechanisms for affirming self-respect. The mere fact of discrimination alone (however arbitrary or unjust its basis) is unlikely to pose a direct threat to the self-respect of its victims. Self-respect is rarely so fragile. But when a scheme of discrimination is rooted in a complex network of degrading and dehumanizing fictions about its victims it can become truly dangerous to self-respect. The more entrenched this network of fictions, the more likely discrimination is to pose a threat to the self-respect of those subjected to it.

Such a scheme demands of those whose choices it restricts that they learn to reconcile two conflicting messages: (1) that self-respect is affirmed and experienced through participation in a particular set of social practices, but (2) that one is nonetheless effectively excluded from these practices. Some who are affected by such a scheme may also fail to discover alternative constructive means to affirm their worth, and they may not recognize the destructive cultural fictions as fictions. For such people, social exclusion is almost certain to weaken self-respect. Moreover, the responses of those who are continually excluded may have powerfully damaging consequences for themselves and their societies. Of course, we cannot ensure that all those who are able to participate in constructive social practices will actually choose to do so; it would be wrong to try if we are to protect the personal liberty that is central to self-respect. Yet we can identify those lingering effects of discrimination that continue to prevent people from choosing to accept or reject the relevant mechanisms. Though these effects are more complex than is often acknowledged, they can be remedied once we understand them.

The Social Construction of Self-Respect

I have so far assumed that the ability to have and affirm a robust sense of self-respect is greatly influenced by social circumstances. Important facts about the contexts in which people initially develop self-conceptions support this assumption. First, the vocabulary in which one learns to give expression to one's self-conception, and even the concepts that initially shape that self-conception, are products of the linguistic conventions of a given community. These conventions embody that community's normative expectations about emotion, thought, and action, and as these expectations change or become more complex so, too, will the self-conceptions of the members of that community. For instance, changes in the way American society views women's choices about work and marriage have changed the way women view themselves and have produced a variety of new and complex expectations about women and their sense of self-worth. Second, a society's normative expectations about emotion, thought, and action have an especially powerful influence on the development of self-respect. Every society gradually develops intricate patterns of normative expectations about what talents and abilities one ought to use in the service of self-preservation—even about what really constitutes survival or self-preservation. A complex society will produce intricate and overlapping patterns of such expectations. Further, self-contained communities within complex societies sometimes produce their own self-contained expectations about selves and self-respect. The self-conceptions of those in such communities will overlap very little with the self-conceptions of those outside such groups. Consider, for example, the self-contained expectations that shape life in America's Old Order Amish communities.[10]

Socially developed patterns of expectations about self-preservation, and about the acceptable means to that end, constitute what I call the *social construction of self-respect*. The social construction of self-respect is so important because it sets down the parameters within which we initially learn to evaluate our worth. In twentieth-century America, for example, a powerful set of normative expectations encourages Americans to link their worth as persons to the kind of work they do. As we might expect, people who conform to such expectation find that their self-respect tends to rise and fall with the character of their employment prospects. But complex societies produce overlapping patterns of expectations governing self-worth. Thus some Americans are more influenced by expectations linking self-worth with material possessions than with honest and productive work. In this regard, the Wall Street stockbroker whose bumper sticker announces that "Whoever dies with the most toys wins" bears important similarities to the urban high-school student preoccupied with getting the latest running shoes or a bigger piece of gold jewelry. Finally, the overlapping patterns of expectations that gradually evolve in complex societies—especially in their coarser adaptations—may conflict with each other. Contemporary American society provides striking examples of the very common conflict between the pursuit of honest work and the pursuit of material possessions. The stockbroker who turns to insider trading in pursuit of his "toys"—and the urban high-school student who sells drugs in pursuit of his—reveal the complexity of the social construction of self-respect in America.

One's ability to conform to any pattern of expectations about appropriate ways to affirm self-respect will be affected by one's social, political, and economic circumstances. A variety of circumstances can be relevant—including geographical location, religion, or native language, as well as class and race. The relevance of any particular circumstance is a function of each society's history and traditions. In a society with a long history of relative ethnic and racial homogeneity, for instance, one's class position may be the most important such circumstance. But in many societies, including American society, there are two such circumstances: class position and membership in a particular racial, ethnic, or religious group. Moreover, in such a society the influence of class position is usually registered most directly on the phenomenon of self-esteem—affecting one's confidence in the worth and attainability of one's life plans. In contrast, the influence of race designations (like that of ethnic or religious group membership) is typically registered most directly on self-respect.

The influence of class is due partly to the typically close connection between life plans and economic resources, but its influence also depends upon each person's understanding of how this connection affects her own life. Awareness of one's class position tends to have the most immediate effects on self-esteem, particularly on one's confidence in one's ability actually to carry out one's life plan. This awareness often determines a young person's sense of what *sort* of life plan she ought to pursue. Indeed, a young person's conviction of severe economic limitations on her life plans may even diminish her confidence in the worth of her most valued plans. Such a loss of confidence, as Rawls has suggested, can have devastating consequences—including apathy and cynicism about the worth of pursuing any constructive projects (TJ 440). Finally, the effects of class on self-esteem and motivation may be compounded by geographical isolation or by membership in a historically disfavored racial group—as the lives of some people in America's Appalachian region, and of some in America's urban underclass, reveal.[11]

Though the loss of self-esteem need not diminish self-respect, those who believe themselves confined in an unfavorable class position may find that circumstances directly affecting self-esteem ultimately pose a threat to their self-respect. The experience of one who believes himself economically confined may even be *phenomenologically* like the experience of legally enforced discrimination: it may be felt as exclusion from accepted social mechanisms for affirming self-respect. To be sure, families can sometimes mitigate the potentially destructive effects of economic limitations. Thus many political philosophers—especially in the liberal tradition—view the family as a private buffer against an array of potential assaults on self-esteem and self-respect.[12] But even in societies where laws protect the internal operations of the family as private, the family is a social and economic institution that registers the effects of social and economic isolation. The strain of membership in economically marginal positions may take a severe toll on the structure and well-being of the family itself. When social and economic marginality persist for several generations of one family, the family may even be the principal vehicle for conveying the belief that social isolation is a permanent fact of experience. As in my example of the child whose mother believes that he is "nothing," the economic isolation of a family may reinforce the tendency for diminutions in self-esteem to be transformed into challenges to self-respect.

The direct influence of racial designations—of "race"—on self-conceptions is registered in different and somewhat more complex ways. Not surprisingly, these designations can have especially damaging effects if a society has ever given explicit legal protection (and implicit social support) to racial discrimination. In such a society, merely outlawing discrimination will be unlikely to immediately undo its effects. For in a country not subject to authoritarian rule, legal rules persist for several generations only if there is relatively widespread acceptance of those rules. In order to understand obedience to law as something more than mere observable regularities in behavior, we must acknowledge the existence of what H. L. A. Hart has called an "internal perspective" on the rules of a legal system.[13] According to Hart, an adequate account of a legal system must recognize the existence of a perspective from which agents subject to legal rules take demands for conformity to the rules, and criticisms of breaches of the rules, to be justified. But if we accept Hart's view, as I think we should, we shall have to relinquish the notion that changing discriminatory laws might automatically eliminate discrimination—or its lingering structural consequences.

Yet accepting the plausibility of this view commits us to two important conclusions about discrimination in America. First, we must acknowledge the existence of a complex internal perspective on the legally supported exclusion of Black people from the social mechanisms for affirming self-respect. A complex set of beliefs and attitudes, transmitted from one generation to another for at least three hundred years, helped shore up the institution of American slavery, and the legally protected discrimination of subsequent periods. Second, it is simply implausible that this internal perspective on the exclusion of Black Americans might have magically ceased to exist with the bitterly contested end of legally-sanctioned discrimination in America.[14] In the "Letter from Birmingham Jail," Martin Luther King vividly describes some of the ways in which legally enforced segregation "distorts the soul and degrades human personality" for both the segregator and those subjected to segregation.[15] I contend that many of the relevant distortions will still be transmitted from one generation to another, as part of the social construction of self-respect, long after the "official" end of segregation.

Thus I claim that in America, the social construction of self-respect continues to bear the complex and often unacknowledged stamp of racial discrimination. What does it mean to claim this? First, in subtle—and sometimes blatant—ways, any group that has been legally excluded from American mechanisms for affirming self-respect will remain a disfavored group for some time. The "conceptual space" that a society historically marks out for a disfavored group places very definite boundaries on what those not in that group will think of them. Changing laws will not automatically alter these boundaries, and many people will unreflectively continue to accept the conceptual boundaries that have been imposed upon the disfavored group. In such a context, even some who actively try not to be "racists" may nonetheless perpetuate the very distortions used to justify discrimination. One of the most dangerous—and least questioned—distortions is the notion that the disfavored group has some psychological and behavioral "essence" that is allegedly genetically transmitted and inescapably possessed by all members of the group.[16] Moreover, beliefs about the alleged essence of some group need not be primarily negative in order to have destructive consequences. For the notion is destructive principally in the way it blinds those who believe in it to the obvious diversity to be found within each group. The Asian American student who neither likes nor excels at mathematics, and the Black American student who prefers physics to basketball alike suffer from the notion of racial essence. Nor is this notion any less destructive when it is unreflectively accepted by the disfavored group themselves as a self-conception. It is particularly destructive when they unreflectively accept a notion of their own "essence" that remains entangled in distortions bound up with a tradition of discrimination. Indeed, to accept such a notion, as I show below, is to participate in one's own victimization.

But the social construction of self-respect typically sustains discriminatory attitudes in a second way. For the social transmission of norms of self-respect continues to encourage many people to believe that they must measure their worth primarily by *comparison* with those in the disfavored group. In particular, some social norms governing self-respect lead many persons to believe that preserving their self-respect depends on being able to prove that they are "superior" to members of the disfavored group. The more precarious the class position of such people, the more they will learn to fear any changes in the "inferior" status of the disfavored group as challenges to the alleged certainties that shore up their sense of self-respect. This phenomenon obviously informs much recent racial discord in the urban centers of America. The more complex the hierarchies of class and ethnicity in a community—and the greater the sense of economic uncertainty there—the more complicated these fears and the resultant conflicts become.

Yet the distorting lessons of discrimination and exclusion are not always manifested in violent conflict: they continually deform and distort the most ordinary social interactions. Consider a college mathematics professor who unreflectively continues to accept unfounded preconceptions about the intellectual capacities of Black students. How might such a professor respond to a Black student's expression of confusion on some point in her class lecture? Coming from a white student, such a confusion would probably be viewed as a simple error, or even as a request for help. But this professor is likely to interpret the Black student's comment as though it were evidence of basic intellectual weakness. If the Black student has expressed confusion on previous occasions, his comments may then become evidence that Black students in general can't "keep up," or won't even try—that they are, in short, "inferior." Similar conduct from a white student would not be taken to support any analogous generalization about all white students. It would simply be a sign that this individual student can't, or even won't, keep up with the class. Moreover, the professor's preconceptions imply that the Black student who has in fact excelled is somehow suspect. Because this professor expects Black students to be weak at mathematics, she will regard a Black student's mathematical success as somehow a "fluke"—she may even question the student's honesty. Crucial social interactions can thus be shaped—one might say deformed—by discriminatory attitudes that commit those who hold them to profoundly *irrational* judgments about the abilities of those in some disfavored group.

Such distortions have consequences that transcend any single social interaction. To understand these consequences, we must take note of two important phenomena identified by social scientists. Robert Merton has described the phenomenon of the "self-fulfilling prophecy" whereby expectations of certain behavior in others often tend to evoke that very behavior.[17] For instance, a Black student might cease to put effort into a class taught by a professor who expects him to be inferior; the student may well presume (correctly) that his effort won't be taken seriously. Of course, he would then do poorly or even fail, thereby seeming to bear out the professor's prediction of failure. But this phenomenon calls attention to a second, described by Gordon Allport as the "reciprocal conduct of human beings in interaction."[18] Allport notes that in social interactions our expectations of others, and the behaviors they then tend to display, will constantly reinforce each other in a complex reciprocal fashion. To be sure, sometimes the effects of this reciprocal process are benign or even beneficial. But when the process begins either with racial exclusion, or with open expression of hatred based on ethnic or religious group membership, dangerous consequences may follow. The experience of hatred and exclusion will sometimes produce extreme anger and bitterness in its victims. Further, those who—for various reasons—come to believe that there is nothing to be gained by restraining their anger may openly display such feelings. But of course, behavioral manifestations of these feelings may then be taken by those not in the disfavored group to "confirm" the culture's reasons for hate and exclusion. Racial and ethnic hatred and exclusion thus initiate processes that distort and deform social interactions by generating mistrust and suspicion, and sometimes violent conflict.

I have so far discussed attitudes that devalue the *abilities* of those in the disfavored group. Yet in many contexts discrimination embodies an effort to devalue, degrade, or discount the worth of persons themselves—not just their talents and abilities. Consider the following example. A dispatcher in an urban police station who has been taught to believe that Black people are not fully human will very likely treat Black victims of crime with less seriousness than victims who are not Black. For instance, he may view a Black person's call for emergency police assistance as relatively unimportant, with potentially disastrous consequences for those who seek that assistance. He may even attempt to rationalize the low priority he gives to emergency calls from Black callers: he might claim that statistics about violence in the caller's neighborhood support his belief that Black people "don't really care" about violence or that giving the call greater priority "won't do any good." The prevalence of such rationalizations, in turn, will have destructive reciprocal effects. People who expect to be viewed with less seriousness when they are victims of crime will learn to mistrust the institutions that view them in this way, and their mistrust can have devastating effects.

Yet the distorting effects of discrimination do not simply shape the attitudes of "outsiders" toward the disfavored group or vice-versa. Discrimination may also have a profound influence on the self-conceptions, and the sense of self-respect, of some within the disfavored group. Of course, even in the face of the cruellest racism, many people are able to affirm a robust sense of their own worth—and of any group with which they identify—in a variety of satisfying ways. Understanding their success, as I suggest below, yields invaluable lessons about the social bases of self-respect. Yet, like King and Clark, I contend that segregation can distort the self-conceptions of the segregated as well as of the segregator. The analysis of self-respect introduced in the first section allows me to show *how* some of these distortions take place. The principal distortions of self-respect take two forms: (1) the mutually reinforcing relation between the two components of self-respect may be undermined, or (2) the minimum content of self-respect may itself be distorted. Ironically, the most important distortions reveal just how valiantly people will fight to retain a minimum degree of self-respect, even in the faces of challenges to their sense of worth.

The first kind of distortion occurs when one's wish to preserve oneself is somehow pried apart from the willingness to develop one's abilities and talents. This separation most often takes place when a person experiences severe disappointment and frustration in the exercise of her abilities. Surprisingly, this process begins as a perfectly ordinary tendency to risk-aversion: in particular, it starts as an aversion to the psychological discomfort of severe disappointment. People with weak voices, for instances, seldom like to sing in public. But what starts as fairly ordinary risk-aversion can develop into extreme self-mistrust, and it may then take on a markedly self-destructive character. Familiar, but distressing, examples of this self-destructive process are common in settings where social and economic isolation compounds the lingering effects of discrimination.

The two components of self-respect are strikingly separated in the tendency of some Black school-aged children in poor urban areas to gradually lower their expectations of themselves, until they effectively relinquish any ambitions of academic success. Hence, the high drop-out rate in these areas. Of course, some students who drop out may have low-ered expectations not of themselves but of the society that they believe excludes them. They may simply lose confidence that it is prudent for them to continue in school. Still others may drop out principally because they mistrust the facilities available to them. But caring and hardwork-ing teachers—many of whom are also Black—conclude that many Black students who drop out have learned to mistrust *themselves* because they have gradually internalized prejudicial assumptions that they cannot suc-ceed. Such students provide distressing evidence of the pervasiveness of the self-fulfilling prophecy: the student who believes that he shouldn't even try certainly will not succeed. Moreover, such a student is liable to mistrust students who excel (or simply try to excel), branding then with the label of what he mistrusts most: they are "trying to be white." Students who make such comments are reluctant to identify successful students as "really Black" because they have come to identify being Black with fail-ure. They have thus internalized the very preconceptions that historical-ly have been used to exclude Black Americans from constructive affirmations of self-respect.

But accepting a view of oneself as intrinsically bound for failure can wreak havoc even on the *minimum content* of self-respect. The student who claims to believe that he is "nothing" provides unfortunate evidence of this second kind of distortion of self-respect. Now it is unlikely that this student consistently believes that he really is "nothing." Rather, his efforts to understand his experience lead him to suffer moments of extreme self-doubt and self-mistrust. Yet few children who experience this degree of self-mistrust could emerge with the minimum content of their sense of self-respect untouched. As I suggested earlier, we are unlikely to find any person totally lacking in self-respect. But one can certainly become unable to distinguish self-destructive behavior from behavior that actually promotes one's well-being. Such a confusion between self-destructive and self-preserving behavior is manifested in the disruptive and ultimately self-destructive classroom behavior of the young boy in my example. His behavior prevents him from learning how to read well or how to manipulate the mathematical concepts he requires to survive economically.

As he develops into a young man, he will become increasingly aware of a set of expectations about selves and self-respect that govern much of his daily life. Some of these expectations will differ very little from those in the larger society: a Wall Street stockbroker and an inner city youth alike may be tempted to measure self-worth by means of their possessions. A second group of expectations will differ radically from those of the larger social group—insofar as they embody a rejection of some of the discriminatory attitudes toward Black Americans. But often, a third category of expectations unintentionally incorporates the exclusion and marginalization that most people in his community would, on reflection, obviously prefer to reject. Familiar patterns of behavior manifest the relevant structure of expectations: membership in youth gangs that promise as great a risk of death as they do protection and camaraderie, drug abuse, and various kinds of violent crime. These patterns of behavior are rooted in dangerous and destructive expectations concerning selves and self-respect.

But the appeal to a Black American teenager of membership in an urban street gang provides an important lesson. For as Rawls once argued, one's sense of one's worth is often bound up with one's sense that one is valued by others; ties of membership in associations and communities typically encourage and support one's sense of self-respect (TJ 440-42). The distressing irony of the urban street gang is that instead of providing a real remedy for the social isolation and exclusion of its members—as a college fraternity, for instance, might—it actually *intensifies* that isolation. Like the young Black student who identifies "Black" with "failure," an older gang member comes to identify "Black" with "marginal." But in viewing his membership in a gang as an affirmation of self-respect, the gang member reveals just how completely he has internalized society's efforts to marginalize him. For he has come to see himself precisely as he is seen by those who wish to exclude him: as essentially a threatening "outlaw," a permanent possibility of danger. Moreover, he will sometimes act on that self-conception in a self-destructive fashion and will often wreak havoc on his community in the process. The gang member's self-conception provides a powerful example of the way in which—even in an effort at self-assertion—one can accept a vision of oneself that remains too entangled in a tradition of discrimination and exclusion to be a constructive category for self-reflection.

The Social Bases of Self-Respect

But how might a young child who claims to think that he is "nothing" learn to seek more constructive categories for self-reflection and self-understanding? An important part of the answer requires reflection on the experience of Black Americans who have been able to disentangle their self-conceptions from a conceptual scheme that threatens to confine them to marginality and failure. Such people have relied upon two principal vehicles to disentangle their sense of self-worth from the legacy of discrimination. First, their experience has typically included membership in various communities and associations that *constructively* affirm their worth as persons. For many, of course, the most important such community has been the family. But associative ties outside the family may supplement the family's influence—or sometimes even remedy the effects of a damaged family.[19] Second, the sense of self-worth of many Black Americans has been sustained by a sense of history and social traditions. Of course, one consequence of American slavery is that many Black Americans have no detailed or particular knowledge of the national (as opposed to continental and geographical) origins of their families. Moreover, discriminatory policies bound up with slavery—and its long aftermath—have often made it difficult, if not impossible, for Black Americans to have access to written history. But the kind of oral history that is seldom preserved in formal educational institutions (for any group) was often an important and constructive alternative. Black Americans who, for many years, managed to develop constructive means for affirming self-respect—often in spite of great hardship—were once a prominent presence in Black communities. Their successes and their failures were an important source of knowledge of how one might preserve one's self-respect—not just in response to exclusion and discrimination but in spite of it. The greater mobility of some Black Americans thus unwittingly deprives other Black people of access to those parts of their history that they may need most.[20] Further, as successful Black residents leave Black communities, many of the communal associations that provided constructive ties of membership leave with them or die off altogether. To be cut off from membership in associations that constructively affirm one's value and to be cut off from an appreciation of how others have found constructive categories for self-reflection and choice in spite of hardship is to be cut off from the two most important social bases of self-respect. Finding ways to develop the social bases of self-respect in communities set apart by class and race will surely require the participation of Black people who have learned to resist internalizing assumptions about marginality and failure. Even small-scale social programs that vividly display the concern of "successful" Black Americans might help provide models of constructive affirmations of self-respect—even if only as an incentive to seek altogether new models.[21]

But no social order can command the respect of people whom it continually fails to respect and for whom (as a consequence) both self-mistrust and widespread mistrust of social institutions come to seem a

rational adaptation to circumstances. The possibility of social cooperation thus also imposes an *obligation* on those not in the disfavored group
to relinquish the discriminatory attitudes that persist. As I have shown,
this requires far more self-scrutiny—and, ultimately, a more serious revision of self-conceptions—than is acknowledged in most discussions of
social reform. The police dispatcher who encourages mistrust of the
police, and the professor who encourages mistrust of her students' abilities, both endanger the complex social cooperation that underwrites the
pursuit of rational life plans for everyone. Still further, restoring the
social bases of self-respect will require social policies that recognize the
important fact that no human being is ever *simply* a victim. Even a victim
retains the fundamental human need to exercise and develop his own
abilities and talents in the effort to help remedy his suffering. One develops the self-trust that is fundamental to a robust sense of self-respect only
by means of experiences that also require that one take responsibility for
the consequences of one's choices—to an extent compatible with one's
knowledge and experience. Some social "reforms" of recent years have
treated the recipients of assistance simply as victims, thus encouraging
the reformers, and those people whom they sought to aid, to ignore
important facts about the nature of self-respect.[22]

Finally, as William Julius Wilson has suggested, efforts to encourage a
robust sense of self-respect can succeed only alongside efforts to remedy
the structural causes of economic and social isolation that seriously
endanger self-respect (TD 1987). I have argued that some of the people
who most need the benefits of economic reform have become deeply
mistrustful of social institutions and—even worse—sometimes, of themselves. Their lack of trust may well hinder their capacity to take advantage of opportunities that might arise with structural changes in the
economy. Finding the remedy for this mistrust will require a concerted
effort to reshape the social construction of self-respect—not just for the
disadvantaged but for any group whose sense of self-worth seems to
"require" them to accept the isolation of the truly disadvantaged (of any
race or ethnic group) as an unrevisable fact of experience.

Notes

An earlier version of this paper was read at a conference at Brown University.
Helpful comments on that earlier version were provided by Howard McGary,
Lucius Outlaw, and Laurence Thomas.

1. Kenneth B. Clark, *Prejudice and Your Child* (Boston: Beacon Press, 1963).
2. Daniel Goleman, "Black Child's Self-View Is Still Low, Study Finds," *New York Times*, Aug. 31, 1987, p. A13.
3. I am indebted to Shirley Moody for this example.
4. A hostage might vigorously attempt to protect her sanity, or her memory of the past, or even simply to keep track of the passage of time—thus exercising, relatively speaking, a significant degree of control over the conditions of her own survival.
5. On some understandings of the self—say, on which one's identity is partly constituted by one's membership in a group—a willingness to sacrifice one's physical body might be required to reveal one's self-respect. See Karl Duncker, "Ethical Relativity? (An Enquiry Into the Psychology of Ethics)," *Mind*, vol. 48: 39–57, for a discussion of the moral consequences of this view of the self.
6. John Rawls, *A Theory of Justice* (Cambridge, Mass.: Harvard University Press, 1971), p. 440 [p. 125, this volume] (hereafter abbreviated TJ).
7. Many important human ends and purposes can be fulfilled only in a context of social cooperation. Thus I reject the libertarian notion that social cooperation is somehow incidental to self-preservation.
8. See Bernard R. Boxill, *Blacks and Social Justice* (Totowa, N.J.: Rowman and Allenheld, 1984), p. 189.
9. Rawls's analysis thus encourages ambiguity: he sometimes treats "self-respect" and "self-esteem" as equivalent expressions (TJ 440–42) [pp. 125–127, this volume].
10. For an intriguing discussion of an Old Order Amish community, see Donald Kraybill, *The Riddle of Amish Culture* (Baltimore: Johns Hopkins University Press, 1989).
11. See David Looff, *Appalachia's Children* (Lexington: University Press of Kentucky, 1971); David Glasgow, *The Black Underclass: Poverty, Unemployment and Entrapment of Ghetto Youth* (New York: Vintage Books, 1980); and William Julius Wilson, *The Truly Disadvantaged: The Inner City, The Underclass and Public Policy* (Chicago: University of Chicago Press, 1987) (hereafter abbreviated TD).
12. See James Fishkin, *Justice, Equal Opportunity and the Family* (New Haven, Conn.: Yale University Press, 1983), for discussion of some problematic consequences of this view for liberal theorists.
13. H. L. A. Hart, *The Concept of Law* (Oxford: Oxford University Press, 1961).
14. Even the Austinian or Benthamite legal positivist must explain the persistence of legally protected segregation in America. This theorist may appeal to the notion of entrenched "habits of obedience"—but *entrenched* habits, as we

all know, do not magically disappear.

15. Martin Luther King, "Letter from Birmingham Jail," in King, *Why We Can't Wait* (New York: Mentor Books, 1964), p. 82.

16. This and other difficulties with the genetic notion of race are discussed in several of the essays in Ashley Montagu, ed., *The Concept of Race* (New York: The Free Press, 1964).

17. Robert Merton, "The Self-Fulfilling Prophecy," *The Antioch Review*, vol. 8: 193–210.

18. Gordon Allport, *The Nature of Prejudice* (Reading, Mass.: Addison-Wesley, 1954).

19. As a matter of historical fact, Black churches and their associated organizations (choirs, youth groups, and so forth) have often been a powerful force in the lives of many Black Americans. Though an organization need not be rooted in shared religious beliefs in order to successfully underwrite self-respect, the experience of the Old Order Amish provides an interesting reflection. When a community is largely self-contained (whether as a result of unchosen external forces, or—as in the case of the Amish—as a result of choice), shared religious beliefs often provide a more coherent and more constructive self-conception than any other phenomenon.

20. Critics of W. J. Wilson's stance in *The Truly Disadvantaged* would do well to consider this fact.

21. Douglas Glasgow, "The Black Underclass," urged similar participation by Black Americans.

22. I discuss the topic of responsibility and victims of economic and social deprivation in M. M. Moody-Adams, "On the Old Saw That Character Is Destiny," in O. Flanagan and A. O. Rorty, ed., *Identity, Character and Morality: Essays in Moral Psychology* (Cambridge, Mass.: Massachusetts Institute of Technology Press, 1990).

15

✤

Toward a Feminist
Conception of Self-Respect

✤

Robin S. Dillon

Self-respect is something most of us want and need. Few things are as important to our well-being as a secure sense of our own worth, or as debilitating and disempowering as its lack. Deep and enduring shame and self-contempt, unremitting doubts about one's worth, a tendency to see oneself as not quite as good or not quite as valuable as others: such things constrict and deform lives, frustrating the quest for self-fulfillment and self-realization. But while the inability to respect oneself is a human tragedy, developing and maintaining self-respect is particularly difficult for women.

Many of us—too many—find self-respect elusive, have little or no confidence in our own worth, feel the need for greater or more secure respect for ourselves. And most of us, I suspect, experience these difficulties in terms of *personal* deficiency or failure, and so seek a solution to

This essay was originally published in *Hypatia* 7 (1992). Copyright © Robin S. Dillon.

our self-respect problems in *personal* amelioration or reformation. Feminist insight suggests, however, that this is a debilitatingly misleading view of things. In "A Feminist Aspect Theory of the Self," Ann Ferguson refers to the "truism that women's sense of self-worth, and consequently our personal power, has been weakened by a male-dominant society".[1] The authors of *Women and Self-Esteem* concur, arguing that a damaged sense of self-worth is a gendered phenomenon.[2] They maintain that the undermining of women's sense of worth "constitutes an insidious form of oppression in its own right" which "facilitate[s] the continuation of women's external oppression in a male-dominated world".[3] Thus, what many of us experience as personal inadequacy may be better understood in terms of what Diana Meyers has called a "politics of self-respect."[4]

But the political dimensions extend beyond the causes and consequences of weakened self-respect. For as Ann Ferguson also suggests, self-respect is crucial to feminist political empowerment, as the source of the strength and confidence needed to effectively challenge and change subordinating institutions.[5] Recognizing in self-respect the promise of liberation, Ann Ferguson calls for a program of feminist education that will enable women to reclaim a secure confidence in our worth. Such a project clearly requires exposing the complex of ways in which political realities, material conditions, and social institutions conspire to deny women opportunities to develop self-respect, work to stunt or deform our sense of worth, and thread the everyday circumstances of women's lives with challenges to the self-respect we do develop. Many feminists have begun this exploration, with illuminating results.[6] But I suspect that the roots of our difficulties lie still deeper, in what we understand self-respect to be.

Moral philosophers have exhibited a great fondness for the concept of self-respect, invoking it in a wide variety of theoretical contexts.[7] One reason for its theoretical power is that self-respect is embedded in a nexus of such profoundly problematic moral concepts as personhood, rights, autonomy, responsibility, identity, virtue, and integrity. But feminist critique has revealed its kin concepts to be imbued with patriarchal poison, thus threatening to render self-respect conceptually dangerous as well as experientially problematic. It is the possibility of conceptual peril that I want to explore.

In the context of developing a feminist account of autonomy, Diana Meyers defends autonomy against charges that it is an androcentric and elitist concept by developing its connections to self-respect, claiming that "self-respect cannot be construed as a masculine or perfectionist value."[8] However, I want to suggest that just as autonomy, once viewed as promising liberation, is revealed by feminist critique to be patriarchally tainted and requiring feminist reconceptualization, so self-respect, similarly emancipatory-seeming, stands in need of feminist critique and revisioning. The project of reclaiming self-respect, then, also requires investigating the possibility that the conception of self-respect that informs social consciousness and philosophical theorizing is itself inimical to women's unimpeded self-respect and to feminist political goals.

My aim in this paper is twofold. First, I want to show that a standard philosophical conception of self-respect does indeed incorporate androcentric elements, rendering it less attainable and less desirable for women and less than conducive to liberation. Second, I want to begin the task of developing a feminist conception of self-respect. I do not claim that there is only one account to be given of feminist self-respect, but I will sketch some central ideas of one way of understanding self-respect that takes seriously women's lived experiences, is safely and coherently accessible to us here and now, and contains resources for an emancipatory transformation of selves and society.

I

Self-respect is a rich complex of beliefs, attitudes, and expectations with regard to oneself, as well as certain modes of acting and reacting. But its core is a kind of valuing of oneself: the self-respecting person has a keen appreciation of her own worth. However, the concept of worth is notoriously vague and profoundly problematic; clarifying it is necessary for understanding self-respect. Our commonsense notion of the worth of persons contains the understanding of at least two different kinds of worth that a person might be said to have. On the one hand, there is the intrinsic worth, which Kant called "dignity," that each of us has simply by virtue of being a person rather than a rock or a tree. One of the fundamental tenets of contemporary Western democratic society is that all persons have this kind of moral worth equally. On the other hand, there is a kind of worth or merit we may earn through what we do and become, which individuals can have in varying degrees, and which some may lack altogether. Now respect is, most generally, a particular sort of response to worth; but these kinds of worth call for different kinds of responses, which is to say, different kinds of respect. A distinction Stephen Darwall has drawn between two kinds of respect and self-respect usefully captures the differential responses appropriate to these different kinds of worth.[9]

One kind of self-respect, which Darwall calls "appraisal self-respect," involves an attitude of positive appraisal of oneself and confidence in one's merit as a person.[10] Individuals with appraisal self-respect judge that they measure up to some standards of excellence, believe they are successfully pursuing a worthwhile plan of life, regard their accomplishments as admirable, and have confidence that they will continue to do and to be what they think it is appropriate and good to do and to be. Appraisal self-respect is something we earn more or less of and which we may rightly lose or fail to earn altogether.

The other kind of self-respect, "recognition self-respect," involves responding to oneself with the kind of respect all persons are owed simply because they are persons. Recognition respect for persons is a matter of taking appropriate account of the fact that something is a person. This involves (1) recognizing that something is a person, (2) appreciating that persons as such have intrinsic moral worth and status, (3) understanding that the fact that something is a person constrains us morally to act only in certain ways in connection with him or her, and (4) acting and being disposed to act in those ways out of that recognition, appreciation, and understanding. Recognition self-respect, then, is a matter of taking appropriate account of one's own status as a person: appreciating one's fundamental moral worth and behaving accordingly.

What, more precisely, does this involve? The most common account focuses on a person's status as a full and equal member of the moral community and as the bearer of certain basic moral rights.[11] The recognition respect to which persons are unconditionally entitled, on this account, is respect for their basic moral rights and dignity. To have recognition self-respect is to understand oneself to be a person with the same intrinsic value and standing in the moral community as every other person and unconditionally owed the equal recognition respect of all persons. In particular, self-respecting persons are those who understand that they have certain basic rights simply in virtue of being persons, who properly value those rights, and who expect others to respect their rights and to treat them in a manner that acknowledges their dignity as persons. The self-respecting person is not servile, does not acquiesce willingly in the avoidable denial of her rights, and resists demeaning or humiliating treatment. Recognition self-respect is something to which all persons are entitled, which all can have equally, and which each of us ought to have, simply because we are persons.

II

Is self-respect so conceived less accessible to women? Does it incorporate androcentric or other problematic values? Does it ignore or fail to speak to or about women's lives or concerns? In exploring these questions I propose to hold constant the idea that there are these two kinds of self-respect. This framework itself no doubt requires feminist revisioning, but one needs some place to stand, though always warily, cognizant of the possibility that the ground may turn out to be quicksand or breaking ice or the cleverly disguised tongue of some patriarchal beast.

There is much that is worrisome about appraisal self-respect, but I want to concentrate in this paper on recognition self-respect, for I believe that personal/political empowerment comes most directly and deeply from claiming one's intrinsic worth as a person. Moreover, a secure sense of one's fundamental worth would seem to be a prerequisite for being able to develop and maintain appraisal self-respect; thus, a reclamation of the former is the more urgent task.

It is, of course, difficult to have recognition respect for oneself in the face of institutionalized denial of one's full and equal personhood. Women's wholeheartedly valuing ourselves as fully and equally persons challenges the prevailing social, political, and economic order. Women's self-respect is thus profoundly insubordinate. It is unsubordinating rebellion—or it can be, if the conception of recognition self-respect is not itself an instrument of subordination. There is this threat, however, in the way the standard account conceptualizes (1) the self and the grounds on which it warrants recognition respect, (2) the attitudes self-respect involves, and (3) the conduct that most typically manifests it. A more fitting and emancipatory conception would, I suggest, involve an alternative conception of the self, other attitudes, different behavior.

To have recognition self-respect is to take appropriate account of the fact that one is a person, to properly appreciate one's worth as a person. We have looked at one version of what this appreciation involves. We can begin to raise worries about this version and to clear some conceptual space for a better understanding of self-respect by noting that, in general, what constitutes appropriate acknowledgement and appreciation of something depends on the kind of thing it is; one does not, for example, appreciate persons in the same way that one appreciates a glass of fine wine. To put this another way, recognition respect is the kind of attitude that must be grounded in certain ways: it is grounded in and responsive to just those features of an object that make objects of that kind worthy of respect. And the nature of the response is shaped by the nature of the grounds. Recognition respect for persons is grounded in what we might call the "morally significant features of persons," that is, those features that make something a person and make persons things that must morally be taken account of. But personhood is an essentially contestable, ideologically malleable concept, and so, therefore, is the concept of recognition respect. We might say that the concept of recognition respect treats personhood as a variable. That is, the concept itself cannot settle substantive questions of what a person is; rather, it requires the antecedent specification of some conception of the person. We must know what the morally significant features of persons are in order to know how to respect them. Thus, different conceptions of the person entail different conceptions of recognition respect and self-respect. What recognition self-respect involves and requires, then, depends on what it is to be a person. So we must ask of present accounts, what is it to be a person entitled to the recognition respect of oneself as well as others?

When we look more carefully at these accounts, we find them informed by a familiar picture. A person, insofar as it is worthy of respect, is an exceedingly thin being wholly constituted by the possession of moral rights, or by the capacity for rationally autonomous moral agency, or by self-consciousness. At the core of the standard understanding of recognition self-respect we find an abstract and essentialist conception of the person that feminists have criticized as male-biased: the neo-Cartesian model of the moral self, disembodied, rational, autonomous, separate, isolated, indistinguishable from every other self. Insofar as feminists have good reason to reject this conception of the person, we have reason to resist valuing ourselves as such a being.

The striking feature of the standard conception is that in viewing us as worthy of respect it abstracts from all particularities, regarding the details of ourselves as irrelevant to our intrinsic moral worth. The morally significant feature of persons is something abstract and generic, not what distinguishes one individual from another but what makes each equally and indistinguishably a person. Individual humans are objects of respect only insofar as they are instances of some universal type such as "being with the capacity for rational autonomous agency." What one is to respect is, to adapt Seyla Benhabib's term, a generalized self.[12] Thus, as one critic puts it, respect "flense[s] the individual down to the bare bones of abstract personhood."[13] In the most extreme versions of this abstraction, the individual disappears altogether from view. Darwall, for example, states that "strictly speaking, the object of recognition respect is a *fact*."[14] Other accounts suggest that self-respect is simply respect for moral rights, for the moral law, or for the capacity rather than for the person.[15]

However, it is difficult to understand how regarding oneself in generic terms could constitute *self*-respect, or how appreciation for a capacity or the moral law could constitute respect for *myself*. Respect, I would argue, is, as its etymology suggests, centrally a matter of focus, of what one's attention is focused on, and such accounts have the focus either on too little or on the wrong thing. But worse, recognition self-respect so understood is compatible with and perhaps even encourages self-alienation, for it allows that I can respect myself without paying attention to who I am, without taking *me* seriously. This is troublesome, for valuing myself in this self-alienated way might discourage the self-understanding needed for self-realization and emancipatory self-transformation.

Moreover, this abstractive conception of recognition self-respect cannot acknowledge the shapes and circumstances of individual human lives, particularly the subordinating circumstances of women's lives. It cannot value our everyday lived experiences, and it cannot take account of the differences among individual human beings. Appraisal self-respect does attend to the details of one's life, but only insofar as they manifest excellence, superior quality, achievement. Neither appraisal self-respect nor the standard conception of recognition self-respect has room for valuing myself for being myself, nor for appreciating both my distinctness and my share in the manifold of human commonalities. The standard account of recognition respect thus involves self-erasure. There is, then, a kind of paradox here: if the particularities of our selves and lives are morally important, as many feminists claim, then recognition respect for ourselves requires disrespecting our selves.

There is another disturbing aspect of the standard account. Insofar as persons are viewed as essentially rights-bearers, we are separated and distanced from one another. For many of our fundamental moral rights function as barriers to protect us from the encroachments of others, and to respect a person's rights is to keep one's distance from her. Staking our worth as persons on being rights-bearers may thus make it difficult to envision ourselves as being-in-relation with others and to value ourselves as connected with others. On the other hand, to the extent that the self-conceptions of many women *do* include regarding themselves as selves-in-relation, as Carol Gilligan and others have claimed,[16] then such an understanding of self-respect does not take seriously the actual concerns of many women. Nor does it take appropriate account of the way in which we are, as Annette Baier calls us, "second persons": beings who become and exist as persons only in relationships with persons.[17] All of this is not to say that we ought not to think of persons as having rights. Rather, it is to suggest that an exclusive or even a strong emphasis on respecting ourselves as rights-bearers does not offer us a way of viewing and valuing ourselves that could serve as the basis for the transformation of society along more integrative lines.

The standard account of the attitude of self-respect is also problematic. The taking-account-of-and-appreciating attitude is a dispassionate, overly intellectualized, arm's-length response that does not engage us emotionally. Not only does this conception of self-respect ignore our emotional being in conceptualizing us as objects of respect, but it also neglects the affective dimensions of ourselves as *subjects* of respect. But recognition, appreciation, and respect are not inherently dispassionate. When I recognize in the crowd a good friend whom I have not seen in years, there is an emotional component, a delight and love, that does not merely follow on the heels of recognizing my friend but is part of the recognition itself. Similarly, an art lover's appreciation of the Mona Lisa is passionate through and through. This is not to say that self-respect ought to be thought of as, say, self-love, but it is to suggest that it might be better understood in warmer, more emotional terms than present accounts allow.

Consider, finally, the implications of regarding the defending of one's rights as the conduct most typically manifesting self-respect. I do not wish to deny the moral importance, nor indeed the particular significance in women's subordinated circumstances, of defending one's rights when they are challenged, of protesting violations of one's rights, of pressing for the recognition of one's rights, of asserting one's rights, and so on. However, this view of respecting oneself neglects a multitude of everyday assaults on a woman's sense of worth that cannot be captured by rights-talk.[18] Moreover, this model does not speak to the ways in which women who are not openly under attack might appreciate and take themselves seriously in the circumstances of their everyday lives. Yet the calm confidence of self-respect is surely part of the weft of the ordinary, while the individual who asserts her rights in the course of tranquil quotidian affairs might be thought to manifest insecurity rather than confidence about her worth.

Further, the oppositional, combative conception of the relations among persons that is encouraged by construing respect as defense of rights is not conducive to the formation of mutually supportive and integrative relationships among persons. Indeed, it neglects the ways in which respect for oneself fosters the realization of self-respect in others. Finally, the focus on defensiveness promotes a preoccupation with victimization—valuing oneself as victim—that is far from empowering.[19] If recognition self-respect is to serve as a source of political empowerment for women, then we need to work away from defensive thinking about what we are and what we are worth, and do more than protect ourselves and protest our victimization. But insofar as our understanding of self-respect is dominated by metaphors of victimization, we undermine possibilities for empowerment.

There are a number of objections, then, that we might raise from a feminist perspective about the various features of the standard conception of self-respect; gathered together, they point to three more general difficulties. First, insofar as self-respect so understood presumes a conception of the person that does not fit women's or some women's self-conceptions, it is less accessible to women or to those women. Second, if we *do* have strong self-respect now that is predicated on this conception of the person, then our self-respect is at odds with feminist goals: we have to choose between transforming ourselves toward liberation and maintaining our self-respect. Yet if recognition self-respect is the source of the strength necessary to effect the transformation, then we are doomed to self-frustration. But third, and most unsettling, is the threat that we will come to fit this conception's model of the self. For self-respect is not a passive or ineffectual response to the self; it is a way in which we actively engage and construct our selves. Respecting oneself is as much anticipation as review; it functions somewhat like a self-fulfilling prophecy: to respect something as *x* is to make it *x* or at least to contribute to its becoming *x*. And if we seek self-respect without understanding what we are after, then we risk losing more than our way.

There is danger here but also promise, for revisioning self-respect empowers us to effect the revisioning of ourselves. Thus, every feminist program must involve not only, as Ann Ferguson says, a process of educating women to respect ourselves but also the reconstruction of recognition self-respect so that the education is empowering and emancipatory.

III

How might we construct a feminist conception of recognition self-respect?[20] I suggested earlier that we will need to reconceive the object, attitudes, and conduct of respecting oneself. This task involves not only rejecting certain aspects of the standard account but also reworking concepts, shifting emphases, highlighting elements the standard account has hidden, recalling actual experiences of valuing ourselves. However, as there are many feminisms, so there may be many feminist revisionings of self-respect. Let me propose one.

Consider first the conception of the self. Feminists and nonfeminists alike have criticized the model of the abstract and general self, arguing that we are *essentially* fully specific and concretely particular individuals, each with our own unique desires, needs, abilities, and emotional constitution, our own peculiar history, concerns, and projects. Rather than disregarding particularity, these critics contend, what we ought morally to take account of is precisely the details that make me who I am. As one writer maintains, "Respect for a person includes respect for this core of individuality...[and] appreciation of...the individual and human *me*."[21] On this view, to respect a person is to treat her not as a case of generic personhood but as the person she is.[22] I believe a feminist conception of recognition self-respect would incorporate the idea of respect for individual "me-ness." Most central to having self-respect would be paying attention to myself in the fullness of my specific detail, valuing myself in my concrete particularity.

Not only does this conception have room for respecting myself *as a woman*, but it also captures an ignored aspect of real experiences of self-respect: the self-respecting person is content in her quirks and idiosyncrasies and does not pummel herself into likeness or conformity. But she also does not rebel against similarity and commonality. She respects the ways she is like and unlike others. Furthermore, respect for one's own particularity also fosters respect for others in their differences. One of the moral functions of self-respect is to facilitate moral relationships among persons, and such relationships are more secure when they acknowledge and value differences among persons than when they try to ignore them.[23]

The upshot of this feminist conception is that nothing about an individual is irrelevant to self-respect. It thus becomes possible to say that one's life has value in all its everyday ordinariness—in the monotony, grime, inadequacy, and despair as well as in the shining moments of achievement. It becomes possible to believe that one's very prosaic self is worthy of respect, deserves attention: one's own and others' alike. This conception also calls us to respect our limitedness and imperfection, and thus to attend to and expect others to attend to our needs and frailties. It encourages us to take seriously our complexity and fragmentation, to not reject or ignore our incoherence but to confront and deal with it, and so to avoid enervating self-deception. It calls us to recognize the extent to which we are open, always in transition, always under construction, and it demands both that we take seriously the task of self-construction and that we appreciate the inherently social nature of the constructive activity. Importantly, a feminist self-respect does not require us to approve of all aspects of ourselves, nor to regard incoherence and fragmentation, for example, as intrinsically valuable. But it does require us to acknowledge what we are, and to see ourselves as valuable *as* we are, rather than despite what we are.

This feminist conception of recognition self-respect also calls us to recognize our interpersonal reality, to take seriously the extent to which we are embedded in relationships of many kinds with others. It gives us the conceptual resources for acknowledging and valuing a self that is both separate in its individuality and connected to other individual selves. Not only does this promote moral relationships with others that are founded on something stronger and warmer than toleratance, but it also provides conceptual room for building appraisal self-respect on what *we* do, on communal activities and achievements, thus moving us toward more integrative and mutually supportive social arrangements.

Some feminists have expressed a concern that the tendency of discussions in feminist ethics to focus on the particularity of the self seems to provide no conceptual resources for recognizing our commonality as persons: our shared humanity, common intrinsic value, and equality.[24] However, I believe a conception of self-respect grounded in the particularity of individual "me's" does have those resources. In the first place, attention to the details of our selves reveals not only uniqueness but also a plethora of commonalities, as well as the many ways in which our lives overlap with and are connected to the lives of others. One very important element in the standard account that is not given much emphasis but that a feminist understanding can recover and highlight is the notion of relatedness. For recognition self-respect involves recognizing one's place in the moral community, as a person among persons, understanding that and how one is related to all other persons. It is this more encompassing vision of the self-in-relation-to-others that distinguishes self-respect from the more narrowly focused self-love. Thus, while recognition self-respect involves attention to oneself, it is not myopic: in appreciating myself I appreciate the others with whom I am connected and on whom I depend. Indeed, it may be that for some individuals the way to develop or strengthen self-respect is to focus on others with whom one is connected rather than on oneself.[25]

Moreover, this conception of self-respect also highlights the way in which our very ability to recognize and value ourselves as persons depends on being recognized and valued by others: we become self-respecters only because we have been and continue to be respected by others.[26] Not only does openly embracing this fact about us have important practical consequences for structuring interpersonal and political relationships, but when we incorporate into the grounds of our self-respect an appreciation of the mutual dependency of self-respect itself, we both acknowledge the reality of our inequalities and open the possibility of finding equality and commonalities in our mutual dependence.

What attitudes might a feminist recognition self-respect involve? I suggested earlier that self-respect should engage us emotionally, thus respecting our affectivity as subjects of respect. Interestingly, respect is not intrinsically dispassionate; cherishing, venerating, and revering are forms of respect that involve profoundness of feeling, treasuring, love. I propose that respecting myself within a feminist framework would involve cherishing and treasuring myself for who I am.[27]

Such a move opens the door to integrating into the conception of self-respect some of the key elements found in feminist discussions of the care perspective in ethics. That is, a feminist recognition self-respect might usefully be seen to involve the understanding, which forms the core of the most mature stage of Carol Gilligan's ethic of care, that I am, in and of myself, worthy of my own care and of the care of others, that it is morally appropriate for me to care for myself, indeed that I sometimes ought to care for myself. This move provides a way of answering one very troubling aspect of the care approach to ethics. Some feminists have objected that in Nel Noddings's account of the ethic of care,[28] although the cared-for is presumed to have intrinsic worth and to be unconditionally worthy of care, the moral worth and worthiness of the one-caring seems to be wholly conditional on her capacity for caring or on her actual engagement in caring activities. But if caring for oneself can be justified only in order to enable oneself to care for others, then the ethic of care has the very potential for exploitation and devaluation of women that feminism seeks to overcome.[29] However, incorporating a feminist conception of self-respect into feminist moral theory precludes the danger of embracing at least some of the ethic of care. For recognition self-respect is the appreciation of my intrinsic worth; it says I may and ought to take care of myself, not only or primarily so that I am better able to care for others, but in the first place because I matter in my own right.

A feminist recognition self-respect would, I believe, also involve two other attitudes: acceptance and patience. For insofar as respecting myself entails acknowledging the extent to which I am always in transition, always under construction, it will require patience. And insofar as I am limited, imperfect, liable to failure and to fragmentation and incoherence, insofar as the details of my life will include much that is not admirable or lovable or nice, self-respect will require a deep and abiding acceptance of myself that goes beyond toleratance. For the self-respecting person's skin does not crawl when she looks at herself, nor does she hide from and refuse to acknowledge what she is. But self-respecting self-acceptance is also not to be confused with smug self-satisfaction, nor with unconditional self-approval, nor with embracing what is bad in oneself: out of respect for her potential for goodness, for example, the self-respecting person will not want to remain in a morally precarious state. But while this secure self-acceptance is not the same as appraisal self-respect, it would provide a basis on which to build appraisal self-respect that is less inclined to perfectionism and less susceptible to soul-shattering experiences of shame and self-contempt in the face of failure and inadequacy.

Finally, what modes of conduct might a feminist revisioning of recognition self-respect endorse? While I would not want to discard or even downgrade the importance (in its place) of defending one's rights, I do want to suggest two more subtle ways of taking oneself seriously. First, I believe a feminist account would give a greater emphasis than does the standard account to the activity of paying attention to oneself, thus recovering epistemological roots of re-spect. This captures the everyday idea that self-respect is incompatible with self-neglect: commonplace signs of self-neglect—unkempt hair, unwashed clothes—are often regarded as signs of lost self-respect. But I also have in mind deeper forms of self-neglect that seem incompatible with self-respect: ignoring one's needs, intuitions, emotional nature, and so on, as women are traditionally encouraged to do.

There is a connection here with issues of self-sacrifice and feminist concerns about the way in which the ethic of care seems to reiterate and encourage the kind of self-abnegation that marks women's oppression. Self-sacrifice in and of itself is not oppressive or denigrating or incompatible with self-respect. For it is possible to give up pursuing my self-interest, even to give up myself, in a self-respecting manner—knowing what I am worth and so knowing the extent and meaning of my sacrifice. Indeed, it can be the case that given the nature of my ground projects and the circumstances in which I find myself, self-sacrifice is a condition of maintaining self-respect—if I do not give myself up, I give up the possibility of being able to respect myself. However, self-abnegation is incompatible with self-respect insofar as it involves not paying attention to oneself in the first place, insofar as one never attends to one's intrinsic worth as a person nor to one's own needs, desires, projects, and so on, in one's construction of the situation and determination of who needs what or to whom one can give what. The first step out of exploitative circumstances that demand self-denigrating self-sacrifice is, I suggest, paying attention to oneself.

There is a caution here, however. For one can pay too much of the wrong kind of attention to oneself, and that is not what self-respect involves. The self-abnegating person is obsessed by the needs of others, but one can also be self-obsessed, and such attention is self-destructively distorting. Moreover, self-respect cannot, conceptually speaking, be self-obsessed, for to respect oneself is to understand and value oneself as a person among persons and to appreciate that one depends for one's moral existence on the mutual recognition of persons. The process of "unselfing" that Sheila Mullett describes may be, paradoxically, what recovering one's self-respect calls for in circumstances of self-obsession.[30] The point here is that self-respect requires an appropriate perspective on oneself, paying the right sort of attention to oneself; what that is and how one achieves it depend on where one starts.[31]

The final element I want to propose for incorporation into feminist recognition self-respect is self-understanding. Having knowledge about and understanding of oneself is surely a necessary condition for self-respect: the appreciation of one's concrete specificity that recognition self-respect involves requires knowing (enough of) the details of oneself, as does the honest and accurate evaluation of oneself that is the heart of appraisal self-respect. And self-understanding would seem to be necessary to avoid becoming alienated from oneself. Self-understanding is also necessary to avoid self-deception, which is incompatible with respect for oneself.[32] But I want to suggest that there is a deeper connection between self-respect and self-understanding: sincerely working toward self-understanding is itself a way of respecting oneself.

Undertaking the effort to understand myself expresses my valuing of myself. It is a way of responding to myself, as the respecting subject, as a knower, a way of taking myself seriously as one who can understand a person. It is also an appropriate response to myself, the object of respect, as the kind of being whose deepest needs include the need to be understood. When we strive for what Lorraine Code calls "knowing oneself responsibly in defiance of stereotypes," we manifest respect for ourselves.[33]

I think of myself in certain ways, and at some level I know my self-image is not accurate. It incorporates distortions and stereotypes, half-truths and whole falsehoods; but it is handy, and it provides a lot of excuses for what I do and why I cannot change, at least not now. But insofar as I "know myself" in this way, I am not respecting my reality. I am not taking seriously the complexity of my self, the ways in which this image may be close to the truth and the ways in which it is far off the mark. I avoid confronting the aspects of myself that I experience as fragmented or contradictory, refuse to acknowledge the ways in which I am alienated from aspects of myself, ignore the fact that there is much about myself that I disown or suppress. But respecting myself involves acknowledging these aspects of myself and my relation to them, regarding them as warranting my attention, and dealing with them: working to integrate, transform, or get rid of them, or learning to live in acknowledged tension with them. The kind of self-understanding that such activities involves lies, I believe, at the very heart of self-respect.

Finally, self-understanding can be self-respecting rebellion against subordination. For as Jean Baker Miller explains, there is a relationship between self-ignorance and domination:

> Subordinates often know more about the dominants than they know about themselves. If a large part of your fate depends on accommodating to and pleasing the dominants, you concentrate on them. Indeed, there is little purpose in knowing yourself.[34]

Under circumstances like these, striving to understand oneself is reclaiming oneself from oppression through one's insistence that one is worthy of being known, that self-understanding is appropriate, warranted, indeed called for—what any self-respecting person must do.

Notes

Earlier versions of this paper were presented at the 1991 Pacific Division meetings of the American Philosophical Society; at the University of Dayton 1990 conference, "Moral Agency and the Fragmented Self: Feminism and Moral Psychology"; to the Midwest Society of Women in Philosophy 1990 Fall Conference; to the Eastern Society of Women in Philosophy 1990 Fall Conference; at Lafayette College; and to the Lehigh Valley Feminist Research Group. I am grateful to members of those audiences for helpful discussion.

1. Ann Ferguson, "A Feminist Aspect Theory of the Self," in *Science, Morality and Feminist Theory*, ed. Marsha Hanen and Kai Nielsen (Calgary: University of

Calgary Press, 1987), pp. 339–356; p. 341.

2. Linda Tschirhart Sanford and Mary Ellen Donovan, *Women and Self-Esteem* (New York: Penguin Books, 1985). I do not mean to suggest that there is no difference between self-respect and self-esteem, for I do believe the two concepts are importantly different. However, there is no widely agreed-upon account of their distinction, and numerous discussions of one concept or the other conflate or confuse the two, incorporating aspects of self-esteem into the account of self-respect and vice versa. I would argue that much of what the authors of *Women and Self-Esteem* discuss concerns self-respect, so that it is not out of place to refer to their claims in the present context.

3. Sanford and Donovan, *Women and Self-Esteem*, pp. xiii, xvi.

4. Diana T. Meyers, "The Politics of Self-Respect: A Feminist Perspective," *Hypatia* 1 (1986): 83–100.

5. Ferguson, "Feminist Aspect Theory," p. 341.

6. In addition to Ferguson and Sanford and Donovan, Diana Meyers makes an important contribution in "The Politics of Self-Respect" and in *Self, Society, and Personal Choice* (New York: Columbia University Press, 1989), especially pt. 4, sec. 2 [chapter 12, this volume]. I read Kathryn Morgan's insightful exploration of the ways women are driven to moral madness as also illuminating the maneuvers of patriarchal culture to undermine our ability to respect ourselves; Morgan, "Women and Moral Madness," in *Science, Morality, and Feminist Theory*, pp. 201–226.

7. For example, self-respect plays a crucial role in grounding Rawls's two principles of justice (John Rawls, *A Theory of Justice* [Cambridge, Mass.: Harvard University Press, 1971]); Kant regards it not only as a duty to oneself but also as a subjective basis of morality, a subjective condition of human beings that makes morality possible (Immanuel Kant, *The Doctrine of Virtue*, trans. Mary Gregor [Philadelphia: University of Pennsylvania Press, 1964], Part I: Duties to Oneself, and Introduction, Section XII, p. 63), while the Categorical Imperative commands respect for all persons, including oneself (Kant, *Groundwork of the Metaphysic of Morals*, trans. H. J. Paton [New York: Harper & Row, 1964]); Darwall invokes self-respect in defense of his account of rationality and intersubjective value (Stephen Darwall, *Impartial Reason* [Ithaca, N.Y.: Cornell University Press, 1983]); Feinberg grounds moral rights in the value of self-respect (Joel Feinberg, "The Nature and Value of Rights," *Journal of Value Inquiry* 4 [1970]: 243–57); Gewirth appeals to it in defense of the Principle of Generic Consistency as the supreme principle of morality (Alan Gewirth, *Reason and Morality* [Chicago: University of Chicago Press, 1978]); Wallace calls on self-respect to explain the value of the virtues of benevolence (James D. Wallace, *Virtues and Vices* [Ithaca, N.Y.: Cornell University

Press, 1978]); Meyers appeals to it to defend the importance of autonomy (Diana T. Meyers, *Self, Society, and Personal Choice* [chapter 12, this volume]); Thomas invokes self-respect in rejecting the Platonic conception of a morally virtuous person (Laurence Thomas, *Living Morally: A Psychology of Moral Character* [Philadelphia: Temple University Press, 1989]); and Taylor appeals to it to explain the nature and moral value of integrity and shame (Gabriele Taylor, *Pride, Shame, and Guilt: Emotions of Self-Assessment* (Oxford: Oxford University Press, 1985) [chapter 9, this volume]).

8. Meyers, *Self, Society, and Personal Choice,* p. 208.

9. Stephen L. Darwall, "Two Kinds of Respect," *Ethics* 88 (1977): 36–49 [chapter 10, this volume].

10. Similar accounts have been developed by others, although terminology often differs. Compare, for example, Rawls, *A Theory of Justice,* where this attitude is referred to as both "self-esteem" and "self-respect"; the discussion of "self-esteem" in Laurence Thomas, "Rawlsian Self-Respect and the Black Consciousness Movement," *The Philosophical Forum* 9 (1977–78): 303–14, and "Morality and Our Self-Concept," *Journal of Value Inquiry* 12 (1978): 258–68 [see also chapter 13, this volume]; what David Sachs calls "self-esteem" in "How To Distinguish Self-Respect from Self-Esteem," *Philosophy and Public Affairs* 10 (1981): 346–60; Stephen J. Massey's "subjective self-respect" in "Is Self-Respect a Moral or a Psychological Concept?" *Ethics* 93 (1983): 246–261 [chapter 11, this volume]; Robert J. Yanal, "Self-Esteem," *Noûs* 21 (1987): 363–79; Joan Didion, "On Self-Respect," in *Slouching Toward Bethlehem* (New York: Washington Square Press, 1968); and "evaluative self-respect" in Stephen D. Hudson, "The Nature of Respect," *Social Theory and Practice* 6 (1980): 69–90.

11. See, for example, Thomas E. Hill, Jr., "Servility and Self-Respect," *The Monist* 57 (1973): 87–104 [chapter 3, this volume]; Virginia Held, "Reasonable Progress and Self-Respect," *The Monist* 57 (1973): 12–27; Bernard R. Boxill, "Self-Respect and Protest," *Philosophy and Public Affairs* 6 (1976): 58–69 [chapter 4, this volume]; Sachs's "self-respect" in "How To Distinguish Self-Respect from Self-Esteem"; Thomas's "self-respect" in "Rawlsian Self-Respect and the Black Consciousness Movement" and "Morality and Our Self-Concept"; and Massey's "objective self-respect" in "Is Self-Respect a Moral or a Psychological Concept?" While this account focuses on the person as rights-bearer and object of others' actions, other accounts of self-respect focus on persons as moral agents, as beings with certain moral capacities and concerns. Recognition respect for oneself so understood involves taking one's capacity for moral agency seriously by acting in ways that express moral agency, committing oneself to live by correct moral principles, taking one's moral

responsibilities seriously, and striving to live a morally unified life. For such an account, see, for example, Mike W. Martin, *Everyday Morality: An Introduction to Applied Ethics* (Belmont, Calif.: Wadsworth, 1989). I do not deal here with this variation on the account of recognition self-respect, although a full critique and reconceptualization of self-respect must do so. For a start on that task, see Robin S. Dillon, "How To Lose Your Self-Respect," *American Philosophical Quarterly* 29 (1992): 125–139.

12. Seyla Benhabib, "The Generalized and the Concrete Other: The Kohlberg-Gilligan Controversy and Moral Theory," in *Women and Moral Theory*, ed. Eva Feder Kittay and Diana T. Meyers (Totowa, N.J.: Rowman and Littlefield, 1989).

13. Edward Johnson, "Ignoring Persons," in *Respect for Persons, Tulane Studies in Philosophy*, vol. 31, ed. O. H. Green (New Orleans: Tulane University Press, 1982), p. 93.

14. Darwall, "Two Kinds", p. 39 [p. 185, this volume]. Emphasis added.

15. David A. J. Richards claims that the object of respect (and by implication, self-respect) is not a person at all but the capacity of autonomy that defines a being as a person: "respect is for an idealized capacity which, if appropriately treated, people can realize" ("Rights and Autonomy," *Ethics* 92 (1981): 16). Compare the wording of the respect-for-persons formulation of the Categorical Imperative: "Act so that you treat humanity, whether in your own person or in that of any other, always as an end and never as a means only." The wording suggests that it is "humanity in us," that is, the defining capacity of human persons, that is the object of the respect we owe all persons, including ourselves. Kant also maintains that "all respect for a person is only respect for the law" (*Foundations of the Metaphysics of Morals*, trans. Lewis White Beck [Indianapolis: Bobbs-Merrill, Library of Liberal Arts, 1959], 18n).

16. See, e.g., Carol Gilligan, *In A Different Voice: Psychology and Women's Development* (Cambridge, Mass.: Harvard University Press, 1982) and "Remapping the Moral Domain: New Images of the Self in Relation," in *Reconstructing Individualism: Autonomy, Individuality, and the Self in Western Thought*, ed. Thomas C. Heller, Morton Sosna, and David Wellbery (Stanford: Stanford University Press, 1986); and Jean Baker Miller, "The Development of Women's Sense of Self," *Works in Progress: Stone Center Working Papers Series* (Wellesley, Mass.: Stone Center, 1984).

17. See Annette C. Baier, "Cartesian Persons," in *Postures of the Mind: Essays on Mind and Morals* (Minneapolis: University of Minnesota Press, 1985); Lorraine Code, "Second Persons," in *Science, Morality, and Feminist Theory*, pp. 357–382; and Caroline Whitbeck, "A Different Reality: Feminist

Ontology," in *Beyond Domination: New Perspectives on Women and Philosophy*, ed. Carol C. Gould (Totowa, N.J.: Rowman and Allenheld, 1984), pp. 64–88.

18. I used to wonder whether I had self-respect, since my rights had never been trampled and I therefore never had the chance to prove my self-respect in defending them. Only later did I come to understand both the subtle onslaughts on my sense of worth and the many other dimensions of self-respect.

19. Meyers, "The Politics of Self-Respect."

20. In working toward a feminist understanding of self-respect, I will be drawing on elements of the so-called "ethic of care." I have argued elsewhere that some discussions of respect for persons and some discussions of care bear such a resemblance to each other as to give us grounds for thinking that care is a kind of respect ("Care and Respect," in *Explorations in Feminist Ethics: Theory and Practice*, ed. Susan Coultrap McQuin and Eve Browning Cole [Bloomington: Indiana University Press, 1991], pp. 69–81). In this paper I begin to develop some of the implications of that view for an understanding of self-respect. I am cognizant of the worries expressed by a number of feminists about the ethic of care (e.g., Claudia Card, "Women's Voices and Ethical Ideals: Must We Mean What We Say?" *Ethics* 99 (1988): 125–35 and "Caring and Evil," *Hypatia* 5, no. 1 (1990): 101–108; Barbara Houston, "Rescuing Womanly Virtues," in *Science, Morality, and Feminist Theory*, pp. 237–264, and "Caring and Exploitation," *Hypatia* 5, no. 1 (1990): 115–119; Sarah Lucia Hoagland, "Some Concerns about Nel Noddings' *Caring*," *Hypatia* 5, no. 1 (1990): 109–14. However, thinking about self-respect from the perspective of care brings to the foreground aspects of our everyday experiences of self-respect that are either downplayed in current accounts or ignored altogether. Development of a feminist conception of self-respect involves as much a reorientation of the discussion, a shift in emphasis and a recovering of certain elements, as a revisioning and transformation of our concepts. In drawing on the ethic of care, I mean to be wary; but I also believe that my account will go some way toward alleviating some of the well-founded worries about care.

21. Melvin Rader, *Ethics and the Human Community* (New York: Holt, Rinehart, Winston, 1964), p. 157.

22. Elizabeth Spelman, "On Treating Persons as Persons," *Ethics* 88 (1978): 150–161.

23. The standard conception of recognition respect for persons aims for moral harmony among individuals by erasing differences among them. By contrast, a feminist conception of recognition respect for persons would, I believe, aim for harmony through acknowledging and dealing with differences. I

explore this idea in "Respect and Care: Toward Moral Integration," *Canadian Journal of Philosophy* 22 (1992): 105–132.

24. Marilyn Friedman has raised this concern in discussion. Alison Jaggar articulates it in "Feminist Ethics: Some Issues for the Nineties," *Journal of Social Philosophy* 20 (1989): 91–107.

25. I owe this point to Marilyn Friedman.

26. See Code, "Second Persons," and "Persons and Others," in *Power, Gender, Values*, ed. Judith Genova (Edmonton, Alberta: Academic Printing and Publishing, 1987), pp. 143–161, for insightful discussion of this point.

27. To forestall a possible misunderstanding, I do not mean to suggest here either that feminist self-respect would involve treasuring every facet of one's self or that a feminist conception of recognition respect should be understood to involve cherishing every facet of others' lives and personalities. For some of those aspects may be objectionable, as I point out below. One of the advantages of distinguishing recognition respect and self-respect from appraisal respect and self-respect is that only the latter involve evaluating the particular aspects of individual selves, thus making it conceptually possible to cherish oneself without cherishing every aspect of one's self.

28. Nel Noddings, *Caring* (Berkeley: University of California Press, 1984).

29. This worry is expressed in, e.g., Hoagland, "Some Concerns," and Houston, "Caring and Exploitation."

30. Sheila Mullett, "Only Connect: The Place of Self-Knowledge in Ethics," in *Science, Morality, and Feminist Theory*, pp. 309–338.

31. I believe, however, that we may start in both places. Some women in contemporary American society are encouraged/conditioned to be both self-obsessed (particularly with superficialities) and other-obsessed.

32. I briefly explore the connection between self-respect and self-deception in "How To Lose Your Self-Respect." Interestingly, the purpose of self-deception, some have argued, is to bolster fragile self-esteem. However, I would suggest that self-esteem is fragile precisely when one lacks self-understanding. For when one does not fully appreciate my own abilities or situation, one sets unachievable goals or unrealistically high standards, or values oneself as x when one is not really x. One thus sets oneself up for the shame and blows to self-respect and self-esteem that accompany failure, and for recourse to self-deception to avoid those blows.

33. Code, "Persons and Others." One interesting consequence, conceptually speaking, of incorporating self-understanding into the conception of recognition self-respect is that respecting oneself becomes less on/off and more a matter of degree. This shifts recognition self-respect closer to appraisal self-respect, thus opening the possibility of moving beyond the

recognition/appraisal dichotomy.

34. Jean Baker Miller, *Toward a New Psychology of Women* (Boston: Beacon Press, 1976), p. 11.

+

Bibliography

+

I. Historical Works

Aristotle. *Nichomachean Ethics*. Translated by W. D. Ross. In *Basic Works of Aristotle*. Edited by Richard McKeon. New York: Random House, 1941.

Descartes, René. *Treatise on the Passions of the Soul*. In *The Philosophical Works of Descartes*. Translated by Elizabeth S. Haldane and G. R. T. Ross. Vol. 1. Cambridge: Cambridge University Press, 1911, 1979 (1646).

Hobbes, Thomas. *Leviathan*. Indianapolis: Bobbs-Merrill, The Library of Liberal Arts, 1958 (1651).

Hume, David. *Enquiries Concerning the Human Understanding and Concerning the Principles of Morals*. Edited by L. A. Selby-Bigge. Oxford: Oxford University Press, 1972 (1751).

Hume, David. "Of the Dignity of Human Nature." In *Essays: Moral, Political, and Literary*. Edited by T. H. Green and T. H. Grose. Vol. 1. London: Longmans, Green, and Co., 1875.

Hume, David. *A Treatise of Human Nature*. Edited by L. A. Selby-Bigge. Oxford: Oxford University Press, 1978 (1739).

Kant, Immanuel. *Critique of Practical Reason*. Translated by Lewis White Beck. Indianapolis: Bobbs-Merrill, 1956 (1788).

Kant, Immanuel. *The Doctrine of Virtue: Part II of the Metaphysics of Morals*. Translated by Mary Gregor. Philadelphia: University of Pennsylvania Press, 1971 (1797).

Kant, Immanuel. *Groundwork of the Metaphysic of Morals*. Translated by H. J. Paton. New York: Harper & Row, 1964 (1785).

Kant, Immanuel. *Lectures on Ethics* [1775–1780]. Translated by Louis Infield. Indianapolis: Hackett Publishing Co., 1963 (1924).

Spinoza, Baruch. *The Ethics and Selected Letters*. Translated by Samuel Shirley. Edited by Seymour Feldman. Indianapolis: Hackett Publishing Company, 1982 (1677).

II. Contemporary Philosophical Works on Self-Respect and Related Concepts

Adler, Mortimer J., et al. "Honor." In *The Great Ideas: A Syntopicon of Great Books of the Western World*. Chicago: Encyclopedia Britannica, Inc., 1952.

Babbitt, Susan. "Feminism and Objective Interests: The Role of Transformation Experiences in Rational Deliberation." In *Feminist Epistemologies*. Edited by Linda Alcoff and Elizabeth Potter. New York: Routledge, 1993.

Balaief, Lynne. "Self-Esteem and Human Equality." *Philosophy and Phenomenological Research* 36 (1975): 25–43.

Bartky, Sandra Lee. "Feminine Masochism and the Politics of Personal Transformation." In *Femininity and Domination: Studies in the Phenomenology of Oppression*. New York: Routledge, 1990. Originally published in *Women's Studies International Forum*, Vol. 7, No. 5. (1984). Reprinted in *Hypatia Reborn: Essays in Feminist Philosophy*. Edited by Azizah Y. al-Hibri and

Margaret A. Simons. Bloomington: Indiana University Press, 1990.

Bartky, Sandra Lee. "On Psychological Oppression." In *Femininity and Domination*. Originally published in *Philosophy and Women*. Edited by Sharon Bishop and Marjorie Weinzweig. Belmont, Calif.: Wadsworth, 1979.

Bartky, Sandra Lee. "Shame and Gender." In *Femininity and Domination*.

Becker, Lawrence C. "Pride." In *Encyclopedia of Ethics*. Edited by Lawrence C. Becker and Charlotte B. Becker. New York: Garland Publishing, Inc., 1992.

Berger, Peter. "On the Obsolescence of the Concept of Honor." *European Journal of Sociology* 11 (1970): 339–347.

Bernick, Michael. "A Note on Promoting Self-Esteem." *Political Theory* 6 (1978): 109–118.

Boxill, Bernard R. *Blacks and Social Justice*. Lanham, Md.: Rowman & Littlefield, 1992.

Braybrooke, David. *Ethics in the World of Business*. Totowa, N.J.: Rowman & Allenheld, 1983.

Campbell, Richmond. *Self-Love and Self-Respect: A Philosophical Study of Egoism*. Ottawa: Canadian Library of Philosophy, 1979.

Collins, Patricia Hill. *Black Feminist Thought: Knowledge, Consciousness, and the Politics of Empowerment*. New York: Routledge, 1990.

Daniels, Norman. "Equal Liberty and Unequal Worth of Liberty." In *Reading Rawls: Critical Studies of "A Theory of Justice."* Edited by Norman Daniels. New York: Basic Books, Inc., 1975.

Darwall, Stephen L. *Impartial Reason*. Ithaca: Cornell University Press, 1983.

Darwall, Stephen L. "Self-Deception, Autonomy, and Moral Constitution." In *Perspectives on Self-Deception*. Edited by Brian P. McLaughlin and Amelie Oksenberg Rorty. Berkeley: University of California Press, 1988.

DeGrazia, David. "Grounding a Right to Health Care in Self-Respect and Self-Esteem." *Public Affairs Quarterly* 5 (1991): 301–318.

Dillon, Robin S. "How To Lose Your Self-Respect." *American Philosophical Quarterly* 29 (1992): 125–139.

Doppelt, Gerald. "Rawls's System of Justice: A Critique from the Left." *Noûs* 15 (1981): 259–307.

Elster, Jon. "Self-Realization in Work and Politics: The Marxist Conception of the Good Life." *Social Philosophy and Policy* 3 (1985–1986): 97–126.

Ezorsky, Gertrude. *Racism & Justice: The Case for Affirmative Action*. Ithaca: Cornell University Press, 1991.

Falk, W. D. "Morality, Form, and Content." In *Ought, Reasons, and Morality: The Collected Papers of W. D. Falk*. Ithaca: Cornell University Press, 1986.

Feinberg, Joel. "The Nature and Value of Rights." *Journal of Value Inquiry* 4 (1970): 243–257.

Ferguson, Ann. "A Feminist Aspect Theory of the Self." In *Science, Morality, and Feminist Theory*. Edited by Marsha Hanen and Kai Nielsen. Calgary: University of Calgary Press, 1987.

Flanagan, Owen. *Varieties of Moral Personality: Ethics and Psychological Realism*. Cambridge, Mass.: Harvard University Press, 1991.

Friedman, Marilyn. "Moral Integrity and the Deferential Wife." *Philosophical Studies* 47 (1985): 141–150.

Gewirth, Alan. "Human Dignity as the Basis of Rights." In *The Constitution of Rights: Human Dignity and American Values*. Edited by Michael J. Meyer and William A. Parent. Ithaca: Cornell University Press, 1992.

Gewirth, Alan. *Reason and Morality*. Chicago: University of Chicago Press, 1978.

Ghosh-Dastidar, Koyeli. "Respect for Persons and Self-Respect: Western and Indian." *Journal of Indian Council of Philosophical Research* 5 (1987): 83–93.

Govier, Trudy. "Self-Trust, Autonomy, and Self-Esteem." *Hypatia* 8 (1993): 99–120.

Grace, Harry A. "The Self and Self-Acceptance." *Educational Theory* 3 (1953): 220–235.

Greenleaf, Nancy P., ed. *The Politics of Self-Esteem. Nursing Digest* 6 (1978).

Gutman, Amy. *Liberal Equality*. Cambridge: Cambridge University Press, 1980.

Haber, Joram Graf. *Forgiveness*. Savage, Md.: Rowman & Littlefield, 1991.

Hampton, Jean. "Selflessness and the Loss of Self." *Social Philosophy and Policy* 10 (1993): 135–165.

Held, Virginia. "Reasonable Progress and Self-Respect." *The Monist* 57 (1973): 12–27.

Hill, Thomas E., Jr. *Autonomy and Self-Respect*. Cambridge: Cambridge University Press, 1991.

Hill, Thomas E., Jr. "Darwall on Practical Reason." *Ethics* 96 (1986): 604–619.

Hill, Thomas E., Jr. *Dignity and Practical Reason in Kant's Moral Theory*. Ithaca: Cornell University Press, 1992.

Hill, Thomas E., Jr. "Humanity as an End in Itself." *Ethics* 91 (1980): 84–99. Reprinted in *Dignity and Practical Reason*.

Hill, Thomas E., Jr. "Self-Respect." In *Encyclopedia of Ethics*. Edited by Lawrence C. Becker and Charlotte B. Becker. New York: Garland Publishing, Inc., 1992.

Holmgren, Margaret. "Forgiveness and the Intrinsic Value of Persons." *American Philosophical Quarterly* 30 (1993): 341–352.

Horsburgh, H. J. N. "The Plurality of Moral Standards." *Philosophy* 24 (1954): 332–346.

Hudson, Stephen D. *Human Character and Morality: Reflections from the History of Ideas*. Boston: Routledge and Kegan Paul, 1986.

Isenberg, Arnold. "Natural Pride and Natural Shame." *Philosophy and Phenomenological Research* 10 (1949): 1–24.

Kekes, John. "Shame and Moral Progress." In *Ethical Theory: Character and Virtue. Midwest Studies in Philosophy*. Vol. 13. Edited by Peter A. French, Theodore E. Uehling, and Howard K. Wettstein. Notre Dame: University of Notre Dame Press, 1988.

Lane, Robert E. "Government and Self-Esteem" *Political Theory* 10 (1982): 5–31.

Lomasky, Loren. *Persons, Rights, and the Moral Community*. Oxford: Oxford University Press, 1987.

Maclaren, Elizabeth. "Dignity." *Journal of Medical Ethics* 3 (1974): 40–41.

Martin, Mike W. *Everyday Morality: An Introduction to Applied Ethics*. Belmont, Calif.: Wadsworth, 1989.

Martin, Mike W. *Self-Deception and Morality*. Lawrence, Kans.: University Press of Kansas, 1986.

Martin, Mike W., ed. *Self-Deception and Self-Understanding*. Lawrence, Kans.: University Press of Kansas, 1985.

Massey, Stephen J. "Kant on Self-Respect" *Journal of the History of Philosophy* 21 (1983): 57–73.

McGary, Howard. "Reparations, Self-Respect, and Public Policy." In *Ethical Theory and Society*. Edited by David Goldberg. New York: Holt, Rinehart, & Winston, 1988.

Meyer, Michael J. "Dignity." In *Encyclopedia of Ethics*. Edited by Lawrence C. Becker and Charlotte B. Becker. New York: Garland Publishing, Inc., 1992.

Meyer, Michael J. "Dignity, Rights, and Self-Control." *Ethics* 99 (1989): 520–534.

Meyer, Michael J. "Kant's Conception of Dignity and Modern Political Thought." *History of European Ideas* 8 (1987): 319–332.

Meyer, Michael J., and William A. Parent, eds. *The Constitution of Rights: Human Dignity and American Values*. Ithaca: Cornell University Press, 1992.

Meyers, Diana T. "The Politics of Self-Respect." *Hypatia* 1 (1986): 83–100.

Meyers, Diana T. *Self, Society, and Personal Choice.* New York: Columbia University Press, 1989.

Meyers, Diana T. "Work and Self-Respect." In *Moral Rights in the Workplace.* Edited by Gertrude Ezorsky. Albany: State University of New York Press, 1987.

Michelman, Frank. "Constitutional Welfare Rights and *A Theory of Justice.*" In *Reading Rawls: Critical Studies of "A Theory of Justice."* Edited by Norman Daniels. New York: Basic Books, Inc., 1975.

Mohr, Richard D. *Gay Ideas: Outings and Other Controversies.* Boston: Beacon Press, 1992.

Mohr, Richard D. *Gays/Justice: A Study of Ethics, Society, and Law.* New York: Columbia University Press, 1988.

Montefiore, Alan. "Self-Reality, Self-Respect, and Respect for Others." In *Studies in Ethical Theory. Midwest Studies in Philosophy.* Vol. 3. Edited by Peter A. French, Theodore E. Uehling, and Howard K. Wettstein. Minneapolis: University of Minnesota Press, 1980.

Morgan, Kathryn Pauly. "Romantic Love, Altruism, and Self-Respect: An Analysis of Simone de Beauvoir." *Hypatia* 1 (1986): 117–148.

Morris, Bertram. "The Dignity of Man." *Ethics* 57 (1946): 57–64.

Murphy, Jeffrie. "Moral Death: A Kantian Essay on Psychopathy." *Ethics* 82 (1972): 284–298.

Murphy, Jeffrie, and Jean Hampton. *Forgiveness and Mercy.* Cambridge: Cambridge University Press, 1988.

Nielsen, Kai. "Capitalism, Socialism, and Justice: Reflections on Rawls's *Theory of Justice.*" *Social Praxis* 7 (1980): 253–277.

Nozick, Robert. *Anarchy, State, and Utopia.* New York: Basis Books, 1974.

Nozick, Robert. *Philosophical Explanations.* Cambridge, Mass.: Harvard University Press, 1981.

Parent, William A. "Constitutional Values and Human Dignity." In *The Constitution of Rights: Human Dignity and American Values.* Edited by Michael J. Meyer and William A. Parent. Ithaca: Cornell University Press, 1992.

Peters, R.S. *Psychology and Ethical Development.* London: George Allen and Unwin, 1974.

Phillips, Michael. "Reason, Dignity, and the Formal Conception of Practical Reason." *American Philosophical Quarterly* 24 (1987): 191–198.

Postow, B. C. "Economic Dependence and Self-Respect." *The Philosophical Forum* 10 (1978–1979): 181–205.

Pritchard, Michael S. "Human Dignity and Justice." *Ethics* 82 (1972): 299–313.

Pritchard, Michael S. *On Becoming Responsible.* Lawrence, Kans.: University Press of Kansas, 1991.

Pritchard, Michael S. "Rawls's Moral Psychology." *Southwestern Journal of Philosophy* 8 (1977): 59–72.

Pritchard, Michael S. "Self-Regard and the Supererogatory." In *Respect for Persons. Tulane Studies in Philosophy.* Vol. 13. Edited by O. H. Green. New Orleans: Tulane University Press, 1982.

Proudfoot, Wayne. "Rawls on Self-Respect and Social Union." *Journal of Chinese Philosophy* 5 (1978): 255–269.

Rawls, John. *A Theory of Justice.* Cambridge, Mass.: Harvard University Press, 1971.

Rawls, John. "Kantian Constructivism in Moral Theory." *The Journal of Philosophy* 77 (1980): 515–572.

Rawls, John. "The Basic Liberties and Their Priority." *The Tanner Lectures on Human Values.* Vol. 3. Salt Lake City: University of Utah Press, 1982.

Sachs, David. "How To Distinguish Self-Respect from Self-Esteem." *Philosophy and Public*

Affairs 10 (1981): 346-360.

Sachs, David. "Self-Respect and Respect for Others: Are They Independent?" In *Respect for Persons. Tulane Studies in Philosophy*. Vol. 31. Edited by O. H. Green. New Orleans: Tulane University Press, 1982.

Scarre, Geoffrey. "Utilitarianism and Self-Respect." *Utilitas* 4 (1992): 27-42.

Seidler, Victor J. *Kant, Respect, and Injustice: The Limits of Liberal Moral Theory*. London: Routledge & Kegan Paul, 1986.

Seidler, Victor J. *The Moral Limits of Modernity: Love, Inequality, and Oppression*. New York: St. Martins Press, 1991.

Shue, Henry. "Liberty and Self-Respect." *Ethics* 85 (1975): 195-203.

Solomon, Robert. *The Passions*. New York: Basic Books, 1977.

Speigelberg, Herbert. "Human Dignity: A Challenge to Contemporary Philosophy." *Philosophy Forum* 9 (1971): 39-64.

Strike, Kenneth. "Education, Justice, and Self-Respect: A School for Rodney Dangerfield." *Philosophy of Education* 35 (1980): 41-49.

Szabados, Bela. "Embarrassment and Self-Esteem." *Journal of Philosophical Research* 15 (1989-1990): 341-349.

Taylor, Charles. *Sources of the Self: The Making of the Modern Identity*. Cambridge, Mass.: Harvard University Press, 1989.

Taylor, Gabriele. *Pride, Shame, and Guilt: Emotions of Self-Assessment*. Oxford: Oxford University Press, 1985.

Thomas, Laurence. "Capitalism vs. Marx's Communism." *Studies in Soviet Thought* 20 (1979): 57-79.

Thomas, Laurence. "Law, Morality, and Our Psychological Nature." In *Social Justice*. Edited by Michael Bradie and David Braybrooke. Bowling Green, Ohio: Bowling Green Studies in Applied Philosophy, 1982.

Thomas, Laurence. *Living Morally: A Psychology of Moral Character*. Philadelphia: Temple University Press, 1989.

Thomas, Laurence. "Morality and Our Self-Concept." *Journal of Value Inquiry* 12 (1978): 258-268.

Thomas, Laurence. "Morality, the Self, and Our Natural Sentiments." In *Emotion: Philosophical Studies*. Edited by K. D. Irani and G. E. Meyers. New York: Haven Publishing Corp, 1983.

Thomas, Laurence. "Rawlsian Self-Respect and the Black Consciousness Movement." *The Philosophical Forum* 9 (1977-1978): 303-314.

Thomas, Laurence. "Sexism and Racism: Some Conceptual Differences." *Ethics* 90 (1980): 239-250.

Vlastos, Gregory. "Justice and Equality." In *Social Justice*. Edited by Richard Brandt. Englewood Cliffs, N.J.: Prentice Hall, 1962.

Wallace, James D. *Virtues and Vices*. Ithaca: Cornell University Press, 1978.

Weil, Simone. *The Need for Roots*. London: Routledge & Kegan Paul, 1972.

Weil, Simone. *Seventy Letters*. Oxford: Oxford University Press, 1965.

Wong, David B. *Moral Relativity*. Berkeley: University of California Press, 1984.

Yanal, Robert J. "Self-Esteem." *Noûs* 21 (1987): 363-379.

III. Contemporary Philosophical Works on Respect and Related Concepts

Arrington, Robert L. "On Respect." *Journal of Value Inquiry* 12 (1978): 1-12.

Atwell, John E. "Kant's Notion of Respect for Persons." In *Respect for Persons. Tulane Studies in*

Philosophy. Vol. 31. Edited by O. H. Green. New Orleans: Tulane University Press, 1982.

Benn, S. I. "Privacy, Freedom, and Respect for Persons." In *Nomos 13: Privacy*. Edited by J. Roland Pennock and John W. Chapman. New York: Atherton Press, 1971.

Benn, S. I. *Theory of Freedom*. Cambridge: Cambridge University Press, 1988.

Brody, Baruch A. "Towards a Theory of Respect for Persons." In *Respect for Persons. Tulane Studies in Philosophy*. Vol. 31. Edited by O. H. Green. New Orleans: Tulane University Press, 1982.

Blum, Alex. "On Respect." *Philosophical Inquiry* 10 (1988): 58–63.

Code, Lorraine. "Persons and Others." In *Power, Gender, Values*. Edited by Judith Genova. Edmonton, Alberta: Academic Printing and Publishing, 1987.

Cranor, Carl F. "Justice, Respect, and Self-Respect." *Philosophy Research Archives* 2 (1976).

Cranor, Carl F. "Kant's Respect-for-Persons Principle." *International Studies in Philosophy* (1980): 19–40.

Cranor, Carl F. "Limitations on Respect-for-Persons Theories." In *Respect for Persons. Tulane Studies in Philosophy*. Vol. 31. Edited by O. H. Green. New Orleans: Tulane University Press, 1982.

Cranor, Carl F. "On Respecting Human Beings as Persons." *Journal of Value Inquiry* 17 (1983): 103–117.

Cranor, Carl F. "Toward a Theory of Respect for Persons," *American Philosophical Quarterly* 12 (1975): 309–320.

DeMarco, Joseph P. "Respect for Persons: Some Prerequisites." *Philosophy in Context* 3 (1974): 33–37.

Diggs, B. J. "A Contractarian View of Respect for Persons." *American Philosophical Quarterly* 18 (1981): 273–283.

Dillon, Robin S. "Care and Respect." In *Explorations in Feminist Ethics: Theory and Practice*. Edited by Eve Browning Cole and Susan Coultrap-McQuin. Bloomington: Indiana University Press, 1991.

Dillon, Robin S. "Respect and Care: Toward Moral Integration." *Canadian Journal of Philosophy* 22 (1992): 105–132.

Donagan, Alan. *The Theory of Morality*. Chicago: University of Chicago Press, 1977.

Downie, R. S., and Elizabeth Telfer. *Respect for Persons*. London: George Allen and Unwin, 1969.

Dworkin, Ronald. *Taking Rights Seriously*. Cambridge, Mass.: Harvard University Press, 1977.

Edel, Abraham. "The Place of Respect for Persons in Moral Philosophy." *Philosophy in Context* 3 (1974): 23–32.

Farley, Margaret A. "A Feminist Version of Respect for Persons." *Journal of Feminist Studies in Religion* 9 (1993): 183–198.

Feinberg, Joel. "Some Conjectures on the Concept of Respect." *Journal of Social Philosophy* 4 (1975): 1–3.

Fotion, Nicholas, and Gerard Elfstrom. "Honor." In *Encyclopedia of Ethics*. Edited by Lawrence C. Becker and Charlotte B. Becker. New York: Garland Publishing, Inc., 1992.

Frankena, William K. "The Ethics of Respect for Persons." *Philosophical Topics* 14 (1986): 149–167.

Fried, Charles. *Right and Wrong*. Cambridge, Mass.: Harvard University Press, 1978.

Garry, Ann. "Pornography and Respect for Women." *Social Theory and Practice* 4 (1978): 395–421.

Gauthier, David. *Practical Reasoning*. Oxford: Oxford University Press, 1963.

Gaylin, Willard. "In Defense of the Dignity of Being Human." *The Hastings Center Report* 14 (1984): 18–22.

Gibbard, Alan. *Wise Choices, Apt Feelings: A Theory of Normative Judgment* Cambridge, Mass.: Harvard University Press, 1990.

Goodin, Robert. "The Political Theories of Choice and Dignity." *American Philosophical Quarterly* 8 (1981): 91–100.

Griffin, James. *Well-Being: Its Meaning, Measurement, and Importance.* Oxford: Clarendon Press, 1986.

Gruzalski, Bart. "Two Accounts of Our Obligations to Respect Persons." In *Respect for Persons. Tulane Studies in Philosophy.* Vol. 31. Edited by O. H. Green. New Orleans: Tulane University Press, 1982.

Honneth, Axel. "Integrity and Disrespect: Principles of a Conception of Morality Based on the Theory of Recognition." *Political Theory* 20 (1992): 187–201.

Hudson, Stephen D. "The Nature of Respect." *Social Theory and Practice* 6 (1980): 69–90.

Johnson, Edward. "Ignoring Persons." In *Respect for Persons. Tulane Studies in Philosophy.* Vol. 31. Edited by O. H. Green. New Orleans: Tulane University Press, 1982.

Katz, Michael S. "Respect for Persons and Students: Charting Some Ethical Territory." *Philosophy of Education Proceedings 1991.* Normal, Ill.: Illinois State University, Philosophy of Education Society, 1992.

Kent, Edward. "Respect for Persons and Social Protest." In *Social Ends and Political Means.* Edited by Ted Honderich. London: Routledge and Kegan Paul, 1976.

Landesman, Charles. "Against Respect for Persons." In *Respect for Persons. Tulane Studies in Philosophy.* Vol. 31. Edited by O. H. Green. New Orleans: Tulane University Press, 1982.

Larmore, Charles E. *Patterns of Moral Complexity.* Cambridge: Cambridge University Press, 1987.

Maclagan, W. G. "Respect for Persons as a Moral Principle." *Philosophy* 35 (1960): 199–305.

Melden, A. I. "Dignity, Worth, and Rights." In *The Constitution of Rights: Human Dignity and American Values.* Edited by Michael J. Meyer and William A. Parent. Ithaca: Cornell University Press, 1992.

Melden, A. I. *Rights and Persons.* Berkeley: University of California Press, 1977.

Shafer, Carolyn M., and Marilyn Frye. "Rape and Respect." In *Feminism and Philosophy.* Edited by Mary Vetterling-Braggin, Frederick A. Elliston, and Jane English. Totowa, N.J.: Rowman & Littlefield, 1977.

Spelman, Elizabeth V. "On Treating Persons as Persons." *Ethics* 88 (1977): 150–161.

Williams, Bernard. "The Idea of Equality." In *Politics, Philosophy, and Society.* Vol. 2. Edited by Peter Laslett and W. G. Runciman. Oxford: Blackwell, 1962.

IV. Selected Works in Psychology on Self-Esteem

Benson, Jann, and Dan Lyons. *Strutting and Fretting: Standards for Self-Esteem.* Niwot, Colo. University Press of Colorado, 1990.

Branden, Nathaniel. *The Psychology of Self-Esteem.* Los Angeles: Nash Publishing Corp., 1969.

Coopersmith, Stanley. *The Antecedents of Self-Esteem.* Palo Alto, Calif.: Consulting Psychologists Press, 1981.

Gilbert, Daniel T., and Joel Cooper. "Social Psychological Strategies of Self-Deception." In *Self-Deception and Self-Understanding.* Edited by Mike W. Martin. Lawrence, Kans.: University Press of Kansas, 1985.

James, William. *The Principles of Psychology.* 2 vols. New York: Dover Publications, 1950 (1890).

Kaplan, Howard B. "Prevalence of the Self-Esteem Motive." In *Social Psychology of the Self-Concept*. Edited by Morris Rosenberg and Howard B. Kaplan. Arlington Heights, Ill.: Davidson Press, 1982.

Lynd, Helen Merrill. *Shame and the Search for Identity*. New York: John Wiley & Sons, 1958.

Markus, Hazel, and Elissa Wurf. "The Dynamic Self-Concept: A Social Psychological Perspective." *Annual Review of Psychology* 38 (1987): 299–337.

Maslow, Abraham H. *Dominance, Self-Esteem, Self-Actualization: Germinal Papers of A. H. Maslow*. Edited by Richard J. Lowry. Monterey: Brooks/Cole Publishing Co., 1973.

Mead, George Herbert. *Mind, Self, and Society*. Chicago: University of Chicago Press, 1934.

Mecca, Andrew M., Neil J. Smelser, and John Vasconcellos, eds. *The Social Importance of Self-Esteem*. Berkeley: University of California Press, 1989.

Miller, Susan. *The Shame Experience*. Hillsdale, N.J.: The Analytic Press, 1985.

Miller, Jean Baker. "The Development of Women's Sense of Self." In *Works in Progress*. Wellesley: Stone Center for Developmental Services and Studies, 1984.

Piers, Gerhart, and Milton B, Singer. *Shame and Guilt*. New York: W. W. Norton & Co., 1971.

Rosenberg, Morris. *Conceiving the Self*. New York: Basic Books, 1979.

Rosenberg, Morris. "Self-Concept from Middle Childhood through Adolescence." In *Social Psychological Perspectives on the Self*. Edited by Jerry Suls. Hillsdale, NJ: Erlbaum, 1986.

Rosenberg, Morris. *Society and the Adolescent Self-Image*. Princeton: Princeton University Press, 1965.

Snyder, C. R. "Collaborative Companions: The Relationship of Self-Deception and Excuse Making." In *Self-Deception and Self-Understanding*. Edited by Mike W. Martin. Lawrence, Kans.: University Press of Kansas, 1985.

Solomon, Sheldon, Jeff Greenberg, and Tom Pyszczynski. "A Terror Management Theory of Social Behavior: The Psychological Functions of Self-Esteem and Cultural Worldviews." In *Advances in Experimental Social Psychology*. Vol. 24. Edited Mark P. Zanna. San Diego: Academic Press, Inc., 1991.

Steffenhagen, R. A., and Jeff D. Burns. *The Social Dynamics of Self-Esteem*. New York: Praeger Publishers, 1987.

Tesser, Abraham. "Toward a Self-Evaluation Maintenance Model of Social Behavior." In *Advances in Experimental Social Psychology*. Vol. 21. Edited by Leonard Berkowitz. San Diego: Academic Press, Inc., 1988.

Wells, L. Edward and Gerald Marwell. *Self-Esteem: Its Conceptualization and Measurement*. Beverly Hills: Sage Publications, 1976.

White, Robert. "Ego And Reality in Psychoanalytic Theory." *Psychological Issues* 3 (1963): 3–203.

V. Other Works of Interest

Bettelheim, Bruno. *The Informed Heart: Autonomy in a Mass Age*. Glencoe, Ill.: Free Press, 1961.

Buss, Fran Leeper. *Dignity: Lower Income Women Tell of Their Lives and Struggles*. Ann Arbor: University of Michigan Press, 1985.

Cannon, Katie G. *Black Womanist Ethics*. Atlanta: Scholars Press, 1988.

Des Pres, Terrence. "Excremental Assault." In *The Survivor: An Anatomy of Life in the Concentration Camps*. New York: Oxford University Press, 1976.

Didion, Joan. "On Self-Respect." In *Slouching Towards Bethlehem*. New York: Washington Square Press, 1968.

Douglass, Frederick. *My Bondage and My Freedom*. New York: Dover Publications, 1969 (1855).

DuBois, W. E. B. "Of Mr. Booker T. Washington and Others." In *The Souls of Black Folk*. New York: Penguin Books, 1969 (1903).

DuBois, W. E. B. "Separation and Self-Respect." In *The Seventh Son: The Thought and Writings of W. E. B. DuBois*. Edited by Julius Lester. New York: Vintage Books, 1971.

Dworkin, Andrea. "Lesbian Pride." In *Our Blood: Prophecies and Discourses on Sexual Politics*. New York: Harper and Row, 1976.

French, Marilyn. "Self-Respect: A Feminist Perspective." *Humanist* 46 (1986): 18-23.

King, Martin Luther, Jr. "Letter from Birmingham Jail" and "The Sword that Heals." In *Why We Can't Wait*. New York: Penguin Books, 1964.

Levi, Primo. *Survival in Auschwitz: The Nazi Assault on Humanity*. New York: MacMillan, 1958.

Lorde, Audre. "Eye to Eye: Black Women, Hatred, and Anger." In *Sister Outsider*. Trumansburg, N.Y.: The Crossing Press, 1984.

Menchu, Rigoberta. *I, Rigobert Menchu: An Indian Woman in Guatemala*. Edited by Elizabeth Burgos-Debray. Translated by Ann Wright. London: Verso, 1984.

Morrison, Toni. *The Bluest Eye*. New York: Pocket Books, 1970.

Sanford, Linda Tschirhart, and Mary Ellen Donovan. *Women and Self-Esteem*. New York: Penguin Books, 1985.

Shoben, Edward Joseph, Jr. "On Self-Respect." *The Antioch Review* 41 (1983): 85-100.

Steinem, Gloria. *Revolution From Within: A Book of Self-Esteem*. Boston: Little, Brown & Company, 1992.

Walker, Alice. *The Color Purple*. New York: Simon & Schuster, 1982.

Washington, Booker T. *Up From Slavery*. New York: Doubleday, 1901.

West, Cornel. *Race Matters*. New York: Vintage Books, 1994.

X, Malcolm. *The Autobiography of Malcolm X*, as told to Alex Haley. New York: Ballantine Books, 1964.

Index

Abilities, 119, 129, 187, 189, 251-66, 272-73
Acceptance, 301-302
Accidents of fortune, 275
Accomplishment, 119, 188
Action and respect, 185-86
Admiration and esteem, 256-57
Affectivity, 31, 297, 301
African Americans
    as children, 271-72, 283-85
    and class, 286-87
    economic isolation of, 272, 287
    and moral status, 260-61
    rights of, 93-103
    and self-contempt, 78-85
    self-esteem vs. self-respect and, 261
    self-respect and, 36-40, 77-85, 93-103, 256-64, 271-87
Agency, 29
    and character, 188-89
    as constraint on choice, 220-21
    and dignity, 221-22
    and integrity, 164-74
Agents, 27, 71, 160, 164, 167, 188, 221
Aims and ideals, 136-37, 143-44, 149
Allport, Gordon, 282
Amish, Old Order, the, 277
Androcentrism, 291-92
Animals, moral status of, 99, 257-58
Appalachian region, the, 278
Appraisal self-respect, 184-95, 292, 294

Aristotelian Principle, 126, 129, 255
Aristotle, 7-11, 12-41 *passim*, 70, 148, 189
"Atlanta Exposition Address" (Washington), 257
Attitudes of others, 24-25, 29, 126, 141-42, 148-49, 257
Auschwitz, 24
Authenticity, 99
Autobiography of Malcolm X, The (Haley), 2
Autonomy, 15-18, 25, 26, 81, 111, 122, 218
    vs. conventionality, 232-33
    episodic, 235
    moral vs. personal, 228-37
    skills of, 222
    and women, 291

Bacon, Francis, 73
Baier, Annette, 296
Bartky, Sandra, 38
Bedau, Hugo Adam, 199
Behavior;
    constraints on, 191-92
    debasing, 172, 220, 221
    standards of, 187
    worthy, 110, 201
Belief, 264
Benhabib, Seyla, 295
Bettelheim, Bruno, 165-66
Blue Angel, The, 118
Blum, Larry, 241
Boxill, Bernard R., 19-41 *passim*
Brown, Jonathan, 240

Brown v. Board of Education, 266

Capitalism, 265-66
Care, ethics of, 301, 302-303
Carlyle, 68
Caste society, 143, 235
Cavell, Stanley, 162-63
Character
    and morality, 29, 188
    and respect, 184, 188-95, 257-58
    and self-respect, 254, 257-58
Childhood and self-respect, 142-43,
    251-53, 271-72, 283-85
Christian tradition, 94
Civil rights movement, 259-64
Clark, Kenneth, 271-72, 283
Class, 143-44, 150, 277-78, 286
Code, Lorraine, 303
Cognitive filters, 233-34
Color Purple, The (Walker), 2
Commitment, 82, 172-75
    and identification, 203
    and maintaining standards,
        220-21
Community, 40, 127, 277, 286, 293
Compromised respect
    causes of, 222-37
    as corrupt, 236-37
    as misguided, 225-26, 229-30
    and moral vs. personal autonomy,
        228-37
    psychological risks of, 237-44
Conative self-respect, 26, 107-116,
    203
Confidence, 23, 100, 149, 159, 174,
    275, 278
Coopersmith, Stanley, 202
Cranor, Carl, 182, 192
Crito, 142

Dangerfield, Rodney, 183
Darwall, Stephen L., 19-41 *passim*,
    292-93, 295

Darwin, Charles, 142-43, 148, 152
Death of a Salesman (Miller), 2
Deferential Wife, the, 78-85, 117
Dependency, 111
Des Pres, Terrence, 24
Desires, 136, 219
Dignity, 7, 21-22, 25-26, 193, 219-20
    annihilation of, 24
    and agency, 221-22
    categorized, 57-59
    ethical problems of, 70-75
    etymology of, 53-54
    "human," 25, 60-64, 74
    and human rights, 22-23, 25,
        60-61
    in Kant, 14-18, 25
    moral, 73-75
    vs. morality, 57
    public availability of, 23-24
    qualities of, 59-60
    as a quality, 63-64
    sense of, 22
Discrimination, 93-103, 245,
    271-72, 276, 279-80
"Doll Study" of racial preferences,
    271-72
Douglass, Frederick, 39, 94-98
Downie, R. S., 181
Du Bois, W. E. B., 93-98, 257
Duty, 17, 22, 76, 85, 89-92
Dworkin, Ronald, 207

Elkins, Stanley, 101
Embarrassment, 134
Emotions, 28, 146-47, 163-76
*Enquiry Concerning Human
    Understanding and Concerning the
    Principles of Morals* (Hume), 11-14
Equality, 203, 259, 294
Erikson, Erik, 142
Esteem, 6-7
Estimative self-respect, 26, 107-16
Excellences, 79, 125-30, 138, 149,

187, 191
Expectations, 272, 277, 282–85

Fairness, 258–60
False shame, 169–75
Feinberg, Joel, 25, 208–10
Fels, Mort, 241
Feminism, 241–42, 290–304
"Feminist Aspect Theory of the Self,
   A" (Ferguson), 291
Feminist critique
   of personhood, 295–97
   of the self, 299–300
   of self-respect, 40–41, 292–304
Ferguson, Ann, 291, 298
Frankfurt, Harry, 234
Friedell, E. 67

Gauthier, David, 181
Generosity, 199
Ghosh-Dastidar, Koyeli, 25
Gide, 141
Gilligan, Carol, 296
Goffman, Irving, 183
Good, self-respect as, 125–30, 226,
   236, 274–75
Good, the, 200
Gordon, Francine, 242
Guilt, 94, 130, 133–34, 168, 170–76

Hall, Douglas, 242
Hampton, Jean, 26
Hart, H. L. A., 279
Hartmann N., 73
Held, Virginia, 193, 209–10
Hill, Thomas E., 19–41 *passim*
Hobbes, 9–10
Homiak, Marcia, 241
Honesty, 166, 189, 219, 254
Honor, 6–7, 17, 112
Honour-groups, 161
Housman, Judy, 241
Housewife-mother, the 240–44

Hume, 10–14, 15–41 *passim*
Humiliation, 7, 24, 84, 159, 173–75
Humility, 70–71

Ice Man Cometh, The (O'Neill), 2
Ideals, 119, 144
Identification, 201
Identity
   ethnic, 144–46
   and integrity, 164
   and sense of worth, 149–53
Injury to self-respect, 24, 36–39,
   128–29, 168–76, 261
Injustice, 38, 93–103
Instantiation of value, 226
Integrity
   as autonomy, 164–66
   as control, 165
   impact on others, 167
   as moral virtue, 164
   vs. self-respect, 174

James, William, 30, 135, 254–55
Jim Crow, 262, 266
Johnson, Samuel, 72
Jünger, E., 72–73
Justice, 127, 130, 260

Kant, 25, 122, 123, 191
   on assessment of persons, 189
   on dignity, 14–15
   on duty and moral law, 77, 85–92
   influence of, 2
   on moral autonomy, 228
   on persons as ends, 181, 203
   on self-respect, 14–18
King, Martin Luther, 38, 280, 283
Kolnai, Aurel, 21–41 *passim*
Krauss, Karl, 67

Legal positivism, 259
"Letter from the Birmingham Jail"
   (King), 38, 280

Levi, Primo, 2, 24
Life plans, 33, 119
    doubt of, 125–26
    and economic resources, 272,
        278
    and self-esteem, 275
    and shame, 129
    as sources of compromised self-
        respect, 239–40, 245

Malcolm X, 39
Mansbridge, Jane, 242
Marx, 265–66
Mashpee Indians, 145–46
Mask of servility, 102
Massey, Stephen J., 19–41 *passim*
Material possessions and self-worth,
    277–78
Meade, G. H., 30
Mechanisms for affirming self-
    respect, 279–80
Megalopsuchia, 7–9, 11, 19
Menchu, Rigoberta, 39
Meretricious, the, 68–70
Merton, Robert, 282
Meyer, Michael, 23–24, 25
Meyers, Diana T., 19–41 *passim*, 291
Miller, Jean Baker, 304
Mills, Earl, 145–46
Modesty, 70–71, 152
Mohr, Richard, 38–39
Moodey-Adams, Michele M., 19–41
    passim
Moral autonomy, 228–37
Moral being, 98–99
Moral community, standing in, 79,
    98, 260, 293–304
Moral law, 14–15, 172
Moral relationships, 299–300
Moral rights, 257–59, 296
    and subjective basis of self-
        respect, 202–204, 207–13
Moral vs. psychological accounts of

self-respect, 222–25, 227–28
Morality, 5
    and character, 188, 254
    and dignity, 73–75
    and integrity, 163–64
    and respect of individuals,
        119–23, 253
    and rights, 253–54
    and shame, 157–58
    and subjective concept of self-
        respect, 208–13
Mrs. Warren's Profession (Shaw), 198
Mullett, Sheila, 303

"Nature and Value of Rights, The"
    (Feinberg), 208–10
Nichomachean Ethics (Aristotle), 7–9
"Noble pride," 17–18
Noddings, Nel, 301

Oakley, Ann, 241
Objective self-respect, 26, 34, 112,
    199–213
Of Human Bondage (Maugham), 138
Old South, the, 263
Oppression, 5–6, 24, 36–39, 93–103,
    256–64, 304
"Outing," 40

Parental love, 251–53, 266
Parks, Mrs. Rosa, 262–63
Passion, 67–68
Patience, 301
Patterson, Orlando, 98–99, 101–102
Personhood, 22, 25–26, 53–104,
    222, 293–94
    feminist critique of, 295–97
Piers, Gerhart, 133–34
Piety, 110
Pilgrim's Progress (Bunyon), 162
Political activism, 40, 291, 297–98
Political theory, 199–200, 207
Politics and self-repect, 5, 36,

93–103, 256–66, 251–304
Presented self, 183
Pride, 7, 11–12, 19, 70, 120, 159, 171, 173–74
Pritchard, Michael, 25
Proportion regarding self and others, 219–20
Prostitution, 118
Protest, 23, 93–103, 263–64, 297
Psychoanalytic theory, 133
Psychology and self-respect, 30, 198–213, 222–46, 254

Race, 144–45, 271–87
Racism, 93–103, 182, 265, 266, 271–72
Rawls, John, 19–41 *passim*, 181, 255, 278
 contemporary influence of, 2, 3
 on rights, 199–200
 account of self-respect, 27–28, 210–11, 274–75
 on sense of worth, 202
 account of shame, 125–30
 account of shame critiqued, 133–54, 158–60
Reality, 66
"Reasonable Progress and Self-Respect" (Held), 209–10
Recognition respect, 183, 191
Recognition self-respect, 35, 183–95, 293–304
Regard, 6–7, 186
Regret, 120–23, 127–28
Respect,
 defined, 182
 and difference, 299
 etymology of, 18–19
 degrees of, 190
 as deliberation, 185
 kinds of, 181–95
 misplaced, 225–27
 objects of, 183

as objective, 205
as triadic relation, 223–45
Responsibility, 165, 166, 244
Ridicule, 141, 142, 153
Rights
 appreciation of, 117–18, 123
 civil, 37, 259–64
 defense of, 22, 83, 95–102, 193, 296–97, 219, 262–64, 302
 human, 21–22, 25, 60–61, 82, 86, 199
 importance of, 199, 207–10
 moral, 5, 22–23, 25–26, 82, 296
 and morality, 253
 possession of and self-respect, 37–38, 60, 203, 256–61
 vs. transformation, 297
 violation of and self-repect, 38–39, 62, 83–84, 193, 219, 256–61
"Rights of Man," 60–64
Rosenberg, Morris, 202
Rousseau, 89

"Sambo" personality, 102
Sappho, 68
Scheler, Max, 60
Scheman, Naomi, 241
Self, the, 173, 295, 299
Self-assertion vs. renunciation, 70–73
Self-conceptions, 276–77
Self-contempt, 78–85, 114, 120–23, 193, 230, 235–36, 290
Self-deprecator, the 77–85, 117
Self-esteem, 7
 and affectivity, 31
 definition of, 135–39
 as determined by others, 126–27
 loss of, 128–29, 133–34, 138, 139
 vs. self-respect, 29, 30, 158–60, 194, 254–56, 261, 275
 as self-worth, 126–28, 254–55

and shame, 127–30, 138
Self-evaluation, 18, 26–27, 99, 107, 163–76, 193–94, 221, 275
Self-perception, 22
Self-pity, 95–96
Self-portraits, 234
Self-protection, 152–53
Self-realization, 290
Self-regard, 9
Self-respect
  African Americans and, 36–40, 77–85, 95–103, 256–64, 271–287
  as androcentric, 292
  appraisal, 184–95, 292, 294
  and change, 234
  compromised, 222–45
  conative, 26, 107–16, 203
  as control, 67–68, 111, 130
  definitions of, 6–7, 272–76
  in drama, 1–2
  as duty, 22–23, 85, 89–92
  estimative, 26, 107–16
  evaluative, 35
  feminist critique of, 40–41, 292–304
  in Kant, 14–18
  injury to, 24, 36–39, 128–29, 168–76, 261
  interpersonal dimensions of, 5, 126–27, 242–43, 278–85
  in literature, 1–2
  minimum content, protection of, 273–74, 284
  moral importance of, 5
  moral vs. psychological accounts of, 222–45, 227–28
  nature of, 2–3
  objective, 26, 34, 112, 199–213
  overview of, 1–41
  phenomenology of, 4
  political dimensions of, 5, 36, 93–103, 256–64, 291–304
  as primary good, 125–30, 210–13,

236
  psychology and, 30, 198–213, 222–46, 254
  recognition, 35, 183–95, 293–304
  robust, 272–87
  vs. self-esteem, 29, 30, 158–60, 194, 254–56, 261, 275
  as separate from abilities, 251–66
  and shame, 161–63
  social construction of, 5, 143–44, 229, 232, 242–43, 255, 264–66, 271–87
  subjective, 26, 34, 112, 199–213
  uncompromised, 34, 222–23, 244–45
  value of, 115–16
Self-sacrifice, 302–303
Self-understanding
  as rebellion, 304
  as self-valuing, 303
Servility, 22–23, 76–92, 117–18
Sexism, 182, 265
Sexuality, 228–29
Shame, 7, 29
  and childhood, 142–43
  and class, 143–44
  classes of, 146–47
  and esteem of others, 141–42, 147–49
  vs. guilt, 130, 133–34, 171–76
  and identity, 145–46
  as injury to self-respect, 168
  as loss of self-esteem, 128–29, 133–34, 138
  vs. loss of self-esteem, 139–46
  as moral, 163, 129–30, 256
  as natural, 127–30
  as self-protection, 152–53
  and self-respect, 161–63, 256
  and trivial things, 140
  as virtue, 168–70
  as useful, 176
  and women, 290

Shaw, George Bernard, 64–66, 198
Slavery, 98–99, 101–102, 256, 264, 266, 280
Slavery: A Problem in American Institutional Life (Elkins), 101
Social institutions and self-respect, 143, 255, 259–61, 264–66, 276
Socrates, 142
Standards, 26, 29, 30, 120–23, 201
Status, 162, 173, 201, 281
Subjective self-respect, 26, 34, 199–213
Success vs. aspirations, 135, 254
Survival in Auschwitz (Levi), 2
Sympathy, 95, 224

Taboo, 170–71
Taylor, Gabriele, 19–41 *passim*
Taylor, Shelley, 240
Teitelman, Michael, 200
Telfer, Elizabeth, 6, 19–41 *passim*, 181, 203
Theory of Justice, A (Rawls), 2, 3, 27–28, 37, 199–200, 202
Theory, thin and thick, 200
Third Reich, 68
"Toward a Future that Has No Past" (Patterson), 98–99, 101–102
Transformation of society, 297
Treatise of Human Nature, A (Hume), 11–14
Tuskegee Institute, 256

Uncle Tom, the, 76–85, 117, 204–205, 256–59
Uncompromised self-respect, 34–35, 222–23, 244–45
Undignified, the, 64–70
Urban underclass, 278
Usher, Sarah, 241

Value, 29, 35, 66, 99, 161, 226
Victimization, 95, 219, 297
Violence, 36, 67, 281
Virtues, 24–25, 26–27, 70–73, 99, 112, 199, 254

Walden II, 205–206
Wallace, James, 24–25, 199
Washington, Booker T., 37, 93–98, 256–59
Williams, Bernard, 172, 181
Wilson, William Julius, 287
Women
    and compromised self-respect, 239–45
    and self-respect, 40–41, 277, 290–304
    as subjects of respect, 297, 301
Women and Self-Esteem, 291
Women's magazines, 69
Worth
    in Aristotle, 7–9
    auteur theory of, 150, 154
    confidence of, 23, 100, 126
    intrinsic vs. earned, 80–81, 292–93, 301
    in Kant, 14–15
    objective, 205–206
    sense of, 19–20, 23, 28, 99–102, 109, 120–23, 126, 149–53, 202–203, 221, 275, 301